INTRODUCTION TO THE BIBLE

INTRODUCTION
TO THE BIBLE

PIERRE GRELOT

TRANSLATED BY G. PATRICK CAMPBELL

HERDER AND HERDER

1967
HERDER AND HERDER NEW YORK
232 Madison Avenue, New York 10016

Original edition: *Introduction aux livres saints,*
Paris, Librairie classique Eugène Belin.

Nihil obstat: Leo J. Steady, Censor Librorum
Imprimatur: ✠ Robert F. Joyce, Bishop of Burlington
April 5, 1967

Library of Congress Catalog Card Number: 66–22603
© 1967 by Herder and Herder, Inc.
Manufactured in the United States

CONTENTS

CONTENTS

CONTENTS

11

PREFACE

EVEN today, when Christians have many excellent translations of the Bible at hand, a meaningful reading of the holy books still requires some kind of introduction. I have not forgotten my own first contact with the Bible and the difficulties I encountered at a time when there were few books to be had on the study of Scripture. Therefore, in this introductory aid I have attempted to gather in brief form those historical, literary, and doctrinal data which seem most important and useful for a fruitful reading of the holy books. Having such a purpose, I have avoided making this introduction too technical, and treatment of technical matters has been kept to a minimum.

Thus in presenting the books of the Bible I have not followed the artificial order of our canonical editions, but, so far as possible, rather the historical order, in an attempt better to coordinate the texts with the living setting in which each of them came to be. As a result I have found it necessary to discuss various books of the Old Testament several times throughout. The reader may refer to Index IV if he wishes to collate all the data about any particular book of Scripture. Likewise, I have avoided any premature abstract exposition of certain general questions with which every reader of the Bible ought eventually to be familiar with—for example, the matter of inspiration and inerrancy in the Bible, or the relation between Scripture and tradition, or the problem of biblical exegesis. The reader will find that these and other questions are taken up in the last chapter, on the supposition that an understanding of the nature of these questions, much less their resolution, cannot be had without a concrete knowledge of the data contained in the preceding

13

chapters. Needless to say, however, this last chapter can be referred to whenever or as often as it is thought necessary.

This *Introduction to the Bible* will not once and for all resolve all of the literary and historical problems concerning the two testaments, of course. Some of them are still matter for lively discussion even among experts. Yet the core of any introduction to the Bible is the presentation of Scripture's doctrinal message, not an initiation into the critical debates which the message may have engendered. Thus my primary concern was to bring this doctrinal message into as sharp a focus as possible, and the only way I could do so was to treat a text first by way of history and literature. Whenever controverted issues presented themselves, I had to take a position, and in doing so I took into account, of course, the opinions expressed on the matter in hand by qualified exegetes. With some of the problems I had to be content with approximate answers; but in most cases a general consensus is in the process of formation, though many details remain to be clarified.

The first edition of this work dates from 1954. The present text is a revision of the second French edition. The sections devoted to the New Testament, and formerly judged to be too succinct by a number of readers, have been considerably amplified, and the chapters relating to the Old Testament have also been revised in varying degrees. I have also thought it best to increase the number of extra-biblical texts cited at the end of chapters by way of documentation. And as far as the ancient texts themselves are concerned, I have reworked the translations from the originals, except for the Egyptian texts. All the texts are classified by number, and the complete list is given in Index II.

For greater utility this revised edition also contains many new scriptural citations. Regarding the New Testament I have referred to it directly, but for the Old Testament I have used a different method. For had I indicated the supporting Old Testament references for each datum proffered, the text would in the end have been unreadable. Thus, rather than cite the Old Testament by chapter and verse, I have chosen a list of typical texts designated by a single number, such as *352*. Opposite that number in Index I the reader will find concrete Old Testament illustration of the general statement in the text. However, although this concordance system is much easier for the reader to handle, it does not dispense him, of course, from reading the books of the Old Testament. But familiarity with selected texts could very well serve as having points of reference for reading the entire Bible.

Moreover, when reading such a sizable block of literature as the Bible, it is helpful to do the reading in two steps. In the first step, the reading of the same passages many times and seeing them from different angles aids the reader to assimilate material which in a cursory reading he may overlook or even misunderstand. In the second step, the reading of the Bible straight through, the reader will then be able to profit throughout by the insights he has gained in his preliminary study of central texts. He will at the same time have acquired a method of reading which will greatly assist him in rereading the Bible or any of its books.

I have also added a bibliography and a study guide at the end of each chapter, for the purpose of further research on the part of the reader. I would have liked to have added illustrations showing various biblical sites and concretizing biblical history by the archeological evidence, but the size of this book made that ambition unrealizable. Happily, other works fill this need. I have retained only those maps indispensable for following the different stages of biblical history.

In conclusion, I urge the reader not to content himself with merely reading this introduction to the Bible, but to go beyond it by reading the holy books themselves. For no introduction to the Bible accomplishes its purpose until it has been set aside for the Bible itself.

INTRODUCTION TO THE BIBLE

I.

ON THE THRESHOLD
OF THE BIBLE

WHAT is the Bible? For many people, even Christians, the Bible is a thick book belonging in a library, or even a bestseller, but few consider it a book to be read. For the Christian alive to his faith, however, it is a book apart from all others. It is the book of books, the book directly linked to the revelation which is the object of his faith. Revelation comes down to us in the teaching of the Church, and the Church has legitimately and trustingly received this book from God as the book which he inspired and which contains his word. According to the measure in which we devote ourselves to the word of God, the living teaching of the Church shapes the content of this book and invites us to open it under her direction: "Take and read!" Hence our reading of the holy Scriptures is no luxury. It is our response to the Church, to her invitation. "Come," says the divine wisdom, "eat of my bread and drink of the wine I have mixed!" (*Prv.* 9, 5). Can we be deaf to such an appeal?

1. A TRADITION OF THE CHURCH

Today, after a period of marked neglect, Catholics are again cultivating a taste for sacred Scripture. This is true not only for specialists in history and theology who must read the Bible out of professional necessity, but also for laymen who wish to refresh themselves with God's word. It would be wrong to view this renewed interest as a passing fad, or as a kind of novelty. Rather, it is the rebirth of a long-standing tradition, a tradition as old as the Church herself. St. Paul, teaching new converts at Corinth, in appealing to the events of the exodus and giving them a Christian meaning in *1 Corinthians* 10, 1–11 gives a clear example of how the New Testament style of interpreting the Scriptures was replacing that of the synagogue. And we still reap the fruits of this interpretation in many other New Testament passages.

This method must continue in the Church; for from the first centuries, preaching, like theology, has regularly taken the holy books as its point of departure, linking those of the New Testament to the ancient Jewish Bible. Thus at Hippo St. Augustine explained the psalms or the Gospel of St. John from the pulpit; and throughout the Middle Ages, in the centers of culture which were the monasteries and later the universities, the Bible was the book most read, most copied, most commented upon. The very art of the period is witness to this fact. In the portals and windows of cathedrals the faithful found a translation in pictures of the very texts which preachers explained from the pulpit.

It is true that later Christianity held itself somewhat aloof from this tradition. An excessive reaction against the biblical fundamentalism of the Protestant movement, and later the indirect influence of modern rationalism, led to a separation of the faithful from the Bible. But we must not exaggerate this separation, for the invention of printing gained a much wider audience for the Bible during this period. In the 16th and 17th centuries, the age of the humanists, editions of magnificent polyglot Bibles appeared in which all the ancient versions of the sacred books were set out side by side. These tomes were monumental in size and tributes to scholarship, but were destined only for libraries. Yet who has not also seen the Bible histories (direct descendants of the "Bibles of the poor" copied in the Middle Ages) which the presses turned out by the many thousands in the 17th and 18th centuries? Certainly, the manner of approaching the texts has differed from age to age, for the culture of the age influences the manner of reading the Bible. But despite superficial differences, the ruling and guiding spirit of Bible-reading remains the same. For the word of God does not change, and to read the Bible is to listen to God, to hear his message and receive it.

2. A NECESSARY AND DIFFICULT READING

Paul Claudel once wrote, "It is a wonderful thing that God has spoken distinctly to men and even more wonderful that this word has been consigned to a written document for all times! This word . . . it is not enough to skim over it lightly. It is necessary to cling to it, remain with it, to be impregnated with it. . . ; not in a spirit of vain curiosity, but of devotion; it is necessary to dwell on it, to store it up, to go to sleep with it and wake up with it. We must be persuaded that it is in its entirety the bread for which alone we hunger." This defines the proper attitude exactly. Reading holy Scripture is not a question of curiosity or culture for the Christian. It is a question of life. It is true that the teaching Church hands the word of God down to us and we give it meaning, and from this point of view its spiritual nourishment does not lead us into error. But it is not for nothing that this word has been fixed in books under the very guarantee of God himself. There is nothing forbidding the ordinary layman to read the texts which the Church tirelessly refers to in order to extract the substance of its teaching. He who reads the Bible in the Church, docile both to its living teaching authority and to the witness of the sacred texts, will find the word of God in the Church and the sacred texts. "It is a Father who speaks to me," Claudel continues, "And overcome with wonder and respect, I listen at his feet to the explanations of this voice which created me." (See Text 1.)

Nevertheless, the difficulty of reading the Bible in a Christian way must not be concealed. It is not enough merely to say that it requires a religious soul, attentive to the interior voice of the

21

Holy Spirit, through whom alone each can find nourishment for his soul. For in the first place, a faith incorrectly over-attentive to this interior inspiration leads directly to the abuse called illuminism. Only the Church, since she is aided by the Holy Spirit, is the authentic mistress in this reading. We must go to the Church in order to avoid being led astray by drawing meaning from the texts which is suggested by mere personal fantasy. But there is more to it than this. Even for the Christian docile to the Church's guidelines, the reading of the Bible, especially the Old Testament, is no easy task.

The Bible is in fact no single book, it is a library. It grew chapter by chapter over some fifteen centuries and it has seen the light of civilizations far-distant from our own. Everything in the Bible is truly the word of God, but the word of God concretized in a multitude of human words; and each human word took shape in a specific time and place which contributed to its form and meaning. Thus the 20th-century reader of the Bible is thrust into a new world where a thousand things uproot him from his own element. In a way, he falls under the fascinating spell of the Orient where only a few of the many passing images are familiar. The texts, because of their religious qualities, sound an immediate echo in his soul, and their expression of doctrine, always concrete and familiar to human experience, is often more understandable to the reader than the abstract writings of theologians.

On the other hand, some biblical elements are baffling: historical references whose importance is not immediately evident, anecdotes for which one sees neither the necessity nor the importance, a way of life, a mentality, a language which disconcerts or surprises us, entire books whose contents seem particularly forbidding. For example, what are we to make of the codes of the Israelite law? And in some cases doctrinal expression must be abandoned. For example, how many books of the Old Testament ignore retribution beyond the grave? Is this the word of God which we must think so highly of? The Gospel and the writings of the apostles certainly are God's word, for there we find Christ, the object of our faith and the source of our hope.

22

Are they not enough? What meaning do the sacred books of the Jewish Old Testament have for us today? Have they not been transcended and replaced by the New Testament?

3. THE UNITY OF THE TWO TESTAMENTS

In reality, the roots of the Gospels sink deep into the Old Testament. As the Letter to the Hebrews says, "In many and various ways God spoke of old to our fathers by the prophets; but in these last days he has spoken to us by a Son . . ." (*Heb.* 1, 1–2). In both cases, it is the same God who has spoken to men and still addresses himself to us. If the Old Testament formerly prepared the hearts and souls of the Jews to receive the Gospel, it plays a similar role in our regard. The Church knows this well. It borrows the words of the Old Testament to form the liturgy, as is evident especially in the texts of the Easter vigil. There is only one Scripture, and Christ forms the unifying bond which gives it all of its meaning. Thus it is not true to say that the Old Testament has no importance for anyone who possesses the New. We must also avoid the temptation to hang back in laziness from the necessary effort. Entry into the world of the Old Testament demands real effort, but the effort is rewarding, for the reward is our fuller understanding of the Gospel. Nevertheless, in order to win the reward the initiate reader needs guidance. To avoid going astray, like the novice explorer in a trackless forest, the reader must be guided. Otherwise he might too quickly become discouraged, and renounce an enterprise which demands perseverance.

The intellectual needs of modern man, the questions which come spontaneously to mind when he is faced with the Bible, are not exactly the same as the needs or questions of the contemporaries of Origen or St. Augustine, or St. Thomas, or Bossuet. Modern man is educated by his culture in the methods of literary and historical criticism in at least a rudimentary way and he tends to apply them to the holy books. Interested in the work of archeologists who can make vanished civilizations live

23

again, he spontaneously tends to reconcile the biblical texts and replace them in the framework of their times. This is not something to be condemned, for God has spoken to men *in human language.* We must apply all the resources of our mind to this language in order to understand what God has said to us through it. All the data of archeology and criticism are not enough to do this. And a climate of faith is necessary lest they form a screen between God and man. But given this climate of faith, one can expect positive help from these modern studies if he knows how to use them and their results judiciously. Pope Pius XII, in the encyclical *Divino Afflante Spiritu* (1943), reminded us of their necessity and practical rules. All things considered, they help greatly to enliven the texts and to bring to light the main threads of the Bible. The Bible is more than a collection of works assembled around a common theme, it is the story of an education, and this gives it an organic unity.

4. THE DIVINE PEDAGOGY

For two thousand years God patiently led the people of Israel from Semitic paganism to the threshold of the Gospel. ". . . the law was our custodian until Christ came," St. Paul wrote (*Gal.* 3, 24). Revelation, therefore, did not enter the world in an atemporal form, indifferent to the fluctuations of history; it was not expressed in abstract treatises. On the contrary, it is through a history of dramatic events, a literature whose sacred character does not overshadow its human variety. Therefore, as a development of beliefs the admirable pedagogy of the Bible is totally unlike the development of dogma in the Church. In applying the rules of literary and historical criticism to the Bible, in comparing it with the data of Oriental archeology, we come nearer to identifying its successive stages of development. Of course, all of this works for the good of the faith, for thus we learn of the true outlook of the Scriptures. Christ comes to crown a slowly maturing revelation. He brings to full light the profound and ultimate meaning of the events, the institutions, and the texts which prepare for the final manifestation of his mystery.

24

Although still wrapped in darkness, the entire Old Testament was already filled with this mystery.

This is the fundamental idea and leading thread of the Old Testament. Its principal object is the history of divine revelation, which guided the people of God up to the time of the Gospel and the Church. This is why, at each of its stages, we find the three elements which help us follow its developments. They are: (1) a brief review of the political history which is the indispensable framework for understanding the full text; (2) a presentation of the inspired literature which is the authentic witness to the word of God; (3) a succinct analysis of the doctrine which develops over the passage of time. At the end of this survey, the New Testament will appear as the supreme flowering of the unique revelation. Political history, literary history, doctrinal history—our perspective, therefore, is fundamentally historical. But on the other hand the progress of revelation is not always comparable to the evolution of human ideas seen throughout the history of civilization. At each instant the word of God transmitted by his legates is the source of progress. God effectively imprints his own rhythm on it by directing the course of events. To retrace this course is not to write a history like other histories, but rather it is a step-by-step following of the spiritual education of men by God himself.

There are other ways possible of studying the Bible. For example, its themes could be classified according to the order of the Creed; or the texts could be meditated upon strictly for their spiritual content. But our approach here will be to follow with an open mind the method God himself has used to speak to men and to lead them into intimacy with himself. In human history, there is a chosen portion which, because God directed it, became sacred history. There is no reason to neglect or disregard this essential aspect of the divine work. We will listen to God speaking under the conditions in which he chose to speak. The message contained in the holy books is basically independent of time, which is why it is still important for us to understand it, but the way in which it is expressed is deeply rooted in the past. To understand the message, therefore, we must situate it in the living context in which it long ago took shape. We will study temporal history in order better to understand the presence of the eternal as it is progressively revealed to men.

Text 1

HOW TO READ THE BIBLE

Paul Claudel was hard on biblical critics. He did not understand their real importance and he often confused their work with the foregone conclusions common to all the rationalist historians who are agnostic, positivist, materialistic, or minimalistic in tone. But he profoundly felt the religious value of the Scriptures, where God speaks to reveal himself to man.

If the Bible is really the *word of God,* with what total respect, fervent attention, ingeniousness in bringing to it reinforcements and favorable resonances should we study its intonations, styles of composition, and developments, and, above all, the intentions of the multiple game of allusions and correspondences! What joy to be at the foot of the Logos and listen with all one's soul and intelligence to that speech! These are not the archives of earth placed at our disposal to explore as well as possible with the miner's pick and the chemist's test tube. This is the history of the universe considered from God's viewpoint and released to our examination, but the very meaning which attracts and harmonizes events and coordinates secondary causes into a continuous teaching, into a *suite.* We do not have here before us the bric-a-brac of a bazaar, a vast number of small incoherent objects which must be reduced to powder by obstinate labor, but vast synclinal areas, a maze of different strata appearing and disappearing, and upset by immersions, a huge school of testimonials worked upon by movements comparable only to geological crackings and recoveries: a limitless significance! It is God himself who with one hand crumples, and with the other goes

26

to the trouble of explaining it to us, in his manner, which is different from ours.

Paul Claudel, *A Poet Before the Cross*

Bibliography

TRANSLATIONS OF THE BIBLE: *The Jerusalem Bible,* with its annotations, scholarly introductions, and textual parallels, is an excellent work aid as well as a superb translation. The *Revised Standard Version* of the King James Authorized Version, a modernization of the beautiful Elizabethan translation done in 1611, was lately given the *imprimatur* of Richard Cardinal Cushing, and thus is officially in use in both the Roman Catholic and Protestant churches. The Confraternity version of the Douay-Rheims translation (New Testament 1582, Old Testament 1609) has been annotated and given special introductions by Joseph A. Grispino; this version is available in a two-volume paperback. Other translations noteworthy for sensitivity of style and the value of their annotation are the *Knox Bible,* translated and annotated by the late Msgr. Ronald Knox, and the *New English Bible,* which was commissioned in 1946 by the General Assembly of the Church of Scotland.

INTRODUCTIONS TO THE BIBLE: We recommend especially, for the Old Testament: *A Critical Introduction to the Old Testament,* by G. W. Anderson, and for the New Testament: *A Historical Introduction to the New Testament,* by R. M. Grant. Both of these introductions are by Protestants. For a work covering the Bible as a whole, there is the masterly *Introduction to the Bible,* edited by A. Robert and A. Tricot.

HISTORY, GEOGRAPHY, AND ARCHEOLOGY: L. H. Grollenberg (compiler), *Atlas of the Bible.* W. F. Albright, *Archaeology and the Religion of Israel* and *Archeology of Palestine* (Penguin paperback). *Geography of Israel* by E. Orni and E. Efrat is also worth while. See also C. Kopp: *The Holy Places of*

27

the Gospels, B. Baly, *The Geography of the Bible,* G. E. Wright, *The Westminster Atlas of the Bible.*

DICTIONARIES: L. Hartmann, *Encyclopedic Dictionary of the Bible.* J. L. McKenzie, *Dictionary of the Bible.* J. D. Davis and H. S. Gehman, *The Westminster Dictionary of the Bible.* Not a dictionary of the Bible, but often valuable nevertheless in this area of research, is *The Oxford Dictionary of the Christian Church,* edited by F. L. Cross.

THEOLOGY AND SPIRITUALITY: L. Bouyer, *The Meaning of Sacred Scripture.* Yves Congar, *The Mystery of the Temple.* A. M. Dubarle, *The Psalms: Their Structure and Meaning,* and *Original Sin in the Bible.* R. Schnackenburg, *The Church in the New Testament* and *The Truth Will Make You Free.* The other available works of this outstanding biblical scholar are well worth reading: *Baptism in the Thought of St. Paul, God's Rule and Kingdom,* and *The Moral Teaching of the New Testament.* Luis Alonso Schökel's *The Inspired Word* is a comprehensive analysis of Scripture in the light of language and literature.

JOURNALS AND MAGAZINES: *The Catholic Biblical Quarterly,* edited by Roland E. Murphy, O. Carm. *The Bible Today,* edited by Kathryn Sullivan, R.S.C.J. *New Testament Abstracts,* edited by J. J. Collins (see the list of journals given in the back of every issue of *NTA* for an alphabetical classification of scholarly theological journals by country of origin).

As a bibliographical aid, one can consult *Theology in Transition,* edited by Elmer O'Brien, S.J. This work contains lengthy critical reviews and bibliographies of all recent major works pertaining in any way to the New and Old Testaments.

II.

ISRAEL:
A SMALL ORIENTAL PEOPLE

ISRAEL occupied a unique place in the circle of ancient Eastern nations, even though, politically, Israel's lot resembled that of many other peoples. Descended from the Hebrew patriarchs and moulded into a nation in the Sinai desert under the authority of Moses, the Israelites settled in Canaan, the place of its ancestors' sojourn. There, under its first kings, it reached the peak of its temporal power. From the point of view of civilization it was no great innovator, and as a vassal of Mesopotamia, Egypt, and Canaan it left no artistic legacy comparable to theirs. There remains only the Hebraic religious point of view, and considered from this angle, Israel is far different from all its neighbors. Israel as a nation worshipped the one God and knew that its history had a particular importance, and that through it, God had begun to realize his plan of salvation on earth. These facts give Israel considerable importance. Its history forms part of the sacred history centering around Christ.

1. THE BIBLICAL LANDS

The Middle East

Before studying biblical history we must first look at the geographical framework in which that history unfolded in the Middle East, and especially in the land of Israel called Palestine. The Middle East is probably the most ancient seat of world civilization. There, at Jericho and some other sites, urban life began in the eighth millennium. The practice of writing came into being in the Middle East, around the fourth millennium, permitting the passage from pre-history to a history founded upon written documents. The Near Eastern culture radiated from two principal centers: the double valley of the Tigris and Euphrates, or Mesopotamia, and the Nile Valley of Egypt. Both centers communicate through a sort of corridor, bounded on the East by the Syrian desert, and on the West by the Mediterranean Sea. The semi-desert plains to the East were a reservoir of uncivilized nations. This overflow probably gave rise to the Semitic invasions linked with the people of the Bible—the last of the invasions was that of the Arabs in the time of Mohammed. To the West, the Mediterranean seacoast was an open corridor from the Syrian backlands to the maritime world of Crete and the other islands, to the shores of Greece and Asia Minor. The Syro-Palestine corridor was a crossroads where traffic routes, paths of invasion, and the currents of civilization all intersected.

Palestine has always offered the spectacle of a well-mixed population and highly unstable political divisions. But above and beyond the surface data, we must recognize certain constant economic factors which help characterize Palestinean society. On the whole, the corridor has four life-zones, each determined by geography and climate. An agricultural zone extends over upper Syria for the most part; then there is a mixed zone, suitable for raising cattle; a third zone, bordering on the desert, comprises the plains where shepherds roam; finally, there is the desert proper, cut by very infrequent trails, and for the most part accessible only to camel-riding tribes. Of course, these theoretical zones are modified by the contours of the terrain. In the northern half, in Syria, the Lebanon chain reduces the littoral plain to almost nothing; but behind, it opens to a vast valley traversed by the River Orontes. In the southern half, the Jordan descends through a deep cleft called the Ghor which extends from the Arabah depressions below the Dead Sea as far as the Red Sea.

Just before the birth of biblical history, the Syro-Palestinean shore and the backlands suitable to a sedentary population were overrun (beginning around 2500) by Semitic invaders called the Canaanites or Phoenicians, from the name of the shore where they had settled (the "shore of purple"). Rapidly mingling with the indigenous population, they founded a series of ports on the coast (Ugarit, Byblos, Arvad, Sidon, Tyre), from which their vessels darted forth on the Mediterranean to supplant the Cretan traders. In northern Syria, towards the beginning of the second millennium, the Amorites (another branch of the Semitic peoples) began to descend the Euphrates valley, until one of them, Hammurabi (*c.* 1700) founded an empire at Babylon (Text 9). But because of their instability we know much less about the nomadic population of the plains. The whole region fell under the preponderant influence of Mesopotamian civilization, in which the contributions of the Sumerians and the Semitic Accadians blended who ruled as far as Asia Minor; even the islands of the Aegean were partially subject to them. Nevertheless, Egypt remained in continued commerce with the ports of Canaan, notably Byblos (see Text 2). Egyptian civilization and religion exercised a certain influence there and the whole South remained, at least in principle, under its political suzerainty. In Asia Minor, around 2000, a warrior aristocracy of Indo-European origin founded the Hittite empire, which as late as the 13th century rivaled Egypt for the leadership of Syria. Several centuries later, tribes from the mountains of Armenia, the Hurrians, infiltrated the great bend of the Euphrates and the upper Tigris, where they set up the empire of the Mitanni around 1600. (See Map 1.)

The Land of Israel

The biblical land par excellence is the land of Israel, which, following the Greeks, we call Palestine after the Philistines who occupied its shores in the 13th century. From the Mediterranean

31

coast inland, there is first a coastal plain (the plain of Sharon) stretching out level with the Carmel headland. Towards the interior are the low lands (Shephelah), and the central mountain range (the Mount of Ephraim and the Mount of Judah) extending into the hills of Galilee, and finally the Lebanon Chain. The trench zone is for the most part located below the level of the Mediterranean. The Sea of Galilee is already 700 feet below sea level and the Dead Sea is 1290 feet below sea level. Beyond the trench the land returns to the level of the central mountains in the mountains of Moab and Bashān, which then extend north to the Anti-Lebanon chain and, in the direction of the Arabian desert, to the volcanic mountain range of Hauran. South of the mountains of Judea are semi-desert expanses, the biblical Negeb. Even further south is the Sinai Peninsula, a vast desert interrupted by less arid regions where there are some oases and rare scrawny pasture lands.

From the Negeb to upper Syria (Djezireh, between the Tigris and Euphrates) and to the western coast of Arabia, the plains, where the raisers of sheep and goats wander, though varying greatly in width extend continuously between the desert and cultivated lands. It was in this region—on the plain of Aram (between the two rivers), in the land beyond the Jordan, on the mountains of Ephraim and Judah, and in the Negeb—that biblical history began. Only little by little were the richest lands won, for they had already been long populated and organized into autonomous city-states when the patriarchs arrived in the land of Canaan. The time was the beginning of the era archeologists call the Middle Bronze.

2. THE TIME OF THE PATRIARCHS

Abraham

Certain texts link the biblical patriarchs to the Amorean sub-group which peopled upper Syria (192), but others indicate that Jacob, the father of the nation, was "a wandering Aramaean" (1). Be that as it may, it is certain that between 2000

32

and 1500 some clans of Semites wandered over the Syrian plains, leading their flocks of sheep and goats. These often turbulent nomads were generally feared by the farming and urban populations. Abraham himself was born of the clan Terah. After a stay in lower Mesopotamia he settled at Haran, a crossroads of caravan routes on the plain of Aram, or Aram of the Two Rivers, between the Tigris and Euphrates. When he became the chief of an independent clan, Abraham quit this land, and crossing Syria descended into southern Canaan and pitched his tent in the nearly uninhabited mountain region (*11*). Some memory of his presence at Bethel, north of Jerusalem, and in the Negeb, and at Hebron and at Beer-Sheba, was preserved. This migration should probably be placed around 1850 B.C., although certain historians put it as far down as 1650 B.C. (Map 1).

The historical context clarifies but does not completely explain Abraham's migration. Its deeper cause was a mystical occurrence: an inspiration from God. The ancestors of the patriarchs were idolators (*2*). They had some idea of the true God, under the name of *El* or *Ilâh,* a word meaning *God* in the biblical tradition and in Islam. All the Semitic peoples knew a supreme God at the head of their pantheon, but like the Arabs before Mohammed, they associated him with gods of nature who personified cosmic forces, or gods of cities who were invoked as protectors. This association destroyed any true idea of God. Abraham, led by an inner inspiration whose exact nature we cannot know, rejected this association, and from that time onward he reserved his worship for the one living God whose call and promise he had heard. (*11, 13*). The import of this religious reform did not as yet reach beyond the bounds of a nomad clan, but it did inaugurate biblical revelation.

From Abraham to the Sojourn in Egypt

After Abraham the history of the Hebrew patriarchs centers around a few names: Isaac, Jacob and his twelve sons (who bear the names of the twelve historical tribes of Israel), and

33

Joseph, the slave who became a minister in Egypt. The Genesis narratives show Isaac leading a sedentary life in southern Palestine (*16*). Then Jacob became a shepherd in the land of Aram again before returning to the land of his ancestors (*17–19*). His sons remembered his varied adventures in this land which the Canaanites dominated (*20*). Finally, at the call of their brother Joseph, they settled in the territory of Goshen (*21–23*). It must be kept in mind that Israel did not leave Egypt until the 13th century, and that the biblical traditions, in gathering up the memories of the patriarchal era, simplified and schematized a history which must have been much more complex. They describe three generations from the time of Abraham to the descent into Egypt; and three more generations from the descent into Egypt to the time of the exodus from Egypt. Clearly, six generations do not cover six centuries; they hardly span four.

But it is difficult to fill in the gaps in the sources. At the end of the patriarchal epoch, the tribes of Israel probably already formed a first confederation in Canaan. Certain adventures of the "sons of Jacob" allow a glimpse of their history (*20*). But these incidents are few and far between and difficult to interpret. As for the descent into Egypt, it is ordinarily associated with the great movement of peoples who, during the 18th century, broke over Egypt like a wave (the Hyksos invasion). The good fortune of Joseph can well be understood in the times of the Asiatic pharaohs. However, some historians lower the date to the 14th century, under the reign of the Pharaoh Amenophis IV. There are several chronologies to choose from. Still, all the Hebrew clans descended from the patriarchs probably did not settle in Goshen on the Asiatic frontier of the Nile delta. Some of them remained in Canaan, the others rejoining them after the exodus from Egypt and the duration in the desert. But the traditions collected by Genesis have no real interest in those Hebrews who stayed on in Canaan, for thus they were not agents in the great biblical history.

3. MOSES: THE EXODUS FROM EGYPT AND THE PERIOD IN THE DESERT

The Exodus from Egypt

After an indefinite length of time the Hebrews dwelling in Goshen were reduced to semi-slavery by a pharaoh who "had not known Joseph" (25). It was under these conditions of slavery that Moses appeared. Hebrew by birth, he bore an Egyptian name and received an Egyptian education, but as a political refugee he led the life of a Midianite nomad. And like the patriarchs of old, he heard the divine call. He was to return to his oppressed compatriots to bring them back to the God of their fathers, whom they would henceforth adore under the name of Yahweh. And he would lead them out from Egypt (26). The whole history of Israel depended upon this key revelation.

Its immediate result was the going out from Egypt, or exodus. The circumstances surrounding this event show the all-powerful God effectively directing the deliverance of the Israelites from Egypt and making them his own people. The exodus was *the great sign* which led the Hebrews to "believe in Yahweh and in Moses his servant" (27–30). It is generally thought that the pharaoh of the exodus was Rameses II, and that the event took place between 1290 B.C. and 1265 B.C., though some historians put it as far down as the reign of Mer-ne-Ptah (1226–1218 B.C.; Text 3).

In the Sinai Desert

After escaping from slavery the Hebrews again lived the life of nomadic shepherds in the plains of the Sinai peninsula, and it was during this period that Moses laid the foundations of a new religious and political organization which would span all the centuries of the Old Testament. At Sinai the tribes of Israel made a pact of alliance with Yahweh their God, with Moses as

35

the mediator and God's law as the charter (32–43). In a certain sense this act founded the nation. Israel was a theocratic nation, with God himself as the head, who was represented here below by Moses, his mandatory. Any injury to the worship of Yahweh or to the institutions intimately connected with this worship would undermine the nation's very life force. The "people of Yahweh" held to the tradition of the patriarchs, their ancestors, but they were not immune to other forces. During this era they admitted some strangers into their society, for the link which united all of the participants was less racial than religious.

The oasis of Kadesh was for a time the center of the confederated tribes. There they gradually became aware of their strength and prepared to step onto the political chessboard of Canaan, which was near the plain where they were living and, as it was the dwelling place of their ancestors, remained the "promised land" for them. Certain of divine help because of the Sinai covenant, they desired to regain their foothold there and rejoin those of the ancient tribes who still lived there. A long migration along the borders of the kingdom of Edom and across the land of Moab led the exodus group, now well reinforced, to the neighborhood of the Jordan (45–47). But Moses died before the river was crossed (48). Israelite tradition assigned the conventional duration of forty years, the length of one generation, to this period (Map 2).

4. IN THE LAND OF CANAAN: JOSHUA AND THE JUDGES

The Conquest

Some texts show each of the tribes of Israel establishing itself in Canaan on its own account, here through the force of arms, there by peaceful agreement with the occupants (49). But this tableau, passed on by the recollections of individual tribes, is overshadowed by the operations of the exodus group under the leadership of Joshua. From the central mountains this group made forays to the north and south of the land (50–54). These events can be dated between 1250 and 1220 B.C. by taking archeological data into account. The first center of the Israelite confederation in Canaan was the sanctuary at Shechem where the ark of the covenant, since Sinai the symbol of the divine presence, was kept. The renewal of the covenant treaty (54) assured unity between all the descendants of the patriarchs as a dynamic and enterprising nation. Then began a period of profound transformation for Israel. The nomads settled on the land and became farmers and mingled with the Canaanite population, whom they conquered by degrees while adopting their language and civilization. This classic process continued for two centuries.

The Time of the Judges

This cultural evolution had repercussions, of course, on the religious level. The sensual paganism of the Canaanites for whom the gods personified the forces of fertility were an especially strong attraction for the new arrivals. And the problem for the religion of Sinai was to resist competition and contamination and still enrich itself with those elements of worship which could be despoiled of their ancient idolatrous meaning. On the political level the crisis was no less grave. The unique basis of Israel's unity was the common worship of Yahweh and the Mosaic Law as preserved in the sanctuaries. No superior authority was imposed on the individuality of the various tribes. Such a structure was badly suited to the times, for Israel had competitors. From the beginning of the 12th century Philistine invaders had come by the sea route and had taken foothold on the coast. They pushed towards the interior. Groups of Canaanites solidly entrenched in strongholds (Megiddo, Taanach, Jerusalem) cut the Israelite territories into many fragments. Finally, profiting from the anarchy found in the land, the plunderers from the plains (Midianites, Ammonites, Amalekites) conducted frequent, fruitful raids.

A number of temporary chiefs also rose up in Israel and

37

carried out the war of deliverance, and these, for a time, exercised short-lived authority over various tribal groupings. These chiefs were the Judges, whose name (*šōfēt*) is reminiscent of the Carthaginian *suffetes*. Such were *Deborah,* the prophetess, who aroused the military campaign of *Barak* (*56*), *Gideon,* and *Jephthat* (*57–58*). Although portrayed as a judge, Samson (*59*) was rather a popular hero whose story shows the dismal situation in the first part of the 11th century. Finally, in the time of the priest *Eli,* the Philistines carried off the ark of the covenant, the battle standard since the time of Moses. The Israelites were practically vassals by the time of Samuel's judgeship.

5. THE MONARCHY, THE HIGH POINT OF THE PEOPLE OF ISRAEL

Saul, the First King

Under stress of danger, Israel obtained a king for herself. A first trial attempt, imitative of the Canaanite monarchies, was made by *Abimelech,* son of Gideon, but it ended in defeat. The revival of the project took place under very different conditions and spirit. The king was to be a permanent chief of all the tribes, bound by the exigencies of national worship and the Law, and it was his mission to guard justice among his people and lead the war of liberation. Although welcomed by some as a divine blessing (*63*), this innovation offended the traditionalist spirits who saw it as an infidelity to the Mosaic institutions (*62*). In any case, it is certain that Samuel hallowed it by his authority as prophet (*62–63*). The first king, Saul, was a Benjamite, a rich peasant who retained a small army of professionals and sometimes conscripted the tribes to himself to lead a more extensive operation. His mode of operation resembled that of Ulysses of Ithaca, much as the battles of the era paralleled those of the *Iliad*. They were very near the same level of civilization, the beginning of the Iron Age. And the Philistines were allies of the Acheans of the Trojan War. Even so, Saul was always successful in containing their power (*64*).

But very soon, the king took offense at the popularity of the captain of his guard, David, a Judean. Faced with morbid jealousy endangering his life, David fled into the desert wastes and finally exiled himself in the Philistine lands (*64*). It was at this hour that war broke out between Israel and her hereditary enemies who were allied with the Canaanite strongholds. Saul perished with his son Jonathan at the Battle of Giboah, around 1015 B.C. (*65–66*).

David's Reign

After this disaster David returned to his tribe, where he was proclaimed king. Some years later, after Saul's son was assassinated, he became king of all Israel (*67*). He then organized the nation and definitively overcame the power of the Philistines. He took possession of the stronghold Jerusalem, at the junction point of the north (Israel) and the south (Judah), and made it the seat of his dynasty (around 1000). He brought the ark of the covenant to Jerusalem and located the combined sanctuary of the tribes there (*68*). This marked the high point of the kingdom. David organized worship, founded the beginning of a central administration, conquered one after another of the "enemies of the neighborhood," and imposed tribute on them. He even annexed the ancient kingdom of Edom. Israel thus became the center of a modest empire exercising its protectorate as far as central Syria (Map 3). During the same period, the kingly office assumed characteristics it lacked at the time of Saul. The king was now fulfilling certain religious functions, a common practice among the monarchs of the times (*68, 70*).

At the height of his reign David received a promise from the prophet Nathan that would have important consequences for the future. Yahweh made a covenant with David's dynasty, who would henceforth be linked to the hope of the people of God (*71*). But every picture has its darker side. The end of the reign was saddened by domestic tragedy and revolts, notably that of

39

Absalom, the heir-apparent (72–73). Upon the death of the old king, Solomon succeeded him in the midst of court intrigues (74).

Solomon

Solomon brought his father's work to completion, though not without some excesses. A strongly centralized administration, a brilliant court, some commercial ventures on the Red Sea, and the construction of a sumptuous palace gave his reign a sparkling brilliance, but it did not quite ring true, for the Israelite monarchy imitated those of the Phoenicians and Egyptians too much (79; Text 4), and on the death of the king (932) the unity of the kingdom could not be maintained. The two states of Israel and Judah led a separate existence during the following centuries (86). Nevertheless, Solomon left two important works behind. He built the temple of Jerusalem (77–78), which remained as the center of Jewish worship, and as a well-educated king he gave wisdom literature a home in his kingdom. This literature was later to undergo considerable development and become more and more impregnated with the religious spirit.

6. CIVILIZATION AND RELIGION IN ISRAEL

Between the time of the Hebrew patriarchs and the reign of Solomon, the civilization of Israel underwent considerable evolution from a nomadic or semi-nomadic pastoral life to a sedentary and urban agricultural life. The federal organization of the tribes, while retaining deep roots among the people, finally fell before monarchical centralization. The rough desert life gave way to a more refined civilization subject to foreign influences, in which written culture played a considerable role. In the meantime, Israel adopted the language of the conquered country and absorbed the bulk of the indigenous population.

Within this historical framework the national religion also developed, but according to its own rhythm, for throughout the events of their history, the people, descended from the patriarchs

40

and linked to Yahweh by the Sinai covenant, recognized the progressive realization of the divine promises: liberation from the Egyptian yoke and the consequent national independence; the covenant and Law; a land acquired by right of victory and held as their own; and finally, the monarchic institution. Each step was the gift of Yahweh to Israel. And, while assimilating the Canaanite civilization, Israel consciously remained the people of Yahweh, despite some experimentations with the religion of Canaan and the apostasy of individual Israelites to those religions. The crisis of the age of the Judges demonstrates the difficulties encountered. Still, the tradition of Sinai overcame all obstacles and finally triumphed under the reigns of David and Solomon. The history of the religions records the triumph of monotheism in the time of Moses as an unprecedented event. If the religion of the Hebrew nomads had evolved following its natural bent exclusively, it would surely have fused with Canaanite idolatry. Yet the paradoxical constancy of the tradition born at Sinai, deepened through the ages thanks to the action of inspired men, constitutes the Hebrew miracle. Not even the marvelous success of the Greeks some centuries later can compare with it.

Text 2

THE GOOD LAND OF CANAAN

The Egyptian tale of Sinuhe was set in the 20th century before our Christian era, a short time before the arrival of the biblical patriarchs in Canaan. The tale presents a vivid picture of the land. Sinuhe, an Egyptian official, voluntarily exiled himself and took refuge in an agricultural country of Asia north of present-day Palestine.

I left Byblos and reached the Orient, where I spent a year and a half. Then Enshi the son of Amou, a prince of upper Retenou, commanded me and said: "You will do well with me, you understand the speech of Egypt." He said this because he knew who I was and he had heard tell of my wisdom. Some Egyptians who had been with him had borne me good witness . . . He set me above even his children, married me to his eldest daughter, and made me choose a portion of his country, the best he possessed, on the frontier of a neighboring land. This was an excellent land called Yaa. There were figs, raisins, more wine than water; honey abounded there, it was rich in olives and fertile; the trees bore all kinds of fruits. Barley and spelt in quantity, and innumerable animals of all sorts were found there. Great privileges were accorded to me by reason of the great love which was shown to me. [Enshi] made me chief of a tribe, among the best of his country. Daily I was furnished nourishment with bread and wine, boiled meat and roast poultry, without counting the game taken by trap for me and brought to me, besides that which my hunting dogs captured.

After this contemporary picture the frequent Canaanite eulogies of the land in the Bible can be understood with less difficulty. "An excellent land, a land flowing with milk and honey" (*26, 111, 152, 156, 157, 179*). Clearly, this must be understood in the contrast between the cultivated lands and the meager pasturage of the desert.

Text 3

THE FIRST MENTION OF ISRAEL IN A FOREIGN TEXT

In a triumphal stele the pharaoh Mer-ne-Ptah, around 1225, pompously recorded his victories over Asiatic and African enemies. Israel is mentioned in it.

A great joy has come to Egypt
  Joy has risen in the cities of Tameri
The victories of Mer-ne-Ptah in Tehenu are recounted:
  "How one loves the valiant leader,
How exalted the king among the gods
  Because he is blessed, the Lord of the empire!"
. . . The princes are prostrated and say: "Peace!"
  No one more raises his head among the Nine-Bows.
Tehenu is ravaged, the Hatti pacified;
  Canaan is pillaged, with all its evildoers.
Ashkelon is deported, Gezer captured;
  Yanoam is reduced to nothingness.
Israel is devastated, its race exists no more.
  The Hurru have become like a widow before Egypt.
All the lands together are in peace:
  whoever were restless have been enchained
by the king of Upper and Lower Egypt. . . ,
  the beloved of Amon, the son of Re Mer-ne-Ptah . . .

This enumeration of geographical names shows the neighbors of Egypt (also called Tameri), the vassal lands (called the Nine-Bows): Tehenu is Libya; Hatti is the Hittite land situated to the north of Syria and in Asia Minor; Canaan designates the maritime cities of the Phoenician coast; Ashkelon, Gezer, and Yanoam are cities of Palestine; Hurru designates Palestine in the Egyptian texts of this period. Israel is situated within the Palestinian framework; nevertheless, its name bears nothing determinative of a homeland, but is that of a people. The Hebrews had not yet settled in a determined territory, for the conquest of Canaan has just begun by this time.

Text 4

THE REIGN OF SOLOMON
AND ARCHEOLOGY

More than once Palestinian excavations have allowed verification of the historical information given by the Bible. An archeologist recounts this verification for the reign of Solomon.

His son Solomon (*c.* 960–922) soon found himself in a difficult position, since he undertook a series of most elaborate building operations throughout the country and also established a powerful standing army of chariotry, both of which occur for the first time in the history of Israel. It is true that scholars used to belittle the tradition preserved in Kings, and reduce his building operations to very modest dimensions. However, archeological discovery at Megiddo since 1929 has shown that Solomon's building activities in a single one of his "chariot-cities" (*Kgs.* 9, 15–19; 10, 26) included well-constructed stables with cement floors for at least 400, and perhaps many more horses. At Hazor and Tell el-Hesi similar installations from the Solomonic age have also been found. Moreover, Nelson Glueck's work at Ezion-geber on the Red Sea since 1938 has demonstrated that Solomon built an elaborate copper refinery there, covering an acre and a half and surrounded by a strong brick wall. Nothing like it is otherwise known from the ancient Near East—yet it was so relatively insignificant an enterprise that it is not even mentioned in our sources. The expense of his extensive and costly building operations and of his relatively huge military establishment was not diminished by his elaborate mercantile and industrial enterprises, such as caravan trade in the desert, naval expeditions in the Red Sea and the Mediterranean, and copper mining and refining in the Arabah (of which nothing was known before Glueck's recent explorations and excavations). Moreover, the scale of his personal life appears to have been proverbially lavish.

W. F. Albright, *From the Stone Age to Christianity*

44

GENERAL HISTORY		BIBLICAL HISTORY
	c. 1850	Migration of Abraham
		Isaac
		Jacob
		The Sons of Jacob
The Hyksos in Egypt	*c.* 1720	
The Asiatic Pharaohs		Joseph
		Descent into Egypt
	c. 1650	Migration of Abraham
		Isaac
Expulsion of the	*c.* 1560	Oppression of Jacob
Hyksos		the Hebrews
		Sons of Jacob
Amenophis IV	1370–1352	Joseph
		Descent into Egypt
Haremhab and Setis I		Oppression of the Hebrews
Ramses II	1292–1226	
	between 1290 & 1265	Exodus under the leadership of Moses
		Sojourn in the Sinai desert and Kadesh
	between 1250 & 1225	Invasion of Canaan: Joshua
Mer-ne-Ptah	1226–1218	
Ramses III repels the sea people	*c.* 1198	Era of the Judges
		The Philistines on the Canaan coast
	c. 1075	Philistine domination over Israel
	c. 1040	Saul
	c. 1012	Death of Saul, David king of Juda
	1005	David king of all Israel
	c. 1000	Capture of Jerusalem
	972	Death of David. Solomon
	932	Death of Solomon. Schism

45

In this chronological table biblical history is set within the framework of world history. However, for all that precedes Moses two hypotheses must be considered: a long chronology placing Abraham around 1850, and a short chronology dating him centuries later. A number of historians place the exodus under Mer-ne-Ptah (see Text 3).

Bibliography

A. Gonzalez, *Abraham, Father of Believers* (New York 1967). H. Renckens, *The Religion of Israel* (New York 1966). J. Plastaras, *The God of Exodus* (Milwaukee 1966).

Study Guides

To put flesh on the simplified schema of this chapter, you should read thoroughly the biblical texts themselves (*1–85*).

Some of the religious personalities preserved in the religious tradition of Israel should be studied in more detail—for example, Abraham, Moses, and David. It is not sufficient merely to retrace their history, for the important thing is the spiritual portrait emphasizing the traits which make them models for Christians even now (see *Heb.* 11, 8–29) and those which show the relative imperfection of their religion.

III.

THE TRADITIONS OF ISRAEL

WITHIN the context of the history sketched here, the blossoming of a national literature took place, and it must be properly understood. Israel, like all peoples, possessed some popular productions of a wholly secular character, though only rare traces of them now exist. But precisely as the people of God Israel formed a literature with the essentially religious purpose of conserving the message brought by the divine envoys and preserving the memory of the acts of God in her history. It was certainly a national literature, but simultaneously and primarily a sacred literature. Thus the collection of inspired books began to form. Naturally, the works of this far-off period are on a level with the mentality and civilization of their times. To understand their origins, the meaning, their literary forms, we must have as precise an idea as possible of the milieu in which they are fashioned and preserved. At the present time they are incorporated into larger works edited in a later age. It must be remembered that before reaching this stage they existed independently, and that most of them were born in oral tradition before being fixed in writing.

1. THE LITERATURE OF THE TRADITIONS

Written Civilization and Oral Civilization

From the time of the patriarchs to the reign of Solomon the history of Israel offers the spectacle of a people slowly progressing towards a written civilization. Starting with the reign of David, official scribes lived in the court. Solomon gave the intellectual culture a vigorous push with a focus on schools (77). And the temple and its priesthood, as in all ancient civilizations, participated in the movement. Undoubtedly, there were also some literate men among the land-owning and merchant aristocracy. Though the peasant masses must have remained almost illiterate, they were no more so than the Western peasants of the Middle Ages. However, at the time of the Judges, of Moses, and of the patriarchs, the situation was notably different. Writing was known in Canaan, and Egyptian hieroglyphics and the Mesopotamian cuneiform had already been used for a long time; but it was in the region of Canaan that alphabetic writing—which would become so convenient and so widespread an instrument—was invented during the first half of the second millennium. In the 14th and 13th centuries, in the time of Moses and a little before him, the Canaanite alphabet was already being written in ink and was a part of daily life. Yet we must not conclude that Israel had already arrived at written civilization by this era.

Among ancient peoples, and especially among nomadic societies, writing was only a secondary memory aid. The items we habitually record in writing—historical recollections, customs and laws, beliefs and rites, poetry and literary works—they preferred to commit to the memories of living men. In transmitting them from one generation to another, the living memory had more chance of enduring than perishable materials. Clay, bricks, wood tablets, papyrus, or prepared hides occasionally served the needs of practical life (lists, enumerations, contracts, etc.). Their usage developed with time, but was very restricted in the beginning, and it was oral tradition which assured the transmission of the diverse lore from which a society draws its spiritual and intellectual nourishment. The recent past still furnishes examples of its faithful transmission. The *Revue biblique* of 1951 published the historical traditions of an Arab tribe moving towards a sedentary life in the region of Bethlehem. The memories they preserved went back as far as 1572, and there is no reason to suspect their general exactitude. It is enough not to ask of them what they do not pretend to furnish.

As late as the reign of David the literature of Israel was essentially a literature of traditions. Writing played a role, but a restricted one. It is important to know the date and reasons for the editions of these traditions; it is even more important to know what to look for in them, to know what literary forms preserved them, what environments shaped them, and what developments they underwent in the course of time. The literary criticism applied to written compositions of our own era clearly is not enough to clarify all of these questions.

Content and Literary Forms of the Biblical Traditions

The content of the ancient traditions gathered in the Bible is at once the law, history, beliefs, rites of worship, and so forth of the people of Israel. And this does not account for the thousand traits defining Israel's spirit, its concept of the world and man, its attitude towards existence. It would be a gross deception to look for nothing except history (that which ordinarily makes up our sacred histories). History is very much there, but it is part of a much vaster ensemble including all the elements of the national culture and religion from their earliest stages of development.

The problem of the literary forms into which the traditions crystalized is no less complex, and, in fact, their type cannot be correctly appreciated in the light of modern literature (Text 5). The man of the Old Testament remained close to primitive civilizations. He did not think in abstractions as we do; his style was spontaneously filled with imagery; poetry permeated his literature; symbolism was part of his intellectual structure. To preserve the fading memory of a striking event, he preferred the warmth of the epic to the dry exactness of a chronicle. To transmit moral and religious ideas, to inculcate principles of law or rules of worship, he frequently used short, concrete, vivid tales whose point was essentially didactic, even if the historical background merited consideration. As for the rest, there are no airtight divisions between the genres, as is the case today. Within the same narrative, he passed easily and without warning from firm historical recollections to poetic embellishments or to details inserted for the moral instruction of the reader. On the other hand, he did not always distinguish an essentially historical tradition from a narrative borrowed from folklore by its literary form. In fact, a profound tendency of spirit led men to cast all narratives in familiar forms, making them conform to stereotyped frameworks.

Origin and Development of Biblical Traditions

Since the traditions preserve the memory of past events, they permit a return to the very facts which gave them birth, whatever the date of their compilation. At the beginning of this century, some suspicious historians were persuaded to minimize the witness of the traditions, as if they represented scarcely anything except the ideas of their later editors. As a matter of fact, verifying archeological discoveries have in almost every instance confirmed their validity (Text 4). From this point of view, then, it is not very important that the Exodus traditions, for example, were not put into writing until the royal era. The essentials of the literary tradition were fixed long before in oral tradition and in their roots the traditions go back substantially to the very events of the Mosaic era. Thus, if we know how to listen to them, the traditions in their own way constitute an excellent source of information for historians.

Nevertheless, the longer the span of oral transmission, the more traditions have the tendency either to be schematized or overloaded with various poetic elements, or to be didactically developed. Thus the narratives of which Abraham is the hero (*11–15*) include more religious or moral teachings than those which recount the adventures of David (*64*), which much more closely approximate the historical details. In the chronicle of the reign of David (*67, 68, 71–74*), the memory of the facts was too recent for epic transformation. This was not the case for the exodus from Egypt (*27–31*) or the conquest of Canaan by Joshua (*51–53*). In short, the variety of biblical traditions reveals both the history and the faith of the people of God. In reading each of the narratives we must therefore consider its particular literary form and try to discover the precise teaching it wishes to convey.

2. THE FIRST FIXED TEXTS

Even during the full flowering of oral civilization some texts were fixed because of their forms themselves—for example, legislative texts and poetic texts. In two very different genres, they already constitute "literary" works in the broad sense of the term, even though other traditions remained in very fluid form or were still on the way towards crystallization.

The Mosaic Legislation

A firm tradition makes Moses the pre-eminent lawgiver in Israel. It shows him exercising the role of judge and pronouncing sentences which have the force of law (*32*). He followed divine inspiration and wrote the Decalogue on tablets of stone (*35*) and gave the people a juridical and ritual rule. On Sinai he concluded the covenant with Yahweh and his Law would be its charter (*36*). There is no doubt that the fundamental principles of Israelite legislation, its spirit, its essential dispositions stemmed from Moses.

But the role of Moses in this area must be clearly understood. He did not invent all the elements of the Law; rather, he chose, corrected, completed, and sanctioned with his authority

51

dispositions borrowed from customary law and Semitic rituals. But the Law continued to live and efficaciously fulfill its role after him, and the Law he established continued to develop in the course of the ages. Moses' continuators, however, interpreters of a Law they preserved, men of tradition and not creators, have remained anonymous. Anxious that the Law retain its full meaning in changing historical circumstances, they merely completed particular points while respecting its original lines. The Law in Israel would always be "the Law of Moses."

In the compilations preserved by the Pentateuch (from Exodus to Deuteronomy) certain more ancient groupings crop up. The Decalogue (37) probably includes, along with some literary developments, the fundamental clauses of the Sinai covenant. The oldest legislative collection is certainly the *Code of the Covenant* (*Ex.* 20, 22—23, 19), which was already adapted to a settled society (38–40). The short Yahwist code of *Exodus* 34, 10–27, also displays a strong primitive viewpoint. But the Mosaic legislation is not limited to these surely ancient documents. In fact, even the dispositions collected in the later compilations, like Deuteronomy and the Priestly Code of which we will say more later, use a traditional base. And in the last analysis, this base was rooted in Moses (38, 39; compare 41 to 29). The normal development of legislation and its adaptations to contemporary needs always respected the Mosaic substance, even in relatively recent editing of the texts.

In the beginning, the laws were expressed in characteristic formulas which clearly indicated their origin. The casuistic formulations ("If a man . . .") call to mind the juridical sentence which gave birth to them (compare 39 to 32). The commandments, brief and energetic, such as those of the Decalogue (37), recall that human conduct has the very word of God for its standard, transmitted by an inspired man. When they receive justifying developments, they assume the character of a lesson in practical wisdom (38). Their content will be treated in the next chapter: "Man before God: morality, law, worship."

52

Some Poems of Ancient Times

Few examples of the poetry of the nomads remain; some brief refrains, echoes of a rugged era, are all that is left (*8, 30*). The period of literary creation began only after the conquest, when the Israelite genius was stimulated by contact with the Canaanite culture. Then the great events of national life found narrators to sing of them. Note the Canticle of Joshua, which unfortunately is only fragmentary (*53*), and the Canticle of Deborah, a direct echo of an episode in the time of the Judges (*56*). Likewise, the ancient refrain of the exodus (*30*) would later develop into a triumphal canticle (*31*).

In these three works, linked by their style, the lyric narration of the event which fired the author's enthusiasm is the high point of the poem. The facts are told in hyperbolic language and Yahweh's overshadowing presence in the theophany of the storm dominates them. The splendor of the images, the vigor of the language, point to a well-mastered art; and though arising from a different mentality, it has no reason to be jealous of the Greek chorus poetry. A characteristic trait of this Semitic poetry is the use of parallelisms in two or three successive half-verses. All of its literary techniques are closely linked to those of Canaanite poetry, which had become known from excavations at Ugarit (Ras-Shamra, in Syria). There, on clay tablets dating from the 14th century, the remnants of a centuries-old epic literature have been found. By analogy these concrete examples clarify the origins of Israelite poetry (Text 7).

Ancient Oracles

In important circumstances the Israelite "consulted Yahweh," either by some imperfectly known processes which were preserved by the priest, or by asking a "seer" (*62–63*). It is in the style of the answers given in such circumstances that the oracles of Jacob (*Gen.* 49), of Balaam (*Num.* 23–24), and of Moses (*Deut.* 33), for example, were drawn up. The oracles of Jacob (*24*) recall the state of the tribes of Israel at the time of the Judges and the beginning of the monarchy. Placed on the lips of

53

the dying Jacob by the compiler of Genesis, they give the reader, especially in the passage which concerns Judah, a perspective of the future showing the continuity of God's plan from Jacob to David. In like manner, the oracles of Balaam (47) include praise of Israel, a people "set apart," and a prophecy of the Davidic monarchy. The book of Numbers also closes with a view to the future. The two texts from these oracles concerning the origins of the person and the dynasty of David would later be applied to the Messiah, the heir of God's promises received by his ancestor (Texts 34 and 38).

The direct proclamation of these promises is found in the oracle of Nathan (71). This marks an important turning point, for it definitely links the race of David to the divine plan being accomplished in the history of Israel. Thus, it lies at the origin of royal messianism. Psalm 110 includes the proclamation of two oracles (70), addressed to the king as warrior chief and as priest. It is supposed with some probability that the king in question was David himself. At least it was a king of his dynasty. As for the oracles of Balaam and of Jacob, the later tradition of the exile applied the texts to the descendant of David par excellence, the future Messiah.

Ancient Liturgical Chants

The poems meant to be chanted in the course of the liturgical ceremonies are called psalms. The genre is very ancient in Israel, and both *Exodus* (15, 21) and *Numbers* (11, 34–36) preserve some refrains dating back to the time of the desert period. A firm biblical tradition makes David the creator of religious poetry and music in Israel. It is certain that David was, in fact, a poet, as his admirable eulogy on the death of Saul and Jonathan shows (56). And there is no doubt that after the transfer of the ark of the covenant to Jerusalem (68), conditions were ripe for religious lyricism to develop in the national sanctuary just as it flourished in the Mesopotamian (Text 25) or Egyptian (Text 26) temples. The construction of the temple by Solomon accentuated this movement and even a fragment of a hymn composed for its dedication has been preserved (*78*). As with the Mosaic Law, the genres developed over the course of the centuries. Recognizing David's historic importance, the sacred poets of every age wished to put themselves under his patronage, sometimes even adapting their works to the circumstances of his life (*281*). Collections were compiled of the poems which were qualified as "Davidic," though this does not necessarily indicate their authorship.

Practically, it is very difficult to date each piece in the Psalter precisely. The antiquity of some pieces is certain. For example, the processional of Yahweh-King (*69*) could have originated with the entry of the ark into Jerusalem (*68*); along the same lines there are Psalms 29 and 93, which have affinities with the poetry of Canaan, and the hymn to Yahweh-King in Psalm 47; the canticle of the exodus (*31*), a liturgical amplification of an old refrain, was intended for the liturgy of the passover time. All the psalms mentioning the king go back at least to the period of the monarchy (*82, 83*), as, for example, the royal *Te Deum* of Psalm 18, which includes a classic picture of the storm theophany (*81*). Some of these royal psalms after the exile will be applied to the future Messiah (*70, 329, 330*). Moreover, in the shadow of the sanctuary a deep piety was born, as is shown by the profoundly moving prayers of the time (*84, 85*).

Fables and Parables

Israelite antiquity possessed a popular wisdom rich in sayings of all sorts. But beginning in the reign of Solomon there arose a wisdom tradition among educated men, wide open to international culture, which found a home among the people of God (*77*). (We will return to this sapiential tradition when we treat the book of Proverbs.) Besides, some examples much earlier than Solomon show that these favorite kinds of literature had been cultivated from the distant past. At the time of the Judges, the fable of Jotham (*61*), which can be likened to the Aesopic fables which inspired La Fontaine, is a satire on the monarchic institution. Under David the parable of Nathan (*72*)

55

inaugurated a form of literature which will crop up often in the rabbinic literature and in the gospels. Here a lesson slowly pierces through a very polished story with striking effect because the listeners' attention has been captivated by the story being told. The subtle genre, so dear to the Oriental mind, enjoyed great popularity in Mesopotamia and in Canaan.

The First Poetry Collections

In the time of Solomon, there were at least two known collections of ancient poetry and many of the pieces cited were borrowed from them. They were the *Book of the Wars of Yahweh* (*Num.* 21, 14–15), and the *Book of the Just,* or the *Book of the Singer* (*53, 66, 78*). Perhaps a rich epic and lyric literature which sung of the ancient heroes, the patriarchs and warriors, existed in Israel as in Ugarit (Text 7) and in Greece, though nothing remains of it but fragments. Perhaps certain prose traditions are a weak echo of them. This would explain the characteristics of some prose of which a classic example is found in the book of Joshua (*53*).

3. THE TRADITIONS

The great majority of the material used by the sacred historians to manifest the first steps of God's plan was fixed in prose by the traditions. In order better to understand their literary structure, we will classify them in great cycles: the beginnings, primitive history, the time of the patriarchs, the era of Moses, the conquest of Canaan, the time of the Judges, the origins of royalty, and the Davidic beginnings.

The Beginnings

To explain the origins of the world and of man, the ancient Orient made use of myths. These myths were not pure products of free and unrestrained imagination, as in our own fiction. Inspired by their experience of life, they expressed their insight in an imaginative and dramatic way, for they were unable to recount it adequately in abstract language. Thus, in analyzing them we touch on the most profound realities of Oriental culture: its concept of man, of life, of the world, of God. But this concept is of very suspect inspiration, for the gods one encounters there and to whom men rendered their worship personify the diverse cosmic forces (Text 8). Biblical revelation, breaking with these erroneous beliefs, firmly established contrary principles, which we will study later: monotheism, a clear distinction between God the Creator of the world and his creatures; the plan of God being realized in the history of man (3–4). Besides, reflecting on the present condition of man, it has a view of his origin and a profound explanation of sin, which troubled the divine ordering of the world. The sin of our first parents is the primary fact of the history in which we live (5–6).

To explain such a doctrine, the Israelites still needed a concrete language, similar to that used in mythologies and the traditions surrounding the beginnings borrowed many expressions and symbols from the other cultures. They purged the polytheistic overtones, filling the expressions with completely new thoughts. For example, there is the anthropomorphic representation of God, or the imaginative description of the creation of man, "fashioned" by God from the slime of the earth, or the symbols of the Tree of Life, the Garden of Eden, the Serpent who personifies the power hostile to God, and so on. Similarities of language must not mask the profound differences in levels of thought. As the encyclical *Humani Generis* says: "Whatever of the popular narrations have been inserted into the sacred Scriptures must in no way be considered on a par with myths or other such things, which are more the product of an extravagant imagination than of that striving for truth and simplicity which in the sacred books, also of the Old Testament, is so apparent . . ." The biblical narratives symbolically translate the things to be given a religious explanation, and the traditions are to be read with this key to interpretation.

57

At the Dawn of History

From the beginnings to the times of the patriarchs, a long train of centuries flowed by and the Israelite chroniclers had almost no verifiable information concerning these ages. Still, these past times had to be treated in order to give a complete idea of the plan of God. So the chroniclers adroitly handled them by using materials borrowed from contemporary popular traditions. We know that among the ancient peoples, the origin of every human group (clan, tribe, city, people) and every facet of civilization (trade, invention, way of life) was conventionally represented by a personage who bore its name, an *eponym*. In chapters 4 to 11 of Genesis there is a genealogy of "patriarchs" which includes a great number of eponyms. They represented both the continuity of mankind, issued from a single stock (Adam, whose name means "man," was its eponym), and the progressive development of civilization, the diversification of humanity where more or less interrelated groups of people appeared.

In addition to these representations where literary convention plays a large part, some vague memories emerged from the more recent past, and served to call proto-history to mind. The figure of Lamech (8) concretely represents the primitive barbarity of the desert. Behind Nimrod are found the great Sumer-Accadian empires (Nimrod is an ancient Mesopotamian city). The historical role of Babylon, metropolis and crossroads of races, with its great temple (the Esagil) and its stepped tower (the Ziggurat), inspired the Tower of Babel episode (10). The story of the flood (9), known from the Mesopotamian epics (Text 6), preserved the memory of catastrophic floodings which devastated lower Mesopotamia in the fourth and third millenniums. In sum, we are here confronted with imprecise and fragmentary traditions organized into a continuous narrative in order to link the time of Abraham to the beginnings.

But we would miss the true value of this narrative if we confined ourselves to its superficial aspect and left out the didactic intentions of the narrators. These chapters, as the encyclical *Humani Generis* says again, "relate in a simple figurative style,

58

adapted to the understanding of a little developed humanity the fundamental truths supposed by the economy of salvation, at the same time as they describe in a popular way the origins of mankind and the chosen people." Imprecise traditions and imaginative stories are charged with profound meaning by the sacred writers and evoke the religious pre-history of mankind. From Adam to Abraham we witness the religious and moral degeneration of humanity further alienating itself from God over and over again. God tries to enter into relation with man to found a universal religion; but each time he fails, and failure results in a worse state for man. The sin of Adam entailed expulsion of the race from Paradise; the sins of Cain's descendants, corrupting civilization, brought on the catastrophy of the flood; the sin of Noah's descendants, engaged in the impious enterprise of Babel, brought on the dispersion of the races and the confusion of tongues. After that, all that remained to God was to choose Abraham, to realize through his race what he could not do through the totality of mankind. This is the meaning of the call of the patriarch and the covenant God made with him.

These seemingly childish anecdotes conceal under their simplicity religious lessons of considerable consequence, for by their representative value they have an immense importance which escapes many readers. It must also be understood that this profound drama is a necessary preamble to the history of salvation about to begin with the election of Abraham.

The Age of the Patriarchs

With the age of the patriarchs we set foot on firmer historical ground. To be sure, the traditions here do not yet correspond to our modern concept of history, but as Roland de Vaux has pointed out, "in their own way they recount real events, giving a faithful picture of the origin and migrations of the ancestors of Israel, of their geographical and ethical links, of their social, moral, and religious behavior."

Old Testament history is not scholarly but popular history, anecdotal in form, spiced with flashes of picturesque customs

(*14*), and stamped with emotion (*15, 21, 23*). This is not a political history, focused on the great temporal events, but the history of a family, landmarked by births, marriages, deaths (*15, 16, 17, 24*). Its framework is that of a genealogy linking the eponyms of the twelve tribes of Israel (the twelve "sons of Jacob") to Abraham, and it excludes from his heritage the eponyms of the neighboring tribes (Amon and Moab, the "sons of Lot"; Ishmael and Madian, the sons of Abraham; Edom, who is Esau, the brother of Jacob) (*11, 17*). Thus, the idea of the divine choice is concretely presented. This election set Israel apart from other peoples as sole heir to the promises given Abraham (*11, 13*), though all peoples will finally participate in the blessing promised by God. Thus the primitive universalism of God's plan will be reëstablished. The history so outlined is religious above all. This is why the role of Providence, directing this history in spite of the obstacles encountered, is constantly underlined (*11, 13, 18, 22, 24*). For the rest, the anecdotes are not reported for mere historical value, but for the moral and religious lessons which can be drawn from them—for example, the efficaciousness of the prayer of the just man (*14*), the grandeur of faith (*15*), courage in the face of trial (*19*), and so on.

In short, the history of the patriarchs is presented as "an epic recalling the important historical facts needed in order to understand the origin and development of revelation" (J. Chaine). It is a detailed memoir of family and rural life, a book full of rich images. On the plane of history the exact importance of the details in the episodes is not always easy to see, especially when the narration becomes more elaborate, but the over-all value is certain. On the plane of faith, all the data have bearing; but as is clear, revelation is only beginning. On the plane of literature, these narratives have all the charm of the most beautiful of Oriental tales.

The Age of Moses

Of more recent origin, the traditions of the age of Moses form a very important cycle. In the books of the Bible they extend from Exodus to Deuteronomy. These traditions show how, under the leadership of Moses, the Hebrew group dwelling in Goshen escaped, wandered for a time in the Sinai peninsula, was there given an organization and a law, bound itself to Yahweh by a covenant, and finally turned towards Canaan. But this slice of history is not recounted merely to exalt Israel's national origins; it is envisaged from the angle of faith. Yahweh, acting through the intermediary of his ambassador Moses, saved Israel in Egypt. In the desert he made them his people by giving them his covenant and his Law, and finally he led them to the promised land.

Perhaps even more than in the saga of the patriarchs, Yahweh is the central personage of this narrative. The exodus is not an action of Moses, it is rather an action of Yahweh. This is clearest in the story of the plagues of Egypt, presented as a combat of God against the pharaoh (26–30), or in the narrative of the covenant at Sinai (33–36). In short, the history became a supernatural drama whose star is God. From then on, the narrators' artistry was aimed at manifesting God's presence in the events taking place and the religious emotion his presence stirred in the memory of them. The salvation of Israel was the sign of grace by which the people of old believed in Yahweh. Along with the creation, this election was the divine wonder of all wonders. The fundamental historical value of these narratives is preserved if they are correctly listened to by taking into account the techniques they used. It must be remembered that this concrete presentation, which strikes the imagination and arouses enthusiasm, served the faith much better than a dry chronicle.

Even so, all the traditions grouped into this cycle are not homogeneous. Besides the epic narratives we are going to treat there are narratives of a much more sober style (32, 36). But what is important to understand regarding all of these different literary forms is the fundamental witness to God which is rendered through them: his way of leading history, his plans for men, his demands on them. The memory of the national past is always subordinate to the religious teaching, although moral education of the readers sometimes rises to a level of prime

61

importance. For example, the traditions retracing Israel's march through the desert continually contrast the ingratitude of a "stiff-necked people" with the manifestations of the divine mercy, and here imagery really preaches the fundamental teachings of the Law (compare *44–46* to *37*).

The Conquest of Canaan

The traditions show the settlement of Canaan from two different viewpoints: in Judges 1 it is a progressive penetration of the tribes acting separately (*49*), whereas in Joshua 1, 11, it is a unified military action under the command of Joshua (*50–54*). Doubtless, the second collection schematizes the plan of history to emphasize the important idea that the divine plan begun with the exodus from Egypt was promoted by the conquest undertaken by the exodus group. Israel was now entering into possession of the inheritance promised to its ancestors by God (*11*). So it can be understood how the crossing of the Jordan is described in terms reminiscent of the crossing of the Red Sea (*50, 51*), for the two events are part of the same over-all plan, and Joshua continued the mission of Moses. At the same time, the capture of Jericho (*52*) and the battle of Gibeon (*53*) are described with an epic tone resembling the account of the plagues of Egypt, but in the details of the narrative the true-to-life touch sometimes surprises us with the crude mentality of this era—for example, the savage extermination of populations "under the Lord's ban" (*52*). It is true that Israel needed such protection from the surrounding paganism; nevertheless, the book of Joshua shows how far they still were from the Gospel. Israel was only at the beginning of her spiritual education.

The Age of the Judges

A great variety of traditions concern the times of the Judges. Centered on important events or great figures, they allow us to reconstruct a very episodic history with an uncertain chronology. Aside from the lyricism of the hymn of Deborah (*56*), the narratives which relate the exploits of Ehud and Barak (*Jgs.* 3–4), of Gideon and Jephthah (*Jgs.* 6–8, 10–12), the foundation of the sanctuary of Dan, and the extermination of the Benjaminites (*Jgs.* 17–21) rarely rise to the level of epic, but they are precious witnesses of the political and religious drama of the era (*57, 58*). The adventures of Samson, which carefully restore the atmosphere and the customs of the time, are retold in racy pages, full of popular zest (*59*). The misfortunes of the hero, occasioned by this romantic adventure, furnish the occasion for a discreet lesson taught more than once by the Wisdom writers (see *Prv.* 7).

The infancy of Samuel (*1 Sam.* 1–3), during the most tragic days of the Philistine wars, is related with consummate artistry (*60*). Here the genre comes closer to pious hagiography, without the critical pretension it took on in the Middle Ages. The religious ideas of predestination and vocation are admirably illustrated in these brilliant pages. In a different genre, the adventures of the Ark of the Covenant after its capture by the Philistines (*1 Sam.* 4–6) gives us some idea of the popular narratives told in its sanctuary when peace was restored.

The Origins of the Royalty and the Debut of David

The traditions which tell of the origins of the royalty are divided into groups. All of them agree on certain important points, namely, Saul was the first king, and Samuel consecrated the new institution. Beyond this they reflect the contrary attitudes taken by the Israelites towards the monarchy and ascribe both to Samuel (*62, 63*). On the one hand, the old judge yields despite himself to the complaints of an ungrateful people, thus preparing the way for future misfortunes (*1 Sam.* 7–8; 10, 17–25; 12); on the other hand, under a divine inspiration, he takes the initiative in anointing Saul to assure the liberation of Israel (9, 1–10, 16; 10, 26–11, 15). The presentation of these recollections is clearly influenced by the mentality and the religious ideas of the collectors who gathered them.

After this, the history and the battles of Saul (*1 Sam.* 13–14), the exploits of David, his glory at the court of Saul, his adventurous life when he fled into the lands of the Philistines

63

(*1 Sam.* 31; *2 Sam.* 1, 1–5, 5), give place to highly colored narratives. These traditions come nearer and nearer to historiography (*64–67*), for they circulated in oral form for only a short time.

4. FROM ORAL TRADITIONS TO HISTORIOGRAPHY

Israelite historiography is introduced by a masterpiece: the internal history of the reign of David (*2 Sam.* 5, 6—*1 Kgs.* 2). This is a work of a contemporary chronicler, who certainly was closely involved in the events, and probably wrote during the reign of Solomon. All we know is that he must be admired for his art as a lively, well-balanced, emotionally restrained narrator, and also for his qualities as psychologist and analyst. Oriental antiquity, where literature of the heart is abundant, offers us nothing else like it. Graeco-Latin antiquity has done no better in style, though it produced more extensive works of history. Thanks to the unknown chronicler, the reign of the great king is reënacted before our eyes in all its glories (the taking of Jerusalem and the transfer of the Ark of the Covenant [*68*]), and its share of pains and sorrows (David's crime, the murder of his eldest son, the revolt of Absalom, his painful old age [*72–73*]). In the plan of God, one stage is coming to an end, and another is beginning. In addition, this history is centered about a prophecy which will dominate the next stage: Nathan's promise to David (*71*), the point of departure for royal messianism.

The History of Solomon

The literary quality of the documentation of Solomon's reign (*1 Kgs.* 3–11) is not equal to the history of David's succession, but it does offer good material for the historian. All the glories of the monarchy are again taken up with pleasure: Solomon's wisdom (that is to say, both his culture and his administrative skill) and his proverbial wealth (*76, 79*), the two traits which complete the portrait of the ideal king. David furnished its first elements, which later would serve to evoke the Messiah-King *(126, 127, 329)*. The temple, as it must, holds the place of honor in this history *(77, 78)*, for was it not God's final touch on the centuries of long work which began with the call of Abraham? But this picture has another side to it *(79)*, which explained the further evolution of the Davidic kingdom *(80, 86)*.

The Written Collections of the Traditions

With the monarchy, Israel came to national adulthood. Heir to many centuries of history, it had come to possess its political and religious institutions, and now had scribes who enjoyed an official status in the court. The close liaison between the palace and the temple, between political life and religion, naturally gave the scribes intimate rapport with the sacerdotal environment of Jerusalem, and made them the depositories of a tradition which the reign of David had brought to final development. In this educated milieu, the need was felt to make a balance-sheet of the past. This was no mere human preoccupation, but a work of faith. A collection of all the traditional materials into one ordered compilation would offer an overall view of the blessings of God upon his people. This collection would be like a detailed commentary on the national creed, whose general tenor certain liturgical formulations preserve for us *(1, 2)*. Besides the juridical collections and some collections of poetic texts, the oral material in many cases had taken on a stereotyped form, so much so that it was transmitted from generation to generation within the confines of the sanctuaries, the tribes, the domestic celebrations, without substantial change. This does not exclude the possibility that some partial collections already existed. Whether they did or not, the royal scribes undertook a work of compilation which would make all of them historiographers and theologians. While respecting the legacy of the past, they enshrined the traditions of Israel in continuous narratives where the anecdotes lose their distinctiveness.

It is difficult to retrace the history of this work exactly. Begun under Solomon, under David for certain sections, it certainly went through many stages. After the schism of 932, it had to

65

go on side by side in the kingdoms of Judah and Israel, and these two great compilations of traditions probably formed the basis of sacred history which extended from the beginning to the death of Moses. Those traditions probably underwent many editions and absorbed preëxisting materials still recognizable by their archaic characteristics. The traditions are conventionally called by the name they give to God in Genesis (Yahweh or Elohim), the "Yahwist" or "Elohist" sacred histories. The Yahwist came from the kingdom of Judah, and from an environment very close to the court, for the court spirit can be seen in this pro-monarchist version of the consecration of Saul (*63*). The Elohist arose in the kingdom of Israel, and in the same milieu to which we owe the anti-monarchistic version of the same event (*62*). In spite of its later date (9th or 8th century?), the Elohist retained a more direct echo of the ancient Mosaic tradition, through the intermediary of an ancient sanctuary, perhaps Shechem (*54*). The connection of the traditions relating the Conquest and the Judges with the two sources is unfortunately unclear, even in passages where there are clearly doublets. And though critical study yields many uncertainties, at least it gives us a glimpse of the fate of the Israelite memories of the past.

Character of These Collections

The compilers of the traditions were truly literary authors. While respecting the content of the materials used, they have sealed the materials with the marks of their own personalities, especially in their style and their doctrinal preoccupations, which were bound up with the problems of their own times. The Yahwist, for example, closely linked to the creator of the Davidic succession, recreated the fall of the first man with great psychological insight and a precise use of symbols (*3–6*), while with equal success the author portrayed a variety of scenes such as Yahweh's visit to Abraham (*14*) and the plagues of Egypt (*28*). Here we are in the presence of a truly great artist. But the Elohist, influenced by the first northern prophets, is no less an artist himself (*23, 44*).

66

The two authors—or, if you prefer, the two schools—so often worked on the same traditional materials that we can compare them where their works have been preserved untouched (*26, 30, 33, 34, 36*), and thus verify both their dependence upon the sources and their originality. Writing at a later date, they undertook a new presentation of the respected data to meet the practical needs of their own eras. In order to maintain the faith of their contemporaries and to present a concrete doctrine of life, they organized the facts concerning the doctrine of the covenant and the Law. Such organizations existed long before them, so that when later Jewish doctors put the first five books of Moses under the direct guarantee of Moses, they interpreted a profound reality in schematic fashion. And the critic faces another problem as important as the literary composition of these books, that of reconstructing the *Mosaic tradition* which was fixed by a complex process.

It should be noted that the first compilers gave their work real unity by the introduction of guiding themes. These first sacred histories sketched out the masterful fresco of the divine plan in which, ten centuries later, Christ would take his place as the central personage. His cross and resurrection would reveal the last secret of this plan: the reunion of all things in Christ (*Eph.* 1, 9–10). But the collectors of the traditions of Israel had already unveiled its first stages.

Text 5

THE IMPORTANCE OF LITERARY GENRES IN THE BIBLE

In the encyclical *Divino Afflante Spiritu* Pope Pius XII shows how important it is to distinguish the literary genres used in the Bible, to understand exactly what they teach us:

67

The ancient peoples of the East, in order to express their ideas, did not always employ those forms or kinds of speech which we use today; but rather those used by the men of their times and countries. What those exactly were the commentator cannot determine, so to speak, in advance, but only after a careful examination of the ancient literature of the East . . .

The same inquiry has also clearly shown the special preëminence of the people of Israel among all the other ancient nations of the East in their mode of compiling history, both by reason of its antiquity and by reason of the faithful record of the events; qualities which may well be attributed to the gift of divine inspiration and to the peculiar religious purpose of biblical history. Nevertheless, no one, who has a correct idea of biblical inspiration, will be surprised to find, even in the sacred writers, as in other ancient authors, certain fixed ways of expounding and narrating, certain definite idioms, especially of a kind peculiar to the Semitic tongues, so-called approximations, and certain hyperbolical modes of expression; nay, at times, even paradoxical, which even help to impress the ideas more deeply on the mind. For of the modes of expression which, among ancient peoples, and especially those of the East, human language used to express its thought, none is excluded from the sacred books, provided the way of speaking adopted in no wise contradicts the holiness and truth of God . . .

For as the substantial Word of God became like men in all things "except sin" (*Heb.* 4, 15), so the words of God expressed in human language are made like human speech in every respect, except error. Not infrequently—to mention only one instance—when some persons reproachfully charge the sacred writers with some historical error or inaccuracy in the recording of facts, on closer examination it turns out to be nothing else than those customary modes of expression and narration peculiar to the ancients, which used to be employed in the mutual dealings of social life and which in fact were sanctioned by common usage.

When then such modes of expression are met with in the sacred text, which, being meant for men, is couched in human language, justice demands that they be no more taxed with error than when they occur in the ordinary intercourse of daily life.

68

Text 6

THE MESOPOTAMIAN NARRATIVE OF THE DELUGE

The biblical narrative of the Flood (*9, 185*) uses the theme of an old Mesopotamian legend which is known in many versions. The most important one, preserved in the epic of Gilgamesh (Text 28), puts the narration on the lips of the story's hero. The gods, in their jealousy, decided to annihilate all life on earth. But Ea, the craftsman-god, reveals their project to his protégé Utnapishtim ("I have found life") and teaches him to construct a ship. Utnapishtim loads all of his possessions on his ship; then he makes his family board, his servants, some land animals and birds. On the day appointed by Shamash, the sun god, the flood begins. Some Mesopotamian gods who appear in the narrative are: Ishtar, goddess of fertility; Anu, god of the sky and head of the Pantheon; Adad, god of the storm, identical to the Canaanite Baal; Shullat and Hanish, his heralds; Nergal, god of the lower regions; Nunurta, god of war; the Annunaki, divinities of the earth.

As soon as the first light of day appeared,
from the lowest point of the heavens a dark cloud arose.
Adad thundered in his chest.
Shullat and Hanish went before him,
they went as his heralds through the mountains and plains.
Nergal tore away the gates [of the sluices];
Ninurta accompanied him, overthrowing the dikes.
The Annunaki lifted their torches,
embracing the earth in their shining.
The rage of Adad reached as far as the heavens,
changing into darkness what was in the light . . .
During one day, the tempest blew.
It blew, rapidly, submerging the mountains,
falling on men, as in a battle:

no one saw his brother any longer,
he could not recognize himself under the heavens.
The gods were terrified by the Flood.
They fled, they mounted up to the heaven of Anu.
The gods crouched like dogs,
they cowered there against the wall of the enclosure;
Ishtar cried like a woman in labor;
she cried out, the Queen of the gods in a loud voice:
"Alas! The days of yesteryear are changed into mud! . . ."

(Tablet 11; 96–118)

The catastrophe lasted six days and six nights. On the seventh day the ship of Utanapishtim came to rest on mount Nisir, the first to emerge from the waters. Still the hero waited seven days before attempting to go out.

When the eleventh day arrived,
I released one dove and set it free:
the dove went out and returned;
not having anywhere to settle, it returned.
I released a swallow and let it go:
the swallow went out and returned;
I released a raven and set it free:
the raven went out and, seeing the ebb of the waters,
it ate, circled, cawed and did not return.
I let them go to the four winds, I offered sacrifice,
I poured out a libation on the mountain peak;
I piled them up under reeds, cedar wood and myrtle.
The gods smelled the odor;
the gods smelled the good odor;
the gods, like flies, gathered themselves above the sacrificer.

(Tablet 11; 145–161)

To finish the story: the gods decide to divinize Utanapishtim and his wife. So they transport them into a paradise located outside the world, beyond the cosmic ocean.

The similarities of the text with the biblical narrative do not need to be underlined. Even if the Bible uses the old legend to relate ancient history, it rethinks the legend and expurgates it.

70

All of its polytheism is suppressed and the flood becomes a judgment type coming down upon sinful humanity in its distant pre-history. The imagery of the god Adad thundering in his cloud will be used again in the biblical storm theophanies (*81*).

Text 7

CANAANITE POETRY

Hebrew poetry developed in the school of Canaanite poetry. A good example of this is the following passage taken from an epic legend of Ugarit. Transcribed in the 14th century, the text could go back to the second millennium. The hero Daniel ("El is my judge") is constantly surnamed "the Rephaite" (it is not sure whether this is the name of a people, but the Bible gives this name to the ancient inhabitants of Canaan), "the Harnemite" (an unknown place name). He is grieved at not having a son (compare Abraham, *13*). In the opening scene, for seven days he carries out a series of rites aimed at obtaining a son; he partakes in a religious feast where he consumes special food, thus sharing the table of the gods; then a nightly sojourn into the sanctuary, which will be the place of the divine manifestation (compare to *18, 76*):

A fifth, a sixth, a seventh day,
   Daniel takes part in the feast of the gods:
at the feast of the gods he eats,
   he drinks at the feast of the Holy Ones.
Daniel removes his tunic;
   he removes this tunic, goes up and lies down to sleep
he removes his cincture and passes the night.
   Then, on the seventh day,
Baal approaches, in his pity,
   at the misfortune of Daniel the Rephaite,

at the sign of the gallant Harnemite,
    who has no son like his brothers
no offspring like his near relations:
    "How does he not have a son like his brothers
offspring like his near relations?
    To him who eats at the feast of the gods,
to him who drinks at the feast of the Holy Ones,
    may you bless him O Bull-El, my father!
be propitious to him, O Creator of Creatures!
    so that there be a son for him in his house,
offspring in his palace,
    who erects the monument to his divine ancestors,
in the sanctuary venerates his ancestors, . . .
    who gives him his hand in his drunkenness
sustains him when he is drunk with wine,
    consumes his [funeral] repast in the house of Baal,
his [funeral] banquet in the house of El . . ."
    Then El touches his servant:
he blesses Daniel the Rephaite
    he shows himself propitious to the gallant Harnemite.

A son is born to Daniel. After some time, while he is at home with his wife, Lady Danatiya, he receives a divine visit. The artisan god brings bows and arrows for his child. The scene is described in these terms:

And behold the seventh day.
Immediately, Daniel the Rephaite,
    on the field, the valiant Harnemite
raised himself and held a meeting at the entrance of the Gate,
    near the heap of grain which is on the threshing floor.
He judges the cause of the widow,
    he states the rights of the orphan.

Raising his eyes, he sees
    at a thousand stadia, at thousands of leagues,
the progress of Kothat [*the Clever*]; as he looks, he sees
    the coming of Khasis [*the Wise*].
Behold him who bears a bow;
    behold him with arrows aplenty.

Immediately, Daniel the Rephaite,
  on the field, the valiant Harnemite with a strong voice calls to his
  wife:
"Listen, Lady Danatiya!
  Bring a lamb from the flock
for the appetite of the Clever and the Wise,
  for the desire of the Expert in craftsmanship.
Feed and give drink to the gods;
  serve and honor them, the Lords of Memphis, the gods of the
  universe!"

She listens, Lady Danatiya;
  she brings a lamb from the flock.
for the appetite of the Clever and the Wise,
  for the desire of the Expert in craftsmanship.
He arrives finally, the Clever and the Wise:
  into the hands of Daniel he places the bow, on his knees he
  places the arrows.
Immediately, Lady Danatiya
  feeds and gives the gods to drink;
she serves them and honors them,
  the Lords of Memphis, the gods of the universe.
The Clever returns then to his tent,
  the Expert returns to his dwelling . . .

Note the balancing paralellisms in the style as in Hebrew
poetry (compare to *31, 56*). The epic legend unfolds in an atmosphere of polytheism; the links between the gods and human
here are very much like those in Homeric poetry. El ("God")
is the supreme god of Canaanite mythology. Baal ("the Lord";
his proper name is Hadad) is the god of the storm and of vege-
tation. The artisan god, analogous to the Vulcan of the Latins,
bears a name composed of epithets drawn from nature: Kothor,
"the Expert"; Khasis, "the Wise"; Hayyan, "the Expert" (in
craftsmanship). The context of his appearance suggests a
double god: the wife of Daniel feeds "the gods"; but this plural
can be understood as a plural of majesty.
  This page can usefully be compared with some biblical texts
(*13, 14, 18, 19*), but a certain similarity in the manner of re-

73

counting the episodes whose theme is very close must not over-shadow the profound differences, notably on the religious level. Still, the biblical narrators do draw from Canaanite art, and it is even probable that their prose editions of the national traditions were preceded by poetic compositions, chanted by the minstrels of Israel.

Bibliography

For an over-all presentation of the critical problem, consult H. Cazelles and J. Delorme in the *Introduction to the Bible*. On particular areas, see B. Vawter, *A Path Through Genesis* (New York 1956), C. Hauret, *Beginnings: Genesis and Modern Science* (Dubuque n.d.), H. Renckens, *Israel's Concept of the Beginning: The Theology of Gen. I–III* (New York 1964), and three books by A. Parrot: *The Flood and Noah's Ark, The Temple of Jerusalem,* and *The Tower of Babel* (New York, n.d.).

Study Guides

Following the indications of the encyclical *Divino Afflante Spiritu* (cited in Text 5), study the various literary procedures seen in the collection of the Israelite traditions: the plan of the narrative, the epic presentation of the facts, the occasional usage of folklore and symbol, etc. If you have a Bible which distinguishes the Yahwist fragments from the Elohist, note the differences between them.

Compare the artistry of the great Hebrew storytellers to that of the historian who wrote the internal history of the kingdom of David.

Indicate how the collections of traditions are constructed on some guiding themes which make them *sacred histories* and commentaries on the Israelite creed (*1, 2*). In tracing the themes in the chapters on the beginning and pre-history (*3–10*), note how the corresponding material details in the narratives are less valuable than their symbolical meaning. For the patriarchal and the Mosaic period, look for events connected with faith (for example, *26, 30, 33*). In what sense can one call these sacred histories a catechism by imagery? If we must look for history, since God revealed himself and realized his plan in real events, do they not also have a real importance in another order? Does not the historical witness assume forms which are different in every way from those to which we are accustomed?

IV.

THE FAITH OF ISRAEL

I<small>T</small> would take too long and often be too difficult to follow the development of the religion of Israel from the call of Abraham to the height of the monarchy. However, it would be good to draw up a provisional balance-sheet of the first stage of its history, before the opening of the age of the prophets. The spiritual education of the People of God was far from over, but God had already set it upon solid foundations, which would come up again in the following stages, even in the age of the Christian faith itself. So we will examine the source of these beliefs, the idea of God, the faith in Israel's unique vocation, its concept of man's proper place before God. For biblical religion had already been totally severed from the paganisms of its neighbors.

1. AT THE SOURCES OF FAITH

The Word of God

The Israelite faith was founded upon the witness of inspired men like Abraham, Moses, and the seers who continued their work. These seers, who soon came to be called prophets, were conscious of having received a message from God which they had to communicate to other men. It is of little importance whether these interventions of God were extraordinary visions or intimate inspirations felt in the depths of consciousness. (The

76

biblical narratives contain events of both orders [*11, 13, 26, 34, 35, 50, 57, 60, 63, 71.*]) Although all we have is the external aspect, the important thing is that the divine word thus received and communicated was afterwards a source of faith. The religion of Israel was extraordinary among the neighboring religions because of the solidarity of its basic affirmations, its intransigence, its original development and continuity in the midst of the gravest difficulties. It was no human tradition analogous to those whose evolution can be followed elsewhere, for faith did not spring up spontaneously from intuitions of reason and a religious sense, but from a revelation of God.

The Signs of Faith

To accredit his messengers, God worked signs. What were they? They were events which felt the touch of his finger, his presence, his intervention, his intentions. But it would be an error to equate the biblical notion of sign with our modern idea of miracle, though there are some cases where the signs performed by the divine mesengers came very near to what we call miracles —for example, the healings worked by Elijah and Eliseus in the royal era (*89, 96*). Signs of this type were quite proper in the narrations of the exodus, at the time of the foundation of a supernatural religion, but events which were the result of natural causes could, in certain cases, also appear charged with meaning. For are not natural causes at the complete disposition of the Creator? This was the case when events fulfilled the predictions of God's messengers or confirmed providential laws revealed by them. For example, in conformity with the doctrine of the covenant, the difficulties of the age of the Judges were seen as a punishment for Israel's infidelity (*55*), while David's success was the reward for his fidelity (*71*). But most often, no distinction was made between the three kinds of signs: miracles, the accomplishment of predicted events, and events consistent with the laws of providence. All three kinds were inextricably intermingled. This was the case for the plagues of Egypt (*28*) or

77

the crossing of the Red Sea at the time of the exodus (*30*); both are divine wonders which led Israel to the faith.

The matter is further complicated by the literary form the witness takes in some narratives. History was transformed into epic, and as a consequence hyperbole and amplification of objective memories took place in those narratives where poetry is present. In such places, the essential facts must not be confused with the stylistic processes the narrators use (*14, 19, 28, 30, 32, 34, 53, 56*). The divine signs must be understood correctly within the marvelous literature where they legitimately occur.

2. THE GOD OF ISRAEL

Who is God?

The ancient Orient was profoundly religious, but divided the divine by multiplying gods. Mythology made its universe the model of the world and of human society. Or rather, it described this model according to terrestrial copies: the immortal gods were represented as the images of man, down to even his vilest passions. So the history of the gods, which took place on primordial times, reflected their loves and battles (Text 8). In Israel, on the contrary, God is unique; he has neither spouse nor children, a characteristic unparalleled in any of the ancient religions. God is the Holy One, not only in the sense that he belongs to a world other than ours (he is the "separated one"), but also, and especially, because he dominates our moral universe by his absolute perfection. By this fact too, he is cut off from all the other gods of the East. He has nothing about him of the abstract principle imagined by some philosopher, for Israelite antiquity ignores metaphysical speculation. Rather, speaking of God concretely in terms of experience, he is represented under human characteristics (that is to say, anthropomorphically), and feelings similar to our own are attributed to him—for example anger, pity. This sympathetic God is truly the living and personal God (*3–7, 9, 14, 26, 28, 32, 48, 58*).

The use of symbols allows a conventionalized representation

of God in the world apart where he resides. He is enthroned in a palace, of which his temple is the terrestrial image (*34, 78*), surrounded by a court of supernatural beings (the angels, the *sons of God*), who are his messengers and instruments of his actions (*18*). To underscore his transcendence, Israel located his palace above the vault of the heavens (*34*), or high on a sacred mountain which recalls the Greek Olympus (*214*), which Sinai is sometimes compared to. His intervention in terrestrial affairs is also depicted in conventional language. Sometimes it is a familiar God descending to earth to see what is going on (*10, 14, 59;* compare Text 7), and sometimes a terrible God, the God of battles, who comes riding the chariot of the storm and manifests himself in clouds and lightning (*13, 30, 31, 33, 53, 56, 81*: Text 6). Or sometimes his mysterious presence is clothed in less definable characteristics: the texts speak of *the Angel of Yahweh* or *the Glory of Yahweh* to name those terrestrial manifestations which both reveal and veil the divine majesty (*19, 26, 35, 51*). The imagery used in the service of faith was mostly borrowed from the common fund of the Oriental religions, but biblical revelation filtered and purified it, adapting it to its own strict monotheism. In addition, some original imagery is without known parallels, denoting the personal character of the experience it expresses. The burning bush is a symbol of this kind (*26*).

The Creator

The gods of the Oriental pantheon were, for the most part, mere personifications of the cosmic elements. There were terrestrial or astral gods (earth, son, moon, the stars, the sea, the underworld) and gods who presided over the phenomena of nature (the growth-force which was manifested in the spring, the terrifying force of the storm). It is easy to find a latent pantheism in such mythology where the gods were multiplied to infinity, for everything in the universe takes on a divine essence, with no strong affirmation of a transcendent God. The pagan of this time, who trembled before his gods and offered them worship, was close to primitive humanity, experiencing a sacral fear in the face of nature, bowing before the forces which gave birth to him and ruled him, hoping to make them incline favorably towards him (Text 8).

These concepts rooted in the remotest ages were radically rectified by biblical revelation. Here, God alone is God and everything else is his creation: earth, sea, stars, plants, animals. As for man, God made him in principle the king of all nature (4). The world's elements are not capricious and unpredictable powers, but things obedient to the laws which God has imposed upon them (9). This ordering of the world is the first of the divine wonders, and gives rise to heartfelt admiration. Far more, it gives natural phenomena a sacred meaning. In their grandeur they manifest God, as if they were the clothing of his awe-inspiring presence (33, 81). If ever they fall upon man to crush him, it is not accidental, for they are signs of God's wrath (9, 14, 31, 56).

The Master of History

In Mesopotamian paganism the gods were thought to have determined from the beginning the destinies which ruled the world. The gods themselves were subject to these destinies, and earthly history, following the law of the eternal return, could only conform to them. The God of Israel, on the contrary, showed himself totally independent. No fixed destinies bind him, but a plan conceived by him from the beginning guides and unfolds through all of history. For though it is true that man is free and responsible for his acts (5–6, 43), God nonetheless governs events by his all-powerful providence (11, 22, 27–30).

The plan of God is the expression of his kindness towards men. He has created them for good and bound them to move towards it (3, 11, 43). But at this point sin came into the world: the original revolt—the prototype of all faults (5); the idolatrous pride of human civilization in full flower (10); the bad will of the powerful who, like the pharaoh, grow proud at

80

their own greatness (27, 28); the hardness of heart of the Chosen People themselves (44–46, 55, 62, 72). In spite of all this, God was not discouraged and he used all his wiles to overcome the obstacles. He is jealous of his glory, but he put this glory aside to show himself merciful and compassionate (37, 44), and he willed that his benevolent plan be successful. This fundamental disposition guides the unfolding of human history. Whatever the face he wears, God is present in every event, whether showing himself a protective power (18, 30, 51, 52), putting his beloved to the test (15, 19), or chastizing sinful men (45, 55).

The Divine Names

The Old Testament borrowed the names for God from Semitic terminology after purifying them of their pagan overtones. *El*, the common name of the gods in Babylon and in Canaan (like *theos* in Greek and *deus* in Latin), designated the supreme God of the pantheon; it is still to be found in the Arabic *Allâh* (*al-Ilâh*, "the God"). In the era of the patriarchs, El was God's proper name and was often accompanied by archaic titles: *El-Elyôn*, "the most high God," an epithet attested to in the pantheon of Ugarit (12, 214); *El-Shaddaï*, probably "the mountain God," alluding to the sacred mountain of the divine residence; *Elôhim*, a plural of majesty and fullness which corresponds to the singular Ilâh, was used throughout the Bible to say "God," in the singular. A whole series of the titles applied to God, especially in the composition of proper names, should be added here: familial titles, such as Father, Brother, Uncle, etc.; lordly titles, like King, Master. Their use shows the links between God and man complexly worded with a mixture of reverence and familiarity.

But the proper name of Israel's God was Yahweh, represented in Hebrew by the tetragram YHWH. This name was probably used before Moses, in an antique form (*Yah* or *Yahô*) which continued to exist for a long time afterwards. But the Mosaic revelation gave it profound meaning (26), for *Yahweh,*

81

related to the verb "to be," means "He who is" in contra-distinction to idols who "are not"; or perhaps "He who makes to be," that is, the Creator; or again, "He who is there," he whose presence and action accompany men everywhere. In ancient times in Israel the name Yahweh, recalling the epics of Sinai and the Conquest, evoked the image of a warrior God marching at the head of a fighting people. This could be the source of the title "Yahweh of Armies" (*Yahweh-Sabaoth*), which is still used in the Sanctus of the Mass, unless it is an allusion to the "Celestial Armies" of angels who form the divine court. Be that as it may, in biblical poetry this warrior image is freely intermingled with the theophany of the storm (*56*), or with the grandiose idea of Yahweh-King developed in Israel after the invasion of Canaan (*62, 69*).

3. THE PEOPLE OF GOD

Israel's Call and the Covenant

To realize his plan in the history of men, God chose a people and revealed himself to them through the intermediary of his messengers, the first ones he called to faith. From among the little peoples related by origin (Aramaeans, Ammonites, Moabites, Ismaelites, Madiamites, Edomites), he "set apart" only the Israelite tribal confederation. Why this predeliction? Here we come face to face with the mystery of divine liberty and grace (*11, 17*). In the Genesis narratives the genealogies are used to highlight the divine choice. At the exodus God openly manifested his will to make Israel his "first-born son" (*26, 29, 30*) by saving them from Egypt in order to make a covenant with them.

At Sinai (also called Horeb) this covenant was concluded (*36*) through the mediation of Moses. He represented God to the Israelites as an inspired person, and represented his people as their leader before God. Sealed in the blood of animals, the covenant required Israel's commitment to observe the Law of

God. In return God promised to protect Israel and lead her into Canaan and to make her prosper there. The covenant was the most important action of all, for together with the escape from Egypt it brought Israel into history as a confederation of tribes united by the sacred link of their religion. At certain turning points in Israel's history this covenant was renewed (*54, 146*), and it dominated the whole development of the Old Testament as a hope for the coming of a new covenant (*181, 204*). The Israelite was especially conscious of the continuity which bound the covenant of Sinai to the patriarchal religion, for Abraham was the first "to conclude a covenant with God" by receiving his promise (*13*).

The Divine Promises

God promised Abraham three things: his blessings, descendants, and settlement of Abraham descendants in the land of Canaan (*11, 13, 15*). This very same promise was renewed when God manifested himself to Moses (*26*) and in the covenant at Sinai (*43*). It was clearly a conditional promise since there were conditons to be fulfilled to receive its benefits, and failure to observe the clauses of the covenant entailed punishments (*43, 54*). The prophet Nathan pointed out to David that God had kept this initial promise fully (*71*), which permitted prediction of everything which would come to pass. At this stage of revelation, the object of the promise apparently did not rise above at terrestrial and temporal prosperity. However, the promise must not be minimized. In fact, in the consecrated phrase, Israel expected the promised land to be "a land flowing with milk and honey" (*26*), an image recalling several themes of Canaanite mythology and evoking a paradise-like prosperity where the evils of the human condition would no longer have a place. The divine promise led Israel to hope for a return at the end of sacred history to the paradise lost (*3*). Since things were not yet so, the total fulfillment of the promise was yet to come.

83

The King

Even after the establishment of the monarchy, a number of people remained attached to the ancient structures of the nation. And to believe them, the golden age of Israel was the period in the desert. With this in mind they criticized the new institution of the kingship (*61, 62*). This viewpoint existed in a latent state among certain circles in the north, and the experience of Solomon's reign followed by some idolatrous kings only reinforced it, although from the reign of David on most of the Israelites, especially in Judah and Jerusalem, saw things differently, for to them the monarchy was a blessing from God (*63*), and the dynasty of David was for all times integrated into the national institutions (*71*). The Yahwist sacred history and the chronicle of the succession of David were written from this point of view. The reign of the great king seemed to be the provincial flowering of a whole series of events since the call of Abraham (*24, 47, 75*).

The king was not a mere political and military leader raised up by God and consecrated by the sacred anointing. The kingship of Saul was this kind (*63*), and it persisted in the kingdom of Israel after the schism. In comparison to this concept, however, the kingship of David was a marked development. Invested by divine authority as a lieutenant of Yahweh, the king was, in the strongest sense of the word, the head of his people, and in a certain way he represented the people before God. For this reason he came to carry out some religious functions (*68, 78*), and there was no hesitation about calling him a "priest" (*70*). The great events of his reign, notably his consecration (*70, 330*), were marked by liturgical celebrations (*81–83*). God was expected to give him riches and glory, victory over enemies (*70, 330*), wisdom to govern his people well (*76*), and justice to make right triumph as the Law demanded (*329*). But he himself had to remain a subject of the Law, which he guarded. If he broke the Law he would be punished, and his people with him (*71, 72, 80*). Such a concept of the monarchy contained the best of the ancient Oriental ideal (Text 7), though it differed radically from that of Egypt, where the king was divinized, and from that of Mesopotamia, where the royal power incarnated the power of the national god.

The Temple

God is present wherever he acts. But his presence was especially accessible in the sacred places where he manifested himself and where he was worshiped. Of old, the patriarchs founded sanctuaries in Canaan (11, 18), and Sinai was particularly venerable since there God appeared to Moses to reveal his name to him (26). In the Yahwist account of the exodus from Egypt, the motive was the accomplishment of a pilgrimage and a feast there (27, 28). It was there that the celebration of the covenant took place as a liturgical ceremony (33, 34, 36). After finally entering the promised land, Israel reëstablished the sacred places founded by its ancestors and took possession of the ancient high places of Baal, the Canaanite divinity (Text 10), transferring them to Yahweh. We know that this was not done without a struggle during the grave crisis of the age of the Judges.

The sign expressing the presence of God in the midst of his people was the ark of the covenant, the memorial of the Sinai covenant (45, 51, 52). After the conquest, the central sanctuary of the tribal confederation was the location of the ark at Shechem (54), and then Shiloh (60). But beginning with the reign of David, the holy places in the north were finally dispossessed, for David transfered the ark to Jerusalem (68), where Solomon later built the temple (77, 78). The ancient places of worship were not yet forbidden, and they remained in use for a long time, but the overwhelming influence of the sanctuary of the ark, and then of the temple at Jerusalem, prepared for the centralization which took place during the era of the monarchy (146). In fact, the temple was the "house of Yahweh," the terrestrial replica of his celestial palace to such a degree that no other sacred place mattered (see 18). When

85

one called upon God in the temple, he answered to his name and made himself mysteriously present in the obscurity of the Holy of Holies (*77*). The temple kept its sign-value until Christ substituted an incomparably greater sign for it in the temple of his body (*Jn.* 2, 21).

4. MAN BEFORE GOD

Man

Established by God as the king of creation (*3, 4, 184*), man is not the plaything of natural forces, for an attentive and benevolent providence rules his destiny. Still, the human condition has its tragic side: death and suffering, the sundering of the fraternal bond between men, the setbacks of civilization, the dispersion of the races and tongues, the cataclysms where nature is unleashed against men. Even so, responsibility for them must not be attributed to the whims of a jealous divinity (Text 6) or to his impotence. They are the effects of sin in our history (*3–10*). In them the solidarity of mankind is manifested, a solidarity of destiny based upon a unity of origin (*1–4*).

When the individual died, the Israelite of this time thought, as did other Semites, that something of him remained, his *shade,* which went down to *sheol,* the Hebrew name of the lower regions. There it led a diminished, unenviable life which was the same for every man regardless of how he had lived. It was, however, still necessary that the body be ritually buried (*24, 65*). Thus, since they were ignorant of any retribution after death, the Israelites saw long life as the mark of divine blessing and the reward for good conduct (*37, 43*). Therefore, Yahweh rewarded a man when he cured him of a sickness or saving him from his enemies, for thus that man was saved from "the snares of death" and "the nets of sheol" already cast over him (81). This was an imperfect concept which clearly demanded amplification, but at least it cut short the temptation to develop a cult of the dead like that of Egypt.

Morality

Israelite morality was essentially religious. It did not rely upon human wisdom flowing from the abstract reasoning of an individual conscience and the experience of past generations to determine what was good or bad for man. God alone "knows the good and the bad"; his will, expressed in commandments or prohibitions, constitutes the rule of human conduct (5). Thus sound morality was based, not upon the desire for the Good in general, but upon the fear of God, that is, upon religious respect for the will of God. This can be understood only within the framework of a personal religion in which man knows himself to be in communication with his Creator, the living God.

The Mosaic Law, of which the Decalogue is the very heart, sanctioned the principle points of natural morality (37). It is remarkable that Israel, though surrounded by the more civilized idolatrous populations of Canaan, still displayed an unequaled purity of morals, uprightness of conscience, and ideal of life. There was human imperfection. Not all the members of the people of God were saints. Far from it! But moral superiority early asserted itself among the Israelites and kept growing right up to the threshold of the Gospel. It surely was not the natural fruit of the Israelite genius, but the result of the persevering action led by God's messengers. Besides, the divine commands did not allow exception. They were imposed upon all, even the king, as is shown by the prophet Nathan's attitude towards David's adultery and murder (72) or the blame cast on Solomon by Israel's historians (79).

The Law

In all civilizations, the purpose of law is to regulate the relations between men so that society is just. In the ancient Orient, because of the close link between social life and religion, the collections of law were put under the guardianship of a god (Text 9). From this point of view alone, it is not surprising that Yahweh was the guardian of Israel's law, for in the final analysis, like the commandments of morality, the law derived from God's word, and the decisions he inspired in his messengers merely clarified the details of his precepts. This reference to the divine authority in apparently profane matters is not surprising if we recall the meaning of the Sinai covenant. By it Israel was not a people like others. God's law fixed the rules she had to follow in order to be a society worthy of him. In this respect, the personality of Moses dominates the whole law of Israel. On Sinai he gave the people their foundations and determined their directive principles; the later precisions were made by men in charge of "proclaiming the law" who adapted the law to the needs of an evolving society. And they always linked their adaptations to the original norms. Thus their adaptations were included in the "Law of Moses" under the same title as the most ancient prescriptions (*32, 34, 35*).

The society of this age still seems crude to us. But note the many prescriptions in the legislation designed to refine customs. The principle of the *Lex Talionis* is not in itself crude. It was aimed at imposing a limit on the right of revenge. This was needed in a civilized society where the central authority did not yet intervene in every question of private rights (compare *8* to *38*). All the canons were preoccupied with defending the weak, smoothing relations between men, correcting the most shocking inequalities (*38*). So Yahweh himself was presented as the avenger of the poor, the widows, the orphans, the refugees, of all people without appeal. He took the cause in hand when unjustly spilled blood cried out to him (compare Text 7). The execution of justice was, in theory, the affair of the leaders (*32*), and beginning with the monarchic era the king was officially the supreme judge of his people. When the Deuteronomic code mentions the Levitical judges of the sanctuaries (*Deut.* 17, 8–13), it is only respecting an old disposition of customary law.

The family institution was strong and healthy in Israel. Revelation had revealed the status of woman as one in whom a man finds not a slave but a "helper like to himself" (*4*). Also, family morality, sanctioned by the codes, was strict. Respect for parents was held in honor. Adultery was severely punished. Nevertheless, marriage had not yet returned to its primitive purity, to the ideal level of the creation narrative (*8*). Divorce remained authorized within the limits made precise by the Law and conformable to the customs of the ancient Orient (*39*).

Worship

The Israelites did not have to invent ritual practices, they borrowed them from the common fund of the Semitic religions, though they expurgated and often reinterpreted them. All that was directly linked to idolatry under all its various forms was carefully eliminated. Thus, the worship of idols and even the symbolic representation of God were forbidden (*37, 44, 57*), as were the sacrifices of first-born infants, current among the Canaanites (*15, 29, 41*), necromancy (*65*), and all other forms of divination, all the rites of fertility cults, and so forth. On the other hand, the same sacrificial rituals were used to express the religious sentiments of the faithful towards God. And there were many kinds of sacrifices: simple offerings, particularly those of the first-fruits (*1, 59*); holocausts, where the victim was burned whole (*78*); sacrifices of expiation for sin (*42*); peacemaking sacrifices followed by a sacred meal (*32, 60, 68*).

After Israel's entrance into Canaan and her adjustment to agricultural life, the year was marked by three great feasts (*40*): the feast of the unleavened bread in the spring, the feast of offering first-fruits at the beginning of summer, and the feast of ingathering in the fall, at the time of harvest. The first was soon merged with an ancient rite of the nomadic period, the sacrifice of the lamb, which had become the memorial of the exodus: this is Passover (*29, 41*). The other two feasts were also reinterpreted, and became memorials of the exodus by being given new names. Pentecost recalled the covenant of Sinai, and the feast of tabernacles commemorated the sojourn in the desert. Thus understood, the three feasts—notably Passover (Text 11)—were to become an essential feature of Jewish tradition for all time.

Among the most prevalent religious practices were prohibitions against all sorts of actions or foods, vows like that of the Nazarite, ritual consecrations of a man to God (*59*). As in all the religions of the time, a state of ritual purity was risked by many profane contacts which accounts for the many purification rites (*33*). Naturally, all these laws of worship developed before being definitively fixed in the priestly legislation (see Chapters VI and IX). In the patriarchal era, the chief of the tribe was also its priest (*11, 13*). This priesthood of the chiefs is prolonged when the kings of Jerusalem, beginning in the reign of David, exercised certain ritual functions (*68, 69, 78*). But from the time of Moses onwards, the tribe of Levi specialized in the service of the sanctuaries. Its members offered the sacrifices and were the preservers and the interpreters of the Law (*60, 74*). Beginning with Solomon the service of the temple at Jerusalem was confined to the descendants of the priest Sadoc, who formed a powerful body jealously attached to the tradition of Aaron.

Sin and Punishment

Every breach of the Law is objectively a sin, which offends God, and displeases and indisposes him, and this is true even of involuntary violations of the precepts. A very ancient liturgical tradition foresees sacrificial expiation for such sins (*42*). This concept of fault ran the risk of remaining very materialistic, though another element tended to correct it. The pure outlook of the Decalogue makes it clearly understood without possible equivocation that the breaches of the moral order are the gravest of faults, especially when they involve that willful clinging to evil which the holy books call *hardness of heart* (*44–46*). Even graver than moral faults, the sin of idolatry constituted a radical infidelity and was irremediable (*55, 79, 80*), for it involved a complete abandonment of God. The narrative of the sin of Adam and Eve (*5*) is helpful for understanding the biblical concept of sin. There, the narrator shrewdly analyzes the psychology of the temptation, the fall, and the guilty conscience. Using the vocabulary of wisdom to explain the symbol of the forbidden fruit, he describes the typical sin, and the malice which is the root of all sin: the sacrilegious pride by which man usurps the divine privilege of deciding what is good or evil for him. This caused a reversal of the divine order of things, the order which the Law of God defined.

All sin demanded punishment. When it was public, some cases in the Law of Israel prescribed social sanctions, which went as far as putting the offender to death. But independently of this, God himself had charge of punishing those who disobeyed him, for he is the Judge of men and master of all things. It was not as yet a question of a sanction in another life. But everything here on earth opposed to the prosperity and happiness of man was interpreted, somewhat simplistically, as the punishment for sin, whether the guilty one himself was punished, or the principle of collective responsibility came into play (6, 9, 10, 14, 28, 45, 55, 72, 80). This doctrine was still imperfect and demanded precisions and completions in the ages to come.

5. THE ISRAELITE CREED

Faith and Sacred History

The faith of Israel, insofar as it corrected and completed the data of the natural religious sense, did not rest on abstract speculation, or on the uncontrollable intuitions of feeling. Founded on the witness of inspired men, the faith was rooted in history, for the prominent events of national life were occasions of enriching and refining it. For example, at the time of the exodus from Egypt, Yahweh not only showed his people that he exists, acts, and is the master of history, he also showed himself to be the saviour of Israel (31). In the difficulties of the desert wanderings or the age of the Judges he expressed his desire for the fidelity of his people. When they were unfaithful, he punished them (46, 55).

Thus, most of the great biblical themes are linked to historical experiences. In fact, in the eyes of believers, the events were

91

not the meaningless result of chance, but acts of God on earth, rich in meaning for the one who knew how to see them in the spirit of faith. It is true that this religious understanding of history was possible only in the light of the prophetic witness, though in return it gave a concrete context to the words of the prophets. For God spoke both by the voice of his messengers and by means of events.

This is why in the Israelite creed (if such an expression can be used), the dogmas of faith and the memories of history are closely intermingled. The Israelite believed "in the one God, who created the heavens and the earth, who chose his fathers and promised them the land of Canaan, who saved them from Egypt and on Sinai gave them his covenant and his Law, who gave them as an inheritance the land of their ancestors" (*1, 2*). The Christian creed will be more complete, but it will retain a similar outlook. It will not enunciate abstract truths. It will recount history: the history of the plan of God, the history of salvation. The Old Testament recalled the first stages; the New will know its last in the cross and resurrection of Christ, the supreme act by which God shows his love for men by accomplishing their redemption.

At the height of the Israelite monarchy this stage had not yet been reached. But it is important to note the place given to hope in the beliefs of the time. Sacred history did not stop with the conquest of Canaan. God did not place Israel in its land merely to fulfill his blessings and make her happy (*43*), and so Israel awaited the full and complete accomplishment of this promise that would come if she remained faithful to the Law. But beginning with David the royal dynasty began to take its place in the creed. The prophecy of Nathan (*71*) linked the race of David to the hope of Israel forevermore. For this reason, their hope acquired a *messianic* character since the king anointed by Yahweh played a part in it. In Hebrew *mashiah* means anointed, and our word *messiah* is derived from it. There is yet no clear and explicit expectation of spiritual salvation and of a saviour to come, but this dynastic messianism is already a sketch of it.

92

Prayer and the Life of Faith

The Israelite lived in a wholly religious atmosphere. In some way everything was for him a chance to secure his relations with God. This did not result on his part in disrespectful familiarity with divine things. On the contrary, his awareness of the presence of God gave rise to a sacred fear (*18, 26, 33*). And fear of God was the fundamental religious sentiment of the Israelite, and was the basis of his prayer and led to obedience to the Law. Of course, spiritually it could be degraded among shallow-spirited men for whom religion seemed a useful means of obtaining divine favors and avoiding many troubles in this life, a deformation of spirit which is to be found in every age. To have a correct idea of biblical spirituality we must look elsewhere, for among more elevated souls we find prayer which is beautiful in the intensity of its adoration and thanksgiving (*18, 31, 81, 83*), trust (*13, 60, 81, 84, 85*), penitence (*72*), and intercession for neighbor (*14, 44, 45*). These ancient formulations, though limited by a still incomplete revelation, are already worthy of Christian prayer, and Christians would do well to use them often.

The Israelite faith does not appear in the Scriptures as a theoretical and beautiful ideal. The important figures of history embody this faith, for their religious portraits are painted to give the believers models; Abraham who is the perfect type (*11, 13, 15*). Jacob (*17–19*), Moses (*26–30, 46, 48*), Joshua (*50, 54*), Samuel (*60, 63*), David (*68, 75*). These heroes remain close to ordinary man because of their human imperfections, which the Bible does not gloss over (*26, 72*), but the dynamism of their lives comes wholly from their faith. This is why the Letter to the Hebrews will still propose them as models for Christians to imitate (*Heb.* 11).

The superiority of the biblical religion over the neighboring paganism can better be gauged by a comparison between the texts which parallel or correspond to similar needs. A common font of literary expressions and ritual actions displays the same level of civilization, but the spirit and the doctrine differ profoundly.

Text 8

THE BABYLONIAN CREATION MYTH

The poem "When on high . . ." was recited in the course of the New Year's liturgy. In inaugurating the year it commemorated the beginning of things and expressed the most profound insights of Mesopotamian thought: its concept of the divine, of the world, and of man. Note the pantheistic and evolutionistic atmosphere which underlies it. The great cosmic forces are personified and divinized. Gods and things progressively arise from the chaos, from which a principle of order (Marduk) finally makes an ordered world. Coming at the end of this evolution, man is to appease the gods by his worship. The poem displays no moral preoccupation at all (compare *3, 4, 184*).

> When on high the heavens had not yet been named
> and below the earth had not yet received its name;
> when the primordial Apsu, their begetter,
> and the roaring Tiamat, who gave birth to all of them,
> mingled their waters;
> when the reeds had not yet emerged,
> the canefields had not yet appeared;
> when no god had yet come into existence,
> nothing had been named, no destiny had been fixed,
> then the gods were created in the womb [of Apsu and Tiamat].

The undifferentiated chaos of the beginnings is thus represented under the form of two sexual principles: Apsu, the sweet waters from below the earth, and Tiamat, the sea waters. From them arise the gods who will preside over the different parts of the universe. But this evolution became "dialectical" when war broke out among the ancient gods; those of the chaotic universe, and the young gods, those of the organized universe. The stormy Tiamat threatened to destroy all her descendants. For this purpose she created an army of terrible monsters and made Kingu their leader. The young gods delegated their power to

94

Marduk, the national god of Babylon, to whose glory the poem was written. Marduk killed Tiamat, cut her into pieces, and overcame Kingu. With the bits of Tiamat he made the different parts of the world, and placed the stars to rule destinies in the heavens.

Finally came the creation of man. Marduk entrusted this to Ea (also called Nudimmud), the craftsman god who used the blood of Kingu, the fallen god, as if man must carry within himself the original curse brought by the war of the gods:

Then Marduk hears the gods,
his heart forces him to create a masterpiece.
He says to Ea the word of his mouth,
he confides to him what he has thought in his heart:
"I wish to shape blood and form a skeleton.
Yea, I wish to raise up a being who will have the name of Man;
I wish to create a being who will be a Man.
The service of the gods will rest on him so that they may be
    comfortable.
I wish to complete the organization of the ways of the gods:
they will be honored together, but divided into two groups."
*Kingu, the prisoner of Marduk, is going to give his blood for
    this creation:*
They chained him and dragged him before Ea.
They punished him by cutting his arteries.
From his blood (Ea) created Man;
he imposed on him the service of the gods so that they might rest
    easy.
After Ea the wise had created Man
and had imposed on him the service of the gods
—a work superior to all understanding
which Nudimmud accomplished according to the marvelous play
    of Marduk,
Marduk, the king, divided
the whole of the gods into gods of the upper-world and of the
    lower-world.
He placed three-hundred gods as guardians of the heavens,
then he determined the ways of the earth.
In the heavens and on the earth he established six hundred gods.

Poem of the Creation, Tablets 1 and 6

95

Text 9

THE CONCLUSION OF THE CODE OF HAMMURABI

Hammurabi, king of Babylon around 1700, reunited the two lands of Sumer and Accad under his scepter. He had a famous code engraved on his statue (today in the Louvre). The articles of the code are essentially practical decisions used to make up jurisprudence. The prologue of the code recalls that the king was summoned by the gods to the kingship to make justice reign in the land. The conclusion exalts the beneficence of his legislative work and calls on men either the blessing or the curse of the gods, according to whether they are obedient to its ordinances or not.

I, Hammurabi, the perfect-king, I have been neither negligent nor slack towards the people of black hair whom Enhil has entrusted to me and whom Marduk has given me the rule over. . . . The great gods have summoned me, and I, I was a shepherd who gave peace, whose scepter was just. My beneficent shadow extended over my city; in my heart I carried the land of Sumer and Akkad. . . . So that the strong do not oppress the weak. To make justice for the orphan and the widow, I have written my precious words on this monument, . . . so as to establish justice and to assure judgment in the land, so as to give rights to the oppressed. . . . I, the king Hammurabi, the just king to whom Shamash confided truth, my words are excellent, my acts are without equal. . . .

If a man listens to my words, which I have inscribed on this monument, if he does not deny my right to me, does not spurn my words, . . . may Shamash extend the empire of that man like my own, like me the just king, who leads his people with justice!

If a man does not listen to my words, which I have inscribed on this monument, if he scorns me, curses and does not hear the curses of the gods, . . . may the great Anu, father of the gods, who called me to kingship, strip that man—king, prince, governor, or anything else that he be—of all royal splendor; may he break his scepter and curse his destiny! May the Lord Enlil, who assigns destinies, assign to him the destiny of a reign of sighs, days of want, years of famine; . . . May he, from his honorable mouth, order the ruin of his city, the dispersal of his people, the fall of his kingdom, the extinction of his name and memory from the land . . .

Extract from Columns 24b to 26b

All the gods are thus called upon to punish the guilty. Among them Anu is the head of the pantheon, like El at Ugarit (Text 7); Marduk is the national god of Babylon; Enlil is the god of the storm; Shamash, the Sun, is the god of right. Compare this concept of royalty with that of Israel (*71, 127, 329*): the covenant between Yahweh and Israel gives a new meaning to the institution. See the biblical parallels (*38, 118, 127, 251, 266*) on the care for social justice which the code manifests. The final statement of blessings and curses is also paralleled in the Mosaic codes, but they call upon God to bless or to punish (*43*).

Text 10

THE CANAANITE HIGH PLACES

The Israelite preferred worship celebrated in the high places which recalled the sacred mountain where God was thought to reside. Archeology has uncovered a number of Canaanite high places. Their set-up is similar to the biblical sanctuaries, but the Israelite religion effaced whatever was reminiscent of the idolatry and immoral practices of Canaan (compare *18, 36, 44, 57, 60, 68, 69, 77, 78*).

In their earliest stage, they seem to have been constituted by an assemblage of cups cut in the rock beside a cavern. After the arrival of the Canaanites, this type was superseded on the same site by a high place, which was in the open air, elevated and detached.

In an enclosure chosen by the divinity, and henceforth reserved for it, were one or more stone pillars, called *masseboth* in the Bible. These were either natural or cut blocks, sometimes having a cup at the top to receive libations. Later an altar was erected near the pillar, such an altar being a block of stone, the projection of the natural rock, or an assemblage of stones. A post near the altar bore the same name as the goddess Ashera and probably represented her. A spring—or in its absence—a cistern, a trough, or a jar furnished the water necessary for purification and perhaps had a symbolic meaning. Trenches received the debris of the sacrifices, votive objects which were no longer to be preserved in the holy place, and sacred vessels unfit for service but which it was forbidden to turn to profane use. Very often, a clump of trees formed a sacred grove. The image of a god, a statue or a symbol, was sometimes placed in a shelter. This shelter later took on larger dimensions and became an actual house or temple. Some places of worship comprised a hall for ritual meals, chambers in which persons might sleep in order to learn by means of dreams what the will of the divinity was, rooms for the clergy . . . and shelters for the faithful. The sacred precinct was inviolable and human justice lost its rights there.

L. Delaporte, "The Canaanite Religion," in *Guide to the Bible,* II

Text 11

THE CELEBRATION OF THE JEWISH PASSOVER

From a distance of 3,000 years the following contemporary witness shows how the paschal celebration continues to play an essential role in the religious consciousness of the scattered Jews (compare *41*).

But the most impressive feast was that of the Passover. The liturgical supper was eaten at the first vespers; the table gleaming with its shining cloth and silver candlesticks, was laid with the greatest care; the family's most beautiful possessions were used. My paternal grandfather presided over the meal, seated upon the highest chair, raised even higher by cushions. Night was falling, and the bitter herbs were eaten; then prayer began. Filled with the mystery of this Passover, I was charged with asking, in Hebrew, questions to which my grandfather replied by the recitation of the Biblical narrative and the explanation of the rites of the Paschal night. It was a long discourse, also in Hebrew, but the meaning had been explained to us in advance, at the same time that I was taught my part in the dramatic dialogue.

The hearts of all those present were wrung by the greatness of the promise and the divine favours, by the pathetic history of so many centuries of suffering which had not extinguished hope. I obscurely felt the immensity of these sorrowful mysteries without realizing, naturally, their significance and their content. Then came the climax of this sacred night: the passage of the Angel. All the cups were filled with a red wine, strong and sweet, the almost liturgical savour of which I have never rediscovered in any wine, even in the wines of France. The Angel of the Lord was to drink from the largest cup, filled with this noble wine—the Angel of the Lord who on that night visited the homes of the Jews. All the lights were extinguished, and in a silence heavy with adoration and fear, the Angel was given time for his passage. Then the candles were all lighted again, the supper was quickly finished, and everyone went to rest, conscious of having taken part in a great action.

Raïssa Maritain, *We Have Been Friends Together*

Bibliography

The books mentioned in the two previous chapters give some insight into Israel's ancient creed. See also the various theologies of the Old Testament. For another specific treatment of the subject, consult R. De Vaux, *Ancient Israel* (New York 1961). On the doctrinal themes which began during this period, see the pertinent articles in the *Encyclopedic Dictionary of the Bible* (Covenant, Creation, God, Israel, Passover, etc.).

Study Guides

Compare the faith of Abraham (*11–15*), of Jacob (*16–19*), and of Moses (*26–48*). Does it reach the same degree of perfection in these three men? How does it resemble the Christian faith (read *Rom.* 4)?

In the narratives of the exodus from Egypt and the covenant at Sinai (*25–36*) anthropomorphic expressions and symbols are repeatedly used concretely to express the divine presence. Would the same language be used today? Does it not have advantages when compared to the abstract language of philosophy?

A parallel can be established between the destiny of the people of God, from the slavery in Egypt to the entry into the promised land, and the spiritual destiny of Christians, snatched from the captivity of sin and led into the kingdom of grace. Inspiration can be drawn from *1 Corinthians* 10, 1–13 and *Hebrews* 3, 7—4, 11. This study will allow a more profitable reading of the liturgy of Holy Saturday, where there are numerous allusions to the biblical texts we have just analyzed.

The biblical idea of sin can be studied through concrete samples cited in the Bible (for example: *5, 9, 10, 14, 27, 44, 45, 55, 72, 79*). However, the resultant doctrine will have to be completed in light of many other texts, chosen from the prophets, the psalms, and the wisdom writers.

V.

THE NATIONAL TRAGEDY

GOD'S plan for the world did not develop smoothly and without setbacks. Men being what they are, divine grace occasionally crashed head-on with sin. Grace finally conquered it, but not before men tasted the bitter fruit of their actions. Their deception and their suffering served to bring them back to God by opening them to his grace. This general law of providential conduct is admirably proven by the history of Israel. From Solomon to the beginning of Judaism a long drawn-out national tragedy unfolded on two different levels: Israel, little by little, abandoned her God, and God seemed to abandon her. During this time Israel's temporal ambitions were defeated, but this uncovered new depths to her true vocation which was in the religious order, and she received the promise of saving grace. Thus, God used her sins as well as the events of international history to educate his people.

1. THE DUAL MONARCHY

The Schism

After the death of Solomon the unity of his kingdom collapsed. The despotism of the monarchy, the administrative annoyances, the too numerous levies, all bred discontent, especially among the northern tribes, while the formalism of the official worship in the temple at Jerusalem displeased the most fervent religious circles, who were attached to the simpler worship of the ancient Mosaic tradition. The tactlessness of Roboam (932–913), Solomon's son and successor, did the rest. Ten tribes revolted, making Jeroboam (932–910) their king. From then on the people of God were divided into two states, living parallel existences: Judah in the south, Israel in the north (86).

Needless to say, this political schism had religious consequences. To take the place of the temple of Jerusalem, Jeroboam established two official sanctuaries in his kingdom, at Dan and at Bethel, though in theory the religion of Israel remained unchanged. Yet there was a new element, for Jeroboam had two golden calves built there. In the imagery of the Semitic religions, the bull, symbol of power and fertility, was the animal sacred to Baal, who was usually represented standing on its back. In the eyes of Jeroboam, the golden calves were not, properly speaking, idols, but their very presence was the great danger of reducing the worship of Yahweh to the rank of Baal worship; or even worse, of practically identifying Yahweh with Baal. By his decision, Jeroboam tried to conciliate the uneducated masses, almost half of whom were of Canaanite origin, though at the time he alienated the prophetic group who had contributed to his seizing the throne (87).

From the political point of view, after Jeroboam Israel fell prey to instability until the coming of Omri (885–874). In Judah, on the contrary, the dynasty of David maintained itself unbroken.

Where the situation of the two kingdoms deteriorated was in relations with the neighboring states, whose vassals regained their liberty one after the other; then too, after 926, the pharaoh Sesac came, ravaging the land and exacting tribute from Judah. The schism thus ruined Israel's fragile power. This is the historical framework for one of the most striking phenomenon of the Old Testament development: the prophetic movement.

102

The Prophetic Movement

All the religions of the Middle East had their seers, their soothsayers. For some centuries, Canaan and Syria had developed confraternities of devotees who gave themselves to ecstatic transports in public. The history of religion knows of similar things in every area, from the Tibetan Lamas to African witchdoctors, from Greek bacchantes to the whirling dervishes of Islam and the convulsionists of Saint-Medard. While in a trance these man were thought to speak in the name of God. Perhaps this is why they had the name *nabi*, which meant prophet, or spokesman for a god (unless it meant: the called, he who has received the call of a god).

To do battle with the idolatry of Canaan on equal terms, the religion of Israel also had its seers, who could be consulted to know the divine will or for enlightenment in troublesome affairs. Then beginning around the 11th century confraternities of prophets grew up around the sanctuaries (95). If their manifestations of religious enthusiasm sometimes took strange forms, the prophets had nevertheless totally broken with paganism, and their practice conformed to the demands of the Law. Thus, because of their prestige among the common people, they were a living force for Yahwism. Among the men who made a profession of prophecy there were many sincere believers, real zealots, but there were certainly mediocre or greedy men too. In brief, institutional prophetism was capable of either the best or the worst, depending upon the individual case. Alongside it there gradually emerged another sort of prophetism, one prolonging the tradition of the great messengers of God, Abraham and Moses. Desire alone did not constitute an authentic prophetic vocation, for the initiative came from God himself. Samuel already represented this vocation of God (60), although he was styled as only a seer (63). Nathan (71, 72) and Ahias (80, 87) are called prophets. After the schism, Elijah, Elisha, and Micah son of Jimal (93) are in close relationship with the prophetic groups, but they received a personal mission

103

from God. After them, institutional prophecy lost more and more of its religious value. Amos would be a shepherd; Isaiah, a member of the aristocracy; Hosea perhaps, and Jeremiah surely, a priest; Ezekiel, a member of the clergy of Jerusalem.

When the prophets of Israel are mentioned, the two meanings of the term prophet must be carefully distinguished. The prophetic confraternities certainly for a time contributed to the maintenance of the religious tradition of the people of God, but it was the action of inspired men, called by a personal vocation, that gave biblical revelation its deeper roots in the time of the kings.

Elijah and the Dynasty of Omri

Omri (885–874), after ascending the throne on the heels of a revolution, ruled brilliantly. Fifty years later the Assyrian annals still spoke of the "house of Omri" to designate the state of Israel. He built Samaria, which he made his capital. In religious matters he followed the lead of his predecessors. Uneasy over the ambitions of the Damascus Syrians, he allied himself against them with the Phoenicians of Tyre and the kingdom of Judah. He sealed these alliances by marriages whose consequences we shall soon see.

Ahab (874–853), the son of Omri, married Jezebel, daughter of the king of Tyre, and under the influence of this queen the Canaanite cults regained their vigor in Israel (88), while Yahweh's faithful were persecuted. The prophet Elijah stood fearlessly in the face of this revival of paganism, laying the blame squarely on idolatry and the exactions of the royal power (89–92). The sons of Ahab, Ahaziah (853–852) and Joram (852–841), succeeded him, while Elisha, a disciple of Elijah, continued his tradition of religious intransigence (94, 95). In his time the last remaining vassal of Israel, the kingdom of Moab, regained its independence (Text 12).

The kingdom of Judah led a tamer life. Jehoshaphat (870–848) was faithful to the religion of his fathers, but he married

104

his son Joram to Athalie, daughter of Ahab and Jezebel (c. 865). The influence of the princess had already been felt during the reign of Joram (848–841) and Ahaziah (841), who should not be confused with the two kings of Israel bearing the same names.

Elisha and the Dynasty of Jehu

Then two bloody revolutions took place. Jehu (841–814), commandant of the army, revolted with the support of Elisha and the prophetic circles. He killed the kings of Israel and of Judah, and became king of Samaria (97). These political shocks had important religious consequences, since the survival of Yahwism as the national religion was at stake.

Little by little the dynasty of Jehu restored the reputation of the kingdom of Israel. For several decades Elisha consoled the kings, but after his death things relapsed. The reign of Jeroboam II (783–743), great grandson of Jehu, was an era of material prosperity almost comparable to the reign of Solomon. But from the moral and religious point of view, the situation was less brilliant. Denouncing the sins he saw under his very eyes, the prophet Amos predicted approaching catastrophes (98–106). The preaching of Hosea some years later sounded exactly the same note (107–113). In Judah, under the kings Amaziah (796–781), Uzziah (781–740), and Jothan (740–736), the atmosphere was no better, as the first works of Isaiah show (114–119).

The End of Samaria

After the reign of Jeroboam II, Israel fell into rapid decline. In six years, five kings followed one after another. Many were assassinated. Assyria was then at the height of her expansion (Map 4): Israel, Judah, and the Arameans of Damascus had to pay tribute to Tiglath-Pileser, as did the other small states of Syria. This heavy subjection gave rise to dreams of independence among the vassals. Upon the accession of Ahaz in Jeru-

105

salem (736), Pekahiah of Israel (737–732) and Racon of Damascus tried to embroil him in a plot against the emperor. Far from giving in, Ahaz called the Assyrian to his aid (*120–125*). A military expedition smashed Damascus and dethroned Pekahiah. The kingdom now came rapidly to its end. Hoshea (732–724), the last king, owed his throne to the Assyrians; but with Egyptian encouragement he also plotted and the end was not long in coming. In 724 Samaria was besieged by the armies of Shalmaneser V. In 721 Sargon II demolished it (Text 13). The upper echelons of the population were deported and Mesopotamian colonists settled in their place. Thus the threats of the prophets were carried out to the letter (*129, 130*).

2. THE KINGDOM OF JUDAH

Hezekiah (716?–607)

During the two centuries after Solomon's death, Judah's religious sentiments rose and fell. Certain reigns were marked by passing reforms, but in the middle of the 8th century the decay was clearly visible. The ruin of Samaria caused many to reflect: should not a similar lot be feared for Jerusalem (*131*)? While this was going on, at a date difficult to ascertain (perhaps 716), Hezekiah succeeded his father Ahaz. Perhaps the young king had already come under the influence of Isaiah. Whether he had or not, the fact remains that, upon his accession, he carried out a profound religious reform (*132*). Not content to combat idolatry by severe measures, he also concerned himself with resettling the remainder of the northern tribes in Jerusalem. Thus a movement towards religious centralization was set up around the temple of Jerusalem and it flowered a hundred years later under Josiah.

This renaissance did not save the king from being drawn into the same political difficulties as his predecessors and all of the neighboring states. Caught between the rival empires of Egypt and Mesopotamia, the little Syrian principalities found it diffi-

106

cult to maintain their freedom. Around 705, trapped by his counselors, Hezekiah entered into an anti-Assyrian league supported by Egypt (*134*). Again the end was not long coming. In 701 Judah suffered the terrible ravages of the campaign of Sennacherib (Text 14). Cut off from a large part of its territory, the kingdom could from then on only submit to Assyria as a vassal. It was during this war, or perhaps during a second siege around 689, that Jerusalem escaped conquest by a miracle (*135–136*).

Manasseh (687–642)

The reign of Manasseh contrasted sharply with that of his father. The Assyrian hegemony had disastrous religious consequences: the official worship of the emperor was linked to that of Canaan and submerged the religion of Yahweh and the moral influence of his Law. It was a true national apostasy, which the king officially supported (*145*). Faithfulness existed only in fervent circles, and the faithful were persecuted by the powers in office. Yet they carried on the tradition of the 8th-century prophets and gathered their works. There also the spirit of the Deuteronomic school, born in northern Israel, carried out the legislative recasting of the Mosaic code (*139–144*). Done in the temple under Hezekiah, this work remained in the shadows for many decades before serving as the foundation of Josiah's reform.

Josiah (640–609)

The beginning of Josiah's reign was marked by the preaching of Zephaniah (*154*) and the beginnings of Jeremiah's preaching (*155–159*). The religious climate was not healthy. Nevertheless, from the political point of view the king began to profit from the decline of Assyria. He could assert independence and extend his authority to the detriment of Samaria. In 622 an unforeseen event gave his action a decisive twist: the Deuteronomic code was accidentally discovered in the temple. With this code Josiah carried out a radical reform, even deeper than that of Hezekiah (*146*). He uprooted every trace of idolatry from the land, suppressed the places of pagan worship, and massacred their personnel. He forbade every sanctuary except Jerusalem: one God alone, one Law alone, one temple alone. This program was vigorously pursued throughout his reign.

But at this hour the Orient changed its master. After years of rapid decline, Nineveh fell in 612 under the blows of the Babylonians and their Median allies (*163, 164*). In vain the Pharaoh Necho tried to rescue Assyria. He himself was wiped out at Carchemish in 605 (*168*). Meanwhile, Josiah profitably strengthened his policy of national independence. In this spirit he forbade the passage of Necho, and Necho annihilated his army at Megiddo (609) and killed him in the battle (*147*). The unexpected death of the reformer king threw all of his work into question, for what good was this religious puritanism if it did nothing for its promoter? With a sort of fatalism the land instinctively returned to some of the errors of the time of Manasseh. Jeremiah spent his last years fighting them.

The End of Jerusalem

Babylon quickly adopted the ambitions of Assyria—not on the upper Tigris and in the direction of Asia Minor, where she left the field clear for the Medes, but in the direction of the vassal states of Syria and Palestine. Caught between Babylon and Egypt, who saw the coming danger, the Israelites were once again in a dangerous position. Nebuchadnezzar led annual campaigns against them. In 598 he besieged Jerusalem, which Egypt had for the first time enticed into alliance with her (Text 15). King Joakin surrendered and was deported along with part of the aristocracy and clergy. Under Zedekiah (597–586), enthroned by Nebuchadnezzar, the Egyptian party provoked a new revolt. This time, after a severe siege, Jerusalem was sacked, and the upper echelons of the population were led away into

108

exile (586). Jeremiah was a powerless witness to this catastrophe, which he tried to prevent by preaching conversion and counseling submission to Babylon (*169–171; 176–181*). Ezekiel, called to the prophetic ministry between the two sieges, was an active agent in the spirtual rejuvenation which will follow (*189–206*).

3. THE BABYLONIAN CAPTIVITY

The Jews in the Land of Exile

After 586, only a miserable population, administratively attached to the prefecture of Samaria, remained in Judah. Some Jews (that is, Judeans) took refuge in Egypt, but the spiritual salvation of the nation did not come from these political emigrants. On the contrary, the deportees of Babylon, listening to and profiting by the counsels of Jeremiah (*177*), organized themselves into homogeneous groupings where tradition remained alive. It was in their midst that Ezekiel fulfilled his mission. The severe punishment imposed by God on his guilty people made the people reflect: there was no longer king, nor state, nor promised land, nor temple, nor organized worship; all the institutions established through the course of many centuries of history had been swept aside. The threats of the prophets had been accomplished to the letter (*207–213*). This was finally the time to listen to the voice of the prophets and be converted, to take seriously the moral and social demands of the Law, which the recent reforms had tried to put into force. Thus a national catastrophe allowed the prophetic preaching and the reforming work of the Deuteronomic circles finally to bear fruit. Thanks to this internal work, the *remnant* of Israel became the point of departure for a new kind of religious restoration: Judaism.

In addition, the Jewish colonies of Babylonia carried out another kind of work. Not only were the older Scriptures collected for meditation (legislative texts, historical ones, prophetic and lyrical ones, etc.), but new books were composed, in answer to the particular needs of the time. These were the historical

109

works impregnated with the spirit of Deuteronomy and some legislative compilations collected among the priestly group. Thus the Jewish restoration was not improvised: these sacred books served as its charter (see Chart).

On the Threshold of the Persian Empire

Nevertheless, the history of the Middle East changed faces once again (Map 5). After Nebuchadnezzar the Babylonian empire declined rapidly under mediocre rulers. On the Iranian plateaux Cyrus reunited the Medes and the Persians under his scepter; in 546, after a campaign across Asia Minor, he annexed Lydia. From there he then turned against Babylon, where King Nabonidus was detested by the local population (Text 16). In 539 Cyrus seized it without striking a blow, and was welcomed as a liberator (Text 17). Departing from the policies of the Assyro-Babylonians, he adapted himself to local situations, and the deported Jews benefited from this mercy. This explains the enthusiasm with which they greeted his approach in that great prophetic work, the *Message of Consolation to the Exiles* (*Is.* 40–45). Israel now saw a new era opening up before her.

4. THE TWOFOLD DRAMA OF THE PEOPLE OF GOD

In the preceding period of history, the plan of God was being progressively realized through the destiny of Israel, his people. Under the reigns of David and Solomon Israel attained a high point; apparently, she could aspire to carve an empire for herself in the Middle East. But this equilibrium had been fragile and provisory. The parallel eclipse of Assyria and of Egypt in the 11th and 10th centuries gave the Davidic monarchy a certain lustre, but the revival of Assyria in the 9th century, and its expansion in the 8th and the 7th, completely changed the situation. Besides, the tenuous union of the north (the house of Joseph) and the south (the house of Judah), realized by

110

David, had not withstood the abuse of the Solomonic era. Once their latent opposition had been revived, Israel and Judah separated; and as they were embroiled in unending quarrels with the small Syro-Palestinian states, the two rival kingdoms drifted further apart. The destruction of both Samaria and Jerusalem was the final blow to national ambitions.

Still, this was something more than a political drama. In assimilating the Canaanite population, Israel absorbed an element which was ill-disposed to the religious tradition of Moses. After the apparent triumph of Yahwism under David, the spiritual drama of the time of the Judges again revived. And in the midst of the unceasing fluctuations revealed in the texts of this period, either a vague paganism had again flared up, or the authentic tradition had at least been corrupted among both the ordinary people and the social elite. Tradition was maintained by a dedicated core alone, composed of a certain number of priests, but directed by the prophets, who were the true guides of the nation. Among this religious elite the faith was again purified, deepened, and enriched. A line of witnesses of God, acting in virtue of their supernatural vocation, held their ground. Once more we sense a trace of God's presence in human history.

Text 12

INSCRIPTION OF MESHA, KING OF MOAB (c. 850)

On this stele, preserved in the Louvre, Mesha, king of Moab recounts how he freed his kingdom from Israel's over-lordship. Victor Hugo includes this inscription in his *Légende des siècles*.

111

I am Mesha, son of Chemosh-Kan, king of Moab, the Dibonite.
My father reigned over Moab for thirty years, and I reigned after
my father. I made this high-place for Chemosh-Qarhoh . . . , because he saved me from all the kings and made me triumph over all
my adversaries. Omri, king of Israel, had oppressed Moab for long
days, for Chemosh was angry at his land. When his son succeeded
him, he also said: "I will oppress Moab." It was during my time
that he spoke thus, but I have triumphed over him and his house,
and Israel had been overwhelmed forever. Omri had possessed the
white land of Medeba, and Israel remained there during his days
and the better half of those of his son, that is forty years. But
Chemosh remained there during my days. I erected Baal-Meon and
I made the cistern there, and I built Qaryaten. The peoples of
Gad had lived always in the land of Ataroth, and the king of Israel
had built Ataroth for them. But I fought against the city; I took it
and massacred all the people of the city, to satisfy the sight of
Moab and of Chemosh. I raised up there Ariel, its chief and dragged
him before Chemosh to Kerioth, and I established there the people
of Sharon and the people of Maharith. And Chemosh said to me:
"Go! Take Nebo from Israel!" I went by night and made war
against her from dawn to noon; I took her and massacred all, seven
thousand men, young men, young women and slaves, for I had
vowed them by anathema for Ashtar-Chemosh. I brought from
there the vases of Yahweh and dragged them before Chemosh. The
king of Israel had battled Jahaz, and he remained there until he
did battle against me; but Chemosh chased him before me: I took
from Moab two hundred men, all first-class warriors, and I sent
them against Jahaz and took it to link it to the district of Dibon . . .

The end of the inscription enumerates the constructions carried out by the king. Notice that, conforming to the ideas of the
time, the war of Moab against Israel is a holy war: the war of
Chemosh, the national god, against Yahweh; the sacred anathema is used (compare to *52*); the allusion to the orders of
Chemosh suggests a consultation of the divinity through official
soothsayers (compare to *93*). No moral preoccupation is evident in this political and religious enterprise, unlike the preaching of the Israelite prophets.

112

Text 13

THE DESTRUCTION OF SAMARIA

Sargon II, in his annals, left a short memorial of the taking of Samaria, which took place the year of his accession to the kingship (compare to *130*).

At the beginning of my reign . . . I besieged and conquered the city of the Samaritans . . . I carried away as prisoners 27,290 inhabitants and appropriated fifty chariots from them for my royal army . . . I built the city better than it had been before and I settled there some peoples of the lands which I had conquered. I set over them as governor one of my officers and I imposed tributes and taxes on them as on the Assyrians [lines 10–17].

Text 14

SENNACHERIB'S CAMPAIGN AGAINST JERUSALEM

In the following text the king reports his victories to Ashur, his national god. The submission and the tribute of Hezekiah are also mentioned by the Bible (*2 Kgs.* 18, 13–16). The miraculous deliverance which is reported in the same context (*136*) is connected perhaps to a second siege around 690.

Hezekiah, king of Judah, had not submitted to my yoke. I besieged about forty-six of his strong-places, surrounded by walls, also the little villages which were in the countryside, beyond count-

113

ing in number, and I seized them by means of siege ramps, infantry battles, mines, and sapping operations. I drove out of them 200,150 persons, young and old, men and women, horses, mules, asses, camels, cattle, sheep, beyond counting, and I accounted them as spoils. Hezekiah himself, like a bird in a cage, I shut up in Jerusalem, his royal residence. I raised an earthwork against him, and whoever left the gates of the city, I made pay for his misdeed. His cities which I had stripped him of, I took and I gave them to Mitinti, king of Ashdod, Padi, king of Ekron, and Sillibel, king of Gaza, and I cut off his territory; but I increased yet again the tribute and the tax to be paid annually as an offering to my majesty, beyond the previous tribute. As for him, Hezekiah, the brilliance of my majesty crushed him. The irregulars and the picked troops which he had brought into Jerusalem, his royal residence, to reinforce it, abandoned him. He sent me then to Nineveh, my ruling city, together with 30 talents of gold, 800 talents of silver, precious stones, antimony . . . and considerable lapis-lazuli, beds of ivory, seats of ivory, elephant hides, elephant teeth, ebony wood . . . , precious treasures of all kinds, his own daughters, concubines, men and women musicians. And to present the tribute and make the act of obedience, he sent his messengers.

Text 15

THE FIRST SIEGE OF JERUSALEM (598)

A recently discovered chronicle of Nebuchadnezzar explicitly mentions the first siege of Jerusalem (compare to *176*).

The seventh year [of his reign], in the month of Kislew, the king of Accad gathered his troops. He marched towards the land of Hatti and camped near the city of Judah. The second day of the month of Adar, he took the city and made its king a prisoner. He appointed there a king of his choice, received his heavy tribute and sent him to Babylon.

Text 16

NABONIDUS, LAST KING OF BABYLON

Nabonidus alienated the clergy of the temples of Babylon. Thus it is not surprising that a priest of Bel-Marduk, the national god, violently criticized him in a chronicle reporting his last years. Nabonidus comes to reconstruct at Harran, around 552, the temple of Sin (the Moon god), where his mother had been priestess.

When he had carried out this project, this work of pure falsehood, when he had built this abomination, this work of impiety, as he was about to begin the third year of his reign, he entrusted the camp to his heir, his firstborn son and in the entire land he placed the troops under his command. He gave his son a free hand, entrusting his regency to him.

As for himself, he left on a long journey, taking with him the military forces of Accad; he went towards Tema, in the west.

Nabonidus lingered in Tema (an oasis of northern Arabia). During this time the liturgy of Marduk was neglected in Babylon. Cyrus made progress, although Nabonidus remained unaware of the danger:

Standing in the assembly, he praised himself:
"I am wise and knowing; I have seen hidden things;
Although I do not know how to write, I have seen secret things;
Ilteri has granted me a vision and shown me all things."

Around 540 Nabonidus planned to consecrate to Sin, his god, the great temple of Marduk in Babylon. This brought things to a head. In the autumn of 539, because of the treason of Gubaru, governor of the city, the troops of Cyrus entered without encountering resistance. The religious policy of Cyrus immediately won over the population. On this point the Babylonian chronicle cross-checks the inscription of Cyrus.

115

Text 17

THE INSCRIPTION OF CYRUS

I am Cyrus, king of the world, great king, lawfully king, king of Babylon, king of the four regions; son of Cambyses, great king, king of Anshan; descendant of Teispes, great king, king of Anshan; of a family which has always exercized the royal power. The gods of Bel and Neo loved my power and desired my reign for the joy in their hearts. Then I entered Babylon as a friend, in joy, and established in the palace of the princes the seat of government, Marduk the great Lord bent the hearts of the sons of Babylon towards me, each day I took care to honor him. . . . On the order of Marduk the great Lord I reëstablished all the gods of Sumer and Accad, which Nabonidus had taken to Babylon to the great anger of the Lord of the gods, in peace in their sanctuaries, there where they find the joy of their hearts.

We know that Cyrus followed a similar religious policy with regard to the Jews, allowing them to return to Jerusalem and to reconstruct their national temple (*229*).

	Death of Solomon *Kingdom of Judah* Roboam	(932) 932 885 874	Israelite schism *Kingdom of Israel* Jeroboam I Omri Ahab & Jezebel
First Assyrian expansion Shalmaneser III (859–824)	Jehosaphat Athaliah (841–835)	870 841	 Jehu
Second Assyrian expansion Teglath-Phalasar (745–727) Shalmaneser V (727–722) Sargon II (722–705) Sennacherib (704–681) Assurbanipal (668–630)	 Ahaz Hezekiah Manasseh Josiah	783 740 722 716 687 640	Jeroboam II Israelite deca- dence *Fall of Samaria*
Assyrian decadence Destruction of Nineveh (612)	Reform of Josiah	622	
Progress of Babylon Battle of Carchemish (605) Nebuchadnezzar (604–562)	Death of Josiah First deportation	609 598	
	Fall of Jerusalem Babylonian Captiv- ity	586	
Nabonidus (555–538) Cyrus (549–529)			
Decadence of Babylon Cyrus conquers Lydia (545) Cyrus takes Babylon (539)	 Edict of Cyrus	 538	

Bibliography

See the various histories of Israel. Also consult three works by A. Parrot: *Samaria, Capital of Israel*, *Nineveh and the Old Testament*, and *Babylon and the Old Testament*.

Study Guides

Look at the biblical texts concerning Elijah, Isaiah, Jeremiah, and the author of the *Message of Consolation*. Study the attitude of the prophets in political matters: what policy do they sanction? Are there not apparent contradictions between them? What meaning do they find in political events? What principles guided their thought in this twofold view?

Does not this attitude of the prophets foreshadow that of the New Testament? What was Jesus' attitude towards political power? Did he not also attribute a religious meaning to certain events? Is it not in this light that one must judge what is called the "politics of the Church"?

VI.

THE PROPHETIC WITNESS

FROM the beginning of its history Israel had divine messengers as its spiritual guides. During the era of its greatest drama these guides were the prophets. The first of them—and not the least: Elijah, Elisha—left no written works. But beginning in the 8th century various collections of sayings of the prophets were gathered. Through them we know fairly well the personalities, doctrines, and actions of many of the inspired men: Amos, Hosea, Micah, Jeremiah, Ezekiel, and others. The influence of the prophets extended far beyond their own times through these first-hand documents. It affected all the literature of the time, whatever its purpose, themes, and genres, to such a degree that they may all be seen as an indirect manifestation of the prophetic witness. This literature is quite varied. Besides the books of the writer-prophets, it contains legislative works, histories, lyrics, even sapiential writings. All the great literary currents begun in the preceding age continued to be developed.

1. THE KINGDOM OF ISRAEL

The Work of the Chroniclers

It is helpful in the beginning to mention the work of the historians who wrote in the kingdom of Israel. We saw above the ancient traditions of Israel collected in both south and north, in the form of the Yahwist and the Elohist sacred histories. The Elohist apparently came from the Israelite centers influenced by

119

the 9th-century prophets, Elijah and Elisha. A narrative like the history of the golden calf (*44*) reflects their polemic against the sanctuary at Bethel (*87, 108*). Likewise, the presentation of the origin of the monarchy (*62*) has an anti-royalist tone explained by the very recent experience of a bad king. It is still doubtful whether the Elohist scribes composed a continuous history which covered all of the ancient times from the beginnings to their own age. In any case, the segments used by their successors do not allow a complete reconstruction.

The official court scribes of Samaria doubtlessly kept annals of the reigns, but almost nothing remains of them, for the destruction of Samaria must have resulted also in their destruction. Still, the editors of the books of Kings had at their disposal a documentation which might be based upon them. Thus they reproduced entire the biographies of Elijah and Elisha, composed in the prophetic circles of the north some time after the death of the two prophets. The Elijah cycle (*1 Kgs.* 17—*2 Kgs.* 1) covers about twenty years, under the reigns of Ahab and his sons Ahaziah and Joram. That of Elisha meshes with Elijah's (*2 Kgs.* 2) but covers a much longer period, from the reign of Joram to that of Joas, grandson of Jehu (*2 Kgs.* 3–13, excepting the intercalary passages taken from other sources).

In some of their pages (see the narrative of Jehu's revolution [*97*]) these works match the qualities of David's biography in psychological finesse, sobriety, sincerity, and warmth. Nevertheless, in other respects the narration takes a more popular turn, as in the judgment of God carried out on Carmel (*90*). The biography of the two heroes follows the memories of the prophetic confraternities. They are basically solid traditions, certainly, but their purposes differ notably from that of modern critics and are sometimes very close to that of the *Little Flowers of St. Francis of Assisi* (*95, 96*). The narrators knew how to give life to the moral atmosphere of the times and the radiance which emanated from Elijah and Elisha. These witnesses of God appear with all their fearless characters (*89, 92, 93*), but other qualities link them to us: Elijah suffers from his lack of success (*91*), Elisha has compassion on human misery (*96*). Besides them, a man like Micah, son of Jimla (*93*), shows that

120

even a vocational prophet must sometimes suffer the hostility of men in bearing witness to the word of God. Closely tied to contemporary politics, their witness stood for the primacy of the spiritual.

Amos

Amos was the first prophet whose discourses and prophesies were collected into a book. He was a herdsman from Tekoa in Judah; but his vocation led him into Israel, to the sanctuary at Bethel, under the reign of Jeroboam II (*c.* 750). His ministry was probably brief: a few weeks, or, at most, several months.

Amos had a profound awareness of his prophetic mission. He proclaimed it loudly when the priest of Bethel wanted to chase him from the royal sanctuary (*106*). He was no professional prophet, he brought the message with which he personally had been charged. A man of the countryside, he used crude words when, in the name of authentic tradition, he condemned all the abuses of his times: the social injustices (*98–100*), the hypocrisy of a formalistic religion where ritual does not express the dispositions of the heart (*105*). He had a lofty concept of the Living God, Creator and Master of all things, of his past blessings to which Israel had responded with ingratitude (*102*). Faced with the hardening of a people who did not listen to the divine pleadings (*103*), he made them listen to threats: soon a *day of Yahweh* would come, when all sinners would be punished (*101*); only a *remnant* would remain to profit by the divine promises (*104*). In announcing this punishment, the prophet extended his horizon beyond the people of Israel: all the neighboring peoples would also undergo just punishment for their crimes. This series of oracles against the nations (*Amos* 1, 3—2, 3) began a literary genre which will recur again and again in most of the prophetic collections. The justice of Yahweh is the same for all men. He is the creator of all and imposes the same morality on all. At the very end of the book there is a prophesy of salvation (*Amos* 9, 11–15) whose literary authenticity is, unfortunately, uncertain.

Amos's style lacks the subtlety and elegance of the language

121

taught in the schools. It is an oral style, which strikes home by its trenchant brevity, its spontaneity, its strength. This peasant knew how to paint a picture of day-to-day life (98), and country life gave him a good supply of images. His speeches are not flowing discourses, but brief oracles alternating with vision-narratives and the proclamation of the evils which will befall sinners. The whole book was apparently collected by the prophet's disciples after a certain period of oral transmission. In its present form the book is composed of three parts: a collection of prophecies of judgment against the nations and against Israel (1, 3—2, 16), a collection of admonitions and threats addressed to Israel (3, 1—6, 14), and a collection of five visions with other diverse fragments (7, 1–9, 10); the oracle of salvation (9, 11–15) forms an appendix.

Hosea

Hosea preached in Israel some years later, at the end of the reign of Jeroboam II (d. 743) and under subsequent reigns until the capture of Samaria (722). The Decalogue could almost be reconstructed (37) by putting end to end the reproaches the prophet addressed to his fellow countrymen. In fact, the discourse opening the second part of his book (107) seems to allude to this synthesis of revealed morality. Elsewhere Hosea explicitly mentions the numerous precepts of the Law (Hos. 8, 12). This shows that he was in touch with a northern sanctuary, probably Sichem (mentioned in 6, 9). But he contrasted this known written law with the conduct of everyone: priests, people, leaders, kings. Vehemently he laid the blame on the worship at Bethel, corrupted by the worship of the golden calf (108), and on the kings of Israel. His hostility extended to the very root of the monarchy, in terms recalling the anti-royalist narrative of its institution (108; see 62). He was particularly sensitive to the basic disorder of idolatry, for all of his thought centered on the covenant relation between Yahweh and his people. It seems that he represented the first as a relationship of love: Yahweh loves Israel as a father loves his child (112), as a husband his wife (111).

122

This is the heart of Hosea's message. On the basis of his own conjugal experience he understood this aspect of the link between God and his people. At God's order he took for his wife a "woman of prostitution," symbol of the sinful people whom Yahweh "married" on Sinai (*110*). Idolatry and infidelity on her part were not only the ingratitude of a prodigal child (*112*), but an adultery. But contrary to the prescriptions of customary law, Hosea also took back into his home the idolatrous wife, as a sign of the mercy with which God would welcome his penitent people (*110*). The Gospel will reveal no greater manifestation of divine pardon, not even in the parable of the Prodigal Son. These symbolic acts involving the prophet's life were commented upon in a discourse on the theme (*111*) of God avenging his scorned love by taking all his previous gifts away from Israel, but only to lead her to repentance. The essential thing is that this repentance be sincere (*113*). Once this point is reached, God will draw his "spouse" to himself, and bind her to himself by a new covenant which will have the freshness of the first betrothal (*111*). Thus the drama which grips Yahweh and sinful men will close on a perspective of paradise regained.

Hosea's style is suited to his message; it is freely emotional. The calls addressed to sinners on the part of the God of love often take on a passionate tone. The book where they have been collected has two parts. The first (*Hos.* 1–3) describes the marital experience of the prophet and discusses it in a running discourse. The second (4–14) is a disordered collection, short fragments juxtaposed and sometimes badly preserved. It ends like the first with a promise of salvation (14, 2–9). The prophet himself could have begun this work of editing, which must have been completed in Judah after the fall of Samaria.

2. ISAIAH AND HIS TIMES

The Prophet Micah

In the same period as Hosea, Micah carried out his prophetic ministry during the reigns of Ahaz and Hezekiah. A peasant, like Amos, he preached in both Israel and Judah. His themes were similar to those of the Shepherd of Tekoa: a denunciation of the sins of society, of superficial worship and idolatry; proclamation of the day of Yahweh (*129*). This divine judgment would first fall upon Samaria, and Micah proclaims its fall as certain (*129*). But beyond this event he also sees the destruction of Jerusalem, if the people of Judah do not do penance (*131*). This shocking message, coming as it did during the dramatic events of 722, made a profound impression. From the book of Jeremiah we learn of its contribution to the reform of Hezekiah (*165*). Nevertheless, the book of Micah does not treat only of Israel's trial (*Mic.* 1–3; 6, 1—7, 8). It includes some beautiful eschatological promises (4–5), in which the temple of Jerusalem (*133*) and the Davidic king (*128*) occupy an important place. The final edition of the book was then completed by later fragments reflecting the eschatology of the Persian era (7, 8–20).

The Prophet Ministry of Isaiah

The personality of Micah is eclipsed by that of his contemporary, Isaiah, whose ministry extended over forty or fifty years. Isaiah was called in 740, in a magnificent vision of the holy God, contemplated under the aspect of his royalty (*114*). He himself belonged to the aristocracy of Jerusalem, and he was probably an educated man trained in the art of writing. In any case, he had access to the court (*121, 122*); even so, his first preaching was not greatly different in theme from that of Amos or Micah. He vigorously denounced the social injustices and practical materialism of the rich (*116*), the hypocrisy of formalistic religion where concern over ritual led to a neglect of God's commandments (*117, 118*), the human pride which rises up against God (*115*), the ingratitude of a sinful people who forgot the blessings of Yahweh (*119*). In the face of this dark picture the prophet announced coming punishments: war, deportation, famine. Doubtless, he was thinking of the armies of Assyria, but these events of contemporary history interested him only so far as they were the realization of the day of Yahweh against sinners (*115*). He says of Judah that Yahweh would leave only

124

a feeble remnant of the just, so that his plan might be accomplished (*114, 125*).

His preaching, however, varied according to circumstances. In the beginning, under the reign of Achaz, it was more violent, because of the king's religious attitude (*120*). Faced by a conflict in which he was opposing both Israel and the Arameans of Damascus, he took a strong position, for, because of the principles of absolute confidence in Yahweh alone, he wished that the king make no appeal to Assyria to defend his threatened throne (*121*). When Ahaz ignored him (*124*), he announced the ravages the Assyrian armies would soon wreak upon Judah (*122, 123*). In the dark days of the war he held on to one hope (*125*), the future king whose name would be Emmanuel ("God-with-us") (*122*). Perhaps it was during this same period that he hailed this King's birth (*126*) and described his ideal reign (*127*). Yet the influence of Isaiah at the court was not connected with the realization of Hezekiah's internal reform (*132*). But time passed, and ten or fifteen years later Hezekiah, in his turn, allowed himself to be carried away by a wholly human policy, inspired by the intrigues of Egypt. Isaiah denounced this lack of confidence in God (*134*) and predicted the siege of Jerusalem by Sennacherib (*135*). However, Assyrians changed the picture. They were only the instrument of the divine anger, but they grew proud of their strength (*137*), and the day would come for God to strike them in their turn (*138*). The book of Kings preserved the memory of this dramatic episode where, in the face of Sennacherib's threats, Isaiah invited Hezekiah to take confidence in his promise of salvation; and in fact, Jerusalem was not taken (*136*). We do not know when the prophet died, though a later legend has him die a martyr under the reign of Manasseh.

The Doctrine of Isaiah

In following in the texts the prophetic ministry and the political role of Isaiah we find that the essential doctrinal themes to which he will return again and again are these: the sanctity and omnipotence of God; the moral and social demands of the faith

125

and the necessity of absolute confidence in God alone; Yahweh's plan for Israel and the world differs radically from that of the politicians and the powerful; all human pride must be crushed for the plan to be realized. Isaiah foresaw this divine judgment (*115*) threatening Israel as well as the foreign nations. He predicted that concrete punishment would soon befall the guilty as a necessary prelude to a salvation which concerned not only the chosen people, but extended to all humanity.

Reference to this salvation to come "in the last times" constituted an essential aspect of the message. It drew inspiration from what Isaiah regarded as the golden age of Israel: the reigns of David and Solomon. That is why he devoted so much space to the ideal king, a son of David, under whose reign the divine promises would be realized (*126, 127*), and to the holy city and to the temple, which would then become the center of the world. Humanity will recover its primitive unity by finding once again the worship of the true God (*133*). At the end of this picture, the image of the future kingdom converged with that of paradise regained (*127, 133*). This was the first time, among the prophets, that the idea of a universal salvation was envisaged in so vast a perspective.

Although vast, the promises were conditional: Isaiah presupposed a profound purification of the people of God before their accomplishment either willingly through conversion, or forcibly through national catastrophe.

The Personality and Influence of Isaiah

Isaiah's style possesses strength, sobriety, and splendid imagery all at the same time. Master of his art, he knew how to paint a picture of the king (*119, 125*) which with the help of splendid symbols evoked the intervention of Yahweh on earth (*115, 138*). He cultivated a great variety of literary forms: invective (*125*), prophetic discourse (*118, 123*), oracle (*123, 124, 126, 127, 133, 138*), cursing (*116, 117*), parables (*119*). Some autobiographical passages (*114*) show that he himself had begun to put his preaching into writing, but the work was carried on in the circle of disciples which gathered around him. Many

126

partial narratives, whose vestiges can still be seen, were thus established.

But the history of the book does not stop there, for Isaiah's influence was prolonged in the following centuries by other inspired men following in his footsteps. And since their oracles echoed his words, all were lumped together in one book. This explains the book of Isaiah's composite literary character, and its diverse historical horizons. The work of the prophet himself figures exclusively in the first part (*Is.* 1–39), and the first two booklets (*Is.* 1; 2–5) are relevant to it. The book of Emmanuel (6–12) includes nothing except later additions (11, 10—12, 6). The oracles against the nations (13–23) are more complex and contain fragments of a later era (13, 1—14, 23; 19, 16–25; 21, 1–10). The great apocalypse (24–27) is later, as is the conclusion of the narrative which follows (33–35); but in between the exilic context is hardly perceptible (30, 19–26; 32, 15–20). Finally, the prose appendix (36–39) has its parallel in the book of Kings but preserves authentic pieces from the prophet. There is also a psalm inserted here (38, 9–20) which was probably composed after the exile.

3. THE DEUTERONOMIC MOVEMENT

The Deuteronomic Code

We have already spoken of the successful reform movement during the reign of Josiah. The Deuteronomic code (*Deut.* 12–28) was its charter (*146*). This code, profoundly traditional in spirit and founded on ancient materials, was a return to the Mosaic Law, but was directed to the needs of the times and was indirectly influenced by the prophetic preaching. Its primitive redaction can be placed in the 8th century, in the Levitic circles of the north (probably the sanctuary of Sichem: *Deut.* 27, 11–13). These reform groups went into Judah after the fall of Samaria, where we discover them in the reign of Josiah. The code was probably completed during that era.

A large part of the code was written in the style of the ancient codes, whose prescriptions it repeats, accentuating their concern to smooth social relations (*39*). Even so, it possessed many important elements of its own, whose usefulness can be understood within the framework of the 8th and 7th centuries: a severe legislation against idolatry (*139–141*); the law of the one sanctuary, rigorously applied by Josiah (*142;* see *146*); rules for the discernment of true prophets, the heirs of the spirit of Moses (*143, 144*). By a stylistic process which authorized the traditional character of the book, it is presented as a discourse addressed by Moses to the Israelites before their entry into Canaan. This literary form echoes, without any doubt whatsoever, the priestly discourses addressed by the Levitic priests to the faithful who frequented the sanctuaries. As interpreters of the Mosaic Law they wished to teach only what Moses had prescribed, so that the people would remain faithful to the message of the unique legislator.

The Deuteronomic Discourses

After the reform of Josiah (622), the code was augmented in following editions by discourses which expressed the spirit of the Deuteronomic school (*Deut.* 1–11; 29). Some other text was added relating the death of Moses (*Deut.* 30–34), notably a great canticle (*Deut.* 32) which again took up the themes of the prophetic preaching. The general object of the discourses was the exhortation to the practice of the Law, which would allow Israel to taste the goods of the promised land (*152*). But it must not be imagined that this was a purely utilitarian morality. On the contrary, the editors insisted at length on the love of God for his chosen people, and on the love Israel must manifest for Yahweh in return (*148–150*). The sign of this love was the observation of the commandments, for the Law brings them before God and is their source of true wisdom (*151*). Such a morality was already very close to that of the Gospel.

The style of these discourses is distinctive in its long periods, full of persuasive unction. It is a classroom style, where a master addressed himself to students to teach them the wisdom of life; or better, it is the style of priestly sermons which, after the liturgical readings of the Law and the recalling of the divine blessings, exhorted the people to obedience and love (2). Through them we catch a glimpse of the ancient "liturgy of the word" in the temple of Jerusalem, at the moment when the trial of the exile was about to come upon them.

The Deuteronomic Historiography

Besides this legislative, theological, and spiritual work, the scribes of the Deuteronomic school undertook another work destined to support it. They retraced the whole history of Israel, placing themselves within it from the point of view of their doctrine of the covenant. To fulfill this program they rearranged an abundant documentation. The ancient collections of the Yahwist and Elohist traditions had probably already been blended together, for under Hezekiah Judah had inherited the religious legacy of Israel. A first edition of the history of Joshua, along with one of the Judges and the first kings down to Solomon, and based upon ancient materials, probably dates from this same era. Besides, there were the biographies of Elijah and Elisha, the traditions relating to Isaiah, and the chronicles of the kings of Israel and Judah, to which readers referred in order to understand political history.

The Deuteronomic scribes were content to be compilers. They preserved entire the original documents, presenting them in their own way to make certain dominant ideas stand out: when Israel was faithful, she was rewarded by God; when she was unfaithful, she was punished; when she was converted, she was saved. The hand of the scribes may be easily recognized, whether in the moral reflections which interrupt the flow of the narratives here and there (50, 130); or in the discourses which they attributed to important persons, although they are written in their own scribal style (80, 87, 92); or in the manner in which they guide the narration itself (145, 146). They tried to make their history as precise as the state of the evidence permitted. The essential thing was not the representation of the past but the doctrine and spirituality drawn from them. In this

129

they come very close to the priestly and prophetic preaching, of which they furnish a concrete illustration.

4. JEREMIAH AND HIS TIMES

From the Time of King Josiah

Born around 650, Jeremiah sprang from a priestly family of Anathoth, an ancient sanctuary located in the territory of Benjamin some miles north of Jerusalem. In 626 he heard the call of God (*155*). In his youthful preaching (preserved principally in *Jer.* 2–6), the influence of the book of Hosea can be felt. Many of Hosea's themes are taken up again: the enumeration of Israel's sins, in reference to the great precepts of the Decalogue; the likening of idolatry to the unfaithfulness of a wife towards her husband (*156*). This pinpoints the spiritual milieu in which the prophet's vocation was rooted. Speaking to a sinful people, he announced to them the coming punishment. Inspired by the reminders left by the Assyrian cavalry, he depicted the arrival of a mysterious northern invader (*158*). This obsession with an impending natural catastrophe took on the terrifying imagery of the day of Yahweh (*159*).

While all this was going on Josiah was carrying out his reform (622). This gave Jeremiah hope of Israel's conversion, as she answered to the invitations he had recently addressed to her (*160*). The Levitic classes, to which Jeremiah was related, were hostile and viewed the suppression of the provincial sanctuaries with a jaundiced eye. Yet Jeremiah supported the reform from his modest position (*Jer.* 11); on the surface the future seemed reassuring. It was during this time, perhaps, that he envisaged a return of the Israelites, scattered since the destruction of Samaria, the rebuilding of the unity of God's people, and the birth of a spiritual and temporal golden age along lines furnished by the sojourn in the desert and the conquest (*161, 162*). This kind of hope again recalls Hosea (*111*). But all of these promises were conditional. The death of Josiah and the brutal halting of his reform work (*147*) soon plunged them back into an uncertain future.

130

The Persecuted Prophet

Beginning in 609 the prophet returned to the themes of his first preaching: a call to repentance, the proclamation of punishment. He saw a thousand signs of the evils approaching Judah. The victory of Babylon at Carchemish in 605 (*168*) allowed him to identify the mysterious northern enemy who would be the instrument of the divine vengeance (*169*). Thus began a difficult ministry for Jeremiah. Alone against everyone, he predicted disaster, since Israel would not really be converted. He was taken for a traitor. After giving a discourse on the destruction of the temple, he escaped death thanks only to the protection of a high official (*165*). Another time, he performed a symbolic action in public, crushing a pitcher to signify the fate awaiting Jerusalem; as a result he was put in chains by the temple police (*171*). Around 604, to make an impression upon men's minds, he had the scroll of his first prophesies read in the temple by his secretary Baruch (probably *Jer.* 2–6). He and Baruch had to flee to avoid the royal vengeance (*170*).

These continuous insults weighed profoundly upon his emotions. The prophet was a recluse. Even as an adult he remained a celibate, as a sign to the people who gathered around him (*166*). The ill-success of his action and the prospect of certain national ruin (*167*) were a cause of moral depression for him, which he has recorded in some very fragmentary autobiographical pages (*172–175*). The calls to the divine justice were no longer enough and he posed the problem of evil for himself, almost doubting his vocation. God had to renew him, calling him to an ever greater intrepidness in the accomplishment of his sorrowful mission (*175*). In these pages the supernatural origin of prophetic inspiration is best evidenced by the witness of one himself inspired.

Facing National Disaster

After the first deportation (*598*), Jeremiah adopted an extremely forthright attitude. This was no longer the moment to nourish illusions and play politics with Egypt and the small

131

neighboring kingdoms. The Israelites must be converted and submit to Nebuchadnezzar, recognizing him as the divine instrument (*176*). For the rest, the hope of Israel lay in the reformed Judean communities of the exile. They would be the point of departure for a new future (*177*). Naturally, these counsels were ignored. The intrigues of the Egyptophile party, which Jeremiah fought forcefully, provoked a second Babylonian campaign. The second siege of Jerusalem (586) brought new sufferings to the prophet. He experienced prison and the danger of death (*178*).

After the destruction of the holy city Jeremiah escaped deportation, but only to be led into Egypt by the fanatical Jews who assassinated the governor Godolias. His last efforts were devoted to the struggle against the idolatry which threatened his compatriots. A later tradition has him die under their blows.

Strangely enough, it was at this dark hour that he delivered his message of hope (preserved in *Jer.* 30–33). The promises proclaimed at the time of the reform (*161, 162*), completed by some new oracles, have a place in his preaching again. After the trial will come a new covenant, he says, which will realize what the old could not (*181*). Then a just king will reign, the Davidic Messiah whom Isaiah had already glimpsed (*180*).

The Personality and Influence of Jeremiah

The contrast between Isaiah and Jeremiah is striking and appears in their very callings (compare *114* and *155*). Jeremiah was a shy, sensitive person who suffered in having to transmit a message of disaster. But the grace of God rendered him fearless in the accomplishment of his task. His destiny marked him as a man of suffering, and among the men of the Old Testament perhaps no one more closely resembles the persecuted Christ. His message, which continued that of Hosea, and presented some affinities with Deuteronomic literature, gave an important place to the reciprocal love of Yahweh and his people, to the religion of the heart. From a literary point of view he does not have Isaiah's dash. But he is a true poet, a writer of elegies.

132

His prophetic discourses, his eschatological oracles, are graced with numerous images, inspired by social life or the countryside (*156, 157, 162, 179*). This side of his genius recalls his provincial origins, for he excels in the art of description, and some of his scenes are very powerful (*158, 159, 168*).

Nevertheless, he did not compile his own book. Baruch, his disciple and secretary, was undoubtedly its first editor. The final literary form of many of the prose oracles is probably due to Baruch (*165*). Most important of all, he has left an admirable biography of his master (*165, 170, 171, 178*). This view of an Old Testament saint is historical witness of the first order, free from artifice and popular imagery. Through it we can penetrate the soul of a prophet and feel the pathos of his unhappy existence. In addition, Baruch's own personality left sufficient impression to have a later collection of some anonymous pieces placed under his name (*331*). In its present form the book of Jeremiah includes many sections which the Hebrew Bible and its Greek version do not set forth in the same order: a collection of oracles against Judah and Jerusalem (*Jer.* 1, 1—25, 13); some oracles against the nations (25, 14–38; 46–49) whose conclusion is an addition of exilic times directed against Babylon (50–51); a book of consolation which includes eschatological promises (30–33); some biographical fragments due to Baruch (26–29; 34–45), completed by an appendix borrowed from the book of Kings (*Jer.* 52).

If the prophet's influence during his lifetime appears slight, it was tremendous after his death. His work, recopied and meditated upon in the Judean circles in Babylonia, contributed considerably to the national conversion. Events proved his prophecies. Thus it became time to obey his voice to return to God by preserving hope in spite of evil times. Jeremiah also prepared the way for a religion more detached from the material temple than Isaiah's. He had even gone so far as to predict the destruction of the temple (*165*), and in fact, it was far from the ruined temple that Judaism reorganized itself during the exile. The spiritual light of Jeremiah made him the first of those chosen souls who called themselves the *poor of Yahweh* (Text 18), and this fervent milieu would become the soul of Israel.

The Prophets Contemporary with Jeremiah

In comparison to Jeremiah the other prophets of the time pale into insignificance. Zephaniah preceded him by a few years. The proclaimer of the day of Yahweh (*154*) apparently was connected with the pious circles who preserved the tradition of Isaiah. He contributed to the establishment of the spirituality of the poor of Yahweh, giving them an important role in the promises of the future (*Wis.* 3, 9–20). His gaze extended to all the people surrounding the kingdom of Judah. Nahum was a little later. In 612 he proclaimed with savage joy the execution of God's judgment on Nineveh, a cruel and proud city, long since doomed to destruction (*164*). As for Habakkuk, he first saw Babylon as the instrument of the divine anger against Israel's sinners (*163*). But after the destruction of Jerusalem his oracle established the theme of a new reflection (whether of Habakkuk or another we do not know) which considered the prosperity of Babylon a scandal and called impatiently for its downfall. In this spirit a series of imprecations were hurled at the conqueror (*Hab.* 2, 5–18). The book finishes with a beautiful psalm describing the theophany of final salvation (*Hab.* 3).

5. THE PRIESTLY SCHOOL

The Law of Holiness

The prophetic circles, like the Levitic ones to which we owe Deuteronomy, insisted upon the moral aspect of the Mosaic tradition and Law, whereas the priests of Jerusalem tended to link all of God's demands to organized worship. They, too, were depositories of an important aspect of tradition. They transmitted from one generation to the other the ritual rules and formularies which began during the time in the desert, and were greatly developed in the course of the ages, especially during

134

the times of David and Solomon. But the reform movement of the 7th century also influenced these circles, much more easily after Deuteronomy finally became the official law of the temple of Jerusalem. That is why the better elements of the priesthood were trying to react against surrounding formalism and to restore an authentic religious spirit to worship. Their work, which paralleled Deuteronomy but was a little later, took shape in the Law of Holiness (*Lev.* 17–26). It is difficult to fix precisely the date when this work was edited and published, on the basis of the traditional customs, but Ezekiel seems to have known of it. In addition, it shows traces of later redaction.

The key idea is impressive: the absolute holiness of God. God wishes a holy people and a holy priesthood in his service. The whole Law, ritual as well as moral and civil, has the purpose of realizing this ideal here on earth (*182, 183*). Doubtless, this sanctity is a ritual rather than a moral purity. This high standard saw all human life as a perpetual religious rite performed, like a liturgy, for the glory of the Creator. In this perspective the moral laws retain their importance. They serve God, like sacrifices and prayers, and the motive of morality is none other than the divine majesty itself: "Be holy because I am holy!"

The Establishment of the Priestly Code

The priestly laws (rules for ritual purity, for sacrifices and offerings, etc.) certainly existed before the exile. They constituted a traditional heritage, enriched through the centuries by the normal development of worship. The possible transmission of certain written rules would have been accompanied in this era by an uninterrupted living tradition. The ways of worship would be taught as much through practice as by the theoretical study of a code of rubrics. But the destruction of Jerusalem (in 586) put an end to most sacred ceremonies. Then it became urgent to collect in writing all the traditional prescriptions, to preserve them exactly until the day of national restoration.

The deportation of the clergy of Jerusalem made such a com-

135

pilation indispensable. The whole legacy of the past was thus gathered up, and on the basis of it a synthesis of liturgical legislation was drawn up expressing the dream of a future ideal. This work led to the *priestly code*, which synthesized a whole school of thought into a complex system parallel to the Deuteronomic school, although it was more developed on the level of worship. How this legislative compilation was done, what its stages were, and at what date it was finished are still much discussed problems. At present, we can only sketch out probable solutions and leave it to the future to refine them.

The Priestly Sacred History

The framework for the writings of the priest-scribes is a *sacred history* leading from the beginnings to Israel's settlement in Canaan. Rooted in pre-exilic tradition, it must have been in use already in the 6th century, before the rebuilding of the temple. Its elements are, at present, scattered from Genesis to the book of Numbers (and perhaps Joshua). In Babylon the milieu of its origin had already come under the influence of Ezekiel. Its editors drew the elements of their synthesis from more ancient traditions which had already been set down in writing or were still circulating orally. But they used them in an original way to highlight the great doctrinal ideas preserved by the Jewish priesthood. They wanted to show how God, concerned for his glory, prepared a holy people here on earth and endowed them little by little with appropriate institutions. They examined the history of God's covenant with men from this angle. They saw four stages in history: the creation of the world and mankind (*184*), which did not close until the disaster of the flood; God's covenant with all mankind, represented by Noah (*185*), which was merely a prelude to the scattering of men; the covenant given the patriarchs (*186*), which proclaimed a new religious economy; finally, the covenant concluded on Sinai, which completed the work by making Israel a holy people (*187, 188*).

This doctrinal synthesis accentuates the transcendent character of the God of Israel. From the historical point of view it intentionally schematizes the presentation of facts and does

136

not always pretend to give precise details in the modern historical sense. To be convinced of this, it is enough to compare its narration of the escape from Egypt (*137*) with that of the ancient traditions (*30*). Then, too, its presentation of creation (*184*) supposed a more elaborate theology than that of the Yahwistic history (*3, 4*). This great historical panorama with the prophetic proclamation of the new covenant, insisted upon by Ezekiel (204), helps reveal the unity of all biblical history, both of the Old and the New Testament.

In the course of the narrative a few laws had also been inserted. These laws were those which could be practiced in exile: the Sabbath (*184*), the dietary prescriptions (*185*), circumcision (*186*), and the Passover (*41*). In point of fact, these practices distinguished the holy people from the nations they lived with. The remainder of the text is the description of the institutions created by Moses in the desert and centered on the tabernacle and the priesthood. These institutions are of no mere historical interest, for they present a concrete program of action, worked out by the priestly caste in exile. The whole code is a formulation of past tradition and a plan for the future. Through it post-exilic Judaism would be linked to the desert theocracy. The first temple had also had its own customs and rituals and the exiles were forced to put them in writing, if this had not already been done. But their definitive codification did not take place until after the rebuilding of the temple and the resumption of the liturgy. So the subject will come up again in that historical context.

6. EZEKIEL, THE PRIESTLY PROPHET

The Preacher of Penance

Ezekiel, a priest of Jerusalem, received his prophetic call in 593. He was to be a preacher of conversion and a foreteller of punishments in the midst of a "house of rebels" (*189, 190*). Fully conscious of this responsibility, he fulfilled his mission for seven years side by side with Jeremiah. It has recently been suggested that he could have remained in Judea until 586, the date in which he would have been deported. Still, it seems that he was in Babylonia from 598 onwards. It is not easy to say on what date each of his oracles was pronounced, for due to its editors the book's order is partly artificial. Even so, this problem is much less important than the prophet's roots in the priestly school and his influence on its later development. From this point of view he seems to be situated between the *code of holiness* and the rest of the priestly compilations.

Before 586 Ezekiel denounced the sins of Israel. Princes, priests, prophets, tribes of the people, all dishonored God by their blameworthy conduct (*191*); they had, he said, brought Israel's century-old infidelity to a peak. So God is going to cast off his people, as an adulterous wife is cast off (*192*). The king of Babylon is to execute this sentence (*195*). In a prophetic vision Ezekiel was present at the future destruction of Jerusalem when the glory of Yahweh left the profaned temple (*193*). The ancients of Judah (probably those of the deported communities) listened to his message with a mixture of respect and skepticism. As for the prophet, he prodded them relentlessly to change their life, insisting upon the necessity of personal conversion, for Yahweh treated each one according to his conduct (*194*). On the day of Jerusalem's punishment, only the just, marked with the seal of God, would be spared (*193*). In order the better to move his hearers, Ezekiel performed strange but meaningful mimes which symbolized the approaching siege of the city, the scattering of its inhabitants, the flight and death of the king, the profanation of the sanctuary (*196, 197*).

Encouraging the Exiles

The national disaster soon came. Still inviting his companions in exile to conversion, Ezekiel received his mission of proclaiming to them the meaning of recent events and maintaining hope in their hearts. The divine glory appeared to him in Babylon (*200*). Thus he saw that the presence of Yahweh was not linked to the temple of Jerusalem, as people tended to believe; Yahweh remained in the midst of his exiled people.

His own time was a test designed to purify Israel, but God would end it and finally rule over them. Jerusalem had experienced the wrath of God, but other nations would feel it in their turn: Ammon and Moab, and Tyre (*198*), and Egypt (*199*), until the turn of Babylon itself comes (*206*).

Henceforth, Ezekiel's attention was given to the future. The people of God would revive (*201*). Yahweh himself would lead them like a good shepherd and put at their head an ideal leader, born of David's dynasty (*202*). God was going to purify them, pour out his Spirit on them, change their heart, reëstablish them in the holy land, and grant them the joy of paradise (*203*). He was going to conclude an eternal covenant with them (*204*). This was the prophet's message of hope to his sorely tried fellow countrymen. In Ezekiel's thought, the eschatological perspective was not distinct from the exiles' return to their homeland. So he traced the plans for the day when this event would take place. And mingling symbolic characteristics with minute prescriptions, he set forth his concept of the ideal Israel: a new holy city and a new temple where the divine glory would return to dwell; a new organization of worship; a new holy land, become marvelously fertile (*205*). On this point once more the prophet's thought seems closely linked to the priestly tradition, while giving it an eschatological outlook.

Nevertheless, at the very end of his days Ezekiel (that is, he or his continuator, for the literary origin of these chapters is disputed) foresaw new trials for the people of Yahweh, a last struggle and an ultimate victory of God over the pagan enemy, after which the glory of God would shine forever among his people (*206*). This section marks a prelude to a literary genre which become very popular in following centuries: the apocalypse.

The Doctrine of Ezekiel

Himself a priest, Ezekiel joined the ordinary preoccupations of his caste with those of all the prophets. He certainly knew Hosea and probably Jeremiah, since he adopted some of their themes, developing them in an original way (*192, 202–204*).

His insistence upon the necessity of conversion is reminiscent of Deuteronomic thought. In brief, his doctrine is, from this point of view, a kind of crossroads of many currents already shaped into sacred books. Yet his repetition of ancient elements was carried out within the sphere of influence of priestly spirituality. Ezekiel had an exalted idea of the glory of the holy God (*200*), and concern for this glory is the only motive determining Yahweh's conduct, both when he punished a people for profaning his name and defiling the holy land, and when he proposed to save Israel to cut short pagan blasphemies (*228; compare 187*).

This representation of God is in strong contrast to those of Hosea and Jeremiah. The difference is noticeable even in the chapters where Ezekiel adopts the image of God as husband (*192*). So, in human sin, he sees less of God's love ignored than his majesty scorned by pride and the hardening of the heart of man (*189, 190, 192*). His strong affirmation of personal retribution deserves special mention (*194*), for as he presents it, it seems to be something new, and it does, in fact, constitute notable progress over the old idea of collective responsibility still present in the Decalogue (*37*). It is not that he rejects the principle of human solidarity, but that he is conscious that, in the new order which will be established after Israel's trial, individual value will break free of the collectivity. From this beginning the doctrine of retribution after the exile will move closer towards that of the Gospel (Text 19).

The Personality and Book of Ezekiel

Ezekiel was a strange man. Certain details of his life (*Ezek.* 4, 4–8) make it seem that he was a sick man. He was certainly eccentric. We have already noted how, in order to impress people, he performed extraordinarily expressive mimes which were parables in action (*195–197*); and if our Western mind is perplexed by them, yet his art was in keeping with his life. Much more often than his predecessors, he presented his prophetic speeches as the explanation of an ecstatic vision (*189, 193, 200*). Naturally, the vision was composed of symbols, for only thus was he able to translate ineffable realities into human terms. He piled up images, not even recoiling from the most bizarre associations (*200*) or macabre evocations (*201*). We can detect the indirect influence of Mesopotamian art on his imagination. As for his style, it was overloaded, bloated with epithets, sometimes choppy. His prose was at times dense (*194*), yet in spite of his faults, noticeable even in translation, he remains a poet of great power. He built beautiful allegories (*192*), whose themes were sometimes adopted in the New Testament (*202*). His lament on the shipwreck of the vessel of Tyre is a masterpiece (*198*).

It is probable that the editors of his book are partly responsible for the present form of his oracles. The last of them dates from 571 (*Ezek*. 30, 17–20). But the over-all organization does not follow chronological order. In the book, after the account of his call, which is probably a composite (*189, 200*), there are, one after another: the message of conversion addressed to the Jews before the siege of Jerusalem (*Ezek*. 3, 22—24, 27), oracles against the pagan nations (*Ezek*. 25–32), oracles contemporary to the siege and after it (*Ezek*. 33–39), and finally the description of the eschatological city and temple (*Ezek*. 40–48). There are also doublets and additions which are difficult to attribute to the prophet. It could even be asked whether the apocalypse of the eschatological section (*206*) does not belong to a continuator of his work. Be that as it may, Ezekiel was certainly important to the direction taken by Judaism after the exile.

7. IN THE LAND OF EXILE

It is very difficult to follow the trail of development of the inspired literature during the exile, because of the dispersal of the Jewish communities. The work of the Deuteronomic and priestly circles was surely carried on during the time in Babylonia. There the book of Ezekiel first saw the light of day. But whether the edition of the book of Jeremiah by Baruch was made in Egypt, in the land of Israel, or in Babylonia cannot be said. The influence of the pre-exilic books grew notably during this time, but their inspired editors did not hesitate to add finishing touches. In the books of Jeremiah and Isaiah, for example, the oracles announcing the fall of Babylon must date from this era (*Jer.* 50–51; *Is.* 13–14; 21, 1–10). After Jerusalem, after Assyria, Egypt, and the other nations, Babylon the proud in her turn will know the day of divine wrath (*214*). But these detached fragments are all eclipsed by the *Message of Consolation for the Exiles* (*Is.* 40–55).

Religious lyricism also finds a suitable theme in the national tragedy. Many elegies on the destruction of Jerusalem have been collected in the book of Lamentations which the Greek translator attributed to Jeremiah. There, sorrow drove the unhappy times to express its heart-rending complaints; but it quickly became an examination of conscience and an avowal of national guilt (*207, 208*). Perhaps the origin of the book must be sought in the liturgies of repentance which were celebrated on the ruins of the temple during the time of exile. However, Lamentation Three parallels the supplication psalms, and could date from a slightly later time. The same tone is found in a certain number of the psalms. "By the waters of Babylon," the Jews more accurately assessed the links binding them to their holy city (*209*) and reminded themselves of God's past blessings, as a motive for both hope and sorrow. The prophetic promises lived on in their minds. They awaited their accomplishment impatiently, and this desire was transformed into ardent prayer (*210–213*).

8. THE MESSAGE OF CONSOLATION FOR THE EXILES

Before Cyrus's Victories

Chapters 40–45 of the book of Isaiah form a unity commonly called the *Message of Consolation for the Exiles,* after its first words (*215*). The victories of Cyrus became, in the eyes of the anonymous prophet, a sign of Israel's approaching deliverance. Cyrus was the providential man chosen by God for this magnificent work. The approach of his armies, depicted in lyric terms *(216)*, furnished the occasion for addressing a message of hope to the Jews in exile. The book possesses powerful unity, but is not composed in modern style. It is a collection of varied pieces, whose dominant themes are quickly noted: the consolation, deliverance, and redemption of Israel; God's unequaled grandeur, as the Creator and Master of history; the approaching fall of Babylon; the return of the exiles and the reconstruction of Jerusalem in an atmosphere of eschatological joy. The historical frame of reference for the entire book are the years before 539. Its presence in the book of Isaiah leads one to suspect that the author belonged to a pious circle of the prophet's disciples who preserved his work and tried to adapt it to new times. The affinities to *Jeremiah* 50–51 are remarkable.

A Message of Hope

The prophet received the mission of proclaiming Israel's deliverance, by which the glory of God would be manifested to the eyes of all *(215)*. He did not have words strong enough to glorify the one God, in the face of whom the whole world is as nothing, who rules events, knows what is to come beforehand and proclaims it through his prophets, creates all things and disposes of them as he pleases. This God is not only Israel's national God, for he alone exists, and idols are nothing and before him every knee should bend *(221)*. This powerful affirmation of monotheism reflected the Jews' reaction against Mesopotamian paganism, against which a biting satire is found here and there. This affirmation blassomed into the proclamation of the universal reign of God, the term towards which his whole plan was tending *(Is.* 45, 14–17. 20–25).

But his unique God is also the special saviour of Israel. Called to be his servant, Israel has known the misery of exile. Now she is reduced to a weak remnant, but this is the hour when God is going to come to her aid *(217, 220)*. Now Israel is enslaved, but Yahweh will free her, as he freed her once before by leading her out of Egypt. The exiles will return to their homeland. The prophet saw the exodus, the crossing of the

143

desert, and the entry into Canaan in the time of Moses and Joshua as the symbol and protoype of this new deliverance and return (*218, 219*). Nevertheless, when he spoke of what was to come he did not distinguish at all between events near at hand and at the end of time, the restoration which was soon to take place and the definitive redemption. While answering the practical problems of his day, his book possesses an eschatological undertone from beginning to end which goes beyond them and touches us directly. This is particularly noticeable in the passages where he proclaims the definitive pardon of past sins (*220*) or promises to the repatriates a joy without equal which will constitute a return to paradise lost (*221*). He called this the *justice* and *salvation* of God, not the justice which judges, but which triumphs and delivers (*220, 221*). These words will henceforth be the technical term for the work of God in the "last times." For this reason, they will be taken up again in the New Testament (*Rom.* 1, 17, etc.).

All the eschatological imagery was grouped around the holy city, whose memory strongly stirred the heart of the exiled children. When Babylon falls into dust along with her tottering gods (*Is.* 47), Yahweh will remember Jerusalem and lead his children back to her (*222*). He pitied her ruin (*221*). He invites her to arise, she who lay on the ground as if dead (*223*). He is going to reclaim her as his spouse and multiply her posterity indefinitely (*224*). This will be a new covenant, which the prophet, following Hosea and Jeremiah, presented under the image of a marriage. The idea of the Davidic covenant, though not absent (*Is.* 55, 5), was little emphasized. And towards the end of his book there is an invitation to conversion and salvation whose tone foreshadows the books of wisdom (*Is.* 55, 1–3).

The Servant of Yahweh

There are four poems in the *Message* which merit special mention (*Is.* 42, 1–7; 49, 1–6; 50, 4–9; 52, 13—53, 12). All have the *Servant of Yahweh* as their subject. This mysterious person is presented as the artisan of the eschatological salvation. He is not a king, it seems, for his traits belong rather to the prophets and masters of wisdom (*225, 226*). The salvation he brings to men is not of the temporal but of the moral order. It is a light for souls, a liberation for darkened hearts; like a new Moses he proclaims a religious rule. He is the mediator and legislator of a new covenant in which all peoples are included. This aspect of his mission contrasts strongly with the picture of the Royal Messiah found in Isaiah.

This contrast is even greater when the earthly fate which God prepares for him is examined. He proclaims his message with faithfulness and courage, but he comes under insults and persecution (*227*). In this section something unheard of is revealed to us. It is not by his visible success but by his suffering that he is going to save man (*228*). Although just, he bears the weight of our sins. For this reason he undergoes an iniquitous judgment, but his death is the expiatory sacrifice by which the plan of God is to be carried out on earth, and his prayer is to gain the pardon of sinners. Thus he finally receives a surprising glory from God.

Without a doubt these pages mark the high point of prophetic promises. Certain historical persons have reflected characteristics of this *Servant of Yahweh* par excellence, for example Moses, or the persecuted prophets like Jeremiah, or even the humble masters of wisdom of this age. It is likely that the author also thought of that humble remnant of the just who, after the destruction of Jerusalem, shared the miserable lot of the sinful masses (*217*). But it is with a view to final salvation that he presents the role of the servant. In this perspective he unveils the redemptive value of suffering. This strikingly anticipates the New Testament where Jesus is seen to be the only just Remnant of a wholly guilty humanity, saving men through the mystery of the cross. Nowhere, however, is this suffering Servant expressly identified with the Royal Messiah (*126, 127, 180, 202*). The two images developed independently in the prophets. The cross and the recurrection of Jesus had to take place for us to see how they fit together, for the Messiah "must die before entering into his glory."

The Literary Value of the Message

While prolonging the work of Isaiah, the *Message of Consolation* is also related to other more ancient books: Hosea, Jeremiah, Deuteronomy, the priestly collections. But it is a profoundly personal work. Its general tone is lyric. The prophetic discourse is fully developed in it and reaches intense persuasive strength *(217, 221)*. It is broken up by oracles, elegies, canticles, and finally blossoms out into eschatological evocations. Its frequent reference to the Scriptures and to the ancient history of Israel leads one to think that it must have been elaborated more than once with an eye towards the prayer-meetings organized by the Jewish exile communities. Be that as it may, with Deuteronomy and Jeremiah it is one of the books most influential upon post-exilic spirituality. Numerous echoes of it are heard in the psalms *(327)* and later writings *(331, 332)*.

Text 18

JEREMIAH AND PERSONAL RELIGION

The primitive Israelite religion was above all a religion of the group. But beginning with the exile a new current developed among those who called themselves the *anawim,* or the poor of Yahweh. A historian writing about Jeremiah shows how the prophet's attitude of mind exercised a strong influence over this religious current (see *172–175, 181*).

The prophet of Anathoth found in his sufferings a springboard towards God and the secret of an unequal dialogue. In the line of the poor of Yahweh he occupies a key place and merits the title of father of the anawim. . . .

Through the dialectic of failure Jeremiah had gained access to a more profound form of religion. Excluded from the temple and re-

146

pulsed by men, he took up the habit of continually conversing with his God. The God of the covenant was thus revealed as the God of mystical dialogue. Jeremiah is the father of prayer. After the death of his master, Baruch collected the precious booklets in which he had set down his "confessions." . . . Jeremiah had let his very soul speak out in sorrowful soliloquies, prayers, and lamentations which expressed his interior life. This piety, however, had its defects. . . : it allows feelings of revenge, a certain fierceness, and if pushed a little further, it would take on overtones of Pharisaism. When the soliloquy became dialogue, Yahweh rebuked his prophet. He called him to abandon his faint-heartedness, impertinence, and niggardliness, and incited him to try to do so.

At a time when the link between religion and the nation was about to be broken it was providential that a man sensed this and realized before his contemporaries "worship in spirit and in truth." In exile a community would be formed around and according to his spiritual model, and his attitude of soul, like his phraseology, would be taken up again to such a degree that the people of God in Babylon would be the church of the poor of Yahweh. In his own lifetime the shining out of this piety must have made itself felt and in any case it is basic to Jeremiah's essential message of the coming new covenant. For he proclaimed it to the people as the religious program of tomorrow. God had begun by making him live it . . . Nowhere has Jeremiah so happily and energetically expressed his thought than when he speaks of religion as an interior commerce uniting the individual to God. God grants it as a gift, man must make the most of it as a personal blessing.

A. Gelin, *Jérémie*

Text 19

EZEKIEL AND THE RELIGIOUS MOVEMENT OF THE EXILE

Though very different from Jeremiah, Ezekiel still began, like the prophet of Anathoth, from religious personalism. But he takes another tack. And, perhaps, it is in Ezekiel that the movement which marked the exile in the development of Israel's religion can best be seen.

Traditionally, up to then, the prophets were men who proclaimed disasters and who warned. Men who preached thus preached conversion. If the people would be converted, Yahweh would repent and not strike them down. Clearly, such affirmations took on many shades of meaning . . . but this is very much their general tenor, and it may be said that, on the whole, they preached conversion, and conversion of the people as a whole.

With Ezekiel, on the other hand, the game is up, the catastrophe has already begun to fall upon Jerusalem and nothing will stop it. It is a settled thing, because conversion had not taken place when there was still time. Thus it can be understood why Ezekiel unexpectedly but explicitly and definitively goes over to an individualistic point of view. In the hour of greatest danger the prophet cries a sort of general "Save yourself if you can." Since the people cannot escape punishment each one must work for himself, abandoning the others to save himself alone. Since the nation is going to perish it is a matter of individuals withdrawing for a time, creating an elite with which a people will be rebuilt, the heir of the old Israel.

This is something analogous to what happened at the outset of Christianity, when, after the nation had refused to receive the Messiah and had rejected the priority of entry offered it into the kingdom, Jesus began to call individually those who would form the Church. Placed at this turning point in history, at this hinge which links two very different eras, instead of remaining obstinately attached to the past and repeating the ancient prophetic themes, Ezekiel inaugurated the individual apostolate.

P. Auvray, Ézéchiel

Bibliography

J. Chaine, *God's Heralds* (New York 1955). J. Dheilly, *The Prophets* (New York 1960). E. Kissane, *The Book of Isaiah* (Dublin n.d.). E. Maly, *Prophets of Salvation* (New York 1967).

T. Sutcliffe, *The Book of Amos* (London n.d.). B. Vawter, *The Conscience of Israel* (New York 1961).

Study Guides

Compare the personalities of Elijah, Isaiah, Jeremiah, and Ezekiel.

With the aid of the testimony of the prophets themselves (*10, 114, 156, 189*) and related texts (*11, 26, 91, 93*) show that revelation is an historical fact, in the sense that its intermediaries clearly attested its supernatural origin, in testimony verifiable by historians. Does this not give the religion based upon it a place apart in the history of religions? Does not the same thing hold true for the New Testament?

The God of biblical revelation is not an abstract idea. He is the "living God." Show this by an inspection of the imagery used by the prophets to depict concretely his presence and action here on earth. Also compare this presentation of God with that found in the Gospel parables. In the images they use are there not some which originated in prophetic literature (*109, 110, 111, 112, 119, 157, 179, 192, 211, 212, 215*)?

VII.

THE MESSAGE OF THE PROPHETS

ALL religions are transmitted as traditions. The permanent functioning of their ritual institutions and the uninterrupted succession of their leaders assure them of continuity. Still, they suffer the setbacks of historical events, the clash of empires, the turmoil of peoples and civilizations, and under these pressures they evolve with the times. It comes as no surprise, then, that the religion of Israel had also clothed itself in tradition. Its originality does not lie here, but in the role which inspired men played in the origin and development of this tradition. In its origins it was dominated by Moses. During the royal era the Mosaic tradition was not content with merely maintaining its position, but refined and deepened its content through new witnesses of God—the prophets. Having discussed their books and actions, it is time now to study their message, to see how they enriched revelation.

1. THE MOSAIC TRADITION
AND THE PREACHING OF THE PROPHETS

Men of Tradition

In the eyes of their contemporaries the prophets were sometimes troublemakers (*90*), even revolutionaries (*85, 97*), and always intruders (*93, 106, 122, 165, 170, 171, 178*). Struck by their bold views, some modern historians make them the creators of

150

a new religion, the initiators of monotheism and worship in spirit. What they really accomplished was something quite different. Though it is true that in their own times these men seemed to be innovators, this is so mainly because the people had forgotten the essentials of the authentic Israelite tradition which the prophets upheld. The authentic tradition was born at Sinai with Moses and triumphed over the paganism of Canaan in the time of David. The prophetic vocation (*106, 114, 155, 189*) followed in the line of Moses (*26*); the prophets' mission continued his, as Deuteronomy rightly points out (*143*). Also, they themselves looked to the national past for the model of the ideal Israel which they wished to revive. According to individual temperament and the school of thought to which they were linked, they looked back to the time of the wandering in the desert (*111, 156, 161, 181, 218, 219*) or to the high point of the Davidic kingdom (*126, 127, 180*). Thus they grafted their own doctrine onto tradition in an attempt to restore its vigor and effectiveness. Revelation progressed through the prophets, but only within its original outlines, deepening those values which it already posessed.

Naturally, the appeal to tradition is more perceptible in the Deuteronomic and priestly works. Their inspired editors were not prophets, original personalities whose very vocation marked them out in sharp fashion, but priests, guardians of the ritual and juridical traditions transmitted in the sanctuaries. Though anxious for reform to prevent degeneration, their only concern was faithful maintenance. Thus they effaced themselves behind the authority of Moses. By comparing their books with the ancient collections of laws and the first collections of historical traditions, we can perceive the development of Israelite thought through the centuries. Because the influence of the prophets so far surpassed them, the Deuteronomic and priestly doctrines reaped its benefits.

The Meaning of God and the Doctrine of the Covenant

The central thought is focused on a profound faith in God. The God of the prophets and their contemporary authors is the

God of the patriarchs and Moses; he is not only the creator of all, the legislator of morality and the lord of history, but also he who speaks to men through his messengers. The Israelites, surrounded by pagan Canaan, tended to reduce Yahweh to the rank of a popular Baal, a personification of the forces of nature whose favors should be sought. In reaction to this temptation the prophets proclaimed God's radical difference from all other gods. In the strongest sense of the term, Yahweh alone was *God* to them (*89, 90, 108, 111, 139–141, 148, 156*). Eventually they found a more and more precise language to explain what his creative activity consisted in (*184, 217*), and they showed his mastery of history by their prediction of future events. Thus events became signs accrediting their teaching (*144*).

In speaking of God the prophets did not abandon the traditional symbols, the normal expressions of a thought-pattern which shunned abstractions. They represented God as a king (*93, 114*) or in the theophany of the storm (*95, 129, 136, 138, 200*). But their religious language tended to strip itself of anthropomorphisms the better to point up the divine transcendence. To get a clear idea of this, it is sufficient to compare the creation narrative or the crossing of the Red Sea in the Yahwist sacred history (*3–6, 30*) and in the priestly sacred history (*184, 187*). The idea of the divine holiness, which sets Yahweh apart and raises him above every creature, has a most important place in a whole segment of the prophetic literature (*114, 191, 203*), as it also does in that of the priestly caste (*182, 183*).

The second fundamental point of the Israelite creed was the doctrine of the covenant. God chose Israel to make her his very own people and to load her with his gifts (*1, 2*). This truth was recalled in vigorous terms, by the prophets (*102, 220*) and by the priests (*149*) and sacred historians (*188*). But the explanation as to why God had acted in this way was given a number of different emphases. Sometimes God was shown to be motivated by concern for his own honor and glory (*184–188, 203*), or the most moving comparisons were used to make it understood that he loves his people (*148–150*). He is like the farmer

152

who cares for his vine (*109, 119, 157*), a shepherd who leads his flock (*109, 202, 215*), a father who cherishes his child (*112, 125, 157, 162, 192*), a husband who clings to his wife (*110, 111, 156, 192, 224*). Thanks to these images of everyday experience the doctrines of the covenant, originally a juridical notion, took on an affective overtone touching man's heart because it revealed something of God's "heart." But it was essential that Israel be faithful to the treaty of covenant. The people of God must not scorn their Lord and Master, ruining his plan, but must honor the tie of affection which God established on his own initiative between himself and mankind. If they did not, God would apply the sanctions proclaimed at Sinai, his betrayal love would turn to wrath, and he would punish Israel.

2. THE PREACHING OF REPENTANCE

The Law of God and the Sins of Men

The prophets and priests operated in the same spirit and had a lively awareness of God's demands. All around them the worship of Yahweh was becoming a religion like that of Canaan, that is, a religion of ritual with no true spiritual depth. To fight this ingrained tendency, which is found even in the Christian milieu, they constantly reaffirmed the primary importance of interior dispositions (*117, 118*), of moral and religious virtues summed up in the Decalogue (*107*). Recalling Yahweh's exclusivism, they thundered against idolatry (*90, 111, 139–141, 145, 146, 156, 192*), to which they likened the worship of the golden calf (*86, 107; see 44*). Their campaigns against the practical paganism of the local sanctuaries helped prepare for the centralization of worship which took place under Josiah (*132, 142, 146*). But this clearly presupposed the reform of the sanctuary at Jerusalem, for without reform its ruin was inevitable (*165, 193*). Besides, attention was brought to bear upon all sorts of social disorders, which were unsuitable to the spirit of the Mosaic legislation, —for example, injustice, bad

153

faith in mutual relation, the practical materialism of the rich, which gave birth to hardness of heart in face of misery (*92, 98–100, 116, 131, 191*). At the root of this situation was pride, a false wisdom which, like original sin (*5*), upset the order of good and evil (*115, 152*).

Thus the notion of sin was greatly refined. Divine law defined good and evil for man, and any material failure in regard to this Law could, in some way, be called a sin. In this sense there were involuntary sins committed through ignorance, and there were rituals for their remission (*42*). But this point of view had to be surpassed. Human guilt is essentially voluntary rebellion against the Creator (*125, 189*), true folly with the dual consequence of defiling man and bringing the wrath of God down upon him. The Christian idea of sin is no different from this. In contrast to this table of human faults the prophets and Deuteronomic scribes praised interior virtues such as knowledge, fear and love of God (*113, 148–150*), obedience, humility, piety, fidelity, a sense of justice and kindness in relations with each other (Text 20). Such a morality was a direct preparation for the Gospels.

The Problem of Conversion

The prophetic preaching was addressed to sinners. Perhaps it was necessary that Israel thus experience its powerlessness to fulfill the divine Law, so that the depths of human evil be revealed. In any case, the prophets saw it with their own eyes. They constantly called for conversion (*118, 125, 160, 165, 190, 194*), and more than once their pressing invitation was supported by present or recent calamities, the signs of God's wrath against a sinful world (*104, 125, 170, 177*).

But the return to God was difficult. Superficial conversions did not reach the depths of a man's heart (*113, 160*)! Isaiah came to think that only a remnant would be converted (*121*). Jeremiah felt that Israel's hardness of heart was unassailable. Ezekiel no longer envisaged a mass conversion of the nation. He summoned his hearers to personal conversion, to escape the disaster which would befall the people as a whole (*194*). These

154

views would seem pessimistic were they not based on experience. In fact, conversion of heart demands a radical transformation of interior dispositions, which is impossible to man alone. Divine grace is needed (*111, 181, 203*), and the discovery of this key point could only happen through Israel's national tragedy.

The Judgment of God

The hardened sinner lulled himself into false security, for he was a threatened man. He could not escape the sight of God, and God is a judge. Certain prophetic discourses took the form of an indictment against the people of God, as if a third party could judge between Israel and him (*107, 111, 118, 119, 129*). But most often they pronounce the sentences he has handed down. For a time he was patient with sinners, but the irrevocable moment came when he decided to punish them (*166, 170, 171*).

The prophetic age did not yet see any deeper than its predecessors into the problem of retribution. God rewarded men according to their conduct. But following the principle of the Sinai covenant, it was thought that he did so here on earth. No distinct light was thrown on the hereafter, except perhaps in the case of the prophet Elijah, whom Elisha gazed upon in a vision as God raised him near to himself (*95*). But no one hoped for anything like this for himself, and death remained a distressing prospect. However, the value of individuals became better separated from the groups to which they belonged. The principle of individual retribution was foreseen in Deuteronomy, and Ezekiel established it firmly (*149, 194*). This was an important doctrinal advance and was not, properly speaking, an innovation. It developed a virtual aspect of the ancient beliefs considerably. In his spiritual life Jeremiah sustained himself through a similar principle. That is why the insults he suffered appeared to him as a refusal of justice (*172–175*). Thus a religious turning point was reached, which would become very clear in post-exilic Judaism (Texts 18 and 19).

Then what reward was there for the just man's fidelity?

155

According to a formula used over and over again by Deuter-onomy, it was the peaceful enjoyment of the goods of the earth (*118, 152*). As for the punishment of sin, it consists in being deprived of these goods, and sin culminated in the scourges of pestilence, famine, and war which befall men (*166, 191*). Thus a current calamity, like a drought, took on a religious meaning (*89, 104*); and there was all the more reason for the incessant wars whose results Israel was suffering from at that time. By these events God chastised his people. According to the prophets, the potentates of the East were the instruments of his vengeance (*122–124, 137, 158, 159, 169, 195*). The destruc-tion of Samaria in 722 and that of Jerusalem in 586 were both clear judgments manifesting God's mastery over history. The same could be said of all evils endured by all peoples, for Yahweh is the God of the universe, and his judgment weighs permanently upon all sinful mankind (*6*). The downfalls of Nineveh (*163, 164*), Tyre (*198*), and Babylon (*214, 216*) were sentences pronounced against these proud communities. The oracles against the nations were not, among the prophets of Israel, simple execrations directed against national enemies but fitted into the over-all concept of the plan of God. The prophets unravelled the intentions of him who guides history. This was how Yahweh taught his people.

The Day of Yahweh

In the light of such events the doctrine of the **day of Yahweh** is understandable. God is the master of history. Since he exer-cises judgment on earth, every sinful nation, the whole sinful world, lives perpetually under the threat of imminent disaster. Yahweh had his day against Sodom (*14*), and against Egypt at the crossing of the Red Sea (*29–30, 187*). The fact that these were pagan groups could lead Israel to a false confidence, as if history had been moving towards a day when Israel would benefit from the victory of its God. In the 8th century Amos protested this erroneous idea. On the day of Yahweh his glory will shine forth and reign fully over men, Amos warned, but let sinners not fool themselves. This day will be a "day of darkness and wrath" for them (*101, 154*), when God alone will be exalted and all human pride brought low (*115*), when the world will tremble, as if at the return of primitive chaos (*129, 159*). Only a small number will be saved: the remnant of just men (*104, 121*).

This evocation, while not precisely affirming an end of human history, still attains cosmic breadth. It is a literary convention, for it does not pretend to give a realistic description of the last day. Even the images used are also found in the texts describing the days of Yahweh which have already come to be. Two ways of presenting such events were available to the sacred writers. One method was the chronicle, attentive to the unfolding of events and their visible causes, but careful to emphasize their religious meaning through theological reflection. The other method belonged to the visionaries and poets, who glossed over visible causes and painted the spectacle of terrifying theophanies the better to bring out the action of God. The two exist side by side in the sacred books, but the second is most used in the prophetic proclamations of the judgment and the day of Yahweh (compare *129* and *130, 135* and *136, 158* and *159, 215* and *216*).

3. ESCHATOLOGY AND MESSIANISM

Prophetic Eschatology

The prophets spoke first to their contemporaries; their message was above all relevant to the doctrinal and spiritual problems of their own times. But their vision of the world embraces past, present, and future. They saw a divine plan unfolding in history and divine promises progressively realized while moving towards their final accomplishment. Their traditional concept of time was not cyclical but finalistic. Human history was moving towards a goal fixed from the beginning, towards a last end which was the object of Israel's hope. This vision took on a fullness unknown up to that time among them and formed an eschatology (from the Greek *eschaton:* extreme, last).

Its chief element is the judgment, which amounts to the day

of Yahweh. Though this was not the longed-for goal, the sins of mankind made it a necessary prelude. The punishment which will befall men on the day of Yahweh, on Israel as on the rest of the world, will not be to destroy them, but to purify the people of God by reducing them to the remnant of the just alone, fully to convert them and make them expiate their past faults. Only then would the plan of God finally be achieved. This *beyond* of the Great Judgment, these *last times* sought by human hope constitute the proper object of eschatology. The term *messianism* is often applied to it, but the expression is a misuse, for the Messiah is only one particular element. One must guard against seeing here a detailed *prediction* of future events, analogous to that of the destruction of Jerusalem. The point at issue is a *promise,* expressed in lyric terms, sufficiently concrete to sustain men's hope, but flexible enough to leave the unfolding of future history in mystery.

The Reign of Yahweh and the New Covenant

Contrary to a prevalent idea, the essential element of this promise was not the coming of a saviour, the Messiah. It was rather the coming of the time when God would reign over all men and the faithful would be totally happy. The idea of the reign of Yahweh was nothing new. It had served, if not since Sinai (*188*), at least since the settlement in Canaan (*62*), to explain the nature of the relation between God and his people. Yahweh reigns by right over all men as he reigns over the universe which he created, but he has chosen a people who must recognize this reign in action. In fact, God was with them only in the measure in which the law of God was observed, his worship carried out, his word cherished. The moral character of Yahweh's reign was thus distinct from all pagan concepts of divine royalty even in cases where both used the same imagery.

In the last times, this reign would be realized in fullness not only over Israel, his first-born people, but over all the nations reunited once again (*133, 221*). Prophetic eschatology was guided by this vision of restored human unity, the unity that

158

preceded the primitive break due to sin (*10*). The vision included a religious universalism which excluded the nationalistic strictures. Yahweh, creator of the universe and of mankind, chose Israel from among all peoples (*148, 149*) only in view of the final salvation of all. This is already a foreshadowing of the catholicity of the Church.

The covenant drawn up on Sinai reveals its true meaning in this perspective. It was only one step in God's plan. At Sinai God had shown that his plan was to *enter into covenant* with man, establishing such relationships with Israel (*188*). This is an important revelation, but it is not the whole of God's plan. The priestly historian was acutely aware of this and he placed two other covenants before the covenant on Sinai. The one with Abraham embraced all who follow the practice of circumcision (*186*), the other and even wider one embraced all people in Noah, their second father (*185*). This meaningful concept underlies the universality of God's plan from its very beginning.

But the prophetic message was completed by the promise of a new covenant which would bring history to a close. To be sure, when Hosea (*111*), Jeremiah (*181*), and Ezekiel (*204*) spoke of this new covenant they saw little except the future of the chosen people after the hard trial of the exile. But in the *Message of Consolation* the perspective was wider. The gates of the new Jerusalem were wide open to the peoples (*224*) who will acknowledge the reign of Yahweh (*221*). The Servant of Yahweh, mediator of the covenant, was sent as the light of nations, so that the law which he gave could recreate the unity of mankind (*225;* see *133*). This will be the character of the new covenant brought to men by Jesus (*411*).

Eschatological Salvation

Recovered human unity was not the only gift in the moral order which the new covenant would bring. It was rather the consequence of a more fundamental grace, for at that future time the heart of man would be healed of sin. On this point the prophets are unanimous. Hosea showed the new covenant bringing to

159

men the virtues they had lacked in the past: justice and righteousness, kindness and love, faithfulness and knowledge of God
(*111*). Isaiah saw a new humanity, bent on knowing Yahweh
and practicing his Law (*133*). Jeremiah announced that God
himself would engrave his Law upon hearts (*181*). Ezekiel
called to mind the purification of the people of God, the gift of
a new heart to men and the outpouring of the divine Spirit upon
them (*203*). The *Message of Consolation* promised radical
obliteration of sin (*220*), and the prophecy of the Servant
promised moral illumination, liberation (*225*), and justification
of sinners returned to grace with God (*228*).

The salvation in question here is of the spiritual order. It
touches the roots of the problem of man, for it touches the
essential question of his relations to God, his practical powerlessness in the face of sin. The promise of a redemptive grace
answers this question. But the question is: Why will God save
men? Have they not already been tried—in the concrete case of
the chosen people? What is to be said for the others? What of
their incurable hardness of heart? But that is just it! God will
triumph over this very hardness of heart—because of his love,
says one section of the prophetic tradition (*110, 111, 161, 162,
221, 224*); for the honor of his Name, says another (*203, 217*).
Here is the heart of the divine promise. The New Testament
will have only to take these formulas up again to speak of Jesus
Christ.

After sin has been wiped away God can give man the un-
mixed happiness for which he was made. On this point it is
true that the texts of the prophets return to the old Israelite hope
more often. But they still look for a mere earthly happiness. At
least they strongly emphasize its fullness. Since sin alone, following an already traditional doctrine, had deprived man of the
happiness of paradise (*3–6, 185*), they concluded that when
sin had been triumphed over, God would reintroduce men into
this original happiness. The promised land, flowing with milk
and honey, is thus identified with paradise regained.

The idea is explicitly expressed in Ezekiel (*203*) and in the
Message of Consolation (*222*). Elsewhere it crops up in the

160

midst of stimulating imagery: a peace treaty between man and nature (*111, 127*); the identification of Jerusalem with the sacred mountain—the divine residence and the site of paradise (*133, 205*); the surprising prosperity of the holy land (*179, 217*), whose marvelous trees, both food and medicine for men, recall the trees of Eden (*205*). The beginnings and the end of human history, though both defying all possibility of description, are depicted in the same symbols. This similarity points out the unity of God's plan, thwarted by sin and underpinned by the historic covenant between God and men.

The History of Israel. Foreshadowing of Salvation

These, however, are not the only images which permit the prophets to depict the last times concretely. The historical experience of Israel also furnished usable material. Without completely attaining its purpose, the providential action of God met partial successes. The history of his people has high points which hint at its finale. Two periods, as we have already said, were privileged above all the rest: that of Israel's beginnings, from the exodus out of Egypt to the settlement in the promised land, and that of the monarchical success, under the reigns of David and Solomon. According to their temperaments and doctrinal preoccupations, the prophets depicted the last times under the features of a renewed exodus or a reformed high point of the kingdom. The first image prevails in Hosea (*111*) and in the *Message of Consolation* (*218, 219*); the second, in Isaiah (*126, 127, 133*) and Micah (*128*). They are intermingled in Jeremiah (*161, 162, 179, 180, 181*) and Ezekiel (*202, 204, 205*). The historic Israel of Moses' and David's times were thus a prophetic foretaste, a figurative prophecy of the eschatological Israel which Jesus would establish here on earth. The escape from Egypt and the wandering through the desert towards the promised land prefigured the spiritual coming of salvation. The royal justice and peace which followed it prefigured the justice and peace which would reign in the last times (*126–128*) in the new Jerusalem (*222, 223*).

161

To take such predictions literally and interpret them as detailed predictions, without taking into account their origin, would be just as wrong as finding them meaningless. God unveils the goal of his plan of salvation through symbols, to which the historical experience of his people gives a very real meaning and great religious content (Text 22).

The Mediator of Salvation

The shaper of salvation, of justice, of eschatological peace, would, of course, be God himself. Some texts place him directly on the scene, without human intermediary (*111, 181, 203, 215–223*). But in the past God had always been represented before his people by ambassadors who acted as mediators. Moses and David, for different reasons, stand out among them. The line of prophets should be added here too. Beginning from this experience, a good number of texts make a place in their eschatology for a man of this type. In Israel the mediator of salvation is an ideal king, a new David, the *anointed* of Yahweh (this is the meaning of the term *Messiah*) (*126, 127*). The same percentage reappears more discreetly in Jeremiah (*180*) and in a humbler position in Ezekiel (*202, 204*).

But the *Message of Consolation*, which makes only passing mention of the promises to David, puts an altogether different personage on the scene: the Servant of Yahweh par excellence, mediator of a new covenant and religious lawgiver (*225, 226*). This man, who in certain characteristics is reminiscent of Moses and the prophets, will be the shaper of a universal salvation in two ways: in proclaiming his doctrine to lead all men to God, and in offering his life as a sacrifice of expiation for sinners (*228*). It is possible that the author was thinking of the small remnant of the Just here, but instead of separating them from the punishment reserved for sinners, he did not hesitate to make them share in it and give his suffering a redemptive value—an exact foreshadowing of what Jesus will accomplish in his passion. Be that as it may, the proclamation of the Messiah and that of the Servant constitute two very different presentations of

162

the future mediator. The one is shown in his royal glory, the other in his function as teacher. The one is associated in the triumph of God by his victories, and the other, by the offering of his life. Only the life of Jesus will show how, by understanding the terrestrial glory of the royal Messiah in a figurative way, the two pictures were in fact of one and the same person. "Did not the Christ have to suffer these things before entering into his glory?" (*Lk.* 24, 26).

4. THE PROBLEMS OF THE SPIRITUAL LIFE

The Schools of Spirituality

The different collections of the royal era—prophetic, Deuteronomic, priestly, not counting the lyric works—all depended on the same fundamental tradition, though they did not develop all of its elements equally. To draw a rule of life from doctrine, each accented one or another aspect: the glory of God or his love, his rights or his engaging kindness. Thus many spiritualities were outlined, each suited to different religious temperaments. All the men of the Old Testament did not go to God by the same route. A similar diversity will be found in Christianity in the era of the apostolic Church. For example, the spirit of St. Paul was not exactly that of St. John.

A prophetic line running from Nathan to Elijah and Elisha, to Amos, Micah, Isaiah, and Zephaniah, seems especially animated by a profound sense of the right of God. Humility before the Creator and obedience to his Law are understood according to its deepest intents and meanings and not only according to its letter. Sincerity of internal dispositions are more important than simple ritual actions. These prophets constantly accentuated these fundamental virtues. The religious attitude thus extolled is a matter of integrity and justice more than feeling. The prophets who preached it appear as strong and fearless personalities. After hearing God's call and embracing his cause, un-

163

flinchingly they proclaim the punishments which unfaithful men will suffer.

This mode of action was common to all the prophets in some measure. But with Hosea it was modified. The prophet's personal experience, carried out under divine orders (*110*), helped him understand a new aspect of what could be called the "psychology" of God. With God as with man there is a conjugal love, demanding, injured, suffering, jealous, but ready to pardon (*111*). So now a certain bond of sympathy arises in the way of conceiving the relation between God and men, and it tempers juridical rigor. The demands of God were clothed with the jealousy of love. What God demanded of man is not only strict obedience, but also tenderness, heart-felt affection. In this new climate the knowledge of God is clothed with an affective aspect. Love and fear of him tend to be mingled, or at least come closer together. On this point Jeremiah and Deuteronomy were written from the same point of view as Hosea. Profoundly imbued with a sense of God's rights, they nevertheless inculcated a religion of the heart (*148–150, 156, 157, 161, 181,* Text 18).

The spirituality of the priestly school developed along a totally different line. The concern for the glory of God and the sense of his holiness gave rise to a desire to realize a similar holiness in the people of God (*182*). The means to this holiness are obedience to the ritual as well as moral Law, and the exercise of worship. They lift man's praises to God and proclaim God's royal prerogatives by imitating the celestial liturgy (*114*). A profound spirit of religion impregnated these men, even though they were attached to the minutest rubrics and canons (*183*). Nothing was too good for the service of God. All life became a vast liturgy. Ezekiel, prophet and priest both, belonged to this school of thought, whose spirituality permeates his message (*203–205*).

The "Poor of Yahweh" and Religious Personalism

From the beginning, little attention was paid the individual in Israel's religion unless he was an important man, a political leader or a prophet. What mattered was the entire people, recipient as a community of the divine covenant. The people had their internal organization, but social cohesion was such that even retribution was seen collectively. Each man's sins had repercussions upon the whole group of which he was a member. But as the prophetic tradition progressed individuals took on greater value. This fact is bound up, at least in part, with social and cultural evolution, but it also had religious implications.

The spiritual experience of the prophets themselves helped promote the importance of the individual. Elijah cried out to God from his distress (*91*); the family lives of Hosea (*110*) and Isaiah (*123*) were involved in their ministry; finally, the personal life of Jeremiah was an inner drama whose echo has been transmitted to us by the humble pages of his "confessions" (*172–175*). Having reached this level, piety could no longer be a group piety, lived essentially according to the rhythm of the communitarian liturgy. This new piety expressed itself in the personal prayers of certain ancient psalms (*84, 85*). And around the time of the captivity the idea of individual retribution and the necessity of personal conversion were ever more strongly affirmed (*102, 150, 194*). Religious personalism thus took a permanent place in Jewish spirituality (Texts 18 and 19).

The most pious members of the communities of the diaspora, who formed the active nucleus of nascent Judaism, called themselves the afflicted, the humbled, *the poor of Yahweh*. The first traces of their internal attitude were found in Zephaniah and Jeremiah. The *Message of Consolation* (*217*) is addressed to them, and the Servant of Yahweh is, in large part, depicted as one of them (*225–228*). But in this text all the preceding spiritual schools still echo for Hosea, Isaiah, Jeremiah, Deuteronomy, and doubtless Ezekiel; and the *Code of Holiness,* too, furnished the elements of the author's doctrine. But it remains something original. The idea of missionary witness first came to light here (*220*), as did an agonizing longing for justce, salvation, the universal reign of Yahweh (*221*). Thus it is that the Jewish soul, beginning with the exile, drank at the spring of a long and varied tradition. Humility and compunction of heart still remained the preferred virtues.

165

Text 20

THE SENSE OF JUSTICE AMONG THE PROPHETS

Looking for the source for the existence of religion, Bergson shows the prophets to be the precursors of the "active mysticism" which will flourish in Christianity.

No school of thought or feeling has contributed as much as Jewish prophetism to the rise of the mysticism we call complete, that of the Christian mystics, the reason being that, if other schools brought some souls to a contemplative mysticism and merit by that fact being accounted mystical, it is to pure contemplation that they tend. To surmount the interval between thought and action there should be a certain drive, which they lack. There is this drive among the prophets. They had a passion for justice, they required it in the name of the God of Israel; and Christianity, which follows in the footsteps of Judaism, owes a great part to the Jewish prophets for having an active mysticism, capable of going out to conquer the world. . . .

How had this justice emerged from social life, to which it was but a dim inner part, to soar above it and above everything, categoric and transcendant? Let us recall the tone and emphasis of the prophets of Israel. It is their voice we hear when a great injustice has been committed and gone unpunished. From the heart of the ages they raise their protest. Certainly, justice has been greatly extended since their times. What they preached above all concerns Israel; their indignation at injustice was the wrath of this chosen people. If some among them, like Isaiah, could have conceived of universal justice, it was because Israel, set apart by God from the peoples, bound to God by a contract, was raised so high above humanity that sooner or later it would be taken for a model. At the least they have given justice the violently imperious character it has retained, which it has since opened out to infinitely wider scope.

Henri Bergson, *The Two Sources of Morality and Religion*

Text 21

CHRIST, WORD OF GOD, AND THE PROPHETS

Bergson's analysis, carried out from a philosophical point of view, does not go beyond the level of phenomenology. St. Augustine, being a Christian theologian, reflected upon the relationship of the prophets to Christ. The prophets brought the word of God to Israel. But Christ is this very Word of God, the Verbum itself (*Jn.* 1, 1–14). On the other hand, he appeared as a prophet to the Jews, the Prophet par excellence, as they said at the multiplication of loaves:

Seeing the sign which he had done, these men said: "this is indeed the Prophet who is come into the world" (*Jn.* 6, 14). Perhaps it is because they had eaten a meal seated upon the grass that they still thought Christ to be a prophet. But he was the Lord of prophets; it was he who fulfilled the prophecies; he who sanctified the prophets. But yet a prophet also. For it was said to Moses: "I will raise up for them a prophet like you" (*Deut.* 18, 18). "Like," it said, a likeness according to the flesh, not according to majesty. That this prophecy must be understood of Christ, is clearly explained in the Acts of the Apostles (*Acts* 3, 22). And the Lord himself says in speaking of himself: "A prophet is not without honor except in his own country" (*Mt.* 13, 57). Thus, the Lord is a Prophet, he who is the Word of God (*Jn.* 1:1–14); and no prophet prophesies without this Word of God. The Word of God was with the prophets, and is himself a prophet. Ancient times had for prophets inspired men, filled with the word of God. But we, we have received as prophet the Word of God himself.

St. Augustine, *On the Gospel of John 25, 8*

167

Text 22

LIGHT AND SHADOW IN THE MESSIANIC PROPHECIES

Christ fulfilled the messianic prophecies, as St. Augustine reminded us. But how should this be understood? The mixture of spiritual promises and temporal imagery they contain is disconcerting to the Christian reader. Pascal, in his *Pensées,* asked himself this too:

On the Figurative Meaning of the History of Israel

God, wishing to make it plain that he could shape a people holy with an invisible holiness and fill them with an eternal glory, made visible things. As nature is an image of grace, he has done among the good things of nature what he would do among those of grace, so that one would conclude that he could do the invisible, since he had done the visible well. Therefore, he saved this people from the flood; he raised up a whole people from Abraham, only to lead them into a rich land . . . God, then, has shown the power he has to grant invisible blessings, because he has shown that he has power other visible things [*No. 275*].

On the Ambiguity of the Promises of the Prophets

Each one finds in these promises what he has in his own heart, whether temporal blessings or spiritual blessings, God or creatures; but with this difference, that those who look for creatures there find them there, but with many contradictions, with having to defend their love, with the order of adoring God alone and loving none but him alone, which is the same thing. And finally, there is no coming of the Messiah for them; instead, to those who look there for God and without contradiction, with the commandment of loving him alone, a Messiah has come in the predicted time to give them the blessings which they ask . . . [*No. 503*].

All that does not move towards charity is figurative. The sole

168

object of Scripture is charity. And all that which does not move towards this one purpose is a symbol for it. For since there is only one purpose, all that does not point to it literally must refer to it figuratively. . . . The Jews loved the figurative things so much, and listened to them so well, that they misunderstood the reality, when it came at the time and in the manner predicted [*No. 270*].

Bibliography

The subjects treated here are presented in the various theologies of the Old Testament. Some articles in the *Encyclopedic Dictionary of the Bible* are also helpful (see under Jerusalem, Judgment, Justice, King, Prophet, Messiah, Salvation, Servant of Yahweh, Time, etc.).

Study Guides

The problem of conversion and hardening of heart is central in the Gospels (*Mt.* 3, 1–2; 17; 11, 20–24; 13, 10–15; *Jn.* 12, 37–43). Seeks out how it was posed in the prophetic era (*44–46, 111–113, 114, 125, 146, 153, 160, 162, 165–167, 171, 181, 190, 194, 203*) and in post-exilic Judaism (*245, 281–284, 290, 294, 357*).

Study the development of the doctrine of God the Creator, from the Yahwist sacred history (*3–4*) to the priestly sacred history (*184*). The formation of this doctrine will continue to be made more precise in times to follow (*220, 253, 259, 300–302, 324, 403*); and the New Testament takes it for granted (*Acts* 14, 14–16; 17, 23–28; *Rom.* 1, 18–23).

The preaching of Jesus centered on the reign (or kingdom) of God (*Mk.* 1, 15). The idea was familiar to the Jews of his time. Study its development through the Old Testament texts

(62, 69, 114, 133, 188, 202, 215, 223, 241, 243, 287, 297, 325–327, 381).

Nathan's prophesy was the point of departure for royal messianism. Follow its trail through the Old Testament *(75, 82, 83, 126–128, 180, 202, 213, 236, 328–330)*. Then find out how, in the New Testament this oracle is applied to Jesus *(Mt.* 2, 5; 3, 17; 9, 27; *Lk.* 1, 32, 67–70; 2, 11; *Jn.* 6, 15; *Acts* 1, 6; 2, 30; 4, 25–26; 13, 33; *Rom.* 1, 3; *Apoc.* 5, 5). But note that the traces of temporal glory are now understood figuratively, in the perspective of Christ's resurrection.

VIII.

THE ORGANIZATION
OF JUDAISM

AT the very hour when Jerusalem was about to meet its doom
Jeremiah transferred his hope to the groups of exiles living in
Babylonia (*177*). Ezekiel, too, subsequently influenced this
remnant of Judah. When the Persian empire marched the relief
troops of Babylon towards the Eastern world, the Jewish restoration used this as its own point of departure. To be sure, the
independent state of Judah, as founded by the first Israelite kings
and, in the end, reduced to the southern districts, would not be
reborn. Now there is formed a completely new organization,
Judaism. Judaism will use the relief to continue, on another
plane, the religious mission vested in the Jewish nation. Under
the benevolent hegemony of the Persians it will slowly acquire
an institutional form whose broad outlines will remain unchanged right up to New Testament times.

1. THE RESTORATION

The Return of the Exiles and the
Reconstruction of the Temple
In 538 the emancipation edict of Cyrus permitted the Jewish
exiles to return to Jerusalem, to return the instruments of worship carried off as spoils a long time ago by Nebuchadnezzar,

171

and to restore their temple. A convoy of repatriates under the leadership of Sheshbazzar, a prince of the royal dynasty, was the first to depart (*229*). The operation was financed by the Jewish communities of Babylonia. But despite royal authorization and the resources at their disposal, the "people of the exile" failed in their project of restoring the temple. For Jerusalem was subject to the prefecture of Samaria, and the "people of the country-side" wanted to take part in the operations and keep the upper hand over the temple. But the repatriates refused this and thus everything came to a halt, and the initial enthusiasm quickly gave way to a profound dicouragement (*231*).

At the beginning of the reign of Darius (522–485), which was marked by savage repression of revolutionary satraps, a second caravan arrived around 520. It was led by the grandson of king Jehoiachin, Zerubbabel, who had been named high-commissioner by the Persian authorities, and the high priest Joshua, descendant of the line established by Solomon. Perhaps the prophet Zechariah was a member too (*232, 233*). In any case, in 520 and 519 the preaching of Haggai and Zechariah stirred up their courage (*234–236*).

Zerubbabel and Joshua actively prepared for the reconstruction of the temple. The opposition of the "people of the country-side" only resulted in Darius's confirmation of the Edict of Cyrus. The edifice was completed in February–March 515. After a solemn dedication the passover was then celebrated there (*237, 239*). Even though this second temple lacked the splendor of Solomon's building, religious enthusiasm was high. Many Jews imagined this to be the predicted fulfillment of the prophetic promises. They felt that the salvation of God was to be realized here below and that Jerusalem would become the religious center of the world (*240, 241*). In greeting Zerubbabel with the pregnant title "Branch of David," borrowed from an oracle of Jeremiah (*236*), Zechariah affirmed Israel's continued hope for a royal dynasty. In sum, taking the temporal side of the oracles of Ezekiel and the *Message of Consolation* depicting the eschatological joy literally, the Jews awaited the imminent coming of the last times.

172

A Stagnant Situation

All these beautiful dreams were quickly scuttled, as if to dissipate the mirage of political messianism once and for all. Zerubbabel, once his mandate ended, disappeared from the scene. The hope of a political restoration under the overlordship of the Persian king vanished. Even further, Jerusalem remained an open city, with no defense against the brigands of the surrounding countryside. The governor of Samaria strengthened his authority over the district of Judea, where the repatriates had settled, and the Samaritans ceaselessly plotted within the central administration against the detested neighbors. Even the material situation of these people was not the best. Though we are poorly informed on the details of their history, a number of the psalms seem to echo the laments of these poor of Yahweh, disappointed by the present and anxious for the future (*231, 270–272*).

In 485 the armies of Xerxes destroyed Babylon, which had revolted at the new sovereign's approach. When Herodotus passed by he found only ruins. To Jewish eyes the event was the execution of the divine judgment long ago pronounced against the proud city (*287*). Still, it is possible that Judea also suffered from the retaliatory blow. In any case, as the realization of the great dreams faded, the initial spiritual fervor also waned. Many prophetic texts show the lax spirit of the "people of the countryside" gaining ground (*284*). Nascent Judaism was again facing a grave religious crisis.

The Missionary Spirit

Despite the crises during these difficult years, the universalist current that had developed towards the end of the prophetic era and during the captivity became strongly affirmed. The contemporary prophets again and again used the image of God's universal reign (*235, 241, 287*). They also looked for the conversion of the pagans (*243, 245*). The gates of the Jewish community were opened to proselytes—foreigners converted to the true God and to his Law (*242, 244*). Thus Judaism, while remaining a national religion, became animated by a true mis-

173

sionary spirit. Doubtless, this preoccupation was linked with the favor the wisdom literature enjoyed later. This literature is a Jewish branch of an international current. It adopted the international language literally and made the witness of Moses and the prophets palatable to pagans of good will. This helped the religion of Israel become the "light of nations," so that the salvation of God reached, according to the expression of the *Message of Consolation,* to the four corners of the world (*226*).

2. THE REFORMERS OF THE 5TH CENTURY

The Mission of Nehemiah

From the reconstruction of the temple to the epoch of Alexander the history of Judaism is fragmentary. The only striking episodes are the missions of Nehemiah and Ezra, and even their chronologies are uncertain, especially that of Ezra. If the biblical chronicler retained the proper grouping of the documents at hand, it would place Ezra in 458. But this order seems artificial, and the date too high. Certain historians, in correcting the biblical text, propose the dates of 437 or 427. Nehemiah and Ezra would then be contemporaries. With a good number of critics we have kept to the "seventh year of Artaxerxes II," that is, 398; but our reconstruction of events is, of course, only hypothetical.

Towards the middle of the fifth century the animosity between the Jews and the Samaritans grew bitter. The Jews tried to rebuild the wall of their city, and Samaria denounced this enterprise as subversive. At this point Nehemiah came on the scene. This Jew of the diaspora had become the cup-bearer at the palace of Artaxerxes I, and in 445 he obtained from his master an official mission to rebuild the ramparts of Jerusalem. With the title of governor he brought letters which accredited him to the satrapy of Transeuphrates (see Map 6), the province including Syria and Palestine (*295*). The Samaritans and their allies tried to stop him, but foiling their attempts at intimidation he restored the ramparts in fifty-two days (*296*). He was to

174

remain in charge for twelve years, securing his tasks through measures of social justice, or settlement, and of civil and religious organization.

Some years later (about 425) Nehemiah returned on a second mission. Now his work was to uproot abuses reintroduced during his absence. The tithes remained unpaid. The service of the temple was deserted by the Levites and the Sabbath was not observed. The custom of marrying foreign women had reached even the priestly families. Nehemiah acted with vigor, even excommunicating recalcitrants and expelling them from Jerusalem. The priests and notables eventually affixed their seal on a solemn and irrevocable written agreement with him (*299*), and this energetic action brought an interior reform to the community of Judea. It also definitively established the independence of Jerusalem from the prefecture of Samaria.

The Mission of Ezra

After the departure of Nehemiah the history of Judea sank into the shadows. The documents of the Jewish colony at Elephantine in upper Egypt show that, under the reign of Darius II (last quarter of the 5th century), the Persian authorities intervened in the internal affairs of Judaism in both Egypt and Judea (Texts 23 and 24). But many details are unrecorded. Be that as it may, it is within this context that the mission of Ezra is most comprehensible. In 398 this priest-scribe of the Babylonian community received an official administrative office, that of "secretary of the Law of the God of heaven," or to put it another way, secretary of state for Jewish affairs, which were regulated according to the Law of Moses. By this title he went to check on the Law's application in Judea, since in this territory it had the force of state law. This was to prove to be a providential mission for Judaism (*292*), for when he arrived in Jerusalem Ezra organized a solemn reading of the Law for the feast of Tabernacles lasting seven days (*293*). Then he occupied himself with the internal reform of the local community according to the Law's demands. Mixed marriages to pagan wives gravely threatened the faith of the young Jews and still

175

figured among the most dangerous abuses. On this point Ezra took more radical measures than those of Nehemiah *(294)*. After his mission was accomplished Ezra probably returned to Babylonia.

It is certain that Ezra, through his work, played a key role in the Pentateuch's definitive fixation of the Mosaic Law. Thanks to this written charter, Judaism was given a stable and uncontestable structure, one recognized by the civil authorities. From then on this formed a ring of shelter (the "hedge of the Law," as the Jewish doctors called it) which let them live among the pagans without being contaminated in faith or in morals by contact with them.

Jews and Samaritans

The tension between the Jews and the Samaritans, already noticeable around 539 and 520 *(231, 237)*, reached a peak in the time of Nehemiah *(295, 296, 299)*. Since 722 the Samaritan population had been of mixed race and religion (130), and after 586 it was ready to use the temple of Jerusalem, all tumbled-down as it was, since its own sanctuaries had been destroyed by Josiah *(146)*. This is not to say that the Samaritans were disposed to practice the Law which Josiah proclaimed in all its rigor! Politically, they hoped to profit by bringing Judea under their thumb; this was the reason for the petty annoyances which they heaped upon the Jewish repatriates *(231, 237)* and the aristocracy's anger against the action of Nehemiah, who had worked to make Jerusalem an independent prefecture. Elephantine documents show that the governor of Judea in 407 was a Persian on good terms with the Samaritans (Text 24). It seems that the Persian administration pressured the Jews and the Samaritans into a single religious community, whose center was the Jerusalem temple, and whose charter was the finally fixed Pentateuch. Part of Ezra's mission could have been realizing this program. In any case, the Samaritans certainly adopted the Pentateuch as a sacred book around this time. But opposition between the two peoples flowed below the surface, and in the 4th century it led to a definitive break. The Samaritans, perhaps

176

in the era of Alexander, built a temple on Mount Gerizim near the ancient sanctuary of Shechem (*54*). This temple must have been destroyed by the Jewish king Alexander Jannaeus. In the New Testament era, Jews and Samaritans were in violent opposition and the Gospels show their hostility on many occasions (*Jn.* 4).

3. FROM THE PERSIAN TO THE MACEDONIAN EMPIRE

After the exile, Jewish communities sprung up throughout the middle East, from Egypt (Texts 23 and 24) to the borders of India. This was called the *diaspora* (scattering). The unification of the East into the Persian empire favored this expansion, although the local communities did not mix with the pagan nations; the religious center of the Jews remained Jerusalem where the high priest lived. There were, however, some important colonies in Babylon, whose intellectual activity is not well known, even though its fruits are visible in the mission of Ezra.

From the 4th century on, nevertheless, Jewish history is almost inacessible. The distant colony of Elephantine must have disappeared when Egypt regained independence (around 399), and the memory of a violent crisis striking the community in Persia has been preserved in the book of Esther (*396–398*). It also seems that the campaign of Artaxerxes III against the satraps of western Asia, around 350, could have been the source of the tradition collected in the book of Judith (*392–395*). But these two books belong to a genre altogether different from historical writings, and are of a later date. Besides these, the Jewish historian Josephus was able to collect only a few imprecise traditions. At the time of Alexander's conquests Judea passed almost without notice from the Persian to the Macedonian empire, which respected the juridical privileges that the Judeans, like the communities of the diaspora, enjoyed under the authority of the high priests. During these centuries of vaguely known political history, Judaism concentrated upon its internal life. The souls of Israel reflected and prayed, meditating upon their heritage—the centuries of past tradition. Proof for this is found in the psalms used over and over again in its worship.

4. JUDAISM: NATION OR CHURCH

At Sinai the people of Israel became a theocracy—a religious and national community led directly by God. Politically, this theocracy was made up of a confederation of tribes linked by a common Law and worship. Beginning with the monarchy, a better constituted, more unified organization would be superimposed upon it, which, though it quickly divided into two states, was still conscious of being but one people. However, this modernization of the state was finally detrimental to Israel's religious vocation, for after the fall of both Samaria and Jerusalem nothing remained of the national institutions, except for the remnant of a people intent upon surviving. Soon the prophets called these to a reconversion to their primordial vocation, and it was in this spirit that the Jews (that is to say, the Judeans) regrouped during the exile. With refound fervor they awaited the salvation promised by their prophets. Then, after the Edict of Cyrus, they returned to their land and rebuilt their temple. They thought they had reached the goal of their dreams and they hoped to see both the national restoration and the eschatological salvation in the very near future. This hope was disappointed, and, in its place, came Judaism.

What was Judaism? Was it a national community strongly imbued with its own religious values, or a religious community limited to a single nation? In either case, Israel no longer had a state as the basis for its existence even though it constituted a distinct people. Although scattered, it formed a single *sacred assembly* called to serve the unique God, like Israel had when she wandered in the desert. This title of sacred assembly, *Qahal,* taken up again by the New Testament, will become the technical designation for the Church. It is possible, then, to speak of a Jewish Church, awaiting the coming of the last times, preparing of hearts for the coming of the Gospel. It was the providential frame of reference into which Jesus was born, lived, preached, and offered his sacrifice. From this church of

178

the expectation, linked to the structures of a particular nation, came the new universal sacred assembly—the eschatological Israel proclaimed by the prophets. Thus the Church of Jesus Christ flowed from Judaism in the history of God's plan.

Text 23

THE PASSOVER AT ELEPHANTINE

On the island of Elephantine, near Aswan in upper Egypt, the archives of a Jewish military colony have been found. The texts, written in Aramaean, date from the 5th century. Originally from Judah, this local community had preserved its ancestors' religion as it existed before the reform of Josiah (*146*). They offered the Pasch in their own homes and had a temple of their own. These beliefs indicate pagan infiltrations, although the Persian administration favored the introduction of the official Jewish law there. In 419, under the reign of Darius II, the Jewish official Hananiah notified his coreligionists of an order sent by the central powers to the satrap of Egypt, Arsames. He gave them practical instructions for the celebration of the feast of the passover and unleavened bread (compare 40, 41). Unfortunately, the document is badly mutilated.

[To my brothers] Yedoniah and his companions, the Jewish garrison, your brother Hananiah. May God [grant] prosperity to my brothers! And now, this present year, the fifth year of the king Darius, the king has ordered Arsames: "... [*gap of half a line*] ..." You, then, count thus fourteen [days beginning from the first day of Nisan] and celebrate [the passover]. And from the fifteenth day to the twenty-first day of N[isan, celebrate the feast of the unleavened bread]. Be pure, and take care: [do] no work [on the fifteenth and the twenty-first day]. Do not drink [beer] and do not [eat] anything at all fermented. [Eat unleavened bread from the fourteenth day of Nisan from] sundown, until the twenty-first day of Nisan [at sunset. For seven days], do not bring [anything fermented] into your dwellings and keep away from it during [these] days . . . [*gap of half a line*] . . . To my brothers Yedoniah and his companions, the Jewish garrison, your brother Hananiah.

The text of the royal rescript has completely disappeared. All that remains is the juridical commentary of the Jewish scribe. The terms he used come very close to the latest strata of the priestly laws (see *Ex.* 12, 15–20). The letter is, then, related to the work of the Jewish legal experts who carried out the fixing of the Mosaic Law. Hananiah seems to have been charged with introducing this legislation to Elephantine.

Text 24

THE PETITION OF THE JEWS OF ELEPHANTINE TO THE GOVERNOR BAGOAS

In 411 the Jews of Elephantine saw their local temple destroyed at the instigation of the priests of the god Khnub. A letter addressed to the high priest at Jerusalem remained unanswered. Evidently, Jerusalem did not admit either the temple of Elephantine, or its local priesthood! The Jews of Egypt then wrote, in 407, both to the Persian governor of Judah, Bagoas, and to the sons of Sanballat, the ancient governor of Samaria and the enemy of Nehemiah (*295, 296*).

To our Lord Bagoas, governor of Judah, your servants Yedoniah and his companions, the Jewish priests of the fortress of Elephantine . . . [*There follow the usual formulas of politeness.*] And now, your servant Yedoniah and his companions speak thus. In the month of Tammuz, in the fourteenth year of the king Darius, when Arsames left to go to the king, the priests of the god Khnub in the fortress of Elephantine plotted with Vidarnag, who as administrator here: "The sanctuary of the god Yaho is the fortress of Elephantine, let it be suppressed! . . ." [*There follows a very detailed account of the destruction. The Jews held a period of solemn mourning, then began to look for support.*]

. . . At the time when this evil had befallen us, we sent a letter to our Lord, to the high priest Johanan and to his companions, the priests of Jerusalem, to Ostanes, the brother of Anani, and to the Jewish notables. They have sent us no response. Since then, the month of Tammuz of the fourteenth year of the king Darius to this very day, we have worn sackcloth and ashes like widows; we have had no more of perfumed ointments nor drunk of wine. Besides, since then to this day, the seventeenth year of the king Darius, we have made no oblations, no incense offerings, nor holocausts in this sanctuary. Now, your servants Yedoniah and the priests and all the Jews living in Elephantine speak thus: If it is agreeable to our Lord, purpose that this sanctuary be rebuilt, since no one has authorized us to reconstruct it. Look upon those who, here in Egypt, are the object of your bounty and favor! Let a letter be sent them on your part on the subject of this sanctuary of the god Yaho, so that it be rebuilt in the fortress of Elephantine as it had been built before: and that there be offered in your name oblation, incense, and holocaust on the altar of the god Yaho. And we will pray for you always, we, our wives, and all the Jews here, if you see to it that this sanctuary be rebuilt. And this will be for you, before Yaho the god of heaven, of greater merit than if you had offered a holocaust and sacrifices at the cost of a thousand talents. As for the gold, we have set out this whole affair in a letter sent in our name to Delaiah and Shelemiah, the sons of Sanballat, governor of Samaria. Again, of all that we have done, Arsames has known nothing. The twentieth of Marheshwan, the seventeenth year of the king Darius.

We know the answer given to this petition thanks to the memorandum of the messenger which was preserved:

Memorandum of Bagoas and Delaiah. Behold this which they have said to me: You must speak in Egypt before Arsames: In that which concerns the house-for-an-altar of the God of heaven which was of old erected in the fortress of Elephantine before Cam-

181

byses, and which that criminal Vidarnag destroyed in the fourteenth year of the king Darius: It must be rebuilt on the place where it stood before, and let there be offered the offering and incense on this altar, conforming to that which was done in times past.

Note that the Persian authorities agree to the reclamation because it corresponds to the secular right of the Jews of Elephantine even though it constituted a derogation of the Law, as the priestly authorities of Jerusalem had understood (*142, 146*). The Samaritans supported this position. Nevertheless, if oblation and incense were permitted by the rescript, there is no question of holocausts. Perhaps these were held in low esteem by the adorers of Khnub, the ram-god. As a consequence, the Jewish community of Elephantine would disappear without leaving a trace when Egypt regained her independence.

Capture of Babylon by Cyrus (539)	538	Edict of Cyrus
Cambyses (529–522)		First Return (Sheshbazzar)
Darius I (522–486)	520	Second Return (Zerubbabel)
	515	Dedication of the Second Temple
Xerxes (486–465)		
Destruction of Babylon (485)		
Artaxerxes I (465–423)	458	(Mission of Ezra?)
	445	First mission of Nehemiah
	427	(Mission of Ezra?)
	425	Second mission of Nehemiah
Darius II (423–404)		
Artaxerxes II (404–358)	398	Mission of Ezra (probable date)
Independence of Egypt (*c.* 400)		
Artaxerxes III (358–338)		
Darius III (336–330)		
Conquests of Alexander (336–323)	*c.* 330	Construction of the Samaritan Temple
In the Middle East (333–331)		
In Iran and India (330–326)		
Death in Babylon (323)		

Bibliography

There are a number of histories of Israel which one can consult. Notable are *The Biblical Period from Abraham to Ezra,* by W. F. Albright (New York n. d.), and *Biblical Archaeology,* by G. E. Wright (Philadelphia 1963). There is also *A History of Israel* by J. Bright (Philadelphia 1959). For a treatment of the chronological problem, see the essay, "The Chronicler's Purpose" by D. N. Freedman, in *The Biblical Archaeologist Reader,* edited by Freedman and G. E. Wright (Chicago 1961).

Study Guides

Using the memoirs of Nehemiah (*295–299*), sketch his psychological and religious portrait.

Throughout the works of Nehemiah and Ezra you will be able to detect concepts of the ideal Jew of the Persian era. Are they not, on certain points, further from the Gospel than those found in certain prophetic oracles (for example, the *Message of Consolation* and especially the prophecy of the Servant of Yahweh) (*225–228*)?

Jerusalem was the religious center of the scattered Jews. Study the role of the holy city in the life and thought of Israel, from David to the threshold of the New Testament (*68, 77, 78, 133, 135, 136, 205, 207–209, 222–224, 241, 297, 298, 317–319, 331, 332*). Try to follow out the theme in the New Testament, and show how it prepared for the Christian idea of the Church (*Gal.* 4, 26–27; *Apoc.* 21).

IX.

SACRED LITERATURE IN THE TIME OF THE PERSIANS

THE history of Judaism in the Persian era is not as rich and spectacular as that of the Israelite and Judean monarchies. Community life centered around worship, prayer, doctrinal reflection. Therefore it is not surprising that its literature, heir to a tradition already witnessed in some sacred writings, continued to develop in its own different lines. This was the time when the law was fixed, when the already existing historical texts assumed their final form and new items were added. Two kinds of literature cultivated in the royal era, wisdom literature and the religious lyricism of the psalms, made extraordinary progress. As for prophetic literature, it was in decline and evolving towards a new form: the apocalypse.

1. PROPHETISM

Haggai and Zechariah

The return from the exile was not dominated by great prophetic figures comparable to Jeremiah, Ezekiel, or the author of the *Message of Consolation*. We know the names of only two prophets from this time: Haggai and Zechariah. Haggai strove to reawaken the courage of the repatriated Jews, from August

to December 520. He exhorted them to rebuild the temple
(*234*), recalling the promises attached to that building by the
prophets of old (*235*). As he made no distinction between the
temple of his time and the eschatological temple confusedly seen
by Ezekiel (*205*), he seemed to see the realization of the
eschatological prophecies as near at hand.

Zechariah probably began his ministry in Babylonia a little
before 520. After he returned to Judea with a caravan of repatriates he exercised a ministry parallel to that of Haggai. He
invited the Jews to sincere conversion. For encouragement he
brought a consoling message: God, he told them, would return
all his dispersed children to Jerusalem. The holy city would be
rebuilt, and the high priest Joshua and the governor Zerubbabel
had been chosen by God to restore Israel (*232*). Thus Haggai
apparently confused the contemporary restoration of Judaism
with the accomplishment of the eschatological promises. This
is noticeable when, following a prophecy of Jeremiah, he hails
Zerubbabel with the messianic title "Branch of David" (*236*).
Moreover, the influence on Haggai of the book of Ezekiel and
of the *Message of Consolation* can be readily seen, for a number
of his discourses are in the classic style, and there are also
oracles of salvation and answers to consultations whose key is
brought by an angel (*232*). All these included a whole system
of complicated symbols, previewing those to come in the apocalypses. Chapters 9–14 form a later section, which we will
examine at the beginning of the section on the Greek era.

In the School of the Message of Consolation

The book of Isaiah, as we have seen, gathers together anonymous texts of various periods. The most important among them
is the *Message of Consolation* (*Is.* 40–55). Some of them are
alive with the enthusiam of the years of the return, with their
universalism and their feverish eschatological longing (11,
10—12, 6; 14, 1–2; 19, 16–24; 31, 19–26; 32, 15—33; 24).
Isaiah 34–35, which is sometimes called the *little apocalypse of
Isaiah,* stands out clearly in this collection. This diptych first

185

depicts the downfall of Edom—the execution of the divine judgment, and then the eschatological gathering together of the people who are saved, in an atmosphere of paradisiac joy (*230*). In this chapter the influence of the *Message of Consolation* is clear. The hostility to the Edomites is explained by the fact that they, thanks to the tragedy of 586, had settled in the south of Judah. This hostility is found again in other texts, for example *Psalm* 137 (*209*), *Isaiah* 63, 1–6, and the little book of Obadiah, which could date from the 5th century. But he had to await 312, when the Nabateans conquered Idumaea, for the judgment of God to fall on Edom.

The last part of the book of Isaiah (*Is.* 56–66) is a collection of pieces related to the school of the *Message of Consolation,* but written by different authors. The diatribes against idolatry are related to the prophetic sermons and the psalms. *Isaiah* 60–62 appears to have the dedication of the second temple in 515 in mind. The glory of the new Jerusalem, to which the nations will flock from all sides (*241*), is also celebrated by the prophet, who was conscious of being a "messenger of good news" (*240*). Jesus' ministry in Galilee would use the explanation of this text as a point of departure (*Lk.* 4, 16–21). A similar universalism is found in the oracles favoring proselytes, *Isaiah* 56, 1–8 (*242*), and in the eschatological texts (*Is.* 65–66) (*243, 285–286*). In contrast to this lyric presentation of the longed-for-salvation is a call to repentance (*Is.* 58–59) which suggests indifference among the faithful and a gloomy situation in the community (*284*). The tone is already that of John the Baptist at the very threshold of the Gospel. It is unfortunately difficult to assign precise dates to any of these texts, which grew by stages from 538 to the 5th century.

The Apocalypse of Isaiah

The *great apocalypse of Isaiah* (*Is.* 24–27) is a later fragment, which prolongs and builds upon the *oracles against the nations* already encountered in the pre-exilic prophets. Some date the work from 485, the era when Babylon was sacked by Xerxes. The author could have seen this event as the execution of the

186

judgment of God against the pagan city par excellence, but later dates have also been proposed, running as far down as the Greek era (4th or 3rd century).

On two alternative themes, the judgment and the reign of God on the one hand, and the two cities and the salvation of the just on the other, the author transported himself in thought to the end of time and depicted the cosmic confusion of the day of Yahweh and the judgment pronounced against the entire earth. In contrast he saw Yahweh establishing his reign in his temple and the joy of the elect taking the form of a liturgical festival offered on the holy mountain, while suffering and death have disappeared forever (287). In this grandiose framework the proud city is overthrown, while the little flock of the elect finds refuge in the city of God. These great images have come through the centuries and will be taken up again more fully in the Apocalypse of St. John, to describe the struggles of the Church in history, the final judgment, and the happiness promised to those who believe. With this text the evolution of the prophetic genre became clear. The prophet did not lose contact with the practical problems of his times, but he was no longer a man of action. Nourished by the ancient Scriptures, he borrowed heavily from them. To console his sorely tried contemporaries he lifted the veils of the future and announced to them "that which is to come at the end of time." Such was the origin of a new literary genre, the apocalypse.

Malachi and Joel

The prophet recorded in the book of Malachi lived towards the middle of the 5th century, before the reform of Nehemiah. His name is unknown, but in one passage we read: "Behold, I send before me *my messenger,*" in Hebrew *Mal'aki,* and this passage has furnished the book's title. The prophet vigorously denounced the lukewarmness of the Jewish community and the rampant abuses—for example, mixed marriages, unpaid tithes, and the negligence of the priests in the choice of the victims offered (288) and in the teaching of the Law. On the day of Yahweh his messenger would come to purify the priesthood,

187

and only the just would then be exempt from the judgment (*289*). Elijah would reappear to convert the people, so that they would escape his anathema. These texts will be applied in the New Testament to John the Baptist (*Mt.* 11, 10; 17, 10–13).

The book of Joel is more difficult to date. A locust plague which was catastrophic for agriculture afforded the prophet an occasion to preach conversion within the concrete framework of a penitential liturgy (*Jl.* 1–2). But the image of this scourge became an evocation of the Day of Yahweh (*290*). Later, the same scene acquired a dual aspect (*Jl.* 3–4): on the one hand, the judgment of the peoples, and on the other, the outpouring of the Spirit of God on the remnant of the saved, who would rejoice in paradisaical bliss at Jerusalem (*291*). Peter was to present the reception of the Holy Spirit by the apostles on Pentecost as the fulfillment of that promise (*Acts* 2, 14–21).

2. THE FIXING OF THE PENTATEUCH

The Stages, from Moses to Ezra

We saw above how the legislative collections containing the Mosaic Law from the ancient collection down to Deuteronomy and the Priestly Code were formed. At the same time, the traditions relating the origins of Israel were collected in the sacred histories. At the beginning of the exile these texts were apparently already grouped into two blocks. On the one hand, Deuteronomy was prolonged in historical literature, but it was preceded by a sacred history where the Yahwist and Elohist materials were combined. On the other hand, the priestly materials pertaining to the Jerusalem temple were still to be collected in written form in the priestly sacred history.

After the Decree of Cyrus (538) this twofold tradition re-settled on Palestinian soil. Perhaps in this period many of the codes found in Leviticus, such as the Code of Sacrifices (*Lev.* 1–7), or the Code of Purity (*Lev.* 11–15), were definitively fixed based upon the ancient customs of the temple. The Law actually in force was Deuteronomy. Finally, the hour of organic synthesis came. The various editions of the laws and traditions were united in a single compilation, the *Torah* (Law), which was divided into five books: Genesis, Exodus, Leviticus, Numbers, and Deuteronomy. These are the "five books of Moses," or the Pentateuch. Genesis recorded from the beginning to the settlement of the Hebrews in Egypt. From Exodus to Numbers the text recounted the exodus from Egypt and the stay in the desert, and it also included the ancient codes and the bulk of the priestly legislation. Deuteronomy kept its hard-earned form and ended with the death of Moses. The execution of this work, which supposes an effort at juridical harmonization, was probably bound up with the mission of Ezra. Perhaps some complementary laws, destined to make the codes agree among themselves and adapt to the needs of the times, can be discerned in some sections (see Text 23). The fixing of the Pentateuch was paralleled by the canonical edition of the *former prophets,* the historical books from Joshua to Kings.

Moses and the Pentateuch

This explanation of the literary origin of the Pentateuch is not accepted by all historians, since it is difficult accurately to follow the living development of the Mosaic tradition and its fixation in written texts through all the vicissitudes of history. The scribes of Israel did not intend to give us direct information about that, so the schema given here is subject to improvement. But a fundamental fact must be kept in mind: Moses' personality dominates the history of the people of God, whether through the Sinai covenant which he mediated, or through the Law which he initiated. The progressive formation of the books embodying his traditions shows that if his work had been fixed immutably in writing, crossing the centuries unchanged, such conservatism would not have been faithful to life. Though no legislator ever added Moses' name to that of the creator of

189

Israel, by staying rooted in the Pentateuch scattered Judaism would authentically perpetuate the people of the covenant born at Sinai.

3. THE HISTORY OF THE DIDACTIC ACCOUNTS

The Memoirs of Ezra and Nehemiah

Historical documents linked to the return from the exile and the life of Judaism during the Persian period are very rare; what remain have been preserved by the chronicler, whose work we will see below. Some are archive materials, analogous to the parallel texts of Elephantine (Texts 23 and 24) and with no literary pretensions at all (*Ez.* 4, 6—6, 18; 7, 11–26), but the autobiographical memoirs of Nehemiah (*Neh.* 1–7; 10, 1—11, 25; 12, 27–43; 13, 4–31) and Ezra (*Ez.* 7–10; *Neh.* 9) have also been preserved. Though fragmentary, these texts give us firsthand information about the personalities of the two reformers. Nehemiah, a man of action, was intrepid in the face of accumulating difficulties. Yet he was very skilled in obtaining the help of the central authorities, showing a strength of mind bordering on fury (*295, 296, 299*). Ezra, the priest expert in the Mosaic Law, was concerned with the juridical and religious formation of the community (*292, 294*).

History and Didactic Narrative

History was never written in Israel merely to satisfy curiosity. Rather, the sacred historian intended to teach his readers moral and religious lessons pertinent to life, and in his own way he completed the preaching of the prophets. To put his plan into operation he used the documentation of the past, from archive materials to popular traditions. He also used many forms, as we have seen, from the Pentateuch to the book of Kings. To highlight the key ideas he schematized his facts, a process already noticeable in the Deuteronomic historians (*48*) and

190

accentuated in the priestly sacred history (*184–188*). This is explained by its purpose and the literary conventions of the times, which were less concerned with presenting a materially exact picture of the past than with giving the present generation a participation in the great experiences of the people of God, by stirring up their faith, hope, and obedience to the divine precepts. Thus the historian's interpretation of his story meant more than its details as known through documents of varying value.

After the exile the scribes of Israel narrowed this formula still more, with the resultant form being a didactic narrative with a dogmatic or moralizing purpose. These narrations were not always of the same value. Sometimes they were excellent historical materials, but selected and presented from a certain angle. At other times they were traditional data used with great literary freedom. At its extremest the data was only a point of departure developed to teach doctrine. *Midrash* is the term used to characterize this type of narration, though in later Judaism this term designated commentaries on Scripture. It is also called *haggada,* a name the Jewish doctors gave to materials intended to edify the readers. These expressions can be used if we remember that the historicity of the narratives can only be determined by examination of each and every passage. Be that as it may, the important thing is to pay more attention to the lessons flowing from them than to the factual details.

The Work of the Chronicler

The chronicler's work, divided into four books (*1 Chr.* [par.] *2 Chr., Ez., Neh.*), is a first-class example of a didactic narrative. It does have an historical purpose, but in reporting the history of Israel from its beginning to Nehemiah and Ezra the author tries especially to justify the foundations of Jewish life: its Law (which for him is the Pentateuch, its institutions—centered around worship and the hierarchical priesthood of Jerusalem), its hope (centered on the Davidic Messiah). It is possible that composition was begun during the struggle against

191

the Samaritan schism (4th century?) and completed some time later.

From the beginnings to David, there is a simple genealogical list. Then the author retains from the books of Samuel and of Kings whatever will serve his purpose, completing his work with information drawn from other sources. He wishes to exalt two institutions: the Davidic dynasty, depositary of the divine promises, and the priesthood of Aaron, which supplies the legitimate high priests. Written from this point of view, the narrative presents several lacunae. There is no mention of the twofold crime of David, nor of the kings of the North. On the other hand, other events are brought into new focus. The whole organization of worship is attributed to David, and the reform of Hezekiah becomes more important than that of Josiah (*132*). In short, this morality tale is above all a work of theology.

For the period following the captivity, we have seen that the documentation at the author's disposal was rather meager. Was he unable properly to organize it? His chronology is the constant despair of historians. He has disjointed the memoirs of Nehemiah and of Ezra and, to emphasize the unity of these two complementary works, he shows them to be associated (verse 425?) at the time of the renewal of the covenant (*Neh.* 8). However, this may be a simple device of composition justified by the conventions of the genre. All this goes to show that, in this period, more importance was given to the profound idea governing the unrollment of history (in other words, to the plan of God realized therein), than to accuracy of detail and chronology.

The Accounts of Ruth and Jonah

The didactic narrative is even more flexible in the books of Ruth and Jonah. The first was built upon a tradition concerning a foreign ancestor of David. The author clearly supports the current universalist movement to throw open the doors of Judaism to proselytes (*242*). Ruth is a type of the foreigner who abandoned her people and its gods to join Israel (*244*). Though the theme is in contrast to the prohibitions of Nehemiah and Ezra against mixed marriages (*294, 299*), this heroine was a sincere convert. Besides, the narrator exalted the family feeling of Ruth and Boaz, and he remembered that these faithful spouses were blessed in their descendants, for from them came the family of David. The book has the literary form of a very charming tale.

The book of Jonah also bears witness to this universalist current of thought. Its author borrowed the name of the prophet Jonah from the book of Kings. But beginning from this he constructed a very successful literary type: that of the chauvinistic Jew, narrowminded, attached to his religious nationalism, who claimed to reserve the blessings of Yahweh to Israel alone. Naturally, God chose him to proclaim repentance to Nineveh, the literary type of the pagan city. We know the rest, how the recalcitrant prophet was brought back to his duty in an unusual way, the divine omnipotence manifesting itself with a touch of humor. Pagan Nineveh was converted and escaped the divine chastisement, while the contrary prophet came to understand that God is concerned for all men (*245*). Thus the story developed according to the lessons it taught. Its fictional character does not detract from the value of the Gospel's two references to the book. Jesus contrasted the impenitence of his hearers to the repentance of the Ninevites (*Lk.* 11, 29–32), and he revealed a symbol of his own fate in the adventures of Jonah, swallowed and spewed forth: death will swallow him up and then cast him forth (*Mt.* 11, 40). Such is the double meaning of the *sign of Jonah*. This literary use of a well-known text does not touch the problem of historicity.

4. THE TRADITIONAL WISDOM: THE PROVERBS

The Sapiential Tradition in Israel

In the ancient Orient wisdom was an international commodity. In Egypt, in Mesopotamia, in Phoenicia, the educated class, which furnished the royal officials, had a tradition of cleverness and good manners. This bordered on good breeding and morality, the knowledge of mores and customs, and psychological acuteness (Text 27). This wisdom had a practical orientation, but reflection on the world and the behavior of man held an important place in it. In many cases it remained independent of religious preoccupations. In Israel the development of a bureaucratic corps introduced this tradition in the normal course of events, but there it had to be adapted to the demands of religious thought. It had to find the rule of human conduct in the divine Law and in the doctrine revealed by God —the rule of true wisdom. To erect a purely human wisdom would have been folly. Wisdom is a privilege of God, who alone "knew good and evil." Encroaching upon his right was the evidence of a sacrilegious excess and this was the sin of our first parents (5). Among men, wisdom can only be a gift from God, as it was in the case of Joseph (22). From these references it can be seen that the problem had already occurred to the Yahwist historian. In fact, it was under the reign of Solomon, the sage par excellence (76), that the sapiential tradition found a home in Israel, as the books of Kings testify. In the following centuries its first literary flowering produced maxims whose number increased with the passage of time.

The book of Proverbs contains two collections of maxims (10, 1—22, 17 and 25–29) which are passed off as Solomon's, though it is clearly stated that the second group was collected by "the people of Hezekiah." But especially at the beginning of the first collection a good number of phrases point to the influence of the prophets and Deuteronomy. The legacy of Solomon was thus enriched at a later date, when the sages had profitably drawn from the sacred Scriptures. Yet it would be irksome, and often impossible, to date each one of the proverbs. It seems best to study the sapiential tradition as a whole at its most vigorous moment in the century following the exile. Here the book of Proverbs furnishes us, besides the two collections attributed to Solomon, with two small books attributed to anonymous sages (22, 17—24, 34), three small collections of which two are of foreign origin (30, 1—31, 9), and an elegy

194

of the virtuous wife (31, 10–31) which serves as the epistle for the Mass of the Common of Holy Women. The whole thing is preceded by a long introduction written by the editor of the book (1–9).

Little need be said about the literary forms represented in this composite collection. For the most part it is composed of brief maxims in highly polished form: a verse with two half-lines in parallel, and, rarely, two consecutive verses. The reader has the feeling that the master carefully chiseled out these striking sentences the better to impress the mind of his disciple, provoking him to silent reflection (246–251). It is the art of an educated man who knows the weight of words, the method of a teacher who loves to stimulate the mind rather than to overload it with long lessons. Some more developed pieces were added, too, in riddles, fables, satires, and numerical or acrostic poems.

The Religious Humanism of the Wise Men

These maxims of the Israelite sages reflect every aspect of ancient Oriental society. They see the world through eyes free of illusion: the king and his great men who flatter him; the more or less venal justice; the arrogance of the rich towards the little people . . . So goes the world! To know the world as it is, is not to approve of it; but the clearsighted man should not be duped (246). The psychological observation of man's defects and good points, the verification of the way things are going, led to a first sketch of a morality, based upon the idea that vice does not pay (247). All the Oriental sages said as much. It is a morality of good common sense whose precepts, on the whole, accord with the Decalogue.

But the sages had a deeper understanding of man not evident at first glance. His joys and sorrows, discouragement and comfort, the delights of friendship, gave rise reflections which surpass the simple practical tact of good bureaucrats (248). We should add that an acute sense of the family and a strict idea of education, common to the ancient Orient, did not rely on

195

the innate goodness of the child, and strongly established firm paternal authority (*249*).

This wisdom was definitely a way of living. The wise man was the complete man, and the fool the man who lacks something. Wisdom and folly were the two ways offered to all on earth. One leads to life, the other to perdition (*250*). Finally, the deepest secret of this wisdom comes to light: man is not the master of his life—he is a creature of God. God's presence envelops man and his gaze penetrates him. It is God who holds the workings of justice in his hands. He is the refuge of man and the master of time. What God detests must be avoided, what he loves must be done. The fear of God is the source of true wisdom (*251*).

We are thus led into the heart of a religious thought fully in harmony with the doctrine of the covenant and the teaching of the prophets. The maxims which accomplish this are probably not the most ancient ones, but they are the ones which give meaning to the whole book. The rest relates to Oriental humanism. In this respect, the sages welcome it. One of them even copies the Egyptian proverbs of Amenope without qualm (Text 27). While integrating international wisdom with the biblical tradition, they rectify it, enrich it, draw it out, and finally they express the ideal of life which they have drawn from hearing the word of God in a language accessible to every cultivated man. In this way their literature became an instrument of proselytism. A sincere pagan could feel drawn to the religion of Israel, attracted by a wisdom superior to his own, either through its monotheism or the purity of its morality. It is interesting to note that this work was carried on in Judaism in the age when Greek wisdom saw the rise of Socrates and then Plato.

The Editor of Proverbs

The book of Proverbs seems to have been edited around the 5th century, in 480 at the earliest. Its editor's introduction (1–9) still includes pieces in a traditional style (6, 1–19), though most often it developed in continuous discourse. Addressing himself to a disciple, whom he calls his son, the sage exhorts him, in long-winded redundant periods, to practice the wisdom which would bring joy to his life if he but followed his father's example (*252*). He particularly warns him against evil companions and adulterous loves, which would lead to his damnation (5; 6, 20–7, 27).

To give more weight to his words the sage finally brings Divine Wisdom onto the scene (1, 20–33; 8–9). For if the source of human wisdom is God, it is because wisdom is fundamentally a divine reality communicated to men by grace. Here Divine Wisdom pleads its own cause. A prophet of new times, it invites all men to follow it, to be converted from their evil ways to take part in its goods. Existing before all the ages, as a child before Yahweh-King, it had been the inspirer and shaper of men (*253*). This is why it invites him who is willing to feast (*254*). The prophetic oracles show people coming from all sides to sit at the eschatological feast at the temple (*287*). Thus the feast of God is spiritualized, for what is this Wisdom if not the word of God addressed to men in revelation and set down in the Scriptures, the very word which will become flesh in Jesus Christ (*Jn.* 1, 14; Text 21)?

5. WISDOM AND CRITICAL REFLECTION: THE BOOK OF JOB

The Problem of Evil

The sapiential doctrine, as taught in the book of Proverbs, sounds a resolutely optimistic note. Certainly it throws no new light on the mystery of the after-life, but it admits as a well-established fact that every wise and virtuous man possesses happiness. The ancient doctrine of the covenant, only lately commented upon by the Deuteronomic scribes (*148–152*), said the same thing, although it was looking at Israel as a whole. The sages individualized it, teaching a theory of terrestrial retribution guaranteed by God. But this theory flies in the face of facts. There are just men who suffer and evildoers who are happy—a problem which was not ignored by the ancient Oriental sages. Babylonian literature records many versions of a poem of the *suffering just man* (Text 28). The problem is truly a serious one, for how can one reconcile the facts with the justice and the omnipotence of God? The question is timeless. Jeremiah faced it, and he triumphed over his agony only by a heroic act of faith (*172–175*). In the Persian era, between 450 and 350, a sage returned to the reflections on Jeremiah (compare *174* to *266*) and came face to face with the double enigma of human existence: retribution and evil. This is the theme of the book of Job.

Job was a famous hero in the Oriental traditions, already familiar to Ezekiel (*Ez.* 14, 14–20). In the book of Job he became the literary type of the suffering just man. A prose prologue (*Job* 1–2) sets the stage and poses the problem. Alternating scenes unfold on earth and in heaven. Job is tested through the successive loss of his goods, his children, his health. In spite of this he remains "just and God-fearing." Three friends, three Oriental sages, come to visit him and their dialogue with Job forms the body of the book. Job sighs his lament (*Job* 3). Three cycles of discourse follow (4–14, 15–21, 22–31) in which each one of the three friends speaks in the order of their age and Job answers each time. His last response (29–31), after contrasting pictures of his past prosperity with his present distress, turns to apology. It ends with a direct appeal to God, calling him to explain himself. God answers Job from the heart of the storm. He rebukes Job and leads him to an act of humility (38, 1—42, 6). Then, in a prose epilogue, he also rebukes the three friends, and returns to Job and doubles all the goods which he had lost (42, 7–17). The neat structure of the book was slightly altered by later editors. The third cycle of the discourse was the first affected. There, besides a poem on the divine wisdom (*Job* 28), unrelated to the context, a speaker, Elihu, who adds nothing, intervenes with three speeches (32–37). God's final discourse probably includes additions as well.

198

The Face-to-Face Confrontation of the Thesis

Faced with a suffering man moaning out his lament, the three friends of Job can only repeat a cold and logical theological thesis: whoever suffers is expiating for his sins, let him be converted, and God will re-establish him. Age-old wisdom teaches that a virtuous man has never been abandoned. In vain does Job boast of his justice, for his state shows that he has committed hidden faults, and his very protestations are culpable arrogance . . . Curious consolers! They develop their preconceived ideas with no regard for the facts, nor the human problem which they have before them.

Job himself sticks to his guns. Certain of his own righteousness, he demands an explanation from God. He asks God about providence, suffering, and sin. In his suffering he cries out and curses the day of his birth (256), for what good is it to be born, if only to suffer? Perhaps no other book has depicted the misery of man and his solitude here on earth with more pathos (258); or the enigma which constitutes the divine justice, when the evildoer lives through happy days and the innocent are bullied (264, 265); or the agony of a man when the formidable presence of a God he does not understand overwhelms him (259–261); or the regret of the man who has known happiness and then lost all joy (266). In spite of all, Job remains firm in his faith, he perseveres through the very heart of his dark night (262). He abandons nothing of his moral ideal, and, when he pleads his own cause, he paints a picture of the just man in tones similar to those of the Gospel (267). Did Job really have grounds against his friends? With the protestations of his humility and virtue Job mingles a strong trace of secret pride. Job has yet to discover the fundamental impurity of man before God, who alone is holy. Job is too conscious of his own righteousness. Reacting against an inexact thesis without a solid viewpoint of his own, he flares up impetuously, failing to keep a sense of his human limitations.

This explains God's answer. God does not answer Job's ques-

199

tions. He is content to call Job back to humility. He is the Creator, whose power is manifested in the unchained elements. He has placed a thousand marvels in nature of whose secrets man is ignorant. How can man be surprised at not knowing the deepest secret of all his existence? How dare he demand an account of God? One does not question God but bows before him, even when overwhelmed by mysteries he does not understand. This invitation to heroic faith will always be a stumbling block to intellectuals who want clear proofs before they commit themselves. Job's friends got their comeuppance too. They were further from the divine truth with their abstract ideas than Job with his burning apostrophes. God is not the imperturbable judge they imagined. He remains close to suffering mankind. For with this Job bows low, confesses his pride and submits to a Providence he does not understand. This is the attitude which will gain him final reward.

The Importance and Literary Value of the Book

The author of the book of Job uses dialogue to reveal every nuance of his thought. Mentally, he confronts the contradictory theses of Job with those of his friends. He feels that the problem of evil has no theoretical solution and that to avoid despair there is no other escape than blind faith and absolute submission. But even this daring view did not satisfy every reader, and one of them tried to complete it by bringing in the character of Elihu. To correct the almost blasphemous words of Job, Elihu expounds at length on the mystery of suffering and he spotlights an important idea: suffering is a providential test which purifies man. But this is as far as he goes, and having said this, no progress will be made towards a solution to the problem until the mystery of the after-life and that of redemptive suffering is clarified by the cross and resurrection of Christ.

The book of Job is a masterpiece of Oriental poetry, and the prologue and epilogue heighten the artistic contours of the work, the elevated tone of the dialogue between Job and his friends. To be sure, we should not look for a logical development of ideas here, a discussion progressing in the manner of

200

the *Dialogues* of Plato. But each facet of the problem is presented successively in an unequaled profusion of images. The great human themes of life and death, suffering and solitude, evil and God, are developed with fervent eloquence which ignores all abstract considerations. The subject gives the book a drama to rival the great works of antiquity, even those of Aeschylus, though its art is of a different order. As for the thought content, it marks an important stage in the development of revelation, for the question it posed demanded an answer, and that answer would be given in the following centuries.

6. THE PSALTER

The Origin and Diversity of the Psalms

David, as we have seen, played an important role in the origin of liturgical lyricism in Israel. The core of the psalter goes back to his era, but the genre developed down through the ages. Many of our psalms already had a place in the liturgy of the royal era, but it is impossible to know exactly how many. The titles of certain pieces do not prove their antiquity, for post-exilic authors often put their works under the patronage of the poet-king. The importance of temple worship in the Persian era and the well-attested existence of confraternities of chanters suggest a great effort at literary creation. In many cases, though, they had to be content with adapting the ancient texts by re-touching them (*329*). There is strong indication of later composition when the psalms intentionally employ expressions borrowed from the holy books, such as Jeremiah, Deuteronomy, Ezekiel, the *Message of Consolation* (*281, 313*). But discerning this is often difficult, for among the pre-exilic authors there was also some repetition of the psalms used in their times. However, the psalter includes pieces from every age, from David to the Hellenic era. Based on partial collections, the complete collection of the 150 psalms was eventually gathered together. (The system of numbering differs in the Hebrew Bible and in the Greek translation; the Latin follows the Greek.)

201

The psalter sums up within itself the whole substance of the Bible. As a mirror of the Jewish soul in the source of all its history, a doctrinal condensation of the whole Old Testament, the book of Psalms merits intensive study.

Stylistically the book of Psalms is very diverse, as diverse as the liturgy for which the psalms were written. In a traditionalist milieu such as the ancient Orient, worship tended to establish fixed formulas, and people's creative imagination did not deviate from these formulas. Mesopotamian and Egyptian literature have preserved some very tightly constructed pieces which show us the genres in use (Texts 25 and 26). The poems in the psalter are divided into general categories too, corresponding to the principal aspects of prayer and worship. There are hymns, or prayers of praise, to which the processional and pilgrimage psalms are related; individual and collective thanksgivings; individual and collective supplications; and didactic psalms, which are related to the wisdom literature from which they draw their subjects. As for the royal psalms, they are linked to various genres, but their common themes permit placing them in a separate category. However, the distinctions among genres are not absolute, and many pieces have mixed forms. For study, then, the psalter lends itself to broader groupings according to the subjects treated.

The artistic value of the psalms varies from one to another. The poetry is slightly conventional in the didactic pieces *(313)* and has little in common with the enthusiasm of the hymns *(104, 302, 323)* and thanksgivings *(81, 307)*, just as the elegant lyricism of the supplications *(270–281)* sounds a different note from that of the psalms of confidence *(308–312)*. Besides prolix pieces like Psalms 118–119 *(314)*, several short poems are pure masterpieces *(308, 310)*. And rich imagery forms an inexhaustible source of nourishment for the Christian poetry of the West.

Praise and Thanksgiving

From the beginning, Israel's worship turned man towards God in an attitude of admiration and thankfulness. This is clear in the hymns of praise or blessing (*300–301, 304, 307, 322–324*) and in the thanksgivings (*81, 83, 238, 321*). Sometimes enthusiasm breaks forth for no particular reason (*324*); but most often the prayer has a well-defined object, like praise of the Creator, whose glory is reflected in his works (*300–302, 322, 323*), or praise of the Lord of history, who has filled Israel with graces (*31, 238, 303, 323*), or praise of the God of mercy, providing for those who hope in him (*307*), or praise of God the all-powerful, who has delivered his people from peril (*81, 321*). This sentiment shines out in the choral psalms, written to be chanted on the days of solemn assembly, to the accompaniment of musical instruments. All creation is invited to take part in this great religious lyric, where even inanimate things are called to praise the Creator (*300;* compare *219, 220, 230*). This preponderance of a collective liturgy embodying individual prayer must not mask the depth of the sentiments expressed. In fact, the psalmists had absorbed the lesson of the prophets, condemnation of superficial worship (*105, 113, 117, 118, 284*). They too desired a worship *in spirit and in truth* whose heart would be obedience to the divine Law (*320, 321*). But they knew the value of external action and wanted to carry this worship over into the temple while taking part in the common ceremonies. The mere thought of the holy city and the sanctuary made their soul tremble with joy (*297, 298, 317*), as can be clearly seen in the pilgrimage chants (*318, 319*). Thus dispositions of heart give the rites a deep meaning. They already have the religious spirit the Gospel will preach.

From the Hope of Israel to Sapiential Reflection

It is natural for the psalms to echo the hopes of Israel. But here we must distinquish between eras, for the prophetic eschatology profoundly modified the narrow perspectives of earlier times. Originally, the liturgy of the temple implored God's blessing on the king, the son of David (*82, 83*). The echo of the promise of Nathan (*71*) constantly resounded in their prayer (*75*), and the fall of the monarchy in 586 brought

203

a veritable crisis of soul to the most pious Jews *(213)*. But after the exile the monarchy could not be reëstablished and their hearts turned to the future King, the ideal Anointed One announced by the prophets, the Messiah *(126–128)*. It was to him that they now applied the old psalms. His enthronement and victories were sung in anticipation *(70, 329, 330)*. Likewise, the psalms of Sion sketched the ideal Jerusalem of the last times *(297, 298)*. Especially was the longing for the reign of Yahweh translated in the psalms which evoke its glory. Their theme is not new: for a long time the processions with the ark of the covenant had acclaimed the Yahweh-King *(60, 326)*; but ever since the prophets had made his eschatological reign the center of all hope *(223, 287)*, this imagery imposed itself on the spirit of what they proposed for the future. At the end of time he would come to judge the world and save the just *(327)*. We Christians beg for the coming of the same reign in the "Our Father."

These themes of judgment and hope, as we have seen, were individualized in the wisdom literature, in answer to the questions posed by human existence. And though the psalmists were not sages, properly speaking, within the framework of prayer they could not avoid meditation on the condition of man, created king of creation *(304)*, but subject to the wear and tear of time *(305)*; and on his situation before God, who alone sounds the depths of minds and hearts *(306)*. The poet of the book of Job had done the same thing. In particular, they questioned themselves on the mystery of retribution. It turns out that the psalmists serenely held the traditional principles on this point: here below, the just are happy *(313)*. But uneasiness was also manifested and the problem of evil troubled some as it had Job *(315)*. On the level of speculative reflection no solution had yet appeared, for revelation of the eschatological resurrection would not come until later. But the psalmists had already discovered a much more important truth: for the religious soul, contact with God is a source of joy *(83, 314)*, and there is no reason for this joy to come to an end *(315, 316)*.

204

The Prayer of the Poor of Yahweh

The last psalms we will treat bring us face to face with the most profound prayer in the Old Testament. They give us a glimpse of the interior life of those fervent circles which after the exile were the very soul of the Jewish community. They loved to call themselves the poor of Yahweh, alluding to the spiritual humility which they cultivated, and also to the state of suffering in which they so often lived. Many of the psalms of supplication come from this milieu, and they reveal its main concerns.

The misfortunes of the people of God caused them intense agony. And his people prayed that God would give his grace (*210–212*). As salvation was slow in coming, they begged for its quicker coming (*238*). But there were individual trials also: injustices suffered, persecution, sickness . . . Why does God permit this suffering of his friends? In the ancient mentality, all suffering was spontaneously regarded as the punishment for sin. Thus, what does suffering mean when it touches an upright man, one trying to practice the divine Law? In time of trial the psalmists poured out their agony before God with more humility than Job. They called God to their aid and expected to see his triumphant justice manifest itself (*270–279*). Jesus himself would make this pathetic lament of suffering humanity his own, praying the psalm of the suffering just men while on the cross (*276–280*).

But this suffering was also a school of humility. The trials of the exile made Israel conscious of its national guilt. Likewise, the poor of Yahweh were conscious of their moral lowliness before the Creator. Their groans of sickness or persecution end with an avowal of guilt (*275*). The *Miserere*, echoing the prophetic writings, admirably sums up the different sentiments which motivated a repentant soul (*281*). The hope of pardon is vivid and the joy and confidence of the sinner justified by grace is sung (282, 283). In this way, prayer of supplication is left and man enters upon the prayer of confidence finding firm ground in the divine mercy. For man can confidently rely upon

205

grace (*308–312*). Again the end of the experience is spiritual joy. In finding God the religious soul enters that blessedness celebrated by the psalmists: "Happy are they whose way is blameless, who walk in the law of the Lord" (*314*). Here again we are very close to the Gospel.

7. THE CANTICLE OF CANTICLES

The Canticle of Canticles (that is, the Canticle above all canticles) is a lyric work written in the style of Oriental love poetry. It must have been edited towards the end of the Persian era. Many commentators regard it as a collection of wedding songs, and some see it as a little drama centering around the fidelity of a wife for her first husband. On the other hand, Jewish tradition, from the beginning of our era, has given it an allegorical meaning and a religious importance. And the Christian tradition, in its turn, has discovered in it the love of God for his Church and for souls.

These two interpretations are not mutually exclusive. The text's point of departure probably flowed from poems singing of human love, a love correctly understood according to biblical tradition (*4, 347*). But since the time of the prophets, human love had become the symbol of God's love for his people as manifested by the institution of the covenant. Introduced by Hosea (*110, 111*), this theme recurred frequently in the later books (*156, 241*). Thus the inspired editors of the Canticle, nourished by the sacred Scripture, probably superimposed a higher meaning on the obvious sense of the text. They made it a lyrical depiction of the eschatological wedding between Yahweh and Israel. The book can be read on two complementary levels: that of human love, and that of the supernatural love represented by the human love, or to put it another way, the love of Christ for his Church (*Eph.* 5, 21–32; *Apoc.* 21). In the first view, the Canticle is the book of nuptial love; in the second, it becomes the book of Christian mysticism, its exuberant imagery lending itself to the freest symbolic interpretations (*333–337*).

206

Text 25

A BABYLONIAN PSALM:
A HYMN TO ISHTAR

Babylonian lyricism preceded that of Canaan (Text 7) and surely influenced it. During the exile the Jews were in direct contact with it, and it stimulated the development of psalmody among them. This hymn to Ishtar is a good example of individual supplication (compare: *81, 211, 213, 270, 271, 273–276, 281*). Ishtar, daughter of the moon-god Sin and identified with the Canaanite Astarte and the Greek Aphrodite, was both goddess of war and goddess of fertility. The planet Venus was her star.

I pray to you, Lady of ladies, Goddess of goddesses!
Ishtar, Queen of every place, Regent of humans!
You are strong, you are sovereign, your name is sublime!
You are the light of the heavens and the earth, O valiant daughter of Sin! . . .
Shining torch of the heavens and the earth, light of every place!
Headlong in attack, without equal, powerful in battle!
Fire-brand who flames against the enemy, causing the ruin of the powerful!
I have known, O my Lady, days of gloom,
Months of darkness, years of grief.
I have known, O my Lady, an unjust and violent condemnation.
They have annihilated me, gave death and misery . . .
I look upon my Lady, my eye strains toward you.
It is you whom I invoke: wipe away my spell,
Remit my fault, my transgression, my misdeed, my sin!
Forget my misdeed, hear my prayer! . . .

How long, O my Lady, will you be irritated and your face turned away?
How long, O my Lady, will you be angered and your heart in a passion?

207

Turn back your face, which is set against me!
Dispose your face, for a favorable word! . . .
My aggressors, like the earth, let me trample them under foot!
Let my prayers and implorations reach you!
Let your great mercies be upon me!
Those who see me on the road, let them magnify your name!
As for me, before the peoples, I will glorify your divinity and
    valor!
Where you look the dead revive, the sick arise;
The unjust become just again, by seeing your face.
I, spent, weak, afflicted, invoke you, I your servant,
Look down on me, O my Lady, receive my prayer!
See me, hear my imploring! . . .
Let your benevolent eyes be upon me!
With your shining face, look down on me!
Chase from my body the evil spells, that I may see your shining
    light!

How long, O my Lady, will my enemies measure me,
In perfidy and falseness dream of evil,
Persecuting me and being envious of me will they laugh at me? . . .
I am tossed about like the waves which an evil wind raises.
My heart soars, it goes and comes, like a bird in the heavens.
I mourn like a dove, night and day.
I am downcast and I weep bitterly.
With oh's! and alas's! my heart is troubled . . .
"Ishtar is sublime! Ishtar is queen!
The Lady is sublime! The lady is queen!
Irnini, the valiant daughter of Sin, has no equal!"

It should be noted that the frequent use of parallelism between the half-lines of the verses is still less regular than in
Hebrew and Canaanite poetry. In this hymn the believer evi-
dences a very vivid and personal religious feeling which surpasses the narrow bounds of the nature worship which centered
upon Ishtar.

208

Text 26

AN EGYPTIAN PSALM:
A HYMN TO ATON

In the 14th century the Pharaoh Amenophis IV (Akhenaton) tried to impose upon Egypt the exclusive worship of Aton, the divinized solar disk, regarded as the fundamental principle of all things. His hymn to Aton bears witness to a great feeling for nature. The author of Psalm 104 seems to have known and partially imitated it, to sing of Yahweh as Creator of all *(302)*.

You radiate with beauty from the horizon of heaven,
O living Sun who lived from the beginning!
When you lift yourself above the eastern horizon,
you fill all lands with your beauty . . .
When you go down on the western horizon,
the earth is in shade equal to that of death . . .
All the lions come out from their lairs,
all the serpents set themselves to strike.
It becomes black, the land is in silence,
for he who made all things rests in his horizon.
At dawn, when you rise above the horizon,
when you shine during the day in your quality as Sun,
when you chase away darkness and dart forth your rays,
the two Lands wake up, joyous, and get to their feet;
because of you they wash their bodies, put on their clothes;
arms are opened to adore your splendor,
the entire earth devotes itself to its work.
All the beasts are delighted with their provider;
the trees and the plants grow green;
the birds which take wing outside the nest
open their wings to adore you.
The lambs skip on their feet.
Everything which flutters its wings and flies,
all live because you have risen for them . . .

How they are numerous, your works
hidden from our sight!
Sole god, who has no one like you!
You have created the earth according to your heart,
while you were alone:
men, beasts, wild beasts,
everything which walks on the earth with its paws,
everything which flies through the heavens with its wings . . .

The earth comes into existence by your hand,
according as you wish it:
you rise, beings live;
you set, and they die.
You are the standard of life,
for nothing lives except through you.
Eyes contemplate your beauty until you go down,
and all work ceases when you sink below the horizon . . .

This adoration of the Creator would be worthy of a place in biblical poetry, were it not for the confusion between the creator and the personified Sun (compare *184, 300*). The psalmist's imitation (*302*) remains on a purely literary level.

Bibliography

On the question of the Pentateuch, see the bibliography for Chapter III. On the post-exilic prophets, see J. Chaine, *God's Heralds* and E. Maly, *Prophets of Salvation*. On the books of Wisdom, see R. Murphy, *Seven Books of Wisdom* (Milwaukee 1960). On the Psalms, see A. Gelin, *The Psalms are our Prayers* (Collegeville 1964), A. George, *Praying the Psalms* (Notre Dame 1964), T. Merton, *Praying the Psalms* (Collegeville 1956), and T. Worden, *The Psalms are Christian Prayer* (New York 1961).

Study Guides

It is always difficult to appreciate the art of poets in translation. Still, it would be interesting to compare, from a literary angle, some authors of the first rank like Isaiah, the *Message of Consolation* (*215–228*), the book of Job, and the most beautiful of the psalms.

Post-exilic literature has a traditionalist character, as the many references to the oldest Scriptures show. This fact can be highlighted through some well-chosen texts by studying the reminiscences which they include. A Bible with parallels will be a necessary tool for this task (see *230, 231, 313*).

By using the references given with respect to the Canticle of Canticles, study the religious symbolism of marriage and human love, from the prophets to the New Testament. In what areas has this symbolism permitted better understanding of God's dispositions with regard to men? How has its use in the Old Testament prepared minds to see marriage as a sacrament?

X.

THE KEY IDEAS
OF JUDAISM

AFTER the slow quiet work of the exile the Persian era saw the Israelite religion reborn in a new form, Judaism. Heir to all the previous tradition and its Scriptures, Judaism also inherited its great doctrinal themes. Thus there is no need to review what we have already studied of the traditions of Israel (Chapter IV) and the prophetic age (Chapter VII). It would be tedious to repeat the many references to these fundamental ideas in the books of the Persian era. Even so, we must highlight the striking aspects of Jewish thought and life which were fixed during these two centuries, for they will come up again and again throughout what is to come and will appear again as the background of the New Testament.

1. AT THE SOURCES OF THE FAITH

From the Prophets to the "Men of the Book"

In the royal era the prophets were Israel's spiritual guides. It is true that the priests, official custodians of the Law and of worship, were *ex officio* the defenders of the Mosaic tradition. And they were effective in this role insofar as they were faithful to

212

the deposit entrusted to them. But this fidelity was conditioned by the influence of the prophets, who made the reform spirit reach even down among the Levitical clergy. Without them, tradition would have hardened and floundered into an uninspired formalism and perhaps it would even have been corrupted by the Canaanite milieu. The most important works, which arose in the priestly circles before the destruction of Jerusalem, Deuteronomy, and the Code of Holiness, show the prophetic influence. Thus tradition was renewed by contact with the living word transmitted by God's messengers.

However, beginning with the exile the situation changed. From the very first the prophetic vocation waned, and prophetism itself evolved. The texts collected in the third section of Isaiah are no longer in the style of living preaching. Its message was from the first fixed in a written form, which would triumph in the apocalyptic literature. This is a sign that the *men of the book* were gaining increasing importance in Jewish society. The exile marked a turning point in this matter. The deported communities were concerned with saving their spiritual patrimony. How could it be done, if not by fixing it in writing from the very first and watching over the preservation of the books thus created? In the areas of the Law and of worship the priests were all appointed to carry out this work. But there were also scribes who could put their science at the service of tradition. These lay *men of the book* had lost their administrative offices in the national catastrophe. Those reformed by the views of the prophets and Deuteronomy would begin to collect other things besides the archives, such as the prophetic books (thus Baruch edited Jeremiah), and the historical books which recalled the great experiences of the people of God.

Thus by force of circumstances the scribes, whether priestly or lay, became the spiritual guides of the community by writing the sacred Scriptures. They solidified tradition. Thanks to them, Moses and the pre-exilic prophets continued to speak to Israel. We have already looked at the process of the formation of the Scriptures. Now that they have been fixed in their essentials, it is important to see their role. They are the crystallization of the

213

word of God which, during centuries past, had never ceased to speak to Israel. The people of God looked to it for the rule of their faith and conduct. In the shadow of the rebuilt temple the young scribes were formed in spirit and in heart while they heard their calling. The sacred texts were engraved in their memory. And when they wrote, their books were full of textual reminiscences. This does not mean that they were scholars. Rather, their thought was rooted in ancient tradition. The new Scriptures they wrote did not carry the authority of the prophetic word, but since they were born of meditation on the ancient Scriptures, they were clothed with the authority of tradition, even though they marked a progression in revelation.

Tradition and Doctrinal Progress

It is important to note the close connection between tradition and doctrinal progress witnessed by the way the Scriptures were interpreted in Judaism. Thus the word of God is not a dead text, a simple historical document relating to the past, but the permanent nourishment of faith and the spiritual life, in the midst of changing historical circumstances. Each fixed text reveals an aspect of the mystery of God and its relationship to man; it had once been revealed in view of determined circumstances, which conditioned its literary form and whose memory was more or less well-preserved, but after these circumstances had disappeared it retained its meaning and value. New events or other texts shed new light on them and gave them a larger and more profound meaning. Thus Nathan's promise to David (*71*) was from the first understood as a promise of dynastic continuity (*75, 213*). Reread in the light of prophecies of Isaiah (*126, 127*), after the abolition of the royal instruction, it took on an eschatological perspective, as the promise of a future messiah. This is how the chronicler understood it when he reproduced it in a corrected version (*1 Chr.* 17, 7–14).

This method of interpretation, which can be seen in the case we have just cited, was applied by post-exilic Judaism to many

214

other texts. Thus Tradition is more than the inert conservation of the past. It is, rather, the on-flowing current of life, within which revelation developed. Up to this point prophetism had been the determining element in doctrinal progress, and now commentary on the Scriptures became another. This explains how Jewish theology never became a fixed synthesis, for though based upon immutable foundations, it still remained open to new elements. When it faced new problems, it formulated contrary solutions side by side. The living unity of this theology, like the Scriptures to which it was related, was not based on rigid correlations of abstract theses, as can be seen in the three principal areas of Jewish interest: the Law and worship, wisdom, eschatology.

2. THE LAW AND WORSHIP

The Law. Foundation of Judaism

Pre-exilic experience had shown the need for a very strong juridical system to maintain the fidelity not only of a small elite, but of the mass of the "stiff-necked people" as well. After the return from the exile this necessity was even more strongly felt. The reform work of Ezra (*292, 294*) reflected this concern, both by definitively fixing the text of the Law (as we saw in the preceding chapter), and by making it relevant. This acted as a kind of wall encircling and protecting Judaism from pagan contaminations. If the people observed the system strictly their thought and their morality and customs would be sheltered. In every life-situation the Jew was ruled by his Law. The explanation given it, whether in the synagogue or in the schools of the scribes, far from minimizing its precepts, tended rather to extend them, so that the faithful were caught in a net of minute prescriptions. Wherever he was, he belonged to a world apart. And though he lived in the midst of the pagan nations he did not mix with them. Circumcision (*186*) was the sign of his belonging to a "holy people," the chosen nation of God.

215

The Ambiguities of Legalism

Without this fervent attachment to the Law, Judaism would have ceased to exist. As St. Paul remarked, the Law was the harsh pedagogue which led Israel to Christ (*Gal.* 3, 24). Nevertheless, this very attachment to the Law was subject to ambiguity or danger. Many currents had intermingled in the books of the Law, particularly the Deuteronomic current and the priestly current. Deuteronomy more sharply insisted on the moral commandments, and was more open to a religion of the heart related to that of Hosea or Jeremiah, than the Priestly Code which was more concerned with the exact observance of rituals and more impressed by the grandeur of the holy God and the need for adoration flowing from that grandeur. Which current finally gave Judaism its fundamental orientation? More profoundly, which element did Judaism prefer in practice, since the spiritual and religious drive of both bordered upon legalistic minutiae?

The tone of Deuteronomy and its religion of the heart are loudly echoed in a text like Psalm 119 (118), though it is sometimes seen as the expression of pure legalism (*314*). But this was not the common reaction in the circles sincerely attached to the Law. Every legalistic school is exposed to the danger of this warping of spirit by a strong institutional structure, for wishing to assure the material execution of the precepts at any cost, it ends by forgetting the spirit which gives it value. The school becomes attached to the small side of things, and founders in withering casuistry. Jewish jurisprudence, whose beginnings certainly date back to the 5th century (Text 23), did not always avoid uninspired and soulless legalism. But despite this partial hardening of a great tradition, we must remember the providential role it played in preparing hearts for the Gospel.

The Ambiguity of the Liturgical Practices

The performance of the liturgy faced the same danger of hardening. But for the priests, the great temptation was to be content with material performance of the obligatory rites of public worship, with all the outward signs of private devotion, but without being too concerned with having suitable interior dispositions. When had the prophets not protested against the hypocrisy of a religion without depth (*105, 117, 118, 284*)! After the exile, Jewish worship was clothed in two forms. On the one hand, everywhere on the Sabbath day they gathered in the synagogue for common prayer (especially through the psalms) and to hear a reading and commentary on Scripture (see *293*). On the other hand, the temple at Jerusalem was the sole center where a sacrificial worship was celebrated. Its feasts, pilgrimages, offerings, and daily prayers played a great role in the spiritual life of the Jews, who went there whenever they could. The priests and Levites formed a privileged class among the people. The high priest was the supreme head of the nation, since there was no longer a king. God relied upon the clergy and their functions to preserve a "holy people" for himself (*182, 183*). But there was the great danger for this clergy of making themselves mere functionaries, and turning worship into ritual formalism.

Fortunately, the profound religious sense of the prophets and Deuteronomy infiltrated the psalms composed or revised during this era. This prayer of the poor of Yahweh, centered upon the interior virtues and personal religion, became the rule in liturgical prayer (*270–283*). The Jews knew the psalter by heart—official chanters learned it through a study of the chant technique, others through hearing the psalms chanted and through participation in their choral execution. Thus the psalter was an excellent source of spiritual formation for them, for the whole substance of Scripture was contained in the sacred canticles. Thanks to them, Jewish worship could really be a worship "in spirit and in truth" (*320, 321*), and could effectively prepare hearts for the future worship of the new covenant.

3. WISDOM

The Doctrine of Wisdom

Though the doctrine of wisdom was not a wholly new thing, after the exile it developed and took on considerably greater importance. We can easily understand why. Among the scribes, who were now the people's spiritual guides, there were laymen who put their literary talents at the service of the word of God, and thereby the ancient tension between the prophets and the counselors of the king, skilled in a wholly human wisdom (*116, 117, 172*), was overcome. The prophets (not the professionals, but those called by God) were conscious of teaching nothing which had not come from God, which had not been inspired by his Spirit. Side by side, the post-exilic sages were conscious that their wisdom, based upon the word of God (*151*), was just as much a fruit of the Spirit (*127*), or better, that its source was divine wisdom itself. That is why their teaching and that of the Law and the prophets were identical. In both cases it was the word of God transmitted to men in different forms. Strengthened by this certainty, the sages did not hesitate to give a new presentation to traditional truths, especially the morality of Moses and the prophets. They gave a very humane presentation, adapted to all mentalities and attractive for the pagans drawn towards wisdom. Despoiled of their strictly national clothing, the teachings of revelation became a message accessible to all.

The Reflection on the Divine Wisdom

Reflection on divine wisdom was the heart of the sage's theology. It is sometimes said that by personifying this attribute of God in a poetic way they prepared from afar the theology of the Holy Trinity, for they elaborated the categories of thought and the language which, in the New Testament, would serve to express this mystery. This does not really get to the root of things, however, for the New Testament revelation of the Trinity can be accounted for only by comparing the doctrine of wisdom and that of the word of God which is more widely attested in the Old Testament. Prophet, psalmist, and sage shared the same worship of this mysterious reality whose activity they saw in creation and in history: the creative and revealing word (*155, 173, 189, 314*). They could not yet know that this Word would become flesh in Jesus Christ and that it would then reveal itself as a Person, but they did see the first tentative steps of his manifestation here on earth, veiled though they were (Text 21).

218

Likewise, when the sages meditated upon the mysterious reality of the divine wisdom, fundamentally identical to the creative word and the Law (*252, 352, 402*), it was no abstraction for them but the object of religious experience. They introduced the presence of him who would later reveal himself as the Wisdom of God in person (*1 Cor.* 1, 30). In the book of Proverbs, this wisdom invites men to take part in the Scriptural banquet (*254, 352*). So we say that this invitation is already a sketch of the invitation repeated by Christ: "Come to me! . . ." (*Mt.* 11, 28; *Jn.* 6, 35).

The Problem of Individual Retribution

Finally, the school of wisdom was the framework for debate on the important and difficult problem of retribution. Ezekiel firmly established the principle of its individual character (*194*). This prophetic affirmation flew in the face of the most ancient orientations of the sapiential thought. What the sage had always communicated to his disciple was a doctrine, a way of acting, a rule of life, capable of procuring happiness for him. In the shape of a *Manual for the Honest Man,* the book of Proverbs tried to teach the secret of the happy life (*252*). To achieve this, it pretended to represent the experience of centuries—a dangerous pretension, for this experience was ambiguous. The observation of the world and critical reflection showed another face to things. Evil exists, not only as punishment for sin, as was still agreed upon, but also apparently without connection with sin. The book of Job, like the psalms of suffering, met this inscrutable mystery head on, a mystery made more inscrutable by a lack of knowledge of life beyond the grave. Therefore, the scribes abandoned the ancient idea of *sheol,* a joyless abode where man was the prisoner of death (*259, 261, 273*). Faced with such a perspective, Mesopotamian thought tended towards a hedonistic morality, counseling men to "Enjoy the goods of this life, since there would be no others" (Text 28). It wrestled with the problem of the suffering of the just without reaching any conclusion (Text 29).

The sage of Israel did not yet have an over-all solution, but

219

when compared to his colleagues in Mesopotamia, his originality and also his superiority soon becomes evident. The difficulty
of the problem of evil never made them question the positive
certitudes of their faith. In the face of the grave awaiting him,
Job was not even tempted to abandon the divine Law. The
author of Psalm 73 did not want "to betray the race of the sons
of God" (315). For in every hypothesis, the spiritual experience of contact with God remained the irreplaceable and supreme good. No image of life beyond the grave illumined the
horizon, but personal relations with God, even if limited to this
life, would be worth the pain and the sacrifice of everything else
for their sake. The psalms highlight this essential discovery (85,
311, 314, 317–319). Already, one or another singer seems to
have had a presentiment of the enduring character of such a
joy (315, 316) and was able to surmount the scandal caused by
the problem of evil (315). This was the first step towards the
revelation of an eternal joy which will be clearly testified to in
the last books of the Old Testament.

4. ESCHATOLOGICAL LONGING AND MESSIANISM

Permanence of the Eschatological Longing

The great disappointment following the return from the exile
(231, 237, 238) did not end the eschatological longing of the
Jews. On the contrary! The value of the prophetic promises was
a certainty nothing could impair. The post-exilic prophets emphasized the meaning of this delay and used it to stir up greater
fervor. If the salvation of Yahweh was delayed, it was because
Israel was not yet converted deeply enough, they said. Let
Israel become more faithful, and the day would come when
the triumphant Justice of God will manifest itself to the world
(284). From that time onwards eschatological longing became
a dominant note of Jewish spirituality on a par with fidelity to
the Law. They are like the two faces of the doctrine of the

220

covenant, for on Sinai God gave his people a Law and promises. The liturgical feasts by recalling each year the past blessings of God also inspired desire for the favors promised for the last times: the new exodus, the new covenant, the new march towards the promised land. . . . The poor of Yahweh, in the midst of great distress, cried out in their prayers for this day when their ills would come to an end (238). More time passed, and the longing became deeper. They lived in a tense atmosphere; they looked for signs showing that "the time is near." In short, they clung to the feeling of its imminence. This longing endured five centuries without losing its ardor. And for the Jews who have not reached the Christian faith, it still endures.

The Development of Eschatological Doctrine

It would be useless to review what has been said about prophetic eschatology and messianism here. After the exile all the elements of their prophecies were drawn towards a single synthesis. If the image of the Suffering Servant of Yahweh (228) was apparently missing from the picture, it is because it served as the spiritual nourishment and consolation of the poor of Yahweh in their trials (278), and because this synthesis, based upon the Scriptures, was not yet a strictly correlated doctrine. Following the source texts, it oscillates between contrary tendencies, as can be seen in the works of the Persian era.

In the first place, the relation of Israel and the other nations to the plan of salvation was left ill-defined. On the one hand, the universalism of the divine plan, already imperfectly perceived before the exile (11, 133), was affirmed more strongly. For the last times would see a universal reassembling of the peoples in the worship of the One God. With some nuances, the idea appears in Haggai (235) and in the third part of Isaiah (241–243), in Malachi (289), and in the Apocalypse of Isaiah (287). It will be found again in the second part of Zechariah (325). Then, it was said, mankind would return to that primitive unity ruined by the coming of idolatrous civiliza-

221

tion (*10*). The closer this concept of an all-encompassing salvation was linked to the theme of the reign of God, the more religious and the less nationalistic it was (*241, 287, 325*). On the other hand, great images flowing from Israel's unique experience continued to structure this representation of the last times. Jerusalem and its temple were the center of the world (*241, 243, 287, 325*). The Messiah, the son of David, even though he had not yet come, usually played the role of the head of the new people (*328*). By applying the ancient royal psalms to him, his glory and victory were sung in advance (*70, 329, 330*). But some of these images were bound to nourish religious nationalism, to make Israel hope for the earthly predominance which seemed to flow from its very vocation.

We run into the same problem in determining the plane on which the promised blessings were seen. On the one hand, in the prolongation of the Sinai promises and the doctrine of Deuteronomy, the people come to view more realistically the enjoyment of earthly goods, which God was bound to secure for his elect (*241, 285*). On the other hand, following a tendency already noted among the pre-exilic prophets, the people transmuted this eschatological joy into the joy of a world restored to its first perfection (*230*), the perfect consolation of the elect (*240, 241*), whom God will take upon his knees like a mother (*285*). It became the creation of a new heaven and a new earth free from sobs or cries of anguish (*286*), and would be the entry into a familiarity with God and the consequent suppression of sorrow and death itself (*287*). The image of paradise regained, which the prophets were fond of, thus expressed the transcendence of the "future world" in relation to the "present world." The ambiguity of the texts follows from the frequent juxtapositions of disparate elements, without explanations telling how they fit together. Was salvation meant in a terrestrial or ultra-terrestrial perspective? Was it based on a universalism or on religious nationalism? On these essential points revelation was indefinite. It would be definite only after the fulfillment of Israel's hope.

222

Text 27

EGYPTIAN WISDOM: THE INSTRUCTIONS OF AMENOPE

Biblical wisdom developed along its own lines, apart from an internationalistic current which antedated Israelite civilization. Among the Egyptian collections, that of Amenope (probably 7th–6th centuries) offers striking similarities to a passage from the book of Proverbs (*Prv.* 22, 17—24, 22). Some of its maxims are cited here:

Keep yourself from stealing from him who is overburdened
and from crushing him who is powerless [ch. 2].

One measure which God gives you is worth more
than five thousand acquired unjustly [ch. 6].

Do not rejoice in goods evilly gotten
and do not be saddened by poverty:
if an archer ventures too far forward,
his squad abandons him;
the boat of the greedy man goes aground,
that of the silent man sails before the wind.
For yourself, when Aton arises make this prayer to him.
"Give me prosperity and health!"
He will give you what is necessary for this life,
and you will be sheltered from terror [ch. 7].

Do not lean upon the scales, do not falsify the weights,
and do not damage the divisions of the measure [ch. 16].

Poverty in the hand of God is worth more
than riches in a shop;
Sharp pain and a joyous heart are worth more
than riches with regret [ch. 13].

223

Do not pass the night in dread over tomorrow:
   at the dawn, what will the next day be like?
No one knows what the next day will be like . . .
God knows success,
   whereas man fails;
what man says is one thing,
   another is what God does [ch. 18].

Do not laugh at a blind man, nor torment a dwarf;
   do not damage the affairs of the crippled;
do not torment a simple-minded man
   and do not be cruel to him if he does wrong.
For man is clay and straw,
   and God is his creator [ch. 29].

This practical wisdom is of a high spiritual level. Still, the monotheistic tendency which appears to be here must not be overestimated. The sage speaks of God while leaving the reader free to put in the proper name that pleases him. Neverthless, he mentions the god Aton explicitly (the divinized solar disk; see Text 26). And very little would have to be done for the counsel given to be joined to the Biblical morality (compare *246–251*).

Text 28

MESOPOTAMIAN PESSIMISM

Mesopotamian tradition carried a somber picture of the abode of the dead (compare *259, 261, 273*), which resulted in a pessimistic concept of existence which the ancient epic of Gilgamesh, fixed before the patriarchal era, enjoyed stressing. Gilgamesh is the hero of many exploits which served as the prototype to those of Hercules. After the death of his friend Enkidu, seized by an obsession with death, he wished to ask the secret of

224

eternal life from his ancestor Utnapishtim, the Babylonian Noah (Text 6), whom the gods let escape the common lot by placing him in an inaccessible paradise. En route, he confides his pain and his desire to Siduri, the divine tavern-keeper.

Enkidu whom I love so much,
who with me had braved all hardships,
he has gone to the destiny of mankind.
Day and night I have wept over him.
I would not confide him to the tomb.
"My soul (I say to myself), he is going to rise to my cry";
That, during seven days and seven nights
until the worm came to him on the face.
Since he has gone, I have no longer found life;
I have wandered like a hunter in the middle of the plain.
O tavern-keeper, now that I see your face,
may I not see the death which I dread!"
The tavern-keeper says to Gilgamesh:
"O Gilgamesh, where are you going then?
The life you look for, you will not find.
When the gods created mankind,
they allotted death to mankind,
and they retained life in their hands.
For you, O Gilgamesh, fill your belly;
day and night, revel!
Of each day make a day of festival;
day and night dance and amuse yourself!
Wear clean clothes,
wash your head and bathe yourself in water!
Cherish the little one who takes your hand;
Let your wife take pleasure on your breast!
Such is the lot of mankind . . ."

In spite of this discouraging advice, Gilgamesh perseveres in his project. He arrives at the home of Utnapishtim, beyond the "waters of death" (see *81*). His ancestor tells him how to find the "plant of life" (see *3, 6*). But on the return road the plant is stolen from him by a serpent (see *4*). The hero will then die: a hopeless prospect! The last word in human wisdom had been

225

given by Siduri. It is hedonism with no spiritual purpose (compare *343, 399*).

Text 29

THE SUFFERING JUST MAN IN BABYLONIAN THOUGHT

Thus orientated, Mesopotamian thought could not avoid the problem of innocent suffering. The suffering just man it presents asks the gods the same questions as Job asked Yahweh (compare *255 to 269*). This is the same lament as the psalms of suffering (*271–279*).

My strength is departing, my appearance is growing gloomy;
my dignity has left me, I have no more protection . . .
The king, flesh of the gods, sun of his peoples,
has his heart in rage and cannot be appeased.
The courtiers scheme intrigues against me;
They gather together and themselves formulate curses.
Their heart is in rage against me, they burn as with fire.
They ponder malice and wickedness against me . . .
My clear voice is reduced to silence;
my haughty head is bent to the ground;
my strong heart, dread weakens it . . .
I who went as a noble, I have learned oblivion;
I the dignitary, I have become a slave . . .
If I walk in the streets, ears prick up;
if I enter the palace, eyes blink.
My city, like an enemy, looks threateningly at me;
my very homeland is foreign and hostile to me . . .

Tablet 1, 47–83

Scarcely had I reached life, when I had reached its end.
I look around me: evil, and yet more evil!

226

My torment only grows, I cannot obtain my right.
I have invoked my god, and he has not shown his face;
I have prayed to my goddess, and she has not lifted her head . . .
Like him who has not made libation to his god,
who in the sacred meal has not mentioned his goddess,
whose mouth has omitted prayer and supplication; . . .
like him who, in his lukewarmness, has forgotten his Lord,
who has sworn vainly by the name of his god,
    such have I seemed.
Still, I, I have been mindful of prayer and supplication;
prayer was my concern, sacrifice my rule;
the day of the worship of god was the joy of my heart,
the day of the procession of the goddess, my gain and my riches . . .
Only let me know whether that pleased the god!
What is regarded as good, is a scandal to the god;
what is kept in the heart, is to the god a good thing.
Who then can know the will of the gods in heaven? . . .
Where will the mortal hear of the way of a god?
He who lived today, is dead tomorrow:
all at one blow he is cut down, suddenly he has been shattered.
He who at one instant was singing in jubilation,
the next instant, he groans like a mourner . . .

Into a prison my house was changed:
my hands in my own flesh were thrown in irons,
in the chains of my own body my feet are shut.
During the whole day, the persecutor pursues me;
even when night comes, he does not leave me one instant . . .
No sorcerer has conjured my state of sickness,
no diviner has procured the end of my infirmity.
My god has not helped me, he has not taken my hand;
my goddess has not had pity, she has not come near to me.
My tomb is still open, that one may seize my goods;
before I am dead, they terminate my funeral rites;
all my land has said: "What a wrong-doer!" . . .

Tablet 2, extracts

There is no ray of hope in this lament (compare *273*). Since
man has no retribution awaiting him in the hereafter, the only

227

desirable good is that of the below. But if man does not find it, what remains to him? The joy of loving God does not enter into this frame of thought as it does in Psalm 73 (*315*).

Bibliography

A. Gelin, *The Poor of Yahweh* (Collegeville n.d.). The different theological questions are treated in the works cited in the preceding chapters, and in the various theologies of the Old Testament.

Study Guides

The quest for a personal interior life was a growing preoccupation in the Old Testament. This can be shown by comparing the attitude of David after his sin (*72*), the discouragement of Elijah (*91*), the concern for a religion of the heart manifested by various texts (*84, 85, 117, 148–150, 160, 181*), the interior life of Jeremiah (*172–175*), and the religious attitude of the post-exilic psalmists (*270–283, 314, 316, 320, 321*). Did this not directly prepare men for the message of the Gospel?

We can follow the development of social morality in the Old Testament through the texts (examples: *38, 98–100, 118, 129, 131, 247, 251, 267, 284, 329, 345, 373*). What did the Gospel add to this morality?

Beginning with the Proverbs and the book of Job, trace the development of the doctrine of retribution in the Old Testament. Study as well, in the time before the sages, the traditional principles bound up with the covenant (*43, 148–153*) and the general doctrine of the prophets, made precise by Ezekiel in an individual meaning (*194*). Look also at the sages themselves, the reflection of the psalmists (*313–316*), and at the end of the

228

Old Testament the new data of Daniel (*383;* see *376*) and of wisdom (*399–401*).

In the Old Testament, souls constantly oscillated between religious nationalism and universalism. This problem can be followed through the texts at the time of the conquest (*49–58*), the prophetic era (*133, 185, 220–223, 225, 226*), the return from the exile (*241–245, 254*), the era of Ezra and Nehemiah (*292–299*), the eschatology of the Persian and Greek era (*325–332*), and the struggles of Maccabean times (*384–398*). How did the Gospel resolve this problem?

XI.

FROM THE CONQUESTS
OF ALEXANDER
TO THE CHRISTIAN ERA

THE Persian era saw the foundations laid for Judaism. But suddenly the Middle East experienced an immense cultural change, for after the conquests of Alexander it became Hellenized. This posed a new problem for the Jewish community. In Palestine as well as in the diaspora the Jews had many contacts with Hellenism. Would they go along with the tide, at the risk of sacrificing their essential values? For a long time they held fast to their tradition, remaining faithful to their vocation and their God. This very resistance finally brought on tragedy. When the king of Syria tried to impose his law and his religion on Judea, though the faithful Jews were violently persecuted, they came out of it strengthened in their faith and freed from the foreign yoke. For a century, Judea formed an autonomous state under the dynasty of the Hasmonaeans. But the dream of national independence quickly faded as Rome now imposed her domination on Palestine. However, at least the Jews had won their spiritual freedom—one which no one contested up to the very threshold of the New Testament. This, in miniature, was the history of Judaism in the Greek era.

230

1. THE HOUR OF HELLENISM

Alexander and Hellenistic Civilization

In the 5th century Greece was at the apex of her civilization, in the glorious hour of her literary classicism. She had been able to defend her independence in the face of Persian aggression during the Median wars, but internally she was worn out by the civil wars which set Athens, Sparta, and Thebes at war with one another. This internal warfare had been profitable to Philip, the king of Macedonia, who finally unified Greece under his own leadership.

Then his son Alexander (335–323), to cement this unity, swept the Greeks off in the great adventure of revenge on the Persian empire. Gaining a foothold in Asia Minor, he conquered Syria, Egypt, and Mesopotamia in lightning campaigns (333–331). He turned to the eastern satrapies and penetrated as far as the valley of the Indus (330–326). When he died in Babylon, in 323, he had united two worlds under his scepter. However, soon after his death this union collapsed. His lieutenants, the Diadochi, quarreled over the sovereignty. Finally, around 275, equilibrium was reëstablished around three monarchies: Macedonia and Greece, Syria and Mesopotomia governed by the Selucid dynasty, and Egypt governed by the Lagides (Ptolemies). The Oriental provinces evolved in their own direction. And beginning in 250, they detached thremselves from the Seleucid empire.

Yet, throughout Alexander's domain there were remnants of a common spirit and culture which was Greek inspired. This was Hellenistic civilization. In the footsteps of the armies, Greek commerce penetrated everywhere. The Greek tongue linked the most diverse peoples, and local civilizations were Hellenized, each one according to its own bent. In return, Hellenism, the unifying principle of these worlds, opened out to the East. It borrowed elements from Egypt and from Iran and rapidly assimilated them. All modes of worship entered into a vast syn-

cretist movement, which glossed over their doctrinal incon-
sistency and promoted their hidden kinships. The Greek Zeus
was identified with Bel-Marduk in Babylon, in Egypt with
Amon-Ra, in Syria with Baal-Shamem. To be sure, Helleniza-
tion remained superficial in more than one area. In the valley
of the Indus and on the Iranian plateau it was the East which
finally absorbed the Greek conquerors. On the other hand, in
the very hour of Athens' decline it was in Egypt, in Syria, and
in Asia Minor that Hellenistic culture found new centers of
diffusion: in Alexandria, Antioch, and Pergamum.

Judaism in the Hellenistic Frame of Reference

In the midst of this world upheaval, Judaism continued to live
its life apart. It is true that the communities of the diaspora
scattered still farther yet in the footsteps of the Greek soldiers,
but the strong originality given to Jewish life by its great organ-
izers persisted in spite of the pressures of the surrounding
environment. The dispersed Jews held on to their Law, their
customs, their traditions, their worship, their Scriptures. Jerusalem remained their spiritual capital, and Yahweh was not
identified with Zeus. This unique fact is worth noting.

During the struggle among the Diadochi, Judea was bandied
back and forth between Egypt and Syria. Finally, in 301, it fell
to Egypt for a century. The reigning Lagides respected its religious and social particularism, as had the Persian empire and
Alexander. Judea thus lived a calm life, favorable to reflection
and prayer. This atmosphere is reflected in the book of Ben-
Sira, Ecclesiasticus. Before long an important Jewish community, which was centered around Alexandria, developed in
Egypt. Its members soon forgot the Hebrew and Aramaic
spoken in Palestine, so a translation of the Bible into the
Greek language was made for them. In the hands of the Jewish
proselytism, this version of the holy books became an instrument of propaganda. We are less well-informed on the other
local communities, scattered from Arabia to India. Those of
Babylonia, near the intellectual centers where Hellenism encountered a strongly Iranized local culture, certainly maintained

great activity, as in the time of Ezra. We find traces of this in later books (Daniel and Enoch). An echo of the thought of the more distant communities of Elam and Media probably reached Judea through them (the books of Esther and Tobit).

2. THE CRISIS OF MACCABEAN TIMES

Judea in the Power of the Seleucids

By the victory of Paneion in 198 the king of Syria, Antiochus III the Great, who belonged to the Seleucid dynasty, snatched Palestine from Ptolemy V of Egypt. Jerusalem quickly rallied to the conqueror, so he confirmed Judaism's previous immunities. The high priest Simon II could even undertake works of repair in the city and temple with the help of the royal treasury. In fact, in this district of the empire the cult of Yahweh had the status of a state religion. Under Seleucus IV, son of Antiochus III (187–175), this peace was disturbed by a minor incident when, being short of money, the king sent his minister Heliodorus to rob the the temple treasury. However, the attempt failed. A little later the same Heliodorus assassinated his master, and Antiochus IV, brother of Seleucus, became king of Syria (175–164). The confrontation of Hellenistic syncretism and Jewish tenacity would take place under him.

For some time a whole party of Jews, the merchants and members of the aristocracy, leaned towards Hellenism. Some had even become royal officials in the time of the Egyptian sovereignty. Separated by their Law from the pagans with whom they kept company, they passed for barbarians; hellenized, they gave the impression that they had attained civilization (Text 30). In a certain measure they were already open to the customs and language of the Greeks. But they never went beyond this, for the Law continued in force over them. But in 175 this party found a leader in the dynasty of the high priest itself. A brother of Onias III, who had taken the Greek name of Jason, profited from the change of rulers to intrigue and obtain the high priesthood by bribe. For, since the Persian era, the royal administration had reserved the right to name the high priests or to confirm them in their office, since they were recognized as the supreme heads of all the Jews. So long as the administration remained respectful of the Law and Jewish customs, this was no inconvenience. But under Antiochus IV, a convinced adept of religious syncretism which he wanted to make the religion of the empire, things went far differently.

Upon his return into Judea, Jason tried to Hellenize his people. He founded a gymnasium in Jerusalem, sent money to Tyre at the time of the quinquinnial games to offer a sacrifice to Hercules, and solemnly received Antiochus in the Jewish capital. These facts show his method well enough. Under the pretext of opening himself to the language and Greek civilization in the form it had in Syria, he practically abandoned monotheism and the Jewish Law (372). Soon Jason was supplanted by the schemer Menelaus, and the lot of the faithful Jews worsened. Not content to multiply his demands and sacrileges, Menelaus made himself the docile instrument of repression when Antiochus decided to Hellenize Judea by force, since things were going too slowly for his taste. In 169 the king pillaged the temple of Jerusalem to boost his weakened finances and Menelaus agreed to it.

The Persecution of Antiochus

Events then rushed headlong towards a climax. In 167 the monarch Apollonius brutally entered Jerusalem. He built a citadel there, the Acra, from which a Greek garrison could supervise the temple. Then a royal decree abolished the exemptions of the Jewish people which Antiochus III had recognized. The Mosaic Law lost all authority in Judea, and the common law of the empire supplanted it. Thus the renegade Jews of the Hellenizing party now played the role of loyal citizens and the traditionalists became rebels against those in power. The pagan cults were established in Jerusalem and bacchanalia were substituted for the Feast of Tabernacles. Finally, the temple was dedicated to the Olympian Zeus, whose worship the king wanted to impose in all his states.

The Olympian Zeus was identified with the supreme god

234

Baal-Shamem in Syria. In Judea, he was supposed to be identified with Yahweh, and in this spirit the temple was consecrated to him. The altar of Zeus, the "abomination of desolation" spoken of by Daniel and the book of Maccabees, stood in place of the altar of holocausts. Moreover, the king considered himself a visible manifestation of the national god, as shown in the title he gave himself, Epiphaneus. "Antiochus, god manifested [*epiphanes*], bringer-of-victory," is stamped on some of his coins. The worship of Zeus and of the king were to be one and the same. So Judaism now faced a totalitarian pagan state (*373*). The state religion was the problem, for the king would let it accommodate itself to worship rendered to the other gods, provided they were seen subordinate to Zeus. Israel could not permit this, for "Yahweh is unique" (*148*). Following the footsteps of the Hellenized Jews, some apostatized. But they were also martyrs (*374, 375*). A great number of Jews took refuge in the desert country where the police hounded them. To put an end to the resistance, the administration compelled the whole world monthly to participation in the official worship. The choice was obedience or death.

The Maccabean Revolt and Jewish Independence

In this tremendous crisis, some groups saw escape only in a divine intervention which, by ending the "present world" through sudden judgment, would institute the kingdom of God proclaimed by the prophets. This spirit was reflected in the book of Daniel (*377–383*). Others, more realistically, turned towards holy war and found in military heroism the practical expression of their faith. In 166, at Modin, the priest Mattathias gave the signal for revolt (*384*). He took refuge in the mountain strongholds and united the objectors around himself. After his death, action was directed by his son Judas, called Maccabee, which probably means "Hammer" (the surname was abusively extended to the whole family), who multiplied surprised attacks on the royal troops and Jewish apostates. The guerrillas defeated Syrian armies one after the other (*385, 386*). Then Judas entrenched himself south of Jerusalem, and the authorities resigned themselves to negotiating with him. Free to re-enter the capital, he purified the temple, and solemnly celebrated its dedication in December 164 (*387*). As Antiochus lay dying in Elam, in the autumn of the same year (*388, 389*), Judas made war on the surrounding countryside of Judea again, against the neighbors whom the Jewish renaissance had stirred up. He finally obtained an edict of toleration for his people (*162*), but in 160 war flared up again, and in spite of new feats of valor (*390*), Judas met his death in it (*391*).

Judas's brother Jonathan succeeded him as head of the Jews. Skillfully playing on the dissensions between the pretenders to the throne of Syria, he concluded advantageous treaties with them. Politically, the land was now autonomous. In October 152, Jonathan was named high priest by one of the pretenders, thus ousting the descendants of Sadoc who had held that office from the time of David to the murder of Onias III (170). But in 143 it was Jonathan who, in his turn, was killed in an ambush. Simon, the last son of Mattathias, followed the same policy. He chased the Greco-Syrian troops from the Acra of Jerusalem, maintained diplomatic connections with the Roman Senate whose help he sought, and was finally recognized by the king as "high priest, ethnarch, and strategos" of the Jews, concentrating the religious, civil, and military powers in his hands (140). He also came to a tragic end, for he was assassinated with two of his sons (134). His government began an era of independence for the Jews.

3. FROM THE ERA OF JEWISH INDEPENDENCE TO THE CHRISTIAN ERA

The Hasmonaean Dynasty

After Simon, power remained in the hands of Mattathias's family, the Hasmonaeans. John Hyrcanus (134–104), son of Simon, obtained confirmation of almost total independence from the king of Syria. Thanks to his fruitful military operations he enlarged his domains little by little, conquering Idumea and Samaria and destroying any schismatic temple. But this temporal renaissance of the nation had another side. The guiding spirit of the nation turned more and more from the religious purpose which the Maccabean wars had sought. John was a pompous and wordly ruler. If the aristocratic party of the Sadducees supported him, the Pharisees alienated themselves. As for the Essene party, they had probably been in opposition since Jonathan had become high priest.

The son of John Hyrcanus, Aristobulus I (104–103), took the title king. This added to the irritation of the Pharisees, for, faithful to Davidic messianism, they saw a sacrilegious usurpation in his action (Text 35). Under Alexander Jannaeus (103–76) the decadence of the dynasty accelerated, in spite of the prosperous appearances of the nation (Map 7). Cruel, debauched, preferring the life of the army camp to the service of the altar, the king shattered his opposition by violence. But after his death, on his own advice, his widow Alexandra (76–67) governed with the support of the Pharisees, who profited by introducing themselves into the supreme council, the Sanhedrin, in strength. Once Alexandra was gone the royalty and the high priesthood quarreled, each supported by rival parties, the Pharisees and the Sadducees. Then Rome intervened.

The Protectorate of Rome: Herod the Great

For more than a century Rome had nibbled at the possessions of the Syrian empire. During their war of independence the Jews had received more moral support than effective help from them. In 65 Pompey made himself master of Syria itself. In 63, when he had reached Damascus, the two Jewish parties sent a deputation, each begging him to support its cause. Pompey seized the opportunity to take a hand in Judean affairs. After storming Jerusalem where one party was entrenched, he organized the land his own way, respecting the religious exemptions which the Jews traditionally enjoyed. The last of the Hasmonaeans, custodians of a religious function deprived of any real political power, were no more than vassals of Rome.

The Idumean, Herod, owed his fortune to these circumstances. His father had been the minister of the Jewish kings. He himself had schemed in the service of Anthony to despoil the high priest Hyrcanus II of all political power (42). But profiting from the Parthian invasion, the last of the Hasmonaeans, Antigone, was recognized as king of Judea by these enemies of the Romans (40). Herod fled to Rome and then, in 39, he returned with a decree of Anthony and Octavian in his hand which made him king. Once installed by force of arms, he rid himself of all the descendants of the ancient royal family in a few years. Then, to conciliate his subjects, he beautified Jerusalem and undertook the rebuilding of the temple (19–18). A wise administrator but an unscrupulous tyrant, he caused ill-will, especially among the Pharisees (Texts 31 and 32). It was at the very end of his reign that, in silence and obscurity, Jesus was born at Bethlehem. Upon Herod's death (4 B.C.) there was a problem with the succession. Rome resolved the question by dividing his states among his sons Archelaus, Philip, and Antipas. When Archelaus was exiled to Gaul in 6 A.D., Judea became a Roman province governed by a procurator.

4. JUDAISM AND GRECO-ROMAN CIVILIZATION

The crisis of Maccabean times was a final purification for Judaism and established it forever in its particular vocation. It is true that the communities of the diaspora do not appear to have been directly influenced. But in assailing Judea the Syrian empire touched the heart of the Jewish institution. This was not only two civilizations face to face, the Greek and the Semitic, nor two tendencies within the Jewish people, the conservative and the progressive; but two totally incompatible religious currents. On the one side was ranged a many-branched paganism, accommodating, openly syncretistic, adoring the same forces of nature or of social life everywhere under different names. On the other was the obstinacy of a people without great political power, without cultural brilliance, but fiercely attached to its worship and its Law because they were founded upon the word of the Living God, the unique God.

In spite of the treason of a great number of Jews infected by modernity and a violent persecution, the political authority of the pagan empire had to bend before the spiritual strength of the faith as before the strength of arms. The tradition of the patriarchs, of Moses, of the prophets, of the builders of Judaism, was able to maintain itself. The rapid decline of the Hasmonaean dynasty showed that survival was not linked to ambiguous political restorations. In fact, its mission lay on another plane, that of eschatological longing, of preparation for the kingdom of God. In spite of the defeat it suffered, Hellenism did indirectly influence Judaism. Just as the civilizations of Canaan, Mesopotamia, and Persia had furnished the Jewish spirit rapidly assimilable materials, as means of expressing revelation and the life founded on it, so the Hellenistic civilization also furnished material. From this point of view the Jews of Palestine, defended by its Hebrew or Aramaic tongue, remained more closed to foreign influences than the Jews of the diaspora, but the interpenetration of cultures must not be minimized even in Judea. As for Alexandrian Judaism, not only did it translate the Bible into Greek, but it created a Greek language literature. Several of these literary works entered the collection of the sacred books. Nevertheless, even there Hellenistic thought had to respect the fundamental data of tradition, for in the eyes of the Jews tradition was not a purely human thing, but a deposit confided by God, over which men had no power at all.

Text 30

JUDAISM IN THE FACE
OF HELLENISM

A historian and student of Judaism makes this analysis of why the faith of many Jews underwent a crisis during the Greek era:

In the midst of the vicissitudes which pushed them back and forth between the hands of the Ptolemies and the Seleucids, many Jews lost confidence in the prospect of independence and were deluded over the prospect of dominating the nations as a society of elite leaders. The ideal held up by the interpreters of the Law was debased, and the tolerant and skeptical spirit of Hellenism infiltrated the middle classes, and especially the aristocracy. It could hardly have been otherwise, considering that the circle of Greek colonies and Hellenized cities grew more and more narrow around Judea. . . .

What struck the Jew from the very first in this Greek-oriented environment was the isolation into which his worship and Law had been plunged. For the Jew, marked out as a barbarian in the eyes of the Greeks, this isolation became unbearable, compared to a way of life which he found flowering the same way in each city. . . . Between the cities, between the kingdoms sprung from the empire of Alexander, there existed a common fund of idea, practices, and institutions which allowed the Greek or the Hellenized Oriental to feel at home wherever Hellenism had become the dominant civilization. . . . The unity of Hellenistic culture easily covered the traits which had but lately distinguished the Syrian, the Phoenician, the Idumean, the Philistine, and the settled Arab. Would the Jews be the only ones to resist the penetration of this culture? On the whole they were obstinate, for the hatred established by their Law between themselves and Hellenism had no equal among other peoples. Thus the party which wished to adhere to the civilization of the conquerors of the Orient had to decide to abrogate the Mosaic Law.

F. M. Abel, *Histoire de la Palestine*

240

Text 31

KING HEROD

The figure of Herod the Great weaves in and out of the first chapters of the Gospel. The following is an interesting portrait of his moral character.

As king, Herod was an intelligent Hellenistic ruler, a seeker after magnificence and display, fond of sumptuous buildings and of the material modernization of his domain. The realm existed, naturally, to serve the throne, and not vice versa; when this service was guaranteed and absolute, little else mattered. Herod knew that he was not loved by his Jewish subjects, and being intelligent, would have preferred to be loved, but this being impossible, there remained for him the principle: *oderint, dum metuant,* let them hate, provided they also fear me. Politically prudent, he hardly ever offended the religious sensibilities of his subjects. He wished to gain their favor by completely rebuilding their temple, but this was done only for reasons of internal politics, and was not a manifestation of his Yahwistic leanings; it simply fitted in well with his passion for sumptuous buildings. A Hellenist and a skeptic, while he was rebuilding Yahweh's temple he was also putting up temples in Palestine in honor (*horribile dictu*) of the living Roman emperor.

G. Ricciotti, History of Israel

Text 32

HEROD IN THE EYES OF A CONTEMPORARY

The Assumption of Moses was written between 7 and 30 A.D. In it Moses is supposed to have predicted the future of Israel (a standard procedure in the apocalypses). Thus he successively depits: the dynasty of Hasmonaean priest-kings, Herod, the sons of Herod, and the repression of Varrus (4 B.C.). He then turns towards the "last times" (compare *383*). The author probably belonged to the Essene sect. He did not recognize the priesthood of the Hasmonaeans and, a little later, bitterly criticized the Sadducees and Pharisees.

Then will arise before them kings who will govern. They will name themselves priests of the Most High God. They will work iniquity in the Holy of Holies.

An insolent king will succeed them, who will not be of the race of the priests. A man shameless and imprudent, he will govern them as they deserve. He will strike down their important men by the sword, and hide their bodies in secret places, so that it will not be known where they are. He will kill the old and young men, without sparing anyone. Thus fear of him will be great in all their land. He will carry out judgments on them as the Egyptians had carried out, during thirty-four years. And he will punish them.

He will give birth to sons who, by succeeding him, will hold back the power for a little time. In their regions will come the cohorts and a powerful king of the West. This one will vanquish them, and take them captive; he will burn by fire a part of their temple and will crucify them around their capital.

Then when these things will have been accomplished, the times will come to their end.

For the author, Herod is an executor of divine punishments, and all of the woes of Israel are the forerunners of the final crisis, which seemed near at hand.

Bibliography

See the various histories of Israel. Also see A. R. Burns, *Alexander the Great and the Hellenistic Empire* (New York 1947), and the Introduction to the Books of Maccabees in the *Jerusalem Bible*.

Study Guides

Study Judaism's motives for resisting Hellenism in the times of Antiochum Epiphanes. You will find help in the books recalling this crisis: Daniel (*377–383*), Judith (*392–395*), the two books of Maccabees (*372–376, 384–391*). Is this conflict analogous to the later opposition between the Roman empire and the Christian Church (see *Apoc.* 12–13; 17–19)? Even so, was not the relation between Church and state different in each period?

In retracing the great steps of the history of Israel, study the attitude adopted by the people of God in regard to the various human civilizations they contacted: Egyptian, Canaanite, Assyro-Babylonian, Persian, Greek. Did Israel not adopt compatible elements from each and yet reject the religious errors of each thanks to its attachment to the word of God? Is this act not the strength of the spiritual leaven of revelation? Is this not close to the essential originality of the Old Testament? Will not the same attitude be found once again in the Church? If it is not, do we not risk equivocation in speaking of a *Christian civilization* as if the message confided to the Church by Christ had the problems of civilization as its essential object, as if it were compatible with only one civilization?

323	Rivalry of the Diadochi	
301	Battle of Ipsus	Judea under the power of Egypt
198	Battle of Panium	Judea in the power of the Seleucids
175	Accession of Antiochus Epiphanes	Jason supplants Onias III
167		Persecution of Antiochus
166		Revolt of Mattathias
Oct. 164	Death of Antiochus	
Dec. 164		Purification of the Temple
163	Struggle for the throne of Syria	
162		Edict of Toleration
160		Death of Judas Maccabeus: Jonathan succeeds him
152		Jonathan high priest
143	Period of civil war in Syria	Death of Jonathan
140		Simon, high priest, ethnarch and strategos
134		Death of Simon: Accession of John Hyrcanus
103		Alexander Jannaeus, king of the Jews
83	Armenian occupation of Syria	
76		Alexandra
69	Roman intervention in Syria	
67		Civil War
65	Syria, Roman province	
63		Pompey takes Jerusalem
40	Parthian invasion	Antigonus, king of Judea
39		Herod, king of Judea
30	Egypt, Roman province	
19		Rebuilding of the Temple
4		Death of Herod
A.D. 6		Judea a Roman province

244

XII.

SACRED LITERATURE IN THE HELLENISTIC ERA

THERE was no break between the sacred literature of the Persian era and that of the following centuries. The wisdom genre enjoyed continued popularity but, taking root in the Alexandrian milieu, Jewish wisdom made use of the Greek language and came into contact with philosophy. Prophetism definitely gave way to the apocalyptic genre, which would consequently occupy a large place in Jewish literature. Historical writing became influenced by Hellenistic models. And didactic narratives were in vogue, for they were the preferred way of teaching doctrine. The picture would be incomplete if we did not glance at the abundant extra-biblical writings which testify to ancient Jewish tradition, just as the works of the Fathers of the Church testify to Christian tradition. It was within the framework of this tradition that the New Testament was born.

1. THE END OF PROPHETISM

Pseudo-Zechariah

After the end of the 5th century there were no active prophets like those of earlier times. Institutional prophetism was forbidden, because it was too like the pagan prophetism of Cybèle

(*Zech.* 13, 2–6). The classic prophetic themes were taken up again in anonymous or pseudonymous writings, similar to the later passages of the book of Isaiah. Some scholars link the Apocalypse of Isaiah (*Is.* 24–27), which has already been treated above, with this era. These scholars' case for the second part of Zechariah is more certain (*Zech.* 9–14). This little collection must have been composed in the 4th century, around the time of the conquests of Alexander, for it seems to allude to them. Its style is labored, the thought obscure; more than once its historical references turn to riddle, as in the allegory of the shepherds (*Zech.* 11, 4–17; 13, 7–9), where the Messiah is described as a peaceful king, just and humble (*328*): a portrait whose traits Christ will intentionally take up again on Palm Sunday (*Mt.* 21, 1–9). But the central theme is the eschatological reign of God, when he will establish himself in Jerusalem and the remnant of the foreign nations will be joined to the people of God (*352*). In this part of the book the writer was clearly inspired by Ezekiel (*205*).

The Book of Baruch

The Greek Bible collected many texts which seem to have arisen in the diaspora but are not linked with Jeremiah under the name of Baruch, the prophet's secretary. In this book are a collective confession of sins (1, 1—3, 8), which recalls the book of Ezra (*294*) and imitates Daniel (*Dn.* 9, 4–19); a short wisdom passage (3, 9–4, 4), identifying divine wisdom and the Law; a prophetic address to Jerusalem (4, 5—5, 9), in which the hope of eschatological restoration is expressed; a diatribe against idolatry (*6*), presented as a "letter of Jeremiah." We can see that these fragments belong to different genres and that ready use was made of a pseudonym in this era. The address to Jerusalem (*331*), inspired by the *Message of Consolation* and *Isaiah* 60–62, shows the influence of these texts during the centuries following the exile, for their reading helped animate the eschatological longing of dispersed Judaism.

246

2. REFLECTION OF HUMAN DESTINY

Qoheleth, or Ecclesiastes

We have seen how the problems of happiness, individual retribution, and human destiny preoccupied minds during the Persian era. A pessimistic and critical current, prone to retain the contradictions opposing the traditional theory to reality, had begun with the book of Job, which in the 3rd century found a follower in the work of a sage who wrote under the pseudonym of Qoheleth, Ecclesiastes. The point of departure for his reflection was not the problem of evil, as it had been for Job, but an acute feeling of universal futility. In the perspective of the Sinai covenant the Israelite hoped for temporal retribution from God. The enjoyment of this world, a long life, numerous descendants, riches, esteem, were the rewards promised to each one who observed the Law and conducted himself wisely *(43, 152, 313)*. Even if the most elevated souls valued the joy of being with God above all else *(314, 318, 319)*, the realism of Jewish thought could not abandon the hope for corporeal goods contained in so many eschatological oracles of the prophets. But Qoheleth coldly saw these much coveted goods at face value and decided they were not worth striving for. Life is deceiving! Pleasure, glory, love, money, even wisdom, all are vanity and chase after the wind. There is no justice here on earth; no sanction for human conduct. All is directed towards death and finds its end there *(338–342)*. Nor does he throw any light on this bitter reflection which strove to be clear and free from illusion.

In spite of this acid critique, Qoheleth was not a religious skeptic. He believed in God, accepted all the doctrines revealed by his word. He insisted that there is in man a craving for happiness which nothing on earth can satisfy, and since he does not know of any life after death, he can only conclude that man can freely abandon himself to his passions, as Mesopotamian wisdom had (Text 28). In his eyes the lot of the just man is not really enviable, since he too must die *(342)*; but the lot of the sinner is worse, though there have been some cases where the sanctions had apparently failed. Thus he said, let a man use the joys God gives him with moderation in his life of deception! Let him beware of too great a love for knowledge or wisdom (*338, 342*). This curt strong morality accorded with the state of the question when it arose, but it is clearly not the morality of the Gospel, nor even that of the book of Job. It is, just the same, a common-sense truth, since it still lacked the perspective of eternal joy. But to come to this latter revelation the Jewish soul had to experience the emptiness of worldly joys. If this world sufficed, why should he stretch towards the "world to come"? To give more bite to his reflections, the author recalls Solomon himself, the king crowned with glory and initiator of the sapiential genre. It is he who proclaimed the vanity of riches, pleasure, and wisdom. This paradox is not without humor. Even so, his style is prosaic and lacks brilliance. It is the style of the discussion between the sages over a tough problem, the author's style of discussion with himself. Some expressions reveal a superficial contact with Greek wisdom. Besides, in the final form of the book the original reflections of Qoheleth are intermingled with diverse maxims belonging to the more classical tradition. It is not known whether they are to be attributed to the same author or to a disciple who edited his work adding an epilogue to it. But it makes the book very disconnected.

The Book of Tobit

The book of Tobit is not an historical account, but a narrative for edification. Its program developed freely according to the lessons the author wanted to draw from it. Mesopotamian wisdom also used such a genre, in which is found the celebrated fictional work of Ahiqar, the legendary wise man of Assyria. Besides maxims and moral discourses it used the marvelous to teach a lesson in wisdom. Thus Tobit, the father of Tobias, was an Israelite deported into Assyria in 722. Though at first he was showered with honors, he was soon persecuted for his fidelity to duty. The crowning blow came when he lost his sight. The very beginning of the story presents the theme of the just man put to the test, just as the book of Job had before (*343*). With the hero begging God to remove him from this world, the scene shifts to Ecbatana in Media, where Sara, whose seven husbands have died on their wedding nights, is also begging God to deliver her from the cause of this affliction (*344*). The simultaneous granting of the two requests is the connecting thread in what is to follow. For lo and behold, Tobit sends his son to bring back a sum of money from Rages of Media. Tobias leaves, accompanied by a guide who is none other than the angel Raphael (*346*). At Ecbatana Tobias marries Sara on Raphael's advice (*347*), and on his return he gives his father a marvelous remedy which heals him (*348*). Tobit, in a canticle of thanksgiving, exalts Jerusalem, hope of the scattered Israelites (*332*).

The book is rich in doctrine. The very theme of the account is based on some great religious themes. There are, for example, the theme of the just man put to the test, which the author treats optimistically after passing a test in which the soul was refined, and the just man recovers all he had been temporarily deprived of (*343, 348*); the theme of prayer granted, which here guides the unfolding of history (*344*); the theme of marriage, understood chastely according to the Law of God (*344, 347*), (on this point, the Jewish ideal reached a level very close to that of the New Testament); the theme of angels and demons, whose struggle forms the backdrop for human life (*346, 347*). The author was also visibly concerned with exalting certain moral virtues: the sense of family, respect for the dead, the duty of almsgiving. This results in the portrait of Tobit (*343*), and in the recommendations attributed to him at the moment of his son's departure (345). The style of the books of wisdom is seen throughout this section, and the morality the old man taught his son is not far from that of the Gospel. The eschatological hope expressed in the final canticle (*332*) echoes the *Message of Consolation* and *Isaiah* 60–62, as does the book of Baruch. The dispersed Jews lived with eyes turned towards their spiritual capital, which would finally become the center for the entire human race.

The author consciously imitates the accounts of the patriarchal times, whose atmosphere he wishes to recall. The narration possesses a penetrating charm—a pleasant sugar-coating for the lessons taught. Interspersed canticles and prayers introduce a lyric note, and very numerous picturesque and homey details decorate the narrative. The world of men and that of supernatural beings, angels, and demons are mingled in a most natural way. The book could certainly rest on historical tradition, but its purpose and genre belong to another order. Many passages link it explicitly to the story of Ahiqar, the cousin of Tobit. It probably arose in the 3rd century, and must have originated in the eastern diaspora, though the redaction could have been made in Palestine. For a long time we knew only of the Greek translation, in two very different recensions. But since 1952 Aramaean and Hebrew fragments have been discovered in the caves of Qumrân, near the Dead Sea.

3. THE WISDOM OF BEN-SIRA, OR ECCLESIASTICUS

The Origin of the Book

Jesus Ben-Sira, or the Siracide, is a master who belonged to the school of wisdom, like the editor of Proverbs, though historically they were probably separated by the reform of Ezra. And Jesus Ben-Sira puts more emphasis upon the Law as the sole source of true wisdom. He is the ancestor of those doctors of the Law whose shadow weaves in and out of the Gospels. It is difficult to say whether he was a lay doctor or whether he belonged to the sacerdotal caste, as his admiration of Aaron (45, 6–22) and the high priest Simon, his contemporary (50, 1–21), could lead one to think. Be that as it may, he received a group of wisdom-thirsty youths in his house of studies and he gave them a traditional teaching to guide them through life. He sketched the portrait of the ideal scribe which gives us a picture of himself (349). He was an eloquent master, in love with the Scriptures, perhaps a little loquacious, one whose fame was on every tongue. Certainly between 200 and 180 he collected the fruit of his reflections and experience into one work.

His book echoes the calm age in which he led a good life

under the tolerant sceptre of the Ptolemies. We should not look for a logical order here. The first part (1, 1—42, 14) is a series of juxtaposed fragments touching just about everything. Nevertheless, the sayings here are better grouped by subjects than the book of Proverbs. The second part (42, 15—50, 29) is a continuous meditation on the works of God in creation and history. The appendix (51) includes a canticle of thanksgiving and an alphabetical poem on the pursuit of wisdom. The whole book was translated into Greek by the grandson of the author towards the end of the 2nd century. Alexandrian Judaism bequeathed this translation to the Church, which formerly used the book for the instruction of neophytes (hence the name Ecclesiasticus). A part of the Hebrew text has been found, but there are many variants between it and the different versions.

The Teaching of Ben-Sira

Ben-Sira prides himself neither on his originality nor on newness. Facing the miseries of life or death, he is not uneasy like the author of Job or Qoheleth. He knows them, it seems, but he has passed them by to find in his faith the secret of serenity (353, 354). He is directly linked to the school of the Proverbs. He has the same realistic view of the world and its inequalities (360), places the same value on friendship (361), and his sense of family (362, 364), and his ideas on the education of children (363) and on the opposition between wisdom and folly (365), are the same as those of the book of Proverbs. The principles of conduct he teaches blend with those of the sapiential tradition, freely mingling moral considerations and counsels for good education (366), since a well-rounded man must excel in everything. But man must not deceive himself on this point, that wisdom is essentially religious. Its source is God and it is nourished by the fear of God (350). If it brings happiness to man (351), it is because God rewards those who fear him (359). Besides, wisdom begins in the divine Law, which should direct the Jew's conduct in every circumstance.

Ben-Sira did not have that legalistic concept of Law for which Christ would reproach certain doctors. A thousand details prove that he understood the Law in the light of the commentaries of Deuteronomy and the prophets. Thus he places much importance in the social virtues of sincerity (*366*), mercy (*367*), pardon of offenses (*368*), without which there would be no sincere religion (*371*). The attitude assumed by man in the face of this Law is the measure of his attitude in regard to God himself. So a man must be conscious of his responsibility and remember the judgment (*356*). He must be converted (*357*) and now adopt an attitude of humility (*369*), and of confidence (*370*), for God is above all merciful (*358*). This practical wisdom definitely goes a long way in its spiritual demands.

The author of Proverbs had personified divine wisdom. And in the same way, Ben-Sira puts it on stage to sing its own praises (*352*). His doctrine on this point is a mark of progress. It more explicitly identifies Wisdom with the word, the Law, the divine glory which has itself come to reside in Israel. Likewise, he innovates timidly when he integrates history to the sapiential reflection in his praise of the Fathers, making the great figures of the past pass in review before the eyes of his disciples.

The Balance-Sheet of Tradition

Such a book does not lend itself to summary since it treats of everything, and that without order. It should not be seen as a major work, either for its style or its thought. It presents no new problems, and often no new solutions. But this is precisely what is interesting: the writer of Sirach presents a balance-sheet of the Jewish tradition of his era. He echoes all the Scriptures. Through his work we can see the values nourishing the Jewish soul as it was about to enter into conflict with Hellenism. Disdaining foreign wisdom, it lived on its own attainments. Even the disquiet caused by certain problems in the preceding century seem to have subsided. It was wholly ignorant of the after-life, and optimistically reaffirmed the thesis of the happiness of the just here on earth. Eschatology translated itself into fervent prayer for the restoration of Israel (36, 1–17), but the longing did not burst into flame. For is not God the master of time? The book does not foresee that twenty years

252

later Judea would be drenched in fire and blood or that supported by the visions of Daniel, religious souls would long for the great judgment, for the resurrection of the dead and the eternal reign of God. It had no inkling that the Maccabees would undertake a holy war, and that the aristocracy would apostatize.

As for the book's style, it has neither the spirit of Job nor the incisive clarity of Proverbs which it imitates. It has a good classical style, florid, a little overdone, rich in well-turned phrases, a minor work of art but worth reading, engaging, and easy to read, often even poetic. On the whole it is very close to the sapiential genre of the New Testament.

4. THE BOOK OF DANIEL

A Message of Hope

Beneath its apparent unity the book of Daniel is a composite. Its first part (*Dn.* 1–6) is a third-person narrative, whereas the second part (*Dn.* 7–12) is in the form of autobiography. And the Greek version includes some supplements (3, 24—90; 13–14) whose originals have been lost. Essentially it is a message of hope addressed by the inspired author to his compatriots under trial, around 165, in the heart of the persecution of Antiochus. Two literary genres intermingle in it, the didactic narrative and the apocalyptic.

The tradition about Daniel, a Jew deported into Babylonia in 598, clearly originated in the eastern diaspora. But it is impossible to follow its development before the principal author of the book gave it its definitive form. The diverse accounts must first have existed separately, for the Greek version (1st century) has gathered parts of it which this author did not know, or which he knew under another form (Daniel in the lions' den: *Dn.* 3 and 14, 23–42). In each part the classification of materials is made according to a supposed chronological order, which presents the following succession: Nebuchadnezzar, Baltasar the Chaldean, Darius the Mede, Cyrus the Persian. This is clearly a conventional representation of history. Also,

Nebuchadnezzar and the other kings are hardly more than literary types. The author presents them to draw out lessons, and the narratives he constructs have one point which is aimed at the people of the time of Antiochus, with the exception of the Greek supplements (*Dn.* 13–14), which are more independent of circumstances.

Daniel and his companions refused to eat impure foods, and this practice gave them extraordinary wisdom (*377*), for to eat of foods forbidden by the Law was an act required of the Jews by their Greek persecutors (*374*). Nebuchadnezzar, because of his pride, saw his reason begin to degenerate (*378*), and thus God will destroy the king who raises himself up against him. The tragic end of Belshazzar (*379*) is a divine judgment which foreshadows that of Antiochus, whereas the deliverance of the faithful persecuted for their faith is prefigured by the two accounts of the young men cast into the furnace and Daniel in the lions' den (*380*). The key to these narratives is furnished by the history of Maccabean times. Not that all the sections had to be created, but the traditional data had to be adapted here to present-day problems. On the other hand, the Greek supplements retained a different character, for they exalted the Jewish ideal of conjugal fidelity (*Dn.* 13), or illustrated the polemic against idolatry (*Dn.* 14; see *Bar.* 6).

The Apocalypse of Daniel

The book also includes materials of the apocalyptic genre. The apocalypse (or revelation) came from the eschatological oracles relating to the day of Yahweh. By literary convention the author puts his prophetic message under the patronage of some man of the past: Enoch, Moses, Baruch, Ezra . . . The hero receives revelations concerning the end of time, that is to say, the times in which the author is living, seen in the perspective of an ever imminent end of time. The fabric of the message is made up of conventional language, woven of reminiscences of Scripture, strange symbols piled up to the point of incoherence, visions, and angelic apparitions.

The prophet's spokesman is the same Daniel whom the

book's didactic narratives had placed on the stage. His clairvoyance and wisdom are constantly opposed to the powerlessness of the magi and astrologers of Chaldea, who were famed in antiquity for their knowledge of the future (*377–379*). This is an indirect polemic against pagan divination, for God alone knows the secret of time and reveals it through his prophets. Daniel interprets dreams (*377, 378*) and the warning visions (*379*). He himself has visions, which an angel explains to him (*381, 383*). He manifests the hidden meaning of the ancient Scriptures (*382*). It is probable that the author occasionally used materials antedating the persecution of Antiochus, but he brought them up to date. In the book from the Babylonian empire to that of Antiochus the succession of empires hurtles towards catastrophe, for the day was approaching when God would destroy the powers of this world to institute his reign on earth. This unique message is seen behind the dreams of the statue and the cosmic tree, the cryptic writing on the wall and the oracle of the seventy weeks, the visions of the four beasts and the Son of man, of the Ram and the he-goat, without counting the grand final vision (*Dn.* 10–12) which explains all history from the time of the Persians to 165.

Eschatology and the Theology of History

In taking a man of the past as his spokesman, the author could step back from the present day to show the outcome of a large slice of history, as foreseen and sovereignly directed by God. Human history, past, present, and to come, appeared to him as a gigantic struggle between God, who pursues his plan of salvation, and the hostile forces incarnate in the proud pagan empires. As this struggle reached its culmination, God pronounced his judgment, overthrew his adversaries, and established his reign here on earth. In this religious interpretation of the facts the present crisis is always seen as the prelude to the imminent *dénouement*. This is a law of the apocalyptic genre. As for the future, all the levels are intertwined: the judgment of the current oppressor and the final judgment are one thing, and the approaching deliverance of the persecuted and the eschatological salvation flow together. The short-term promises, which the victories of Judas Maccabaeus and the death of Antiochus fulfilled, were less important than the prophetic announcement of the definitive judgment and salvation.

But this salvation is depicted through symbols. The reign of God is the rock crushing the statue and changing it into a mountain (377), it is the Son of man who arrives on the clouds and strikes the power of the evil beasts (378). The people of God are not forgotten, for the saints of the Most-High will participate in the royalty of the Son of man (378). Those put to death for the faith sleep in sheol and will rise from it to enter into life eternal (383). This promise of the resurrection, symbolized by the deliverance of the young men cast into the furnace and Daniel thrown into the lions (380), resolved the agonizing problem of the suffering and death of the just. In this eschatology the images of national triumph, of temporal glory and terrestrial happiness, ceded to the grandiose vision of a transfigured world. The Gospel of the reign of God which Jesus will preach will not be understandable except to the souls formed at this school.

5. THE BOOKS OF JUDITH AND ESTHER

The book of Judith unfolds in an atmosphere of apocalyptic struggle, recalling the atmosphere of the book of Daniel. Was its point of departure a tradition relating to the revolt of western Asia against Artaxerxes III, around 350? This is possible, but uncertain and a secondary question. The accumulation of anachronisms opening the book (392) quickly tell us that we are faced with something other than history. The parallelism of the situation described with that of the 2nd century is the convincing argument that what we have here is a didactic narrative.

This Nebuchadnezzar who wants to dominate the whole world and to make himself adored as a god (392) is not the historical one (176), but a literary type, already met in the book of Daniel (Dn. 1–4), where it was easy to recognize Antiochus Epiphanes (373). But, as in Maccabean times, only a single people dares to resist his sacrilegious design: the Jewish people, a people invincible as long as it is faithful to its God (*393*). Their resistance is incarnated in a widow with the symbolic name Judith, "the Jewess" (*394*). Relying upon the strength of God, she conceived a plan to triumph by ruse. She went to the enemy camp, seduced the general Holofernes, killed him, and thus delivered her people (*395*).

Judith, in a certain way, personifies the spirit of resistance and warlike courage which sustained the Maccabean revolt. A tone of holy war, at the same time religious and chauvinistic, echoes through this book. It forms a companion to the book of Daniel, but has a different outlook. Not content to wait for God himself to smash the tyrant and establish his reign here on earth, and knowing that God used human instruments to realize his purposes, the author of Judith believed that the strength of faith must flower in military valor. But this must not stifle men's longing for salvation as a grace. So in Judith, Israel was not delivered by force of arms, but by the hand of a weak woman (*394*). This lesson has not lost its value, though the theme of the book is closely linked to the conditions of the life of Judaism; and beginning with the New Testament the idea of a holy war must now be transposed onto another plane (*Eph.* 6, 10–17).

The Book of Esther

The book of Esther probably first appeared in a community of the eastern diaspora, between the 4th and 2nd centuries. Possibly it preserved the memory of an historical incident which took place under the reign of Xerxes. But in spite of its precise local color the incident is surely fictionalized. This is a secondary question and can safely be left to the discussions of historians. In point of fact, the book is a didactic account with a twofold purpose: to show a providential deliverance of Israel, and to justify the Jews' adoption of the feast of *Purim* (or of Lots) on the 14th of Adar. This feast, which is of disputed origin, was introduced first into Oriental Judaism, and does not seem to have been adopted in Judea until after the war of independence. It was more or less confused with the annual celebration of the victory of Judas Maccabaeus over the general Nicanor on the 13th of Adar (*390*). It was a day of nationalistic and religious joy when God was thanked for Israel's triumph over the enemies who had plotted her destruction, a theme which was open to multiple applications. The book of Esther concretizes it and was the text read on the day of Purim.

The book of Esther shows the direction of Jewish thought in the last centuries before the Christian era, particularly beginning with the Maccabean wars—religious nationalism. The idea of a providence directing history is present throughout, but the original Hebrew nowhere mentions it explicitly. That is why supplements which are preserved in the Greek translation (*396–398*) were added as an afterthought correcting this impression. Under this form the book has been received as sacred Scripture in the Christian Church.

6. THE BOOKS OF MACCABEES

The First Book

Hasmonaean times saw the reflowering of historical writing in two works of very different characters. The first was written after the death of John Hyrcanus (*104*). Its author set out to recount the course of events which led from the oppression of Antiochus (*175*) to the death of the last son of Mattathias (*134*). A convinced partisan of the Hasmonaean dynasty, he composed his book to the glory of the heroes who directed the war of independence, and to the glory of God who gave them success. Well informed on the events, he recounted with fair accuracy the feats of Judas Maccabaeus and his brothers. Instinctively he returned to the concerns and literary forms of the ancient historians of Israel, whose procedure he occasionally imitates. But he was not content merely to compile his sources. He composed a continuous narrative, in the manner of the Greek historians.

His images are sober and precise, like those in the persecution of Antiochus (*373, 374*), the revolt of Mattathias (*384*),

258

the purification of the temple (387), and the death of Judas (391) and of Antiochus (388) where his chronology seems faulty. If he highlights the guiding action of providence, it was always in a discrete manner (385). However, this valuable book was not retained by the learned men of Palestine in their list of the holy books. The animosity of the Pharisees against the Hasmonaean dynasty explains this exclusion. Also, though written in Hebrew, the book has come down to us in its Greek version only.

The Second Book

The second book of Maccabees has nothing in common with the first. It is a summary, written in Greek around 124, from a work of Jason of Cyrene composed a little after 160. However, the original source is lost today. The period of time it covers is very brief: from 175 to160.

A work of edification based upon history, the book often takes a certain liberty with the factual details. It does contain some excellent information (372), but it is developed for moral instruction, by going back to the literary processes of what Hellenism called pathetic history. Thus it reported the death of Antiochus (389) and that of Nicanor (390) in an ample and grandiloquent style, and the accounts of the martyrs' deaths (374, 375) were a pretext for edifying sermons. In contrast to the first book, its narrations are liberally ornamented with marvelous details which strike the imagination of the reader (386, 390). All these elements date it. But taken as it is, the book does show, in its own way, the religious meaning of the Maccabean wars. Also, explicit affirmation of the resurrection and eternal life for the martyrs is found in it (376). The author thus echoes the message of the book of Daniel (383).

7. THE GREEK VERSION OF THE BIBLE

The translation of the Bible into Greek for the faithful of the community of Alexandria was done by stages beginning in the 3rd century and starting with the books of the Pentateuch. The

INTRODUCTION TO THE BIBLE

version is called the Septuagint because, according to an ancient legend, it was translated by seventy-two old Jews, commissioned by King Ptolemy. Certain later works have been integrally preserved only here. They are Judith, the Maccabees, Baruch, Tobit, Ecclesiasticus, and certain parts of Daniel and Esther. This version has great importance, not only because of its antiquity, but especially because it was the biblical text used by the Apostolic Church, beginning from the moment the Gospel was preached to the Greek-speaking Jews and to the pagans living around them. For example, St. Paul and St. Luke usually follow it in citing the Scriptures. The religious language of the New Testament (in Greek) was also largely borrowed from it. Many ancient ecclesiastical authors held the translation to be inspired, but this point is still disputed. The Septuagint is nonetheless the authorized representation of the Alexandrian Jewish tradition. By this title it must be cited in a history of biblical revelation and of the holy books, for it marks a further step in the development of revelation. It also testifies to a certain doctrinal progress over the original Hebrew on certain points. In fact, as literal as it generally is, it sometimes contains interpretations manifesting Jewish thought on the threshold of the Christian era—for example, the translation of the prophecy of *Isaiah* 7, 14: "Behold the Virgin shall conceive and bring forth a son" (*123*).

8. THE WISDOM OF SOLOMON

The Origin and Purpose of the Book

This book, written in Greek in Alexandria between 80 and 30 B.C., deliberately put itself under the patronage of Solomon, the sage par excellence. By this fiction the anonymous sage hoped to stress the traditional character of his doctrine. His compatriots were exposed to a persecuting power and the peril of idolatry and he wished to warn them against this twofold danger of apostasy. In a long parallel between the just and the impious man (*Wis.* 1–5), he meditated on human destiny and scrutinized the mystery of individual retribution (*399–401*).

260

Then he put a hymn on the lips of Solomon (*Wis.* 6–9), praising wisdom as the source of all goods (*402*). Finally, in a long historical section (*Wis.* 10–19), he showed the directive action of wisdom in sacred history. Thus, by nearly unnoticeable transition, he arrived at a parallel between the Hebrews and the Egyptians illustrating the preceding parallel of the just and impious man. This last section, certainly the most ancient in the book, constitutes a free *midrash* on the narratives of the exodus (*404, 405*). Polemic considerations on the origin and folly of idolatry are also scattered (*403*) through the book, and in it we catch an echo of the synagogical preaching in Alexandrian circles.

The Book's Doctrine

As heir to the whole sapiential tradition the book of Wisdom marks an advance in revelation. In the first place, it cleared up the problem of individual retribution, no longer seeing it from the perspective of the present life (*252, 313*), but in the perspective of the divine visitation (*400*), that is, of the great judgment which would come to close history and inaugurate the "world to come" (*401*). Then the just would receive the immortality for which God had created man from the beginning (*399*). Then too, the book's reflections on the divine wisdom (*402*), while not yet seen as a distinct person in God, very directly prepared for the presentation of Christ as the Word and Wisdom of God. Also, the communication of the divine wisdom to man, which makes him a friend of God, foreshadowed the doctrine of sanctifying grace. Finally, the meditation on the history of the people of God which closes the book (*404, 405*) shows the propensity of Alexandrian Judaism for searching past history for proper examples to illustrate very doctrine, a process which will be widely used by the Fathers of the Church.

Though drawn up in a Greek milieu, the book of Wisdom is an essentially Jewish work, and an inspired work forming part of the Scriptures. Wisdom also shows, in its own particular way, the victory of Jewish tradition over Hellenism. The books opposition to pagan idolatry is absolute (*403*), but it is still

261

quite evidently open to Hellenistic culture. Retaining Hellenism's compatible elements, it turned them against the paganism to which they had been coupled. For example, it uses the language and the concepts of popularized Greek philosophy to express certain traditional doctrines. Thus it speaks of the soul and of the body (*402*), of immortality and incorruptibility (*399*), in terms which would not shock the educated men of Alexandria. But this translated concept of man is free of any Greek dualism where the spiritual soul was opposed to an essentially evil body, for it explicitly refers to the first chapters of Genesis (*399*). Wisdom's idea of the soul is still that of the Old Testament, where the word concretely designates the entire human person.

Even more characteristic is the sage's promise of everlasting life to the just (*400, 401*). It is sometimes said that the Platonic concept of the immortal soul facilitated the progress of revelation on this point, but in reality eternal life was essentially linked to the context of the eschatological judgment, as it had been in the book of Daniel (*383*) and in the other Jewish apocalypses (book of Enoch). The book's silence on the resurrection of the body is a tactical silence, for to speak of it would have flown in the face of Greek sensibilities, for whom this idea would be unintelligible (*Acts* 17, 31–32; *1 Cor.* 15, 12). But the same silence was kept in regard to the time-gap between death and the divine visitation. The important thing was to make the traditional Jewish eschatology attractive to pagans of good will, who were already attracted to monotheism. Thus Judaism affirmed both its originality and its power of assimilation, its solidity and its conquering strength, in a world where the ferment of ideas generally moved towards syncretism. Christianity would do the same when it developed its apologetics and theology.

9. EXTRA-BIBLICAL JEWISH LITERATURE

All inspired literature was collected into the Bible, and the Septuagint translation made it known even in the literate circles of the Greek world, while the Jewish diaspora of the Mesopotamian and Iranian Orient diffused it in the Aramaean spoken there. But side by side with it another abundant literature also developed in the diverse surroundings of Judaism, around the turn of our era. Through it we can discover the living milieu in which the New Testament was born.

The Old Testament Apocrypha

As early as the end of the Old Testament, some more ancient tendencies were continued which had already been visible in Deuteronomy (*139–142*) and the priestly sacred history (*184–188*). For the biblical books loved to put themselves under the patronage of the heroes of the past. Ecclesiastes (*338*), Daniel (*381, 382*), Wisdom (*402*), and one edition of the book of Tobit (*343*) used this current procedure, so it is no surprise to find a good number of other books, notably the apocalypses and "testaments," using it. The name *apocrypha* given them should be abandoned, as should the term *pseudepigrapha* which the Jews and Protestants prefer. The book of *Enoch* (Texts 33 and 37) is in reality a compilation, whose most ancient pieces date back to Daniel. The books of *Jubilees,* the *Testaments of the Twelve Patriarchs* (Text 36), and the *Assumption of Moses* (Text 32) are linked to the Essene sect. On the other hand, we find the spirit of Phariseeism in the *Psalms of Solomon* (Text 35), the apocalypses of *Ezra* and *Baruch,* and perhaps the *Ascension of Isaiah* too. The composition of these books took place from Maccabean times to the end of the 1st century A.D. As works of instruction and edification they exercised a profound influence on various Jewish circles.

The Literature of Palestinean Judaism

The greater part of the apocrypha belong to two currents of thought, the Essene or the Pharisee. The first has become directly accessible through the discovery in the caves of Qumrân, near the Dead Sea, of manuscripts hidden there in the time of the Jewish War (around 70 A.D.). This first-hand documentation is composed of, among other things, various rules of the organization of the sect (*Manual of Discipline, Damascus Document, Manual of Discipline for the Holy War*), religious hymn-

263

meditations, some commentaries on Scripture, and so forth (Text 34). All the texts discovered have not as yet been published. Pharisaism has left us nothing as ancient. But since, after 70, it took the guidance of Judaism in hand, the works composed or collected in the rabbinic milieu are strongly colored by its thought. The "traditions of the ancients" rejected by Jesus (*Mk*. 7, 1–13) were later turned into compilations called the *mishna* (end of the 2nd century), the *tosephta,* and the *talmuds* (Text 36). The commentaries on Scripture elaborated in the synagogal preaching and in the rabbinic schools form the various *midrashim* (plural of *midrash*). Finally, the Aramaean interpretation of the biblical texts which always followed their liturgical reading was fixed in the *targums* (Text 34). Through this documentation the spirit of teachers contemporary with Jesus becomes accessible to us, and even though the works were edited well after Christ, they have only gathered up a tradition long since fixed in its essentials.

The Literature of Alexandrian Judaism

Besides the Greek translation of the Bible and the apocrypha, and some inspired books, Alexandrian Judaism produced an entire religious literature of its own. It has its historians (Demetrios, Eupolemes), its poets (Exekiel the tragedian, the *Sybilline Books*), its apologists (*The Letter of Aristeus,* which includes the legend of the translation of the Septuagint), its moralists (the third and fourth books of Maccabees). The most important work is that of the philosopher Philo of Alexandria, born about 20 B.C., who tried to unite biblical revelation and Greek thought in one synthesis. The influence of his work, though attenuated, is found in the Letter to the Hebrews, and especially in the works of Clement of Alexandria and Origen. Finally, the historian Flavius Josephus must be mentioned (1st century A.D.). To him we owe the *Jewish Antiquities* (Texts 41 and 43) and the *Jewish War,* as well as an apologetic work *Contra Apion.* For the historian of the New Testament this documentation gives an idea of the intellectual life of the Jewish communities of the diaspora in the Greek world, the very ones in which the Gospel would spread rapidly in apostolic times and from which it will go out to find followers in the pagan world.

Text 33

THE HOPE OF LIFE ETERNAL

At the end of the Old Testament period the hope of entering into eternal life on the last day resolved the problem of individual retribution. The apocrypha largely echo the last of the inspired books on this point. The last part of the collection of Enoch (the *Book of Exhortation and Cursing*) speak of it in these terms:

Fear not, just souls!
 Have confidence, you who die in justice!
Do not be troubled lest your souls
 descend into hell in pain,
if during life your bodies of flesh
 were not rewarded according to your virtue. . . .

When you die, sinners say of you:
"As we die, the just die also,
 And what profit do they draw from their works?
See! They die as we do in pain and distress,
 and what have they more than we?
From now on, we are equals:
 What do they receive, what will they see forever?
See! They are dead, they too,
 and henceforth they will no longer see the light. . . ."
Be it so! I swear to you, O just,
 by the honor of the Great and Glorious,
of the Powerful who has the rule,
 by his very greatness, I swear to you!

265

I know a mystery,
I have read it in the heavenly record-books;
I have seen the sacred books,
and on the subject of the just I have found written
that goods and joy and glory are prepared,
inscribed for the souls of those who die in justice;
that is the price of your labors, numerous goods will be given you;
that your lot will be better than that of the living.
Your soul, oh you who die in justice,
will live, will be joined together, will exult;
nor will their spirits disappear
nor their memory before His Majesty,
during all the cycles of the centuries,
No longer, then, fear dishonor!

Book of Enoch, 102–103

Compare this doctrine to that of Daniel (*383*) and Wisdom (*400–401*). The author of Wisdom could have known this passage of Enoch.

Text 34

A SYNAGOGAL COMMENTARY ON SCRIPTURE

The Aramaean Targums on the Bible are not simply translations, but echo the synagogical commentary which strove to nourish Jewish piety. This amplification of the prophecy of Jacob (*Gen.* 49, 10–12) links the messianic hope of Israel to the text of Genesis (compare *24*):

Kings will not be lacking to the house of Judah,
nor doctors of the Law to the children of his children,
until the Royal Messiah will come
to whom the royality will return
and to whom all kingdoms will be submitted!

266

How handsome he is, the Messiah-King
who will arise from the House of Judah!
He girds his loins and he leaves
to fight against his enemies
and he kills kings and generals
The blood of those killed, it reddens the mountains;
the fat of their warriors, it whitens the hills.
His clothes are filthy with blood,
he resembles a treader of grapes.
How handsome he is, the Messiah-King
who will arise from the House of Judah!
His eyes are more beautiful than pure wine,
for with them he does not look upon either base nakedness
nor the spilling of innocent blood.
His lips are whiter than milk,
for with them he eats neither what is pillage nor stolen.
His mountains redden with vines
and his presses with wine;
His hills grow white with the abundance of grain
and with flocks of sheep.

These two pictures of the messianic reign have a point of departure in Scripture (see *70, 329, 330*). Still, they do express a
certain religious nationalism.

Text 35

AN IDEAL FOR THE SPIRITUAL LIFE

On the shores of the Dead Sea, some miles from the spot where
John the Baptist preached, an Essene community stood in the
time of Christ. A part of its library, hidden in 70 during the
war against the Romans, was found in 1947 in the neighboring
caves (called the Caves of Qumrân). It is interesting to see the
spirituality of this circle with John the Baptist's and Jesus'
hearers could have been in contact. Here are several passages
from the hymn which ends the *Manual of Discipline:*

267

At the coming of day and of night,
  I will enter into the covenant of God;
at the departure of evening and of morning,
  I will enunciate his commandments,
and so long as they endure I will there make my domain
  without swerving from them.

At the outset of my work and my goings
  I will bless his name;
at the beginning of every activity,
  when I lie down and when I rise,
and when I settle on my couch,
  I will acclaim him.

I will bless him, offering the tribute of my lips,
  when I leave the table of men
and before extending my hand to eat
  the delicious produce of the earth.

When fear and terror rise up,
  when agony and desolation are at hand,
I will bless the extraordinary marvels which he does;
I will meditate on his power,
  and on his graces I will rely all day.
Knowing that the judgment of every living thing is in his hand
  and that his works are the Truth,
I will praise him in the midst of my distress,
  and when he saves me, I will praise him also.

Column 10, 10–17

For myself, I belong to sinful humanity,
  to the company of the flesh of iniquity;
my offenses, my faults, my sins
  the same as the perversion of my heart
put me in the company of the abject
and those who go in darkness.

But I, if I waver,
  the graces of God will ever be my salvation;
and if I stumble through the disorder of the flesh,
  my judgment will be made according to the justice of God
  who exists forever.

268

If he prolongs my agony,
   he will deliver my soul from perdition
   and will strengthen my steps on the way.
He has made me approach in his mercy,
   and my judgment will occur by his grace,
He has judged me in his truthful justice,
   and in his great bounty he will efface all my offenses.
In his justice, he will purify me of the impurity
   and of the sin of the sons of Adam,
so that thanks are given to God for his justice
   to the Most-High for his magnificence.

Blessed are you, My God,
   who open to understanding the heart of your servant!
Establish all my works in justice,
   and grant to the son of your servant,
as you will it for those you choose from among men,
   to stand before you forever! . . .

Column 11, 9–17

This spirituality prolongs that of the Old Testament while accentuating certain aspects, like the sense of sin and of the divine mercy (compare to *210–283, 304–312, 316*).

Text 36

A JEWISH MORNING PRAYER

The synagogal liturgy gathered together some ancient prayer formularies. In the morning prayers, before the recitation of the biblical text "Hear, O Israel . . ." (*148*), a *blessing* was said, certain elements of which seem to antedate our era.

Blessed be you, O Lord our God, you the King of the world who form the light and create the darkness,

269

who make happiness and create everything,
who illumine the earth and those who dwell on it with mercy,
who in his bounty, each day, continually renew the work of
Genesis . . .

Blessed be you, O Lord our God, for the excellence of the work
of your hands;
for the light-bearer which you have created, may you be glorified!
[*All*] Blessed be you, Lord, who form the lights!
You have loved us with a great love, O Lord our God!
You have shown us an immense excessive pity, O our Father and
King,
because of our fathers, who confided in you and to whom you
taught the precepts of life!
Likewise show us mercy and teach us!
Illumine our eyes by your Law, bind our heart to your commandments.
apply it to love and fear your name,
and never will we be confounded. . . .
For you are the God who effects salvation;
you have chosen us from among all peoples and all tongues,
and you have brought us near to your great Name, in truth,
to praise you and confess you as One with love.

[*All*] Blessed be you, Lord,
who have chosen Israel for your people with love.

This spirituality is on a par with that of the teacher of
Qumrân; but it is less personal in character. It shows that the
attachment to the Law among the Jewish teachers did not confuse itself with heartless legalism. It was based on the awareness
of the love of God for his people and was meant to lead to love.

Bibliography

On the last of the prophets and the sapiential books, consult the
bibliography cited in Chapter IX and also the various biblical
dictionaries and encyclopedias. In Vol. I of the *Introduction to*

the Bible, see the articles by A. Lusseau and A. Lefevre. On extra-biblical Judaism, see C. F. Pfeiffer, *Between the Testaments* (Grand Rapids n.d.), and C. C. Torrey, *The Apocryphal Literature* (New Haven 1945). Consult the introduction and bibliography in Vol. II of the *Introduction to the Bible* for the various schools of extra-biblical literature and the principal sects. On Qumrân and Essenism, the recent bibliography is abundant: R. E. Murphy, *The Dead Sea Scrolls and the Bible* (Westminster 1956), J. P. van der Ploeg, *The Excavations at Qumrân* (Mystic 1958). Both of these are introductory works. M. A. Dupont-Sommer, *The Jewish Sect of Qumrân and the Essenes* (New York 1955). T. H. Gaster, *The Dead Sea Scriptures* (New York 1956). The problem calls for some critical work, however, and among the best examples we find *The Ancient Library of Qumrân and Modern Biblical Studies* by F. M. Cross (New York n.d.) and *Ten Years of Discovery in the Wilderness of Judea* by J. T. Milik (Mapierville 1959), both of which presuppose a certain familiarity with the question. Consult also M. Burrows, *The Dead Sea Scrolls* (New York 1955) and *More Light on the Dead Sea Scrolls* (New York 1958), J. Daniélou, *The Dead Sea Scrolls and Primitive Christianity* (New York 1962), and G. Vermes, *Discovery in the Judean Desert* (New York 1956).

Study Guides

Study the development of the apocalyptic genre, from the prophets to the New Testament. Note its stages: prophetic evocations of the day of Yahweh (*101, 104, 115, 129, 135, 154, 159*); the evolution of prophetic eschatology towards the apocalypse (*206, 287, 289–291, 297, 298, 327, 330*); the flowering of the genre (*337, 383;* Texts 32–33, 38); the use of the genre in the New Testament (*Mt.* 24, and the parallels; *1 Thess.* 5, 1–3; *2 Thess.* 1, 7–10; *2 Tim.* 4, 1–8; *2 Pet.* 3, 9–13; *Apoc.* 16, 3–21; 18; 19, 11–21). Show that the basis of this genre is a belief in God's mastery over human history, which in itself belongs to biblical revelation.

Taking as a starting point the didactic narratives written after the exile: Ruth (*244*), Jonah (*245*), Tobit (*343–348*), Daniel (*378–380*), Judith (*392–395*), and Esther (*396–398*), study the art of the story in the Bible. Show how this art puts itself at the service of doctrinal teaching. In spite of the cleverness of the narrators of the latest era, has the art of the collectors of the traditions and the ancient historians been surpassed?

Compare the manner of the ancient sages (*246–251*), the editor of Proverbs (*252–254*), Ecclesiastes (*338–342*), Tobit (*345*), the writer of Sirach (*349–371*), the Wisdom of Solomon (*399–405*). Has there not been a great variety of styles within the same sapiental genre? Is not something of this found again in the New Testament in the discourses and parables of the Gospel, in the Letter of James?

272

XIII.

JUDAISM ON THE THRESHOLD OF THE GOSPEL

As the heir to a long tradition and possessor of the holy books from which it drew the substance of its thought, the Jewish community was forced to organize its teachings into a synthesis, to cast light upon its own system of values. Here we will take up only the final doctrinal completions which the writings of this time put on revelation. Finally, we will examine the sects and tendencies manifested within Judaism on the threshold of the New Testament.

1. JUDAISM AND THE TRADITION OF ISRAEL

The Continuity of the Tradition

The Mediterranean world, during the three centuries preceding our era, was a melting-pot where races, currents of ideas, and religious beliefs intersected and fused in a climate of absolute syncretism. Within this framework Judaism intentionally made itself a world apart. Not that it completely escaped from its environment to the point of borrowing nothing from it, for the techniques, arts, and civilization of this milieu penetrated even the land of Israel. The very fact that the doctrine was set forth by authors like the author of Wisdom who were imbued with Greek culture implies a certain usage of the elements furnished by Hellenistic civilization.

But even while using this new language, and evolving in its level of civilization, Judaism still managed to escape the syncretistic current to which the entire East was bound. Its tradition proved stronger than the surroundings into which it was plunged. For Israel was less occupied with modernizing itself and fitting itself to the tastes of the day, than with faithfully conserving the ancestral heritage which was peculiarly its own, its Law, liturgy, wisdom, and eschatological hope. The Scriptures made known the words of its God, the One True God. But Israel was content to bind itself to the Scriptures unconditionally. Even more, Judaism was conscious of having been set down, by divine choice and covenant, in a situation superior to that of the surrounding pagans. It even felt charged with a mission to them, to bear witness to God so that they would recognize him and be converted to him, and would long for the day when he would establish his eschatological reign here on earth.

Some works like Ecclesiasticus, the books of Tobit and Baruch, of Judith and Esther, only restated these very traditional doctrines to their readers. When Ecclesiastes apparently tried to be critical, it still stayed within the narrow limits of this traditional framework of ideas. And when Daniel and Wisdom introduced new elements, they still prolonged tradition and developed its potentialities.

The Causes of Fidelity

Was it the peculiar Jewish genius, so singularly tenacious and attached to its own national pecularities, which explained such fidelity? For this genius was flexible in adapting itself to circumstances, although it did occasionally fall into an apostate modernism, as we saw in the time of the persecution of Antiochus Epiphanes, when Israel contacted the civilization of Canaan and the great Mesopotamian empires (55, 57, 90,

274

139–141). No, this permanence of the tradition was due to a peculiar mysterious quality of the Jewish faith itself. From Moses to David, in spite of the crises of the times of the Judges; from David to post-exilic Judaism, in spite of the crisis of the time of the kings; from the end of the exile to the time of Christ, in spite of the crisis of the Greek era, there is a fundamental continuity. At each crisis, new inspired men arise, and thanks to them fidelity is maintained around and against everything, and at the same time the traditional doctrine is deepened and enriched, profiting from the very crises which had threatened to overwhelm it.

This phenomenon has no exact parallel in the history of religions, and thereby poses a problem, though the role of the inspired men gives a glimpse of the profound causes for this fidelity. The religion of Israel is a revealed religion, and if Israel remained faithful to it in spite of contrary currents it was by the grace of God. Thus Judaism, which served as the framework for the Gospel, even in the scattered Greek-speaking communities around the circumference of the Mediterranean, did not produce a hybrid fusion between the Israelite tradition and the Greek culture and religious spirit, but slowly matured under the direction of God himself.

2. THE DOCTRINAL FINISHING TOUCHES

The World of the Angels and Demons

The belief in celestial messengers, executors of the commands of God, always existed in the Old Testament (*6, 18, 93, 114, 200, 205*). After the exile it seems that the contact of Jewish thought with the religion of the Persians, which had been strongly implanted in Babylon since the time of Cyrus, stimulated the development and facilitated the systematization of an angelology. The book of Tobit reaped this angelology's fruit, in a strictly individual perspective. Against the background of the world in which men live, this book gave glimpses of

275

the presence of invisible spirits, good and evil, who attack or defend them (*344, 346–348*). In the book of Daniel, attentive to the spiritual drama acted out within human groups, the powers inimical to God are certain earthly empires. The author represented them under the bestial traits of demoniacal symbols (*381*), and he knew that the people of God would only be delivered from them by the intervention of "Michael the Great Prince" (*383*). Finally, the book of Wisdom identified that mysterious being veiled by Genesis under the traits of the Serpent: as the Devil, through whose envy death entered into the world (*399*).

To announce this doctrine authors used many symbols. The names of the angels and demons (*344, 382*), their concrete representation, their division into classes according to certain hierarchical orders, rose out of these conventional procedures. The apocryphal books (notably the book of Enoch) are much less restrained on this point than the inspired writings. But the key point does not lie here but in the light which this doctrine throws on human existence, and particularly on the problem of evil. At the time of Christ, Judaism would see the signs of Satan's reign over the world, not only in sin, but in all suffering and sickness. Even at the risk of the masses' superstitious exaggeration, it must be acknowledged that the view is fundamentally just, for Jesus himself did not hesitate to present his redemptive action as a victory over Satan, "Prince of this world," master of souls and bodies (*Mt.* 12, 22–29; *Jn.* 12, 31–32).

Eschatology and Messianism

Eschatological hope remained very much alive during these centuries when the people of God saw their time of trial incomprehensibly prolonged. But the pertinent sacred texts were so diverse that it was very difficult to cast all the elements into a coherent synthesis; if one excepts Ecclesiastes, all the books of the era express this eschatological hope in one way or another, at least by recounting past deliverances which presage the great deliverance (*378–380, 392–398, 404, 405*). The writer of Sirach composed a beautiful prayer for the liberation of Israel (*Sir.* 36, 1–17); the books of Baruch and Tobit chanted the glory of the new Jerusalem (*331, 332*); Daniel and Wisdom clothed the day of Yahweh and definitive salvation with grandiose imagery (*377, 381–383, 400, 401*).

The terrestrial artisan of this salvation is most often represented as a king, the son of David. If the inspired texts do not make this point, the apocrypha and the rabbinic writings supply for their unexpected silence (Texts 34 and 37). In addition to royal messianism, the Essenes also awaited a Priest-Messiah who would have precedence over the Messiah-King (Text 38). On the other hand, the image of the Suffering Servant completely disappeared and nowhere is it ever applied to the Messiah. The book of Daniel introduced a new personage into eschatology: the mysterious *Son of man* who will come on the clouds of heaven (*387*). Originally, this was only a symbol, which represented both the reign of God coming to earth and the just remnant ("the people of the saints of the Most-High") who had part in it. As a consequence, one part of the Jewish tradition, attested to by the book of Enoch, identified this Son of man with the Royal Messiah of Isaiah (*125*) and the Chosen One of God, that is, the Servant of Yahweh considered in his teaching role (but not in his passion [*225*]). This longing for a transcendent Messiah (Text 39), which is of mysterious origin, is presupposed by certain Gospel texts (*Jn.* 6, 41–42; 7, 26–27); Jesus will use the same image to depict his role on the last day (*Mt.* 24, 30; 26, 64).

Individual Destiny

After the agonies of Job and the disillusioned reflections of Ecclesiastes, after the intuitions of some of the psalmists who had experienced the joy of being with God (*315, 316*), the problem of individual destiny was finally clarified along an original line of thought which found its way into the Scriptures themselves. This clarification came not by way of speculation on the divine justice or the immortality of the human soul, as one would find in Greece, but by again taking up the page of Ezekiel depicting the symbolic resurrection of Israel after the exile (*201*) and transposing his theme to the end of time (*285–287*). The apocalypse of Daniel saw in this the promise of a real resurrection of the just who would rise from the kingdom of the dead to participate in the eschatological reign of God (*383*). This doctrine was new, but was still linked to to ancient tradition and was a message of hope sent by God to the persecuted Jews. Thanks to it the martyrs found the strength to die for their faith (*376*). Beginning in this era, this idea was commonly accepted in the various pietistic schools, with the exception of the Sadducees. It is also found in the apocrypha, notably the book of Enoch (Text 33), and in rabbinic literature.

On the basis of this belief in eternal life, in the "world to come," the book of Wisdom elaborated its own doctrine of the hereafter (*400, 401*). In spite of the book's silence on corporeal resurrection of the just, and insistence on the peace which accompanies their death, the author clearly links their entry into immortality and their eternal life with God to the time of the "divine visitation." Thus he takes up again, from an individual point of view, the pictures of eschatological happiness painted by the apocalyptic literature. Naturally, in contrast, the ancient sojourn of the dead, sheol, the lower regions, place of shadows and oblivion, becomes the place of perdition, where sinners are relegated far from the face of God. The Gospel will presuppose that these doctrines are accepted by the Jews.

3. THE JEWISH SECTS IN
THE TIME OF JESUS

The Sadducees

From the time of the Hasmonaeans, the Jewish community saw the continuation of religious parties formed by the consolidation and formalization of more ancient currents, though the name "sects" is not properly given to them. The high priest-kings had, in fact, slowly alienated themselves from vast sectors

278

of public opinion until they finally found firm support only among the Sadducees recruited mostly from among sacerdotal circles and the aristocracy. From the point of view of religious ideas, they represented an archaizing Judaism, for they recognized only the books of the Pentateuch as sacred, and denied all authority to the oral traditions of the lay doctors. They were also hostile to the doctrinal progress carried out in the course of the latest centuries. Notably, they rejected belief in angels, the resurrection, and retribution beyond the grave (*Acts* 23, 8). Messianic hope, which had few roots in the Pentateuch (*24, 47*), was almost dead among them. Provided that worship could be carried out and the Law observed, they accommodated themselves to the unfavorable political conditions of Judaism. Practically, afted supporting the Hasmonaeans, they accepted the yoke of Rome.

The Pharisees

The Pharisees formed a pietistic current springing from certain loyalist groups which rallied to the Maccabees on account of their religious fidelity (*374, 384*). Their disagreement with John Hyrcanus was probably caused by the secular character which the Hasmonaean dynasty had taken on. When he restored the monarchy for his own benefit, their attachment to Davidic messianism hardened their opposition. Thus they were persecuted by Alexander Janneus. Membership in the Pharisees came especially from the lay doctors, who were specialists in the Law. Before our era, it seems, they were organized in confraternities. As minute observers of the Law and oral traditions amplified by custom, they nevertheless tried to adapt the demands of the Law to the necessities of practical life, through a highly developed casuistry. Jesus would reprimand them for this with asperity (*Mt.* 23, 13–32; *Mk.* 7, 1–13). But they were open to the most recent doctrinal progress, like the belief in the resurrection. Their fidelity to the messianic ideal of the nation rested on a literal interpretation of the prophetic texts (Texts 34 and 37), for they awaited the Messiah-King who would deliver Israel from the yoke of the pagans. Spiritual

guides of the Jewish masses, in the service of whom they enjoyed a great prestige, they took charge of the destiny of
Judaism after the national catastrophe of 70 A.D.

The Essenes

Up to now we have had only secondhand data on the Essenes,
but the texts discovered in the caves of Qumrân document, if
not the whole of Essenism, at least the group which they relate
to. The Essenes must be linked, like the Pharisees, to the
"Zealots" who supported Judas Maccabaeus (*384*). It was
probably from fidelity to the legitimate sacerdotal dynasty of
Zaddok that they were opposed to the Hasmonaeans when they
became high priests. The Jewish writers Philo and Josephus
show them organized into little local communities, with some
among them practicing celibacy. The excavations of Qumrân
near the Dead Sea have in fact rediscovered the traces of a
settlement with all the characteristics of a monastery. In some
ways this current formed a conservative reaction, strongly influenced by the sacerdotal circles. It had its own juridical traditions, even more rigorous than those of the Pharisees. This
intransigent legalism was, nonetheless, allied to a high spirituality (Text 35). Eschatological hope among the Essenes generally retained a very pronounced nationalistic character.
Besides the Davidic Messiah, they awaited a priestly Messiah
(Text 38). But the most recent section of the book of Enoch,
which appears to be linked to the sect, speculates on the character of the Son of man from the book of Daniel (Text 39). In
longing for the "last times" the "penitents of Israel" grouped
at Qumrân regarded themselves as the faithful remnant of the
people of God, the depository of the national hope. That is
why they lived in solitude, so that their influence on the masses
cannot be measured.

The Other Parties

The Zealots and Herodians were less religious sects than political parties. The first were fierce nationalists who could have
been influenced either by Pharisaism or by Essenism. Their

agitation freely took advantage of messianic pretexts, which translated itself into armed revolts which the Romans bloodily quelled. The Jewish war of 67–70 was their work.

Outside of Palestine, the Judaism of the diaspora presents its own peculiar characteristics which varied greatly from place to place. We have seen how Judaism, living in contact with Hellenism, gradually developed widened horizons. The missionary spirit of the post-exilic period (*242–245*) remained alive among them and they recruited proselytes from among their pagan surroundings and forged an apologetics. In that, they anticipated the Christian apostolate. The book of Wisdom is a good example of the doctrinal orientations of the diaspora. But it is also possible that, on the fringes, certain members were contaminated by the rampant syncretism.

We must remember that in the diaspora as in Palestine, the Jewish masses did not belong to any sect, even if the influence of the diverse religious parties was felt among them. Thanks to synagogal worship, the reading and commentary on the Scriptures (Text 34), the chanting of the psalms, the recitation of the most ancient prayer formularies (Text 36) were the spiritual nourishment of those simple souls who, on the whole, showed themselves more open to the Gospel than the Sadducees and Pharisees.

4. ON THE THRESHOLD OF THE NEW TESTAMENT

The Spiritual Problem of Judaism

Every tradition runs the risk of becoming stagnant over the years. At the time of Christ, Judaism found itself in an ambiguous situation in this regard, for while it formed a homogeneous block which had never been so attached to its faith, its Law, its worship, on three essential points this very attachment contained dangers.

In the first place, the worship of the Law turned more than once into withering legalism. Meticulous attention to the letter of the Law overloaded with various traditions finally concealed

281

the Law's spirit and profound meaning. The great vitality of the prophets, of Deuteronomy, of the masters of wisdom, was snuffed out, and formalism invaded religious practices. It was forgotten that "the Sabbath is made for man, and not man for the Sabbath" (*Mk.* 2, 27). This was the price of five centuries of struggle to keep faithful to the Law. The Jews now risked forgetting that inside this Law there existed a hierarchy of values, that the Law and cultual observances had to be put in their proper place, which was not first place. The very external barrier which protected Israel from the contagion of pagans, the Law, must not stamp out the vitality of souls.

In the second place, the sense of national vocation often hardened into religious nationalism. By repeating that Israel was the people of God they were tempted to annex Yahweh to Israel, to confound his glory with that of his people. Thus national self-love found nourishment in the freest of divine gifts, the call of Israel, first of all the peoples, to enter into the kingdom of God. This is far from the spirit of Deuteronomy (*149*) and far also from the religious universalism which the prophetic preaching (*133, 225, 241*) and post-exilic Judaism (*242–245, 287*) had already emphasized. Even the proselytism of the communities of the diaspora risked being subordinated to Israel's human interests.

Under such conditions it is not surprising that messianism was dangerously inclined to a nationalistic and temporal meaning. The texts which fed it are of all ages and they contain contradictory materials, for side by side were found images of the Royal Messiah in his battles and his glory, and those of the Servant of Yahweh in his life of teaching and suffering; the aspirations to warlike triumph, and the most spiritualized evocations of the reign of God; the most realistic promise of the goods of this earth, and that of an entry into a transfigured world. Only Christ, by coming to earth, could dissipate the ambiguity of the prophecies (Text 22). While awaiting him, many Jews were attracted to the earthlier pictures, whose literal fulfillment they longed for. They longed for the reign of God and the salvation of Israel, but in a feverish hope where human passions were dangerously mingled with religious hope.

The picture must not be painted too black, as if these deformations were common to all the Jews, or even to all the members of the sects. The Gospel itself shows simple and profound souls among whom fidelity to the Law is wholly interior and whose messianic longing is pure and lofty. Such are the people found in the first two chapters of the Gospel of St. Luke, especially Zachary, Elizabeth, Mary and Joseph, Simeon and the prophetess Anna. And cases of this kind were not rare. In such souls, the preaching of Jesus would find immediate response, and would be fervently welcomed. It is then that the Old Testament, having fulfilled its educative role, attained its fulfillment. But the others, anchored to their preconceived notions, turned away from a teaching which seemed deceiving or dangerous to them. The drama of the Gospel will rise from this context.

John the Baptist

John the Baptist was a man of the Old Testament, the last of the inspired men. It has been suggested that his retreat into the desert involved a stay, more or less long, in the community of Qumrân. If this is so—which is by no means proven—it is certain that John went far beyond Essenism. In proclaiming the judgment to be at hand (*Mt.* 3, 7–10), the coming of the reign of God and the Messiah (*Mt.* 3, 2. 11–12), the necessity of conversion "to prepare the way of the Lord" (*Mt.* 3, 2), in administering a baptism which signified this conversion (*Mt.* 3, 6), John renewed real prophecy and he resumed its key themes. Far from linking himself to ritual formalism, like the Pharisees and Essenes, he tried to revive "the religion of the spirit" in the Jewish community. To all those who came to him he gave the appropriate advice (Lk. 3, 10–14). The Jewish authorities, priests and scribes, Pharisees and Sadducees, whose faults he denounced (*Mt.* 3, 7), remained reserved and defiant towards him (*Mt.* 21, 24–26). But among the simple people he aroused an awakening of religious feeling which would

283

persist even after his arrest and death. Due to his preaching, messianic longing was more pressing and hearts were more attentive to the conditions necessary to enter into the kingdom of God. Thus the authentic religious tradition of Israel is found in John the Baptist, and in him the Law and the prophets fulfilled their mission (*Mt.* 11, 13). The Gospel message would bear its first fruits in the environment prepared by his preaching (*Jn.* 1, 35–51).

Text 37

THE LONGING FOR THE MESSIAH-KING, THE SON OF DAVID

The *Psalms of Solomon* were composed in a Pharisaical milieu between 68 and 42 B.C. The fragments of Psalm 17 cited here show the state of messianism at this time. In the exasperation caused by Roman domination, the Jew's nationalistic tendency came strongly to the fore and, in spite of the great religious spirit of the author, his dreams of the future do not rise above the plane of temporal history.

Look upon him, Lord, and raise him up
  your king, the son of David [*71*],
in the time which you know, O God,
  so that he, your servant, may rule over Israel;
invest him with strength
  so that he may destroy the unjust potentates [*127, 330*]! . . .

He will gather up the holy people
  whom he will lead with justice [*329*];
he will govern the tribes of the people
  sanctified by the Lord its God [*203, 204*].

284

He will not allow iniquity
  to remain in the midst of them;
no man used to evil
  will remain any longer with them . . .
He will govern peoples and nations,
  in his just wisdom [127];
he will hold the pagan peoples
  under the yoke, to serve him [330],
and he will glorify the Lord
  in the sight of all the earth.

He will purify Jerusalem
  sanctifying it as of old;
so that the nations will come from the ends of the earth
  to see the glory of it
bringing as offerings
  their sons to it, at the end of a tether,
and to see the glory of the Lord
  whose God will have glorified him [241, 243].
For he, like a just king
  educated by God, will reign over them [127];
and there will be nothing of iniquity
  during his days in their midst,
for all will be holy,
  and their king will be the Anointed One of the Lord [330] . . .
He will be free from sin
  to rule innumerable peoples,
 to capture the leaders and destroy the sinners
  by the force of his work [127].
He will not bend, during his days,
  depending upon his God,
for God will have made him
  strong through the Holy Spirit,
and wise with a counsel full of wisdom
  accompanied with strength and justice [127].
Happy those who will be living
  in those days,
to see the happiness of Israel
  in the gathering together once more of the tribes!
O God do it!

O God hasten his mercy towards Israel!
Deliver us from the defilement of impure enemies!

Psalm 17, 23–51

Most of the characteristics of the prophetic oracles can be found reassembled in this picture (*71, 126, 127, 202, 223, 241, 328–332*). The poet expects God to realize here on earth a holy people (*182, 203, 223*); nevertheless, this religious hope is still very nationalistic.

Text 38

THE LONGING FOR THE MESSIAH-PRIEST, THE SON OF LEVI

The *Testaments of the Twelve Patriarchs* is a hybrid work. Its Essene literary basis has been reworked and adapted by a Christian author. The prophecy of a Messiah-Priest, the son of Levi, certainly reflects Essene doctrine, but the Christian adapter identified this person with the Messiah-King, and has referred the whole portrait to Jesus Christ by inserting Gospel allusions into the text (star of the Magi, baptism of Jesus). In spite of this revision, the text still gives us a glimpse of Essene thought.

Then the Lord will raise up a new Priest [*70*],
   to whom all the Words of the Lord will be revealed.
He will pronounce a true judgment
   on the earth, on all ways,
His star will rise in the heavens, like that of a king [*47*]
   making the light of his knowledge shine forth. . . .

The heavens will be opened and, from the sanctuary of glory,
   holiness will come upon him,
with a fatherly voice,

286

like that of Abraham to Isaac [15, 225, 330].
The glory of the Most-High will be proclaimed over him
and the Spirit of knowledge and holiness will repose on him in
the water [127].
The nation, by his priesthood,
will be filled with knowledge on earth,
and they will be enlightened by the grace of the Lord [225, 226].

By his priesthood, sin will come to an end,
and the impious will cease to do evil.
He will open the gates of paradise
and wipe away the sword raised against Adam [6].
He will make the saints eat of the tree of life,
and the Spirit of holiness will be upon them.
Belial will be enchained by him
and he will give power to his sons
to trample the evil spirits underfoot. . . .
The Lord will rejoice in his children,
he will delight in his well-beloved forever.
Then Abraham, Isaac and Jacob will exult.
and all the saints will be filled with Joy.

Testament of Levi, 18, 2–14

The allusions to the Scriptures are noted in the course of the text, but some of them presuppose the New Testament for their full meaning. From this point of view, compare: *Matthew* 2, 1–12; 3, 16–17; 12, 29; *Luke* 2, 32; 10, 19; *John* 5, 22–27; 9, 56; *Apocalypse* 2, 7; 20, 2; 22, 2.

Text 39

THE LONGING FOR THE SON OF MAN

In the central section of the book of Enoch, which is called the *Book of Parables,* God's envoy is no longer presented as an earthly king, but as the Son of man who comes from heaven.

287

This representation develops the data of the book of Daniel
(*381*), identifying the Son of man and the Messiah, the son of
David and the Servant of Yahweh (excluding the aspect of his
suffering).

The names given God belong only to the book of Enoch: the
Eternal, literally: the Head (one in charge) of days (see *381*);
the Lord of Spirits, probably a paraphrase of Yahweh of Hosts.

There I saw the Eternal,
> whose head was like clean wool;
and with him another,
> whose visage had a human look;
his face was full of favor,
> like that of one of the holy angels [*381*].

I questioned the angel who accompanied me on the subject of this
Son of Man and he let me see all the mysteries: Who was he?
From whence did he come? Why did he go with the Eternal? He
answered and said to me:

"This is the Son of man who possesses justice;
justice dwells with him,
> and he reveals all the secrets of the mysteries" . . . [46, 1–4].

At this moment,
the Son of man was named before the Lord of Spirits,
> and his name was pronounced before the Eternal.
Before the very sun and the constellations were created,
> before the stars of the heavens were made [*253, 305*],
his name was mentioned before the Lord of Spirits.

He will be the rod of the just,
> so that they will lean on him and not fall;
he will be the light of nations [*225, 226*];
> he will be the hope of those who are brokenhearted [*240*].
All those who inhabit the earth
> will fall down before him and render him homage [*328, 329*],
> praising, blessing and chanting of the Lord of Spirits.
This is why he was chosen and called before him,
> before the creation of the world and for eternity [84, 2–6].

The Elect stands before the Lord of Spirits;
his glory will endure for endless ages,
   and his power, from age to age [381].
In him dwells the Spirit of Wisdom,
   the Spirit which gives understanding,
the Spirit of knowledge and strength [127],
   the Spirit of those who fall asleep in justice.
He will judge secret things,
   and no one will be able to lie before him,
for he has been chosen before the Lord of Spirits
   according to his good pleasure [225] [49, 2–4].

In those days, the earth will give back what was entrusted to it,
   sheol will give up that which it received,
   Hades will give back what it owes [383].
For in these days, the Elect will arise;
   he will choose from among them the just and the holy,
for it is near, the day
on which they must be saved . . . [51, 1–2].

The Lord of Spirits has seated him upon his throne of glory,
   and the Spirit of justice has been poured out upon him.
The sword of his mouth will make all sinners perish,
   all the impious will disappear before his face [127].
They will answer the summons on that day,
   the kings and the mighty
   the great and powerful of the earth.
They will see him and recognize him,
   when he will sit upon his throne of glory.
Justice will be rendered before him,
   before him no deceitful word will be pronounced. . . .

They will look upon one another;
   they will be terrified and hang their heads,
   and sorrow will grip them [401],
when they see this Son of Man
   seated upon his throne of glory . . . [62, 2–5].

The source which inspired this powerful evocation could be
sought in the prophetic oracles. Compare the apocalyptic pic-

289

ture of the judgment to that of the book of Wisdom (*401*). The New Testament will use the same images: *Matthew* 19, 28; 25, 32; 26, 64; *Luke* 4, 18; 21, 28; *John* 5, 27–30; 8, 12; *1 Thessalonians* 5, 3; *Philippians* 2, 9–11; *Apocalypse* 1, 13–14; 15, 14; 19, 11–15; 20, 11–13.

Bibliography

On the belief of Judaism, see the treatment in the *Guide to the Bible* by A. Tricot. In the *Encyclopedic Dictionary of the Bible*, see the pertinent articles (Angel, Demon, Satan, Messiah, Son of Man, Retribution, Heaven, Resurrection, Life, Hell, etc.). See also A. Retif, *St. John the Baptist* (Westminster n.d.).

Study Guides

Study the longing for messianic times, from the return from the exile to the threshold of the New Testament (*215–224, 229–241, 284–291, 325–337, 337–383, 406–408*). How does the Church's longing for Christ's return differ?

What was the idea of the Messiah and messianic times on the threshold of the New Testament (Texts 34, 37, 38, 39)? Is not the doctrine of the Scriptures very complex? Is not this complexity reflected in the New Testament?

How did the doctrine of the divine wisdom prepare for the revelation of the mystery of the Holy Trinity (*253, 352, 402*)? Does not the depiction of the benefits conferred on man by the communication of this wisdom flower in the doctrine of grace (*252–254, 350–352, 399–402*)?

XIV.

JESUS, MESSIAH AND SON
OF GOD

THE person of Jesus merits a much more profound study than
we can give it here. Jesus himself wrote nothing, but he is the
center of the whole Bible. On the one hand, the whole Old
Testament converged upon him, since its sole function was to
prepare for his coming. On the other hand, the New Testament
begins with him, since its sole function is to transmit his message and proclaim the salvation he brought to men. Two points
concern us here. In the first place, by his life, words, and his
work, Jesus fulfilled the Scriptures which preceded him, and it
is important to see how the Scriptures have been fulfilled.
Secondly, the words of Jesus and the events of his brief career
are the point of departure for the apostolic preaching and the
books which gathered it. Thus it is also important to see how
we can reach back to his public life beginning with the texts
which bear witness to it.

1. THE HISTORY OF JESUS

The Paradox of Jesus

The life of Jesus unfolded within the framework of Palestinian
Judaism, which, for all practical purposes, he never left (Map
8). Indeed, through the eyes of the faith, his birth, his preach-

ing, his death and resurrection constitute a group of privileged facts. Not only are they the center of gravity of Jewish history, but they constitute the event of events dominating the whole of human history. Nevertheless, this is not apparent on the surface. There was here no break in history's continuity, neither in Judaism nor in Rome. For the citizen of Rome, the tragic adventure of the young Galilean rabbi was only a news item from an obscure province. The event would have remained forever unknown if Christianity had not arisen out of it. In fact, this was all that Tacitus remembered (Text 40). To the Jews of Judea or the diaspora who did not adhere to the Gospel, Jesus seemed a fascinating man, but they would resist this very fascination, for Jesus had committed the triple offense of teaching on his own authority without having gone to school, of proclaiming blasphemous pretensions which led to his condemnation to death, and of founding a sect rejected by the leaders of Judaism. His death would have silenced his unhappy efforts, if the Christian "sect" had not become the Church, recruiting its followers even among pagan surroundings.

This is the paradox which overthrew the logic of history. Thus the life of Jesus must be studied from both points of view: as it appears to us after the event, in the light of the faith; and also in its humble reality, as it unfolded within the framework of Judaism. It is through this humble reality that the mystery of the Son of God become man slowly reveals itself to the believing soul.

The Stages of Jesus' Life

From the viewpoint of modern history it is difficult to reconstruct a biography of Jesus. The apostolic testimony collected in the Gospels does not completely lack critical value, but its purpose was not to satisfy human curiosity by making the life of the Master live again in full detail; rather, it was to nourish the faith of believers. To be sure, as early as the primitive Church, Christians were interested in the earthly life of the Lord, but they only selected those meaningful characteristics

292

which would reveal the mystery of his person. When they gave their memories a literary form, it was through those events designed to bring this mysteriousness to light.

In spite of the incomplete character of the sources, the broad lines of the drama appear with sufficient clarity. The exact chronology remains under discussion, but the following dates can be taken as most probable: 7–5 B.C. for the birth; 30 A.D. for the death, which is a little better established. It would have been around the year 28 that Jesus left Nazareth, his hometown (Map 9), to lead the life of an itinerant preacher. In the eyes of the Galilean crowds he first appeared as a prophet of the reign of God—like John the Baptist, whom Herod Antipas was about to arrest. But quickly, as more and more disciples attached themselves to him, he became more like a rabbi, although he had received no instruction from any master and he kept himself aloof from the accepted traditions. In relation to the sects, especially the Pharisees and the Essenes, he is unclassifiable. From the beginning, his preaching and miracles captured the popular enthusiasm; but the Pharisaic scribes remained defiant, and gradually their defiance became open hostility. Under their influence the spiritual climate in Galilee changed. At the same time, King Herod Antipas, who was now about to execute John the Baptist (Text 41), was disquieted by the messianic ferment running rampant among his people.

After a crisis emphasized by the four Gospels, Jesus stayed within the confines of the province he had been raised in, then he went over into Perea and into Judea. In Jerusalem he ran into the opposition of both the lay doctors and priestly circles, the Pharisees and the Sadducees. At the time of the Feast of the Passover he was arrested, condemned, and put to death, after both a religious and a civil trial (Map 10). Judging by the narration of the Synoptic Gospels, the adventure lasted one year and some months, although the Fourth Gospel mentions many journeys to Jerusalem and three Passover Feasts, which tempts us to lengthen this span of one year. Whether three

293

years or not, this brief career totally changed the religious face of the world.

2. THE FULFILLMENT OF THE SCRIPTURES

The Doctrinal Completion of the Old Testament

"Do not think that I have come to destroy the Law or the prophets. I have not come to destroy, but to fulfill" (*Mt.* 5, 17). This saying shows what role Jesus claimed in relation to the revelation which had preceded him. Addressing himself to the Jews, he presupposed that all of the positive teachings of the Old Testament had been acquired. He confirmed them by completing them. His own teaching, given with singular authority (*Mk.* 1, 22), is substituted for "the tradition of the ancients" to furnish an authentic interpretation of the Scriptures.

Thus the study of biblical revelation, in its progressive elaboration, is not useless or a matter of secondary importance for the Christian, as it forms a part of the study of the Gospel. The doctrine of the Old Testament, which Judaism contemporary to Jesus attempted to organize into a synthesis, sets the thought of Jesus in relief. The spirit of Moses, the prophets, and the sages flowered in the Law of perfection which Jesus formulated (*Mt.* 5, 17–48). All the great religious ideas encountered up to this point retained their value, but they were refined and acquired a new dimension. For example, Jesus intransigently maintains the Jewish faith in the sole God (*37*): the obligation to love him alone (*148*) is the first commandment which includes all the others (*Mk.* 12, 28–34). But he does give us a glimpse of his relations with the Father (*Mk.* 12, 6; 14, 36; *Mt.* 11, 27; *Jn.* 8, 42. 54–58; 10, 22–42), casting marvelous light upon the inmost mystery of God. This completion of revelation constitutes a primary fulfillment of the Scriptures (Text 42).

When we read the words of Jesus as collected by the evangelists, the texts of the Old Testament referred to must be kept in mind, for then the words and symbols which it includes take

294

on their real rich and profound meaning. Learning to read the Gospels is in large part learning to find the substance of the whole Old Testament gathered up and brought to completion. This work of investigation clarifies the continuity of biblical revelation.

The Establishment of the Reign of God

To his hearers, Jesus announces the Good News (*240*), the Gospel. The first object of this Gospel is the coming of the reign (or kingdom) of God (*Mk.* 1, 14). The use of this expression, found in most of the parables, stresses that with Jesus "the time is fulfilled" (*Mk.* 1, 15), or to put it another way, the history of the Old Testament has reached its goal. By the covenant at Sinai, God had made Israel his people and his kingdom (*188*). This was a provisional dispensation, since the prophets had announced the coming of a new covenant at the end of time (*181, 204, 225*), and one aspect of this future dispensation was the extension of the reign of God to all the nations (*133, 225, 243, 287*). Jesus proclaimed that this eschatological reality was already present. He inaugurated the kingdom of God here on earth. It is true that the unbelieving Jews will be excluded, especially the official authorities of the people (*Mt.* 21, 31–32. 43); but now the pagans take their place along with the faithful remnant of Israel (*Lk.* 13, 28–29).

As signs of the establishment of the kingdom of God, Jesus worked miracles which fulfilled the eschatological prophecies (*408*). It is true that the kingdom of God does not manifest itself in the brilliance foreseen in the apocalyptic literature (Text 39); nor does it take the form imagined by Jewish nationalism (Texts 34 and 37). However, it does take shape amid the surrounding realities of this world, though it does not depend upon the surroundings, for Jesus founded a new institution which would form the visible structure of the kingdom here on earth, his Church (*Mt.* 16, 17–19). In this way Jesus

295

brings the object of Israel's hope and the prophetic promises to men. This is a second fulfillment of the Scriptures.

The Glorification of God

The religion of the Old Testament did not consist in exterior actions alone. The actions had to translate the interior dispositions of souls. A powerful spiritual movement gradually raised this to a quest for a pure interior religion, uniquely concerned with the fear and the love of God, passionately desirous of procuring his glory (*105, 118, 148, 182, 284*). This was the special concern of the poor of Yahweh, whose prayer is heard in the psalms (*314, 320, 321*). Their tradition was maintained among these groups of the pious who preserved the best elements of Judaism. But how could such a force be reconciled with the profound consciousness of human sin (*281–283*)? What real value did the prayer of impure lips have before God (Text 35)?

This aspiration to a religion worthy of God was realized in the prayer of Jesus. Is it possible to imagine his interior dialogue with the Father? Very few words introduce us into this intimate secret of his personality (*Mt.* 11, 25–27; 26, 39; *Lk.* 23, 34; *Jn.* 11, 41–42; 17). On the other hand, we know that he participated in the Jewish ceremonies and prayed with the words of the psalms. After the Last Supper he chanted the great Hallel with his disciples (*322–324*) and on the cross, he murmured the psalms of suffering (*276–280*). Thus he adopted the spirituality of the poor of Yahweh. By sharing their experience of human suffering, like the mysterious Servant of Yahweh presented by the book of Isaiah (*225–228*), he integrated their spirituality with his own religious attitude towards the Father. Consequently, those sacred texts so often repeated by the Jewish masses found a new fullness of meaning in his mouth. This again is a fulfillment of the Scriptures. The religion of the Old Testament finally realizes its promise when the heavenly Father receives unequaled glorification from his Son made man.

296

The Sacrifice of Salvation

Finally, Jesus presented himself as "he of whom the Scriptures have spoken." This allusion to the eschatological oracles of the prophets make it clear that he fulfills them. The Old Testament presented the future mediator of salvation from very different angles: the Messiah Son of David, the Servant of Yahweh, the Son of man. These images fused in the person of Jesus, but they are related to one another. Refusing political messianism (*Jn.* 6, 15), Jesus nevertheless let himself be recognized as the Messiah (*Mt.* 16, 16; see *71, 330*) and the son of David (*Mt.* 21, 9; see *328*). But he made it clear that the Messiah must suffer before entering into his glory (*Lk.* 24, 26; Mk. 8, 31–33; 9, 12. 30–32; 10, 32–34). This disconcerting perspective fused with the prophesy of the Suffering Servant (*228*). Jesus had to give his life as a ransom for the multitude, in remission of sins (*Mk.* 10, 45; *Mt.* 26, 28). His death was the expiatory sacrifice which sealed the new covenant (*181, 203, 204*) and at the same time the paschal sacrifice of the new exodus (*29, 218–220*). By thus revealing the meaning of the cross, the Last Supper takes on profound meaning for it inaugurates, through visible signs, a sacrificial feast recalling that of wisdom (*254*) and foretelling that of the kingdom of God (*287*). But after the cross came glory. By his resurrection from the dead (*383*), Jesus realized on a high plane, the images of the Royal Messiah "seated at the right hand of God" (*70*), awaiting the end of time when he will return "on the clouds of heaven" to carry out the divine judgment (*381*). This conformity of the destiny of Jesus to the diverse presentations of the Saviour that had been sketched out is also a fulfillment of the Scriptures (*406– 411*).

3. THE WORDS OF JESUS

The words of Jesus are the point of departure for Christian tradition. To be sure, Jesus spoke in Aramaic, and the Gospels were written in Greek. But the sayings which were preserved often retain, under Greek clothing, a Semitic flavor. It is not surprising that the disciples of Jesus preserved the teachings of their Master not only in their general sense, but sometimes word for word. Such memory feats were common at the time. The disciples of the Jewish rabbis also engraved the teacher's sayings and casuistic solutions in their memories and in their turn, they transmitted the sayings to others. This chain of oral tradition could perpetuate itself for a long time before being set down in written collections. In Jesus' case a tradition of this sort was formed which conveyed the discourses and often repeated on the same themes (and perhaps in the same terms). The striking sayings were quickly memorized, the aphorisms linked to such and such a determined situation, and so forth. Already during the lifetime of Jesus, the disciples had been sent on a mission to proclaim the Good News of the Reign of God, that is to say, to repeat everywhere what they had heard him say (*Mt.* 19, 5–7). From the very origins of the Church, these same disciples were concerned only with retaining the words of the Master, which held an intangible value in their eyes. The events which had taken place during the public life—the cross and the resurrection—clarified them with a new light, without changing their profound meaning.

So we are assured of possessing the substance of Jesus's thought in the Gospel, faithfully gathered up by his disciples, and often in the very words used by Jesus. Yet it is false to imagine a wholly material fidelity, and a purely verbal repetition. The differences between the parallel texts of the Gospels suffice to show that, in details, the words of Jesus were retouched in their literary presentation to fit the needs of catechesis or the spirit of the hearers. From this point of view we can compare, for example, the beatitudes in Matthew (5, 3–11) and in Luke (6, 20–26), the eucharistic words of Jesus in the various accounts of the Last Supper, the twin parables of the talents (*Mt.* 25, 14–20) and the gold pieces (*Lk.* 19, 12–27). The living fidelity of the disciples was less concerned with a verbal exactitude than a substantial transmission, in keeping with the spirit of Jesus.

298

The Literary Form of Jesus' Words

The words of Jesus, as the evangelists have transmitted them, have a varied literary style. They sometimes adopt the customary forms of the teachers of his time: casuistic discussion supported by scriptural arguments. This was especially true when the Jewish scribes attempted to embarrass Jesus or to lead him into compromising statements—Jesus was willing to pursue them on their own ground. He seems accustomed to this dialectic style and capable of overcoming the most artful adversaries (*Mt.* 9, 3–6. 10–13; 12, 1–8; 15, 1–11; 21, 14–16. 23–27; 22, 23–46).

But when he speaks to the crowd Jesus adopts a very different and original manner, which stands out clearly from that of the scribes and amazes his hearers (*Mk.* 1, 22). Sometimes he enunciates precepts to regulate human conduct, not only as an interpreter of the Law, but as a true lawgiver (*Mt.* 5, 20–48; 18, 15–18), and that points to him as a new Moses. Sometimes he renews the preaching of the prophets by again adopting their manner of expression: curses (*Mt.* 11, 21–24) 23, 13–32; *Lk.* 7, 24–26; prophetic discourse (*Mt.* 23, 33– 39); eschatological oracles, which flows easily into apocalyptic (*Mt.* 24, 4–36; 25, 31–46). On the other hand, in his familiar teaching he also returns to the tone of the ancient masters of wisdom. There are beatitudes (*Mt.* 5, 1–11), proverbs (*Mt.* 6, 34; 7, 7; etc.), more developed sapiential discourses (*Mt.* 5–6; 10, 9–42; 23, 1–12). The use of the parable, frequent among the Jewish teachers, receives considerable development at his hands, for besides the great parables his words are embellished with comparisons and images of all sorts. Within these diverse forms, his speech follows the rhythm of oral, and more properly, Semitic language. As soon as he lifts his tone, parallelism appears in striking expressions which catch the ear of his hearer and reappear like refrains in the flow of the discourse (for example, *Mt.* 7, 24–27; 23, 13–36). All this places us in the presence of real literary creativity.

299

The Word of Jesus, Word of God

The words of Jesus fully realize what the prophets said of their preaching: it is the word of God. Yet the prophets were nothing more than *witnesses, messengers;* they spoke, neither on their own initiative, nor on their own authority. Jesus, on the contrary, is the Son of God who speaks (*Heb.* 1, 1). His words express absolutely (though in Semitic turns of phrase, long prepared for by the Bible) the thought of God, as he wished to communicate it to us. This is why revelation reaches its summit here. The human spirit enters into the most direct contact imaginable with the God who speaks—with the Word of God made flesh, according to the expression of St. John (*Jn.* 1, 1–18; *1 Jn.* 1, 1–4; Text 21).

Text 40

JESUS SEEN BY A ROMAN PAGAN

Writing before 117, Tacitus recounted in his *Annals* the burning of Rome in 64. He wrote that Nero, accused by popular rumor of having set it, diverted popular discontent onto the Christians:

Having presented as responsible those whom the rabble, who hate them on account of their crimes, called Christians, he punished them with some tortures of unheard refinement. The name of the Christians comes from Christ, who, under the reign of Tiberius, was delivered to death by the procurator Pontius Pilate. Repressed for the moment, this detestable superstition appeared anew; not only in Judea, where the evil had been born, but in Rome itself, where all the atrocities and all the shameful things of the world flow and find their followers.

Annals, 15, 44

The disdain of the Roman for the "detestable superstition" born in Judea governs his appreciation of its founder. His information is materially correct, but it reduces the episode to just another insignificant fact.

Text 41

THE DEATH OF JOHN THE BAPTIST

The Jewish historian Flavius Josephus, in his *Jewish Antiquities* (published in 93/94), also spoke of Jesus, but his text was soon revised by Christian copyists. On the other hand, the passage dedicated to John the Baptist shows well the impression John made upon the Jewish crowds.

Herod put him to death, this excellent man who exhorted the Jews to apply themselves to virtue, to practice justice towards one another and piety towards God, and to come to receive baptism. Immersion appeared to him a good thing, not to obtain pardon of certain faults, but to procure purification of the body, once the soul was purified of its stains by justice. All the people gathered around him, for they were struck by the hearing of his word. Also Herod feared him lest he use his influence over men to drive them to some revolt, as they seemed disposed to do following his advice. Thus he believed it preferable to forestall his teaching and had him killed to prevent any mischief he might cause and not bring himself into difficulties by sparing a man who might make him repent of it when it was too late. Following this suspicion of Herod, John was cast in irons and sent to Machaerus, the fortress already mentioned, and there he was put to death.

Compare this to the Gospel account (*Mt.* 14, 3–12; *Mk.* 6, 17–29; *Lk.* 3, 19–20). The political context mentioned by Josephus explains the arrest of John; but the Gospel tradition is more explicit on his death.

301

Text 42

JESUS "FULFILLS" THE OLD TESTAMENT

The place of Jesus in relation to the entire Old Testament is defined by Scripture as a "fulfillment." We mean that he clarifies its definitive meaning, as Henri de Lubac explains:

If the Old Testament was to be understood in its "true," "absolute" meaning, it was imperative that the time should be accomplished and that Christ should come. For he alone could "break the mysterious silence, provide the clue to the riddles of the prophets"; he alone could open the book sealed with seven seals. He alone, the one cornerstone, could join the two arms of the arch of history, as he was also the junction of the two peoples. For the Christian to understand the Bible means to understand it in the light of the Gospel . . . For it is the cross which disperses the cloud which until then was hiding the truth. "Behold the page between the two Testaments all set in vivid red." At the very moment that Christ, having finished his work, gave up the ghost, the veil of the temple was rent: a symbol with a double meaning like the reality which it signified. For it signified at the same time the downfall of the letter of Jewish worship and the manifestation of the mystery foretold in figure by this worship.

Yet the act of redemption is not a key which by unlocking the Old Testament reveals a meaning already present in it. This act in some sort creates the meaning. It is only for God, from the eternal point of view, that the Old Testament contains the New already in a mystery. . . . The value that Christianity accords to time, that is, to the *act* that is registered in time, is here revealed in its full meaning:

Before the coming of Christ, writes Origen, the Law and the prophets were not yet, one may say, the announcement of what came to pass in the Gospel, since he who was to make their mysteries clear had not yet come. But when the Saviour had come to us and had given a body to the Gospel, then, by means of the Gospel, he effected that the whole [of the Scriptures] should be like the Gospel.

H. de Lubac, *Catholicism*

302

Bibliography

Classical summaries of the life of Christ: H. Daniel-Rops, *Jesus and His Times* (New York 1958), L. Grandmaison, *Jesus Christ* (New York 1961), M. J. Lagrange, *The Gospel of Our Lord Jesus Christ* (New York n.d.), J. Lebreton, *The Life and Teaching of Jesus Christ Our Lord* (London n.d.), F. Prat, *Jesus Christ: His Life, His Teaching and His Work* (Milwaukee 1963), G. Ricciotti, *The Life of Christ* (Milwaukee 1952), F. Sheed, *To Know Christ Jesus* (New York n.d.). From the point of view of historical criticism, however, these books are dated. Other contributions include J. Guitton, *The Problem of Jesus* (New York n.d.) and R. Guardini, *The Lord* (Chicago 1954). Daniel-Rops describes the milieu in which Jesus lived in *Daily Life in the Times of Jesus* (New York 1964).

Study Guides

To lead men to believe in his word, God supported it by *signs*. The Old Testament idea of such signs was wider than our concept of a miracle (see *26–31, 45, 55, 80, 89, 90, 96, 102–104, 122, 123, 143, 144, 165–171, 216, 303*). We must refer to the Old Testament concept if we are to understand the meaning of the Gospel miracles (*408*) as well as that of the destruction of Jerusalem in 70 A.D. (see *Mk.* 13, 14–19).

Study the literary genre of the parable in both the Old and the New Testaments. For the Old Testament see: *61, 72, 119, 192, 202, 245, 339, 378–380, 392–395*. Compare, too, the symbolic actions of the prophets (*80, 91, 195–197, 246*) and those of Jesus.

XV.

IN APOSTOLIC TIMES

PROPERLY to locate the apostolic writings in the development of revelation it is necessary to sketch the history of the Church from the death of Christ to the end of the first century. In addition to the indications given by the apostolic epistles and the data preserved by the ancient Christian writers, our only source of information is the book of the *Acts of the Apostles*, which is far from a complete and detailed history of this period. Thus the chronology of certain events is difficult to establish. It is even more difficult to assign an exact date to the composition of certain New Testament writings. Among the suggestions of the historians, we have kept those which appear best to account for the texts. But we must be prepared to come across some very different positions on these unsettled questions which are not matters of faith.

1. THE CHURCH IN JEWISH SURROUNDINGS

The Jerusalem Community

The Acts of the Apostles gives only sketchy indications of the origins of the Church at Jerusalem (1, 1—6, 7). After the death of Christ, his disciples were very discouraged. They regained courage after a series of apparitions certified their Master's resurrection. They saw that it was truly the Messiah who had entered into his glory and is seated at the right hand of God. The gift of the Spirit of God, which Jesus had promised them, confirmed them in these new dispositions. Then from Pentecost on, profiting from the fact that pilgrims were numerous in Jerusalem, they began proclaiming the Gospel openly. To the ancient object of this *Good News,* the reign of God, a new element was now added: the witness rendered to Jesus, Messiah and Son of God, enthroned as Lord by his resurrection. Those who "believe in the word" formed a more and more numerous group, around Mary, the "Twelve," and the "brothers" of the Lord, those near relatives of Jesus who played a great role in the Church at Jerusalem as late as the 2nd century. The newcomers joined them by receiving baptism "in the name of Jesus." This did not happen, however, without opposition from the Jewish authorities. And after only a short time, Peter and John were brought before the Sanhedrin, which tried in vain to silence them.

Even before leaving Judaism, the community included two distinct groups: the faithful who spoke Hebrew (or Aramaic) and those who spoke Greek, the Hebrews and the Hellenists. To fit the latter into the community the Twelve associated seven men with themselves, whom they consecrated to "service" (*diakonia*) of the community. We see them as the first *deacons.* But it is not certain that their function and powers corresponded to the diaconate as it was later organized (*Phil.* 1, 1; *1 Tim.* 2, 8–13). The life of the Church, in its first fervor, is depicted in glowing terms by the book of Acts. The Church had not yet broken with Judaism, but did form a distinct group within it. Continuing to frequent the temple, it expected to win the Jews over as a group to faith in Jesus Christ, the crowning point of the Jewish faith. The little Church awaited the return of Christ in his glory as the Son of man, according to the prophecy of Daniel (*381*) and Jesus' own promise (Mt. 26, 64). Conforming to the tradition of the apocalyptic circles, it lived with the vital impression that his return was imminent. In

305

this perspective it celebrated the *breaking of bread,* that is, the eucharistic meal, in memory of Jesus. On this point particularly its prayer and liturgy were altogether distinct from those of ordinary Judaism.

First Struggles

The first conflict broke over the little community because of the preaching of Stephen, one of the seven Hellenist "deacons." A formidable controversialist, he was accused by his hearers of having blasphemed against Moses and against the temple and was stoned without due process of law. Among his accusers stood Saul of Tarsus. This young Pharisee, in spite of the moderation of his master Gamaliel, fiercely pursued the disciples of Jesus. It is difficult to date the death of the first martyr precisely, although it could have followed very close upon the foundation of the Church (around 33–34?). Following Stephen's murder, the Hellenists who were part of the Christian community had to disperse, which resulted in the extension of their apostolate. Philip proclaimed the Gospel in Samaria, where Peter and John went to inspect the communities he founded. Others did likewise in Phoenicia, on the island of Cyprus, and as far as Antioch in Syria, which would be the stepping off point for the mission to pagan circles. A little later, Saul of Tarsus was suddenly converted near Damascus by an apparition of the Risen Christ (around 35). After a stay in Arabia he made a short journey to Jerusalem, returned to his homeland, and then set out to proclaim the Gospel.

After peace had been reëstablished the apostles returned to Judea and Samaria. During his inspection tour Peter was inspired to go to the pagan town of Caesarea to receive the Roman centurion Cornelius into the number of the faithful. While wholly committed to Jewish monotheism, Cornelius was not joined to the community of Israel by circumcision. His conversion, while confusing for the Christian of Jewish origin, proved a turning point in the development of the Church. But

306

in 44 the community of Jerusalem was again troubled by a violent persecution. Herod Agrippa, king of the whole land for some years, executed James, the son of Zebedee, and imprisoned Peter. Peter was miraculously freed, but the apostles had to scatter. The local Church was still led by James, the "brother" of the Lord, who probably did not belong to the group of the Twelve. He was assisted by a college of elders (the *presbyters*). This virtuous and austere man and his followers remained attached to the practice of the Mosaic Law. On these events the Acts are still the sole consultable source (6, 8—11, 19; 12), except for what concerns the conversion of St. Paul.

2. THE CHURCH IN PAGAN SURROUNDINGS

First Success

The admission of Cornelius into the Church was regarded by the Judeo-Christians of Jerusalem as an exceptional favor. But in the diaspora, Christian proselytism became much more boldly involved in the apostolate to the pagans. The Hellenists who returned to Cyprus and Antioch in Syria after the death of Stephen did not hesitate to proclaim the Gospel to the pagans and to administer baptism to them without first receiving them into Judaism. The Jerusalem community was disturbed by this. Barnabas was sent to Antioch to look into the affair, where he sided with the innovators and, to direct the Church at Antioch, associated Saul of Tarsus with himself. Around 45 both departed on a missionary tour, taking John-Mark, the future evangelist, with them as a companion. This first apostolic journey of Saul and Barnabas (45–48) took place on the island of Cyprus and in the provinces of Pisidia and Lycaonia, in Asia Minor (Map 11). In each town they used the same method: the Gospel was proclaimed first to the Jews; then, when they opposed it, the preachers turned to the *Gentiles*. And the faithful of pagan origin formed the majority in these local communities (see *Acts* 13–14). It was in the course of

307

this journey that Saul made a habit of calling himself by the Greco-Roman name Paul.

The Judaizing Crisis

In the Judeo-Christian circles of Jerusalem the positions taken by the community of Antioch and the apostolic methods of Paul aroused growing opposition. They thought that if one wished to participate in the salvation brought by Christ Jesus he must first be incorporated into the people of God by circumcision and by practicing the Mosaic Law. Strong in this conviction, some of the followers of James arrived in Antioch and, from the first, refused to eat at the common table with the uncircumcised Christians. This position split the eucharistic communion. In the ensuing troubles, Peter, who had arrived a little later at Antioch, dodged and vacillated. Barnabas let himself be carried away by the prestige of James whose name the disturbers used, but Paul rose to the defense of the authentic Gospel and Christian liberty. He reprimanded Peter, attacked the Judaizers with vigor, and absolutely refused to impose the yoke of the Jewish Law on the Christians coming from paganism (*Acts* 15, 1–2; *Gal.* 2, 11–21; in the Acts, Luke omits every allusion to the incident at Antioch).

To resolve the problem an assembly was held in Jerusalem (49). Paul's position was approved by the apostles present, Peter and John, as well as by James (*Gal.* 2, 1–10; *Acts* 15, 3–21). But to spare the susceptibilities of the Judeo-Christians the group adopted a compromise measure, applicable to the Churches of Syria and Cilicia. The pagano-Christians would practice certain abstinences which would allow community at table (*Acts* 15, 22–32). If this measure momentarily appeased spirits, the intransigent Judeo-Christians were not appeased by anything and they organized a veritable counter-mission in Paul's path, which he had to face many times (*Gal.* 1, 6–7; *Phil.* 3, 2–16; *Cor.* 10–13; *Rom.* 16, 17–18).

308

The Missionary Journeys of St. Paul

After the convocation of Jerusalem the great period of Paul's missionary activity began. From 49 to 52 he went on a long journey through the Mediterranean East (*Acts* 15, 35—18, 21). While Barnabas left for Cyprus, he himself visited the Churches of Lycaonia, penetrated into Galatia where he founded several communities; then, following a heavenly sign, he passed over into Macedonia. He founded churches in the towns of Philippi and Thessalonica. When Athens showed itself unreceptive, he descended to Corinth, where he stayed two years. There he wrote the letters to the Thessalonians (Map 11).

After a return through Ephesus and a brief stay in Jerusalem, Paul retraced his steps for a new mission (*Acts* 18, 22—21, 16), which lasted from 53 to 58. After Galatia he went to Ephesus, the Asiatic metropolis. There he carried on a fruitful apostolate for almost three years. Still there were troubles. In Galatia the Judaizers attacked his work, and he had to write a very firm letter to set matters straight. The Church at Corinth passed through a crisis. He sent instructions in two letters (one of which has been lost). While still at Ephesus he very likely endured an imprisonment, during which he wrote to the Philippians. Finally, he left for Macedonia, because of some alarming news from Corinth. He wrote again twice to this Church which was very dear to him, before going there in person. It was in the course of this last stay that he sent the Christians at Rome a long letter preparing them for his visit. But after seeing the Corinthians he returned to Jerusalem, to bring to the mother Church the fruits of a collection made during his missions (Map 11).

The Church at Rome

We are totally ignorant of the origins of the Church at Rome, as with many other churches. Without doubt it was born in Jewish surroundings, where the Gospel had been brought by

309

some obscure converts. It already existed under the Emperor Claudius, and it was probably after internal dissensions caused by the Christian propaganda that Claudius expelled the Jews from Rome in 49. A reliable tradition, attested to in the 2nd century, mentions the coming of Peter to Rome, but does not precisely date his coming. It was certainly after 60. The first letter of Peter would have been sent from Rome, in the time of the persecution of Nero (around 65).

Paul also came to Rome, but as a prisoner. In 58 Jewish fanatics had him arrested in Jerusalem; and he remained a captive at Caesarea for two years. Finally, to free himself from the maneuvers of his accusers he appealed as a Roman citizen to the tribunal of the emperor, and after a long and eventful voyage he arrived at Rome in 61 (Map 11). He was a prisoner there for two years, but the indications given by the Acts of the Apostles (*Acts* 21, 17—28, 31) leave off before his liberation by the imperial court (63). The letters to the Colossians, to Philemon, and to the Ephesians probably have this Roman captivity as their background. The last apostolic activities of the apostle (63–66) are known only through brief allusions in the epistle to Titus and the first epistle to Timothy. It is doubtful that he went to Spain, as he had planned (*Rom.* 15, 24–28; see Text 44). In any case, he surely returned to the East, passing through Crete, and it is while returning into Macedonia that he must have sent these two letters (64–65).

The Persecution of Nero

In 64 the Christian community at Rome suddenly faced a violent persecution by the imperial powers. Tacitus has told how Nero, to ward off the suspicion of having burned Rome, blamed the Christians (Text 40). An "immense multitude" (these are his very words) perished in punishment. A firm tradition links the violent death of Peter to these circumstances, which the fourth Gospel alludes to in John 21, 18–19. He was buried on the Vatican Hill, near the Circus of Nero. A little later Paul also died at Rome (66–67). His second letter to Timothy shows him, during this last captivity, resigned to all things, having no one with him except Luke, his "dear physician." This double martyrdom is firmly attested to from the end of the 1st century and the beginning of the 2nd (Text 44). We do not know how the Church at Rome rebuilt itself after this bloody trial.

3. JEWISH CHRISTIANITY

Before the Fall of Jerusalem

The facts had to be reviewed briefly to understand the evolution of Jewish Christianity. After the Council of Jerusalem (49) the local community retained its traditional attitude of attachment to the Mosaic Law. This position assured it of a certain prestige in Jewish surroundings. When Paul was arrested, James was not disturbed. The Letter of James (around 60?) is a good witness to his spirituality and austere asceticism. However, in 61–62, profiting from the momentary absence of the Roman procurator, the high priest Annas had James and other Christians put to death (Text 43). The affair occasioned upheaval, and James was replaced as the head of the Church by another relative of Jesus, Simon.

At this time Judaism was also in upheaval, led by groups of Zealots. In 66 troubles broke out in Jerusalem which soon spread to a general uprising, although the Christians, with a good number of Pharisee teachers, did not take part in political action. At the beginning of the war they emigrated to Pella, in the Transjordan. In 70 the Roman troops laid siege to the holy city, captured it, plundered it, and burned the temple. Recalling that Jesus had warned Jerusalem of the divine wrath because of its refusal to believe in the Gospel (Mk. 13, 14–19), the Christians saw in these events a divine sign confirming Jesus' words.

311

The Break Between the Church and Judaism

After 70 Judaism rebuilt itself under the leadership of the Pharisee scholars; it survived through entrenchment in tradition. But this restoration was accompanied by a hardening of positions, notably in regard to the "sects" foreign to Phariseeism. The Christian movement was less and less tolerated and around 80–85, its followers were definitively excluded from the synagogues and Jewish life. Although some Jewish Christian communities in communion with the other churches continued to subsist as far down as the 4th century. Certain groups, on the other hand, perpetuated the traditions of the ancient adversaries of Paul under the name of Ebionites. They finally constituted a sect outside of the Church. During this time Judaism lived through its own tragedy; new insurrections were again defeated in Palestine in 117 and 135, when the Emperor Hadrian drove the Jews from Jerusalem once and for all. The survivors retreated to Galilee, where they began to reorganize, and it was in the Galilean schools that, around the end of the 2nd century, compilation of rabbinic literature began.

4. THE GENTILE CHURCH

The Development of the Church

Thus it was in the communities of Gentile origin, that is, the pagan nations, that the Church took root, in the last third of the 1st century. This is an obscure period in history, on which we possess very few documents. What had become of the apostles, besides Peter, Paul, and John? Who founded the churches in Alexandria, in Mesopotamia, in Persia? Many problems are nearly insoluble. Within even the churches which have left us some mementoes, it is certain that there were pastoral problems, for there was a certain spiritual relaxation, accompanied by heretical infiltrations. The letters of Paul to Titus and Timothy, and the first letter of Peter, already show concern. From the reading of the Letter of Jude, from the second letter which has come to us under the patronage of Peter, and from the "letters to the churches" included in the Apocalypse we get the impression that the danger was grave. After the persecution of Nero, a wholly local affair, the Church enjoyed a period of calm during which it could make many converts, although number endangered quality.

For the rest, we have little precise data on this period. Around 95 Clement of Rome intervened to reëstablish peace in the Church at Corinth (Texts 44 and 48). In 96–97 a new wave of terror rolled over the Church, under the rule of Domitian. Beginning from this date Christians entered an age of intermittent insecurity, which lasted more than two centuries but did not prevent the spreading of their faith.

The Parties of the Asian Churches

The churches of Asia Minor (Map 12) form a separate group on which we are a little better informed. According to a firm tradition (Text 45), the apostle John came to reside in Ephesus, at an unknown date. His personality dominated the life of the Asiatic communities. As the last survivor of the twelve, John was still living during the persecution of Domitian, when he was exiled on the Island of Patmos. The definitive edition of the Apocalypse dates from this era. According to converging indices which go back as far as the 2nd century (Text 51), John's Gospel and his letters would be later still. Thus we come to the end of the 1st century closing the apostolic era. Be that as it may, the struggle against the nascent heresies is equally visible in the last writings linked with John's name.

After his death, the history of the Asiatic church is still known thanks to many texts. A letter from Pliny the Younger, legate to Bythinia, occasioned the rescript of Trajan regulating legal procedure against the Christians. Around 110–115 Ignatius, bishop of Antioch, sent to the Eastern churches several wonderful letters while on his way to Rome to be executed

313

(Texts 44 and 49). Papias, bishop of Hierapolis in Phrygia, gathered up precious traditions on the origins of the Church (around 125?) partially reproduced by the historian Eusebius of Caesarea (Text 46). But the living tradition of the communities still conserved very nearly the same memory of Jesus and the "elders" who had gathered his sayings (Text 45).

5. THE CHURCH, THE NEW PEOPLE OF GOD

The Church and Israel

During the first century of its existence the Church founded by Christ was conscious of being the legitimate heir of Israel. Its faith showed the Old Testament ending in Jesus, the Son of God made man, the Messiah of Israel, the mediator of the new covenant and founder of the kingdom of God here on earth. The Jewish people, beneficiary and trustee of the preparatory revelation, had been called to form the nucleus of the new people of God, now open to every nation. Even after the death of Jesus this vocation was not taken away from her. That is why the Judeo-Christian apostolate originally sought to convert Israel first of all, so that it would fulfill its providential mission towards the pagans. But things turned out otherwise. That is why the Hellenistic Christians, and especially Paul, were triumphant by another method. For faced with the resistance of the Jews, the Gospel was proclaimed directly to the pagans and the Church was opened to them.

The drama of Israel is thus bound up with the Gospel. Only a remnant had fulfilled its vocation by coming to the Christian faith. The authorities, not content with their guilt in the trial of Jesus, opposed the Christian preaching with all their might and kept the mass of the nation away from it. But even though the Jewish people thereby refused to enter the Church as a whole, pagans came in great numbers. Thus the construction of a people of God formed of all the nations had its practical

314

point of departure in the hardening of the heart of Israel. How mysterious this plan of God, which was already the object of St. Paul's reflections (*Rom.* 9–11)! Judaism from now on would pursue its own separate course in history. The remnant of Israel would grow century by century, in the measure that the Jews would be led to Christ by their holy Scriptures. Here they would finally hear the profound message and would wait for the day in which "all Israel would be saved" (*Rom.* 11, 26).

While Awaiting the Return of Christ

During the hour of Judaism's great tragedy in Palestine the evangelical seed was taking root in pagan soil. This made it easier for the Church to understand its separation from the synagogue. However, it did not, for all that, break with the Old Testament, nor did it reject the *Jewish Scriptures*. The Church knew that the Scriptures played an essential role in the plan of God, that they witnessed to Jesus and the Gospel. The Church laid claim to the Scriptures by explaining them in the light of the word of Jesus (Text 42). Very soon the apostolic writings were added to them as a direct echo of the teachings of Jesus. How could they fail to have unparalleled authority?

Thus in the religious history of mankind, Judaism is replaced by the Church, as it awaits the *kingdom of God* to come to completion with the glorious return of the Lord. Then only will the divine promises, renewed and made precise from the era of Abraham down to apostolic times, be realized in their fullness. As had Judaism, the Church remained tense with this expectation (*Apoc.* 22, 12–20). There is, however, a difference between this Jewish hope and the Christian hope. For the Church, the hope of Israel had already begun to be realized. The kingdom of God is present in the heart of history; the Church itself is its "sacramental" realization, adapted to the temporal condition of man. In a hidden way it is the new Jerusalem (*Gal.* 4, 26), more beautiful than the old, which

315

Christ prepares in view of "wedding feast of the Lamb" (*Apoc.* 21).

Text 43

THE DEATH OF JAMES

Flavius Josephus, in his *Jewish Antiquities,* recounts the death of James, the head of the Christian community in Jerusalem. Better attested than the traditions gathered in the 2nd century by Christians, his account shows the situation of the Judeo-Christians of Jerusalem shortly after the arrest of Paul.

After learning of the death of Festus, Caesar sent Albinus to Judea as governor. Annas the Younger who, as we have said, had received the sovereign pontificate, was very bold and enterprising in character and belonged to the Sadducee sect, those among the Jews who were the most severe in their judgments. . . . So disposed, Annas thought to find a favorable occasion in the death of Festus. While Albinus was still on the way, he assembled a court of judges and led before them the brother of Jesus called the Christ, named James, as well as some others. Accused of transgressing the Law, they were condemned to be stoned. All those who in the city were considered most moderate and the strictest observers of the laws supported him only sorrowfully. In secret they sent messengers to the king [Agrippa], begging him to forbid Annas to act in this manner, and informing him that up to now he had done nothing good. Some of them even went to meet Albinus, who had reached Alexandria; they told him that Annas did not have the power to convoke the tribunal without him. Persuaded by this report, Albinus wrote angrily to Annas threatening him with punishment. As for king Agrippa, he withdrew from him for this reason the sovereign pontificate which he had exercised for three months.

316

The Procurator Festus is mentioned by the Acts of the Apostles, at the time of Paul's trial (*Acts* 25, 1–12). Agrippa II, the son of Herod Agrippa I (*Acts* 25, 13—26, 32), without exercising political power in Palestine nevertheless held jurisdiction over the religious institutions of the Jews. The government of Albinus would precipitate the evolution of events leading to the armed revolt of the Jews.

Text 44

THE MARTYRDOM OF
PETER AND PAUL AT ROME

The Bishop Clement wrote from Rome to the Christians of Corinth, around 95, to restore peace in their community. He cites for their example, as a thing known to all, the recent martyrdom of Peter and Paul:

Let us come to those who have very recently struggled, let us take the noble examples of our generation. Those who were the most lofty and the most upright pillars, as a result of jealousy and envy, they were persecuted and put to death. Let us place before our eyes the excellent apostles. Peter, as a result of an unjust jealousy, bore not one or two, but numerous sufferings, and having borne witness, he went to the place of glory which was his due. Paul, because of jealousy and strife, obtained the reward of his long-suffering: seven times put in chains, exiled, stoned, this herald [of the Gospel] in the East and the West received the noble renown which suited his faith; having taught justice to the entire world, reaching the limits of the West and having rendered his witness befor governors, he quit this world and went to the holy place, having become the illustrious model of long-suffering. To these men, whose conduct had thus been so holy, are to be added an immense multitude of the elect who, as a result of jealousy, suffered

317

many outrages and tortures and left among us the most magnificent example.

St. Clement, *Letter to the Corinthians*, 5, 1—6, 1

The allusion to the persecution of Nero dovetails with the account of Tacitus. Some interior dissentions within the Christian communities are also mentioned. Fifteen years later, en route to Rome to "bear his witness" (that is, to undergo martyrdom), Ignatius of Antioch wrote to the Romans recalling in his turn the double martyrdom of the apostles:

Pray for me, so that by the teeth of the wild beasts I be offered as a victim to God. I do not order you as Peter and Paul. They were apostles; I, a condemned man. They were free men; I, up to now, a slave. But by suffering I will become a freedman of Jesus Christ and in him I will rise free. For the time being, in chains, I study to learn to desire nothing.

St. Ignatius of Antioch, *Letter to the Romans*, 4, 2–3

This allusion supposes that Peter and Paul had "borne their witness" in Rome, giving on this occasion their instructions to the Christian community. Other extracts from the letters are quoted below (Text 49).

Text 45

THE TRADITION OF THE APOSTLE JOHN IN ASIA MINOR

Around 190 Irenaeus of Lyons wrote to reëstablish the faith of Florinus, his childhood friend, who had fallen into the agnostic heresy. He appeals to the living tradition by which, through the intermediary of the bishop of Smyrna, Polycarp, they both are linked to the apostle John:

318

These doctrines, Florinus, are not in accord with the Church, they throw those who believe into the greatest impiety . . . These doctrines the elders who preceded us and who associated with the apostles have not transmitted to you. For I saw you, as a child, in lower Asia, near Polycarp, when you shone in the imperial court and you tried to win his regard. I remember it better, in fact, than what has taken place recently, for that which one learns as a youth grows with the soul and is a part of each one. I can then say in what place the blessed Polycarp sat down to teach, his manner of entering and leaving, his way of life, his aspect, the speeches which he made to the crowd, what he said of his relations with John and with the others who had seen the Lord, how he recalled their words, and what things he had heard them recount about the Lord, his miracles and his teaching. Having received all this from eye-witnesses of the Word of Life, Polycarp reported them in conformity with the Scriptures. That also by the mercy of God, I have then listened to carefully; I have preserved their memory, not on paper, but in my heart.

Eusebeus of Caesarea, Ecclesiastical History, 5, 20. 4

Elsewhere, Irenaeus returns to this theme:

As for Polycarp, not only was he the disciple of the apostles and associated with a number of persons who had seen the Lord, but it is through the apostles that he was made bishop for Asia in the Church of Smyrna. We ourselves saw him in our youth. For he lived a long time afterwards, to a very advanced age, glorious and brilliant he bore witness, and then quit his life. He never had but one teaching: what he had learned from the apostles, what the Church transmits, which alone is true.

St. Irenaeus, Against Heresies, 3, 3. 4

	Events of the Apostolic Era	Apostolic Writings (except the Gospels of Matthew and Luke and the Acts of the Apostles)
30	Pentecost	
c. 33	Martyrdom of Stephen	
c. 35	Conversion of Paul	
44	Persecution of Herod Agrippa	
45–48	Journey of Paul and Barnabas	
49	Quarrel with Judaizers Council of Jerusalem	
49–52	2nd missionary journey of Paul	Letters to Thessalonians
53–58	3rd journey of Paul	Letter to the Galatians Letter to the Philippians Letters to the Corinthians Letter to the Romans
58–60	Paul in prison at Caesarea	
c. 60		Letter of James(?)
60–61	Journey of Paul to Rome	
61–62	Martyrdom of James	
61–63	Paul a prisoner at Rome	Letters to the Collossians, to
after 60	Peter in Rome	Philemon, to Ephesians
64–66	Last journeys of Paul	Letter to Titus and 1st Letter to Timothy
64	Persecution of Nero	1st Letter of Peter
c. 65	Peter's martyrdom at Rome	
66	Paul's final captivity	2nd Letter to Timothy
c. 67	Paul's martyrdom at Rome	
66–70	War in Judea	Letter to the Hebrews Gospel of Mark
70	Destruction of Jerusalem	First texts of the Apocalypse (?)
70–90	Period of calm for the Church	Collection of Paul's Letters Letter of Jude 2nd Letter attributed to Peter
c. 95	Letter of Clement of Rome to the Corinthians	
96–97	Persecution of Domitian	Edition of the Apocalypse Letters of John
98–100	Death of John	Edition of John's Gospel

320

Bibliography

The history of the Church in the apostolic era is presented in all of the histories of the Church, for example, *The Church of the Apostles and Martyrs* by H. Daniel-Rops (New York 1960), which is good on the whole, despite some insufficiencies in criticism of the sources.

Study Guides

Study the Christian apologetic at the beginning of the Church according to the discourses in the Acts of the Apostles (*Acts* 2, 14–39; 3, 12–26; 4, 9–12; 5, 29–32; 10, 34–43; 13, 16–41). What place does it give to the fulfillment of the Scriptures? (See section II of Chapter XIV on this idea.)

To throw light on the crisis of the Judaizers, look for indications in the history of Judaism which will make its motives comprehensible (*186, 188, 235, 241–243, 325, 393, 396–398;* see Text 37).

XVI.

THE PROCLAMATION
OF THE GOSPEL

The Christian Bible is the Jewish Bible completed by the writings which summarize the apostolic witness. These writings are often divided into three categories: historical works (the Gospels and Acts of the Apostles), epistles or letters, and an Apocalypse. In reality, however, the problem is much more complex. And to understand the exact nature of these books, it would be better to classify them differently. All have their place in the pastoral work of the primitive Church, but some directly concern the concrete proclamation of the Gospel (Acts of the Apostles) or gather together the message itself (Gospels). Other books regulate the life of the churches and they assure the accuracy of the faith (epistles, or letters). The writings grouped under St. John's name fall into these two categories (a Gospel, three epistles, and an Apocalypse). This is the classification followed in the next three chapters along with a summary doctrinal statement of each book's contents.

1. THE PRIMITIVE PREACHING

From the Pentecost day on, the main task of the Twelve was the proclamation of the Gospel. All those who, under the authority of the apostles, gave themselves to the ministry also took on

322

preaching as their principal activity. Even though the books of the New Testament were written much later, they give us some idea of this preaching. The catechetical discourses of the Acts of the Apostles preserve the key themes of this proclamation in summary form (2, 14–41; 3, 12–25; 4, 9–12; 5, 29–32; 7, 1–53; 8, 26–35; 10, 34–43; 13, 16–41; 26, 12–23), while the apostolic epistles recapture several outlines of the preaching from which it was derived. St. Paul explicitly alludes to a "tradition" which he had "received," without doubt at the time of his conversion or his first journey to Jerusalem (*1 Cor.* 11, 23–25; 15, 1–5). This proclamation of the Gospel is made up of three closely linked elements.

The Gospel of the Kingdom of God

The first element was the Gospel of the kingdom of God, which had already been preached by Jesus. During his lifetime, the Twelve and the seventy-two were sent out, commissioned to proclaim the kingdom to the surrounding masses (*Lk.* 9, 1–6; 10, 1–20). At this time their preaching was certainly not original; rather, they limited themselves to repeating, wherever they went, what the Master had said to those who heard him directly. After Pentecost, they naturally resumed this same activity, reporting with the same scrupulous care the words of Jesus which were the foundation of their authority: sayings, parables, casuistic solutions, and so forth. And the unexpected happenings since the end of his public life—the passion, resurrection, the reception of the Holy Spirit—considerably clarified the deeper meaning of his words. The apostles emphasized elements of its teaching according to the preaching occasion, establishing all the needed connections between the words of Jesus and the present experience of the Church. The practical necessities of preaching aso entailed certain literary adaptations, in order to make their proclamation of the mysterious kingdom of God clear to various audiences.

The Gospel of Jesus, Messiah and Son of God

The second element of the apostolic preaching is directly related to the mystery of the resurrection: Jesus, Son of God, is the Messiah promised by the prophets; he died for our sins, according to the Scriptures; rose on the third day, and has been enthroned in glory at the right hand of God, from whence he will return as Judge on the last day. Such a proclamation did not focus on abstract *ideas* but implied an historical witness to certain essential *facts* by which the salvation of men was accomplished and the promises of the prophets had come true. But the proclamation also included a doctrinal explanation of the religious *meaning* of the role and person of Jesus himself; the key element was the application of the eschatological prophesies to recent events (for example, *Acts* 2, 15–21; 2, 30–34). Finally, the agreement of the facts with Scriptures gave a foundation for an apologetic aimed at Jewish hearers, justifying the scandal of the Messiah's passion (*Acts* 2, 23; 3, 18; 8, 28–35) and proving that Jesus clearly was the prophesied Saviour (*Acts* 3, 2–24).

The precise object of this preaching was not a *past* event, but a *present* reality: the lordship of Jesus, who is enthroned in his glory and whose return is awaited. Everything rested, finally, on the experience of the apparitions and events which corroborated the reality of the resurrection. But apart from these, the witnesses of Jesus saw the mysterious nature and meaning of his life unveiled. When the witnesses looked into the Scriptures to apply the texts to Jesus, they found that he had exceeded the bounds of their frame of reference. In their eyes Jesus was not only the Messiah Son of David (*Acts* 2, 30), the Servant of Yahweh (*Acts* 3, 13), and the Son of man (*Acts* 7, 55–56). He was the Son of God in the strongest sense of the term. For, having entered into the glory of God, he participated in his Father's prerogatives and thus received the name Lord (*Phil.* 2, 9–11). As this became a conscious element and more explicitly expressed, it dominated all apostolic

324

preaching and, in retrospect, shed light upon the whole history of Jesus.

The Actions and Conduct of Jesus

The Christ in glory, who is the object of faith, is Jesus of Nazareth, the man whom the Jews had known, heard, and finally rejected. The proclamation of the Gospel is based upon this constantly affirmed identity of the two titles (*Acts* 2, 22–24; 4, 10–12; 10, 37–40; 13, 23–30). This is why the witnesses of Jesus' life, who had followed him since his baptism by John, played so important a role in the origins of the Church (*Acts* 1, 21–22; 10, 37–39). The link between the Gospel and historical reality is thus forcefully brought out. That is why the memory of the actions and conduct of Jesus had to be preserved. These certainly were not preserved to satisfy curiosity, but only because of their religious interest. Thus the apostolic catechesis was repeated in short accounts, showing Jesus accredited by his miracles (see *Acts* 2, 22), depicting his concrete attitudes or emphasizing his sayings which unveiled the mystery of his person (like those of the baptism and the transfiguration). Only the unit made up of the Last Supper, the passion, and the resurrection was amplified and more developed.

So the proclamation of the Gospel itself demanded the authentic preservation of the memories relating to Jesus. This also explains the character of their formulation which is often disconnected and so different from our scientific concept of history.

To prepare men for the reception of baptism, an elementary catechesis used parts of the proclamation. After baptism the faithful continued to learn through the teaching of the apostles, to whom they listened attentively (*Acts* 2, 42). This was the cradle of the Gospels, where traditions were still transmitted orally. The role of the apostles, the leaders of the Christian community, was clearly eminent in this process of formation.

325

According to the book of the Acts, the personality of Peter stands out with particular clarity.

2. THE APOSTOLIC TRADITION

The Life of the Primitive Church

We would like to have more detailed information on the life of the primitive Church the better to understand this formation of the Gospel witness, since the information found in the book of Acts is unhappily very fragmentary. For besides the sermon outlines, which we will discuss, the facts reported are scarce and the accounts rarely detailed (*Acts* 1–12; 15). The Christian liturgy must have had great importance at this time for it was the milieu in which the tradition about Jesus took shape. The liturgy of baptism included, before the rite of immersion, a profession whose formulation already foreshadowed the Apostles' Creed (*Acts* 2, 38–41; 8, 35–38; 10, 34–48; *1 Cor.* 15, 3–5; *Rom.* 6, 3–4; 8, 34; 10, 9; *Eph.* 2, 5–6); the accounts of Jesus' baptism evidently had this liturgy as their background. The liturgy of the Lord's Supper, still called the Breaking of the Bread (*Acts* 2, 42; 20, 7–11), reproduced the action of the Last Supper "in memory of the Lord," to "proclaim his death while awaiting his coming" (*1 Cor.* 11, 26). It was to answer this precise need that the accounts of the Supper took shape (*Mt.* 26, 26–29; *Mk.* 14, 22–25; *Lk.* 22, 19–20; *1 Cor.* 11, 23–25); and these in their turn have influenced the accounts of the meal at which Jesus appeared (*Mk.* 8, 6; *Lk.* 24, 30).

The First Collections of Christian Texts

All these traditions could have been transmitted orally for a long time without corruption, especially while the apostles were still at the head of the community. Nevertheless, the rapid extension of the Church soon required the fixing of at least the essentials and their preservation in writing. There the preachers of the Gospel, as they became more numerous, found

326

a firm basis for their catechesis and for the celebration of the liturgy in the communities which they founded. Fragments of this primitive literature still remain in the Acts and in the epistles as outlines of sermons (repeated in the sermons in Acts); chains of Scripture texts, used to proclaim the Gospel to the Jews or to explain doctrine (*Acts* 6, 9–10; 13, 33–43; 18, 28; 28, 23–28; *Rom.* 3, 9–20; 9, 6–29; 10, 5–21, etc.); psalms (*Acts* 4, 24–30) and hymns (*Phil.* 2, 6–11; *Col.* 1, 15–20; *Eph.* 5, 14; *1 Tim.* 3, 16; 5, 15–16); official formularies of the profession of faith; rules for the rites of baptism (*Mt.* 28, 19) and the Eucharist. We possess only scattered fragments of all this, but the phraseology of the apostolic letters must have felt their influence, and besides the New Testament, the most ancient of Christian writings is their direct descendant (Text 47).

From the Oral Gospel to the Written Gospel

Finally, partial collections of the "sayings of the Lord" from which the Gospel narratives probably were gradually formed included the passion narrative; a list of appearances (*1 Cor.* 15, 5–7); episodes grouped by affinity (*Mk.* 2, 1—3, 6); sayings linked by the similarity of themes (*Mk.* 4, 1–34). The passage from the Aramaic version to the Greek translation was no problem, since the Church at Jerusalem was soon bilingual (*Acts* 6, 1), and the Greek version of the Old Testament furnished suitable language. St. Luke, in the prologue to his Gospel, refers to many works of this kind (*Lk.* 1, 1–3). It is within this framework that the Gospel of Matthew "in the Hebrew language" (actually Aramaic) must be located—a 2nd-century tradition makes it the most ancient of the Gospels (Text 46). Unfortunately, its text is lost, and it is hard to determine its order and content from the Greek Gospel bearing Matthew's name. But we do know enough about it to understand that our Gospels are the result of a long, involved process of development.

The first three Gospels (Matthew, Mark, Luke) are closely

327

related to one another. Since they can be put in parallel columns for immediate comparisons of their texts, they are called *synoptics*. Such a resemblance together with a thousand differences in detail poses a peculiar problem which is not yet

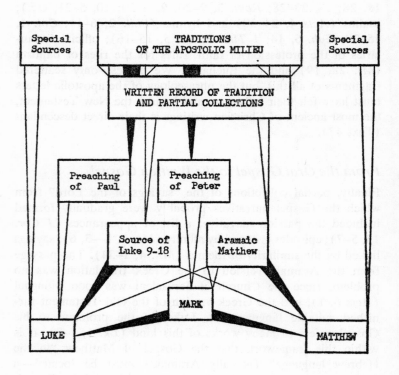

completely clarified. Oversimplifications must be abandoned for the processes of formation probably followed one of these patterns. These three little books could be the independent summaries of the oral catechesis of the apostles; or better, Mark and Luke could have used Matthew, the one abridging

328

him, the other completing him; or again, Matthew and Luke could have combined the text of Mark with that of another source unknown to the others. In fact, certain literary contacts between the three works at least suppose the use of a common written document. The use of Mark and Luke by the final editor of Matthew is also probable, but Mark himself could, in his turn, depend on an older written Gospel, the Aramaic Matthew, which was soon translated into Greek. But this is only hypothesis. At the time of their writing, oral tradition still existed and could also have influenced them. In brief, the process of the formation of the Gospels can only be probably sketched, as the diagram shows.

The Importance of the Apostolic Tradition

The problem of the writing of the Synoptics, of their dates, their authors, loses much importance once it is established that the Gospels are rooted in the tradition of the primitive Church, which itself depended on the apostolic witness. Of course, the composition and presentation the materials of this tradition by the three authors of these three little books does not affect the antiquity and values of these materials. At this early age, the fundamental element of life of the Church was not books, but a living tradition—the writings of the New Testament are only occasional and incomplete witnesses of this tradition. The tradition is the essential link between them and the Lord. But it is important to note two complementary points.

In the first place, the purpose of writing was the integral transmission of a received deposit (*1 Tim.* 6, 20; *2 Tim.* 1, 14): what Jesus had said and done, the meaning of his life and death perceived in the light of the resurrection, the meaning of the whole Old Testament veiled through faith in him. These are the contents of this intangible deposit. From this point of view, the faith is a conserver, and the leaders of the Church have the mission of watching over this deposit and guaranteeing the fidelity of the Gospel accounts. Secondly, as time went on the Church faced new problems that had to be settled (for example, the problem posed by the conversion of the pagans). So it penetrates to a deeper understanding of the Scriptures which concern Jesus and comprehends more fully the meaning of his acts and the mystery of his person, expressing with greater precision the essential points of its faith. As a consequence, under the shield of the apostles and then the responsible ones who took their places, doctrinal progress began. While the apostles, witnesses to Christ, were living, revelation was completed and fulfilled. Preservation and progress conditioned one another. Preservation without progress would have ended in the archaic Christianity of the Judeo-Christians, and the desire for progress without holding firm the received deposit would have given birth to heresies.

3. THE GOSPEL ACCORDING TO ST. MARK

Mark, the Interpreter of Peter

The harmonizing testimony of 2nd-century authors makes Mark the "interpreter of Peter," who fixed his preaching in writing (Text 46). The peculiarities of his book confirm this view. Peter is the apostle whose portrait stands out with the greatest relief. In Mark's Gospel certain highly colored picturesque accounts, closely resembling the oral preaching with no concern for correcting style, indicate an eyewitness (4, 35–41; 5, 1–43; 8, 22–26; 9, 14–28; 10, 46–52; compare these with the parallel accounts of Matthew and Luke); the citations in Aramaic also point to the same source (5, 41; 7, 34; 15, 34). The explanations given to the Greco-Roman readers who were ignorant of Jewish customs (7, 3–4) give us a glimpse of Mark's public. Thus a "Gospel according to Peter" can be spoken of, if we mean the oral Gospel of the apostle.

The Work of the Evangelist

The selection of the ideas preserved and the construction of the whole belong to Mark. Certainly, he used preëxisting collections

of anecdotes (2, 1—3, 6; 11, 27—12, 37) or sayings of Jesus
(4, 13). Likewise, he probably depended on the Aramaic Gospel of Matthew, even though this cannot be proven. But Mark
used these traditional materials in his own way, sometimes
summarizing them schematically (1, 1–20; 6, 7–13), sometimes enriching them with concrete details gathered from the
lips of Peter. To dispose souls to faith in Jesus, Mark relied on
the impression of religious fear produced by the miracles (2,
12; 4, 41), more than on the fulfillment of the prophecies. This
proves that he was not writing for Judeo-Christians, though nowhere else is the human sensibility of Jesus (his affections,
wonder, impatience, wrath) noted with so little toning down.
The words of Jesus are especially well preserved when presented as an anecdote, while sermons are reduced to a minimum (4; 13).

The plan is clear when you see the Gospel as a whole starting
with chapter 9. Up to 8, 27, it is the proclamation of the kingdom of God, in Galilee, then in the surrounding territories, supported by signs and miracles. At the end of this first period, we
note a crisis among the crowd (6, 1–5) and signs of hostility
manifested by Herod Antipas (6, 14–16) and by the Pharisees
(8, 11–15). Peter confesses in the name of the Twelve his faith
in Jesus as Messiah (8, 27–30); six days later, at the transfiguration, Jesus reveals his role as Son of God to three privileged apostles (9, 2–10). But immediately, in contradiction to
their dream of a temporal success, he orients them towards his
approaching passion (8, 31–33; 9, 12. 30–32; 10, 32–34),
which is bound up with the coming of the kingdom of God (9,
1). His life takes on the character of a journey towards suffering and death, the necessary prelude to the glorious resurrection. Paradoxically, it will be at the foot of the cross that a
pagan will recognize him as Son of God (14, 39). The sayings
and anecdotes are unequally distributed within this very broad
framework, which follows the outline of the primitive preaching (*Acts* 2, 22–24; 10, 37–41; 13, 23–37). The end of the
Gospel (16, 9–19), recognized as an inspired text, was never-

theless written by another author, as the original ending has been lost.

The Evangelist

We know Mark through others. His family belonged to the Church at Jerusalem from the very beginning (*Acts* 12, 12). From this passage in Acts it has been supposed that the Cenacle, the first meeting place of Christians (*Acts* 1, 13; 2, 1–4; 4, 23–31; see *Mk*. 14, 12–16), was located in the house of Mark's mother, who also owned the enclosure of Gethsemani. Mark was the unidentified young man mentioned only by his Gospel at the time of the arrest of Jesus (*Mk*. 14, 51–52). These are plausible hypotheses, but by no means certain. In any case, Mark was linked at a young age to the apostolate of Paul and Barnabas (*Acts* 12, 25; 13, 13; 15, 37–39). He accompanied Paul during his first captivity at Rome (*Col*. 4, 10; *Philem.* 24). He is found accompanying Peter in Rome, at the beginning of the persecution of Nero, in 64–65 (*1 Pet*. 5, 13). But he had left the city when Paul underwent his second captivity, in 66–67, and Paul regretted the absence of this helper "useful for the ministry" (*2 Tim*. 4, 11). The composition of his Gospel could have taken place at Rome, or at least in Italy, between 67 and 70, for it makes allusion to the war in Judea as already underway (*Mk*. 13, 14: "let the reader understand"). Apparently, he did not know the concrete details of the destruction of Jerusalem (*Mk*. 13, 19).

4. THE WORK OF ST. LUKE

The Evangelist and His Two Works

Luke, a Greek physician originally from Antioch, was Paul's companion beginning with Paul's second missionary voyage. Luke frequently refers to memories of the trip in the Acts (in the first person plural) indicating his presence with the apostle (*Acts* 16, 11–17; 20, 5—21, 18; 27, 1—28, 16). Also Paul mentions him at the end of his letters during the first Roman captivity (*Col.* 4, 14; *Philem.* 24). During his last captivity (66–67) Luke was the only one with him (*2 Tim.* 4, 11). So it is not surprising that his work contains Pauline echoes, which are, nevertheless, very discreet, because of his fidelity to his sources of information (Text 46).

Luke himself speaks of his painstaking inquiries (1, 3). He gathered together the memories of persons linked to the Gospel events: Mary (*Lk.* 2, 19. 51); the members of Jesus' family (3, 23–31); the holy women (7, 36–50; 8, 1–3; 23, 49. 55); Cleophas (24, 12–35). But analysis of his book also gives evidence of written sources: the Gospel of Mark; a well-ordered collection which Matthew also used (perhaps Aramaic Matthew, already translated into Greek); another collection of selected Gospel fragments, reproduced in 9, 51—18, 14. When Luke is working with already formed materials, he is generally content to juxtapose them without blending them together; at other times he enjoys his freedom of composition (for example, in chapters 1–2, 15, and 24).

The date of the final edition of his book is placed in the years following the publication of Mark (around 67), when the war in Judea had at least begun. Basing themselves upon allusions in Luke 19, 43–44, and 21, 20, which make the formularies of Mark more precise as if to insist upon Jesus' prediction, some Catholic exegetes try to place it in the decade following the destruction of Jesrusalem, but this conclusion may go beyond the data it is based upon. In any case, the discussion is over a small period of time, and besides, the question is secondary, since the antiquity of the materials used can be verified.

The Key Ideas of the Gospel

In his choice of episodes and sayings, and especially in his manner of presenting them, Luke was guided by several dominant ideas. He seems to have been preoccupied with chronology (3, 1–2), but for the public life of Jesus the state of the tradition did not permit a true ordering of events, so he juxtaposed the episodes while retaining the great divisions of Mark's outline

333

and inserting in it two sections of his own (6, 20—7, 17; 9, 51—18, 14). He also gave the abrupt accounts of Mark a more literary form. His portrait of Jesus is sketched in the most pleasant colors, and his version of the sayings of the Master follows the Semitic original less closely than that of Matthew, for he tries to make the Gospel more accessible to the Hellenistic public. This caused a flood of corrections in detail.

Luke had reasons for passing lightly over Jesus' relations to official Judaism, for he intended to show Jesus as the *Light of Nations* as well as the Messiah of Israel. This is perceptible in the infancy narratives (1, 68–78; 2, 29–32) and in the genealogy of Jesus, which he traces back to man's first parents (3, 23–38). Among his favorite themes are the mercy of God towards sinners and suffering mankind (6, 11–17. 36–50; 15), those of the virtues which characterize Christian spirituality: true poverty (6, 20. 24; 12, 13–34; 14, 25–33; 16), fraternal charity (10, 25–37), and the joy and praise of God (repeatedly heard in the infancy narratives, which punctuate the canticles, or in the conclusion of his Gospel, 24, 52–53). These themes hold an eminent position in the chapters where the material is proper to Luke (1–2; 11, 51—18, 14).

The Mystery of Jesus Christ

Of Jesus' infancy, Luke did not relate facts merely to satisfy the curiosity of feelings of his readers. The first Christian catechesis was not interested in the infancy and it is not contained in the sermons in Acts nor in Mark's Gospel. But having collected firsthand information on it, Luke used it to present the mysterious person of Jesus concretely. These accounts, very carefully worked out, consciously imitate certain pages of the Greek Bible, and have a didactic purpose. The relationship of Jesus and John the Baptist is insinuated by the parallel presentation of the two annunciations and births. The dignity of Jesus, the Davidic Messiah and the Son of God, and his virginal conception are clearly indicated (1, 30–38). The episode of the shepherds at the manger foreshadows Jesus' preaching on the poor (2, 8–18); the presentation in the temple presages his future sacrifice (2, 22–35), and the episode with the teachers, his teaching mission (2, 41–50). So the memories are put at the service of the Christian catechesis. Luke is not an historian in the modern sense of the word; he is an *evangelist* who loads his accounts to convey a real theology. Even in telling the public life he succeeds in doing the same thing. For example, he constantly shows Jesus, during the last month, on the way to Jerusalem (9, 31. 51; 13, 22. 33; 17, 11; 18, 31; 19, 11) where the sacrifice of salvation would take place. This is not by chance, for after the resurrection the proclamation of the Gospel will also start from Jerusalem (24, 47–49). Thus the place of the holy city in the Gospel account symbolizes its place in the plan of God.

The Acts of the Apostles

The Acts of the Apostles is a follow-up to the Gospel like the second panel of a diptych. The prologue is a literary device which marks the junction of the two books (*Lk.* 24, 36–53; *Acts* 1, 3–11). And as the Gospel concluded in Jerusalem, so the Acts start there. The story of the Acts of the Apostles also constitutes a concrete commentary on the risen Christ's address to the eleven apostles: "When the Holy Spirit will descend upon you, you will be clothed with power and you will bear me witness in Jerusalem, in the whole of Judea, in Samaria, and even to the ends of the earth" (*Acts* 1, 8). From Pentecost, the Church was established in Jerusalem, where it developed (*Acts* 2–7). The persecution, by scattering the Hellenistic Christians, carried it to Judea and to Samaria (8; 9, 31—11, 18; 12, 1–24) and even to Cyprus and Syria (11, 19–30; 12, 25). In this first part of the book, attention is centered on the Jerusalem community, where Peter occupied the central place. One episode, however, foreshadows the second part of the book: the conversion of Paul, the persecutor (9, 1–30). Beginning with 13, 1, the account is tied to the apostolic journeys of Paul, with the exception of chapter 15, which treats of the Judeo-Christian problem and of the council of Jerusalem—the hinge between the evangelization of the Jewish world and the pagan world.

In writing the first part Luke used many sources of information—for example, the traditions of the Church at Jerusalem and the witnesses of the Palestinian community, which he could have gathered in his travels there (*Acts* 21, 7–17). But this information gives an imprecise idea of the actual events. Concerning the information on the Church at Antioch, we must remember that this was Luke's home town. Companion to Paul during the sea-voyage, he must have heard the story of Paul's conversion more than once. Having himself taken part in the missions of the apostle, he could speak at first hand, even if he did not have a log of the journey to reproduce (17, 1—20, 4; 21, 18—26, 32). But whenever he cites this log he shows himself an excellent stylist, as exemplified in the account of his shipwreck (27–28).

The book stops abruptly after St. Paul's arrival in Rome, but it would be improper to conclude from this that Luke composed his two-volume work then. More simply, having brought the proclamation of the Gospel as far as the political center of the pagan world, he thought that his program was finished. The book was published at the earliest around 68–69, at the latest around 80–85. His text, however, makes no allusion to the persecution of Nero or the destruction of Jerusalem. Perhaps during the calm years which followed 70, Luke tried to obtain the good will of the Roman world towards a religion which could no longer use the name Judaism, but whose legal standing was poorly defined. But who knows if he had the time to put the finishing touches on his work?

The Historical and Religious Value of the Acts

The text of the Acts remains very close to its sources, often reproducing them literally. The different character of the accounts flows from the different sources—Luke's log of the trip, for example, or the primitive traditions collected at Jerusalem long after the events. In these various cases, the details are not reported with the same degree of precision, and on the level of historical criticism their value is uneven. But Luke's purpose was not critical history. He wanted to show the religious mean-

336

ing of history, by recalling the events as best he could. Every-thing in his account hangs together because of the leading threads which criss-cross it: the word of God is always pro-claimed at greater and greater distance; the Holy Spirit makes it fruitful; the Church spreads from the remnant of Israel (6, 7; 9, 31; 12, 24) even to the pagans among whom it grows fruit-ful (28, 23–29).

Within this broad framework the spiritual themes dear to Luke reappear from place to place: poverty, charity, joy, praise of God (3, 42–45; 4, 32–37; 6, 41; 11, 18). The at-mosphere of the book is full of serenity which neither the account of the martyrdoms (8, 54–60; 12) nor the remem-brance of difficulties alters. Luke preferred to slide over these without delay (16, 35–39), when he did not pass over them in total silence, as he did with the incident at Antioch between Peter and Paul (*Gal.* 2, 11–14). Only the positive side of the events interest this kind-souled narrator, who wondered at the marvels of divine grace rather than attend to human pettiness. The Acts do not give us a complete history of Christian origins, but such as they are they furnish precious teachings and, what is more, edify the soul of the reader and invite him to medita-tion.

5. THE GOSPEL ACCORDING TO ST. MATTHEW

The Origin of the Book

The Aramaic Gospel of Matthew, condensed from the apostolic tradition, could have been composed very early, though its text has been lost. Our present Gospel is not simply a translation of it but a new edition painstakingly composed, recast and en-riched. The sources it used are still discernible, and the author seems to have been acquainted with the Gospel of Mark. He also used a collection of selected Gospel fragments parallel to that which *Luke* 11, 51—18, 14, reproduced, but he scattered them throughout his narrative. Finally, he borrowed from his own sources for the chapters of the infancy narrative (*Mt.*

1–2), some episodes of the public life (17, 24–27), a great number of sayings or parables, and many details in the passion account and in the resurrection. The book forms a synthesis, behind which we can sense a whole process of elaboration in Christian catechesis.

Was the author Matthew or an inspired continuator? It is impossible to say. But in the second case, the book has so well preserved the link with the original book of Matthew that it has been transmitted under his name. The exact date of composition is also debated, as in the case of Luke. Indications suggesting a date later than 70 are tenuous (22, 7, taken as an allusion to the destruction of Jerusalem), but the polemic against the unfaithful Jews supposes an era of tension between the Church and the synagogue. In any case, the critics vie with one another in establishing the antiquity of the materials used, making a distinction between the elements drawn from written sources already fixed for a long time, and the elements drawn from oral tradition. In the first case, the memories crystallized very early because of the Christian catechesis. In the second, they have been transmitted in a freer fashion, and they, especially those of the infancy of Christ, would already have begun to recede into the past.

The Plan of the Gospel

Apart from the infancy narratives (1–2) and the passion narratives (26–28), the plan of the Gospel is tightly hinged around five sermons, which all treat of *the kingdom of heaven,* the central theme of Jesus' teaching. They are: the charter of the kingdom, or the Sermon on the Mount (5–7); the instruction to the apostles, missionaries of the kingdom (10); the teaching in parables on the nature of the kingdom (13); the instruction to the disciples on the spirit of the kingdom (18); the discourse on the destiny of Israel, in the perspective of the eschatological consummation of the kingdom (24–25). This intentional disposition shows the pedagogical purpose of the work, which tried not only to depict Jesus as a teacher but to serve effectively in teaching the faithful.

Between these sermons, the events of the public life are distributed in large blocks, where a number of the sayings of Jesus are found. Arrangement of materials is often made according to a logical order (ten miracles in chapters 8–9; a collection of sayings against the Pharisees in chapter 23). However, the plan of Mark reappears, notably in the great turning point of the Gospel—Peter's profession of faith and the transfiguration (16, 15—17, 23). From one stage to another even a certain progression in the drama can be followed: the enthusiasm of the crowds (4, 24–25), the reserve of the Pharisees and the first conflicts between Jesus and them (9, 1–17); calumnies against Jesus, who is accused of driving out devils by Beelzebub and who is driven out of Nazareth (12, 1–4. 22–45; 13, 53–58); Jesus' refusal of a sign in the heavens, and his warning the apostles against the spirit of the Pharisees (15, 39—16, 12); the violent arguments of the last week (21, 1—23, 39); and the final conspiracy (26, 1–5).

Jesus, Messiah of Israel

The chain of events prepared for the tragedy of the passion. But this is only the apparent side of things. On a deeper level, Jesus gradually revealed the mystery of his person, linked so closely to the mystery of the kingdom. He is the prophet of the kingdom (4, 17. 23); he is the teacher, as a new Moses (5, 17–48); he is the Messiah of Israel, whose works fulfilled the eschatological prophecies (11, 2–6); he is the Son of the Heavenly Father (11, 25–27). At the end of his mission in Galilee, he calls forth an act of faith from his own: "You are the Messiah, the Son of the Living God" (16, 16). From then on he begins to teach them that "the Messiah must suffer before entering into his glory" (16, 21; 17, 22–23; 20, 17–19). The legitimate heir of royal messianism as "Son of David" (20, 29; 21, 1–10. 15–16), only Son of the Father sent to the "vine-dressers" of Israel (21, 37–39), he realized by his death the prophecy of the Suffering Servant (26, 24. 31), namely, finally to seal in his blood the new covenant (26, 26–29). But then having entered into his glory, he will come as Judge on the last day (26, 64). The revelation of the personality of Jesus culminates in the hour of his passion. But it is there also that the drama of Israel comes to a head. Through the voice of their leaders the chosen people refuse their Messiah and fail to recognize the Son of God (26, 63–68; 27, 39–43). Here the accompanying perspective is that of the judgment and of Yahweh (24, 14–36).

Such a presentation of events shows that the evangelist wrote for Jewish readers. He selected sayings of Jesus to shock the hardest of rebellious Judaism to grace (21, 33–45; 23). Did they have no value for the present, in a time when the Christians saw themselves definitively excluded from the synagogue? No, for at the same time, by a positive apologetical preoccupation, the evangelist insistently pointed out the fulfillment of the messianic prophesies which could be seen in the life of Jesus. Using, perhaps, an already existing collection, he inserted in his text ten witnesses from Scripture which constitute a proof for the Jews (1, 22–23; 2, 15; 2, 17–18; 2, 23; 4, 14–16; 8, 17; 12, 17–21; 13, 14–15; 13, 34; 21, 4–5; 27, 9–10). His Gospel is, then, above all others, that of the Messiah of Israel.

It was in this spirit that Matthew developed the infancy narratives. Drawing material from an oral tradition further separated from the details of the events than the parallel source of Luke, he is in agreement with the essential points: the virgin conception, the birth at Bethlehem, settlement at Nazareth. For the rest, he constructed accounts with a didactic purpose. Jesus is the true heir of the promises made to David and Abraham (1, 1–18). Conceived by the action of the Holy Spirit, he is the Messiah prophesied by Isaiah (1, 18–25). Born at Bethlehem according to the prophecy of Micah (2, 4–6), he is at birth the king of the nations (2, 1–12), prophesied by Balaam, the pagan prophet (2, 21; see 47). But foreshadowing his future passion, he is persecuted by the great of this world, as had been Moses before him (2, 13–21). Thus the evangelist examined the mystery of Jesus and led the faithful to reflect on it from the earliest years of the Saviour.

340

6. THE CANONICAL GOSPELS AND THE APOCRYPHAL GOSPELS

The books of Matthew, Mark, and Luke obviously used the same material. But each evangelist used this material in his own way, giving each edition of the one Gospel a different character. It is characteristic of a living tradition to avoid fixation into stiff formulas and to adapt the presentations of material to the concrete needs of the community which nourished it. This profound fidelity to the apostolic teaching was shown by the Church of the 2nd century, when it adhered to the three Synoptics (and at the same time the Gospel of John) as Scripture inspired by God. From this time on the discernment of the authentic Gospels was necessary because a certain number of apocryphal ones were written using the names of the apostles. Some developed the memories of the infancy (Protogospel of James) or the life of Joseph and Mary and pious legends. Others amplified the narrative of the passion and the resurrection (Gospels of Peter and Nicodemus). Others constituted collections of sayings of the Lord, drawn from canonical Gospels or taken from more suspect sources (Gospel of Thomas). Detached from the apostolic tradition, this literature often tried to nourish popular sentimentality. But heretical infiltrations rapidly cropped up there, and sects used them (notably the Gnostics) as a medium of propaganda.

Text 46

WITNESSES OF THE 2ND CENTURY ON THE ORIGIN OF THE GOSPELS

Papias, Bishop of Hierapolis in Phrygia around 125, wrote an *Explanation of the Words of the Lord*. Echoing an older tradition, he wrote:

As for Matthew, he collected the sayings of the Lord in the Hebrew language, and each one should interpret them as best he may.

And on Mark:

Here is what the Elder says: Mark, who was Peter's interpreter, wrote down with exactness but without order all that he recalled of the sayings or actions of the Lord. In fact, he had been neither a hearer nor a disciple of the Lord; but he was later, as I have said, the disciple of Peter. But, Peter taught according to need, without attempting to put the sayings of the Lord in order. Mark, then, is not at fault if he has not written of certain things, as much as he recalled of them. His only care was not to omit anything of what he had heard and to speak no lie.

Eusebius, Ecclesiastical History, 3, 39. 15–16

In his Dialogue with Trypho, around 155, St. Justin referred to a passage in the Gospel according to St. Mark in terms which tend to link the Gospel with St. Peter (see Mk. 3, 16–17):

It is said that he [Jesus] changed the name of one of the apostles, calling him Peter, as is written in his memoirs of him; and equally, that he changed the name of two brothers, the sons of Zebedee, calling them Boanerges, that is Sons of Thunder.

Around 180, in his book Against Heresies, St. Irenaeus sums up his knowledge from tradition on the origin of the four Gospels (compare Text 45):

As for Matthew, it was among the Hebrews and in their own language that he undertook to write the Gospel, while Peter and Paul preached the Gospel at Rome and founded the Church there. After their death, Mark, Peter's disciple and interpreter, also left us in writing what Peter preached, while Luke, Paul's companion, set down in a book what he preached. Finally, John, the disciple of the Lord who leaned on his breast, also wrote a Gospel while he resided at Ephesus in Asia.

St. Irenaeus, Against Heresies, 3, 1. 1

Between 160 and 180 an ordered list of the books accepted by the Church at Rome (the *Muratorian Canon*) says about Luke:

The third book of the Gospel, according to Luke. This Luke was a physician; after Christ's Ascension, Paul had taken him with him because of his experience [of a sea-voyage?]. With his assent, he wrote what seemed good to him. Nevertheless, as he had not himself seen the Lord in the flesh, he did it after learning of him as best he could, beginning his account from the birth of John . . . [lines 2–8]. The Acts of all the Apostles were written down in a single book. Luke gathered up together for the excellent Theophilus all that he had seen, as the omission of the passion of Peter and the departure of Paul for Spain clearly shows [lines 34–39].

The passage relating to Matthew and Mark has been lost. The author seems to have deduced his teachings from the text of the Gospel and the Acts of the Apostles alone. This is why he attributes a very late date to the Acts (around 62–63). The allusion to the journey of St. Paul to Spain already figured in the letter of Clement of Rome (Text 44). It is nevertheless doubtful, since it could have been inferred from *Romans* 15, 28.

Text 47

THE ANCIENT EUCHARISTIC LITURGY

There are few eucharistic texts in the New Testament. But the *Teaching of the Twelve Apostles,* an account originating from Syria dating from the first century of the beginning of the sec-

ond, traces the archaic liturgy going back perhaps to the times
of the Apostles.

When you come together on Sunday, the day of the Lord, break
bread and give thanks, after having confessed your sins so that
your sacrifice is pure. He who has a quarrel with his neighbor, let
him not be with you before having been reconciled, for fear of
your sacrifice being profaned. This is in fact what the Lord said:
"That in every place and every time, there be presented to me a
pure sacrifice, for I am a great King, says the Lord, and my name
is marvelous among the nations" [14, 1–3].

On the necessary reconciliation, see *Matthew* 5, 23–24; 15,
11–20. The text cited is taken from the book of Malachy
(*288*). Here, from another section, is a liturgical formula:

As for the Eucharist give thanks thus. First for the chalice: "We
give you thanks, O our Father, for the holy vine of David your
servant, which you have made known through Jesus your Servant.
Glory be to you through the ages!" Then for the broken bread:
"We give you thanks, O our Father, for life and the knowledge
that you have made known to us through Jesus your Servant. Glory
be to you through the ages! Just as this broken bread was scattered
on the mountains and has been gathered into one, so let your
Church be gathered from the ends of the earth into your kingdom.
For to you is the glory and the power, through Jesus Christ,
through the ages." Let no person eat or drink of your Eucharist,
except those who have been baptized in the name of the Lord, for
the Lord has said of this: "Do not give to dogs that which is holy"
[9, 1–5].

This eucharistic prayer (that is, this thanksgiving) supposes
that the meal of the Lord was celebrated following the apostolic
ritual. On the "vine of David," see *Luke* 22, 17–18, and *John*
15, 1–8. On the one bread which the faithful form, see *1 Corinthians* 10, 17. The end of the text cites *Matthew* 7, 6. After

344

this chapter there is a prayer of thanks to be said "after one has been satisfied."

Bibliography

An excellent introduction to each of the Gospels and to the process of their formation may be found in *Explaining the Gospels* by W. Harrington (New York n.d.) and *To Know Jesus Christ* by A. George (Notre Dame 1964). See also Vols. I–IV of the *New Testament Reading Guide Series*.

Study Guides

Keeping in mind the prophetic proclamation of the reign of God in the Old Testament (see above, Chapter VII, *Study Guides*), study the theme of the kingdom of God in the preaching of Jesus, and especially in the parables. The Gospel according to St. Matthew will furnish the best point of departure (the expressions *kingdom of God* and *kingdom of heaven* are equivalents). Note the two times of realization of the kingdom: its inauguration by Jesus, and its eschatological consummation (especially: *Mt.* 13, 24–30. 34–36).

Keeping in mind the prophets' attitude towards sin and the promise of forgiveness "in the last times" (*181, 203, 220, 281–284*), study the attitude of Christ towards sinners. For the basis of this study, take the Gospel according to St. Luke (note especially: 5, 17–32; 7, 36–50; 15; 18, 9–14; 19, 1–10).

How did Jesus reveal his nature as Son of God? In the Synoptics note the texts which bear upon this theme: those which concern a personal experience of Jesus (*Mk.* 1, 11); those where Jesus speaks of his relations as Son with the Father (*Mt.* 11, 25–27; 21, 37–38; 24, 36); those where he speaks of "my

Father in heaven" and speaks familiarly with him (*Mt.* 15, 13; 16, 17; 18, 10. 19. 35; 20, 23; 26, 19; 26, 53; *Mk.* 14, 36; *Lk.* 23, 34. 46); those in which the Father reveals him to the disciples (*Mt.* 17,5); those where Satan uses the title equivocally (*Mt.* 4, 3. 6; *Mk.* 3, 11; 5, 7); those which include a yet imperfect profession of faith (*Mt.* 16, 16); those where the title is used in derision (*Mt.* 26, 63; 27, 40. 43); the confession of faith at the foot of the cross (*Mk.* 15, 39; *Mt.* 27, 54).

XVII.

THE APOSTOLIC EPISTLES

THE proclamation of the Gospel was the first task of the apostles and their aides. Thus, once the Gospel was preached, and believers baptized, they founded churches. Responsibility in the churches was confided to local authorities, *presbyters* ("elders": *Acts* 14, 23; 20, 17), set up as *bishops* ("over-seers": *Acts* 20, 28) of their communities, with a president (*Rom.* 12, 8; *1 Thess.* 5, 12) at their head. But the founding apostle, as pastor, kept his rights and exercised them through emissaries or through letters. Independent of the government of the churches, there were also frequent letters for edification or exhortation. This was the origin of the apostolic letters. Deeply concerned with the concrete problems of a determined time and place, they were occasional writings, not treatises of abstract theology, and so must be replaced in the framework where they were formed and read as living documents with the whole pastoral activity of the primitive Church behind them.

1. THE FIRST LETTERS OF ST. PAUL

The Preaching of Paul

The book of the Acts gives us some idea of the preaching of St. Paul. The sermon outlines reproduced in it are clearly not firsthand documents like the epistles, but they do evoke a

347

preaching which must have ceaselessly returned to the same themes. The preaching of the Gospel to the Jews (*Acts* 13, 16–41) is not substantially distinct from what we find elsewhere on the lips of Peter, but nevertheless Paul stamps the mark of his doctrine on them by insisting on justification through faith in Christ (13, 38–39). His failure in the face of a closed Judaism soon led him towards the pagan nations (13, 46–47; 17, 5–13; 18, 6. 12–17); thus began his reflection on the drama of Israel (*1 Thess.* 2, 15–16). To the pagans he first proclaimed abandonment of idols and faith in the living God (*Acts* 14, 15–17; see *1 Thess.* 1, 9–10); Jewish apologetics had already prepared the way for Christian preaching among them (*403*). Only once did Paul try to gain hearers by looking into paganism for the basis of an argument leading to the Gospel—while speaking to the cultivated audience of Athens (17, 22–31). The ensuing failure made him renounce once and for all the use of this "human wisdom" (*1 Cor.* 2, 1–5). With the pagans as with the Jews, he wished to know only the "folly of the cross."

The Letters to the Thessalonians

After experiencing the disappointment of Athens, Paul, on the same missionary journey, now went to Corinth, where he remained for two years (50–52). There he wrote to the community of Thessalonica, which had been founded a little earlier. The first letter begins with a long heartfelt outpouring which cannot be read without emotion. Recalling the memories of his brief but fruitful apostolate (*1 Thess.* 1, 1—2, 12), Paul rejoices that his converts, imitating those of Judea, have shown themselves to be faithful to the word of God (2, 13–20), as his envoy Timothy had told him (3, 1–13). He exhorts the Thessalonians to persevere in purity, fraternal love, and the other Christian virtues (4, 1–12; 5, 12–22). In passing, he completes his teaching on an important point, the hope of the return of the Lord which occupied a great place in early Christian spirituality (see 1, 10; 2, 12. 19; 3, 13; 5, 23). But the faithful were stirred up on this subject. Would those already dead take part in the glory of Jesus? And when will that come? Paul recalls the certainty of the resurrection of the dead. Using conventional images drawn from Scripture, he sketches a grandiose picture of the return of the Lord (4, 1—3, 18). While awaiting it, as the date remains secret, the Christian must live as a son of light and hold himself ready for the day of the Lord (5, 1–11). The series of recommendations closing the letter brings us close to the actual preaching of the apostle (4, 1–12; 5, 2–24), which he was undoubtedly then presenting to the Church at Corinth.

Some time later a second letter repeated and clarified the same questions. The eschatological revelation of Jesus constituted a constant basis for development along with the perspective of the judgment which is linked to it (2 Thess. 1, 3–12), but Paul had to cut short the eschatological fever which believed the day of the Lord to be very near. He recalls that this day must be preceded by a flowering of the enemy Power, a mysterious reality depicted in the language of the apocalypse (2, 1–13). While waiting, Christians must persevere in fidelity to the traditions they had received (2, 14—3, 5). They must avoid idleness particularly and earn what they eat (3, 6–15). This helped prevent the Christian longing for the return of the Lord from degenerating into a valueless illuminism.

2. THE LETTERS OF THE THIRD MISSIONARY JOURNEY

The Letter to the Galatians

After having visited the churches of Galatia for the second time, Paul settled at Ephesus, where he stayed two years and three months (54–57). Then at an uncertain date he received alarming news from Galatia. Preachers of Jewish origin, still not appeased despite the council of Jerusalem, had organized a veritable counter-mission in Paul's footsteps. They accused Paul of preaching a mutilated Gospel, since he did not compel the pagans to have themselves circumcised in order to join the

349

people of God, and dispensed them from observing the Mosaic Law. To put things back in order, Paul sent a letter to the Galatians intermingling polemics, doctrinal exposition, and pastoral exhortation.

To prove the authenticity of his Gospel, he begins with precise autobiographical data, by recounting his conversion (1, 11–24), his participation in the council of Jerusalem (2, 1–10), and his altercation with Peter at Antioch (2, 11–21). This gave him the occasion to proclaim, in an abridged form, his doctrine of justification through faith in Jesus Christ and not through the works of the Law (2,15–21), which constitutes the only Gospel (see 1, 6–10). He shows evidence of this doctrine in Scripture for Abraham and his descendants, but his descendant is the Christ (3, 1–18). The Jewish Law was only a pedagogue charged with leading men to Christ. Since he has come, we are no longer under the pedagogue, for we have received the Holy Spirit who makes us children of God (3, 19—4, 7). Let the Galatians, who have been snatched by Christ from slavery to idols, not fall into another slavery (4, 8–20)! For the two Testaments have the same difference between them as there was of old between the two wives and the two sons of Abraham. On the one hand is slavery, on the other, liberty (4, 21–31). They must, then, live as free men: free as regards the circumcision (5, 1–12), free but full of charity (5, 13–15; 6, 1–6), free with the interior liberty which guarantees the triumph of the Holy Spirit over the *flesh,* that is, over sinful nature (5, 16–26; 6, 7–10). The final exhortations return to the principal theme of the letter. Written in the heat of battle, this exposé will be taken up again with more fullness in the Letter to the Romans.

The Letter to the Philippians

Paul, this time, was a captive. But rather than his captivity at Caesarea or Rome, it is better to postulate an obscure trial endured at Ephesus, referred to in the second letter to the Corinthians (*2 Cor.* 1, 8–10). The stay in the capital of Asia would then have been almost over. The Christians of Philippi

350

sent an alms with Epaphroditus to the apostle. Paul thanks them immediately with tenderness (4, 10–23), and this short fragment seems to have been at first a separate note.

A little later, Paul sent a hearfelt letter to the Philippians, which is an outpouring of his fatherly tenderness (1, 1—3, 1, followed up in 4, 4–7). Facing possible martyrdom, he aspired to go to them to "be with Christ" (1, 12–26). Facing death, he exhorts his spiritual sons to the practice of the Christian life (1, 27—2, 18). In the course of this fragment he cites a celebrated lyric passage briefly retracing the whole career of Christ Jesus (2, 6–11). To conclude, he announces the approaching mission of Timothy, who will prepare for his coming (2, 19–24). Apaphroditus, the bearer of aid, who meanwhile had been deathly sick, will leave bearing this letter (2, 25–30). The conclusion is an exhortation to joy while awaiting the return of the Lord (3, 1, following 4, 4–7).

This conclusion is bruskly interrupted by a diatribe against the Judaizers, similar in tone to that of the letter to the Galatians. This insertion is probably a third short note artificially joined to the preceding (3, 1—4, 1, finishing in 4, 8–9). Some new autobiographical elements reveal the interior life of Paul who scorned the advantages of Judaism to attach himself to Christ alone, in the expectation of the resurrection of the body (see 3, 8–11. 20–21). If the division of the letter into three notes is accurate, its present ordering would have been made by the recipients.

The First Letter to the Corinthians

Corinth, a cosmopolitan port and dissolute city, possessed a spirited church which caused her founder much trouble. Nothing remains of a first letter inviting the faithful to flee the immodest (see *1 Cor.* 5, 9) except a doubtful fragment which interrupts its present context (*2 Cor.* 6, 14—7, 1). But around Easter 56 or 57, Paul received alarming news at Ephesus through the "servants of Chloe" (*1 Cor.* 1, 11). He then wrote to correct abuses brought to his attention: divisions among the

351

faithful about preachers of the Gospel (1, 10—4, 21); an incestuous marriage (5, 1–13); trials before pagan judges (6, 1–11); a false interpretation of Christian liberty being used to justify license in morals (6, 12–20). Faced with these difficulties, Paul quickly rose to the debate, giving his readers admirable developments on the true Christian wisdom, that of the cross (1, 17–3, 4), and the role of preachers of the Gospel (3, 5—4, 13); on the conditions of entry into the kingdom of God (6, 9–11) and the Christian dignity of the body (6, 12–20); not to mention an outline of a sermon for the Christian Easter (5, 7–8).

In a second part (which some regard as a new letter), Paul treated a series of cases of conscience, which the Corinthians had written to him: the respective value of marriage and chastity (7); use of food ritually sacrificed to idols (8, 1—11, 1); use of *charisms* or spiritual gifts (12, 1—13, 39). With clear and practical casuistry, Paul nevertheless gave solutions only by constant reference to the great principles of the Christian life. The time of the Church, straining towards the return of the Lord, assures the state of virginity a sure superiority over the state of marriage; but in this domain one must not go beyond the gifts of the Holy Spirit (7). Idols are nothing, nor is ritual immolation anything (8, 1–6); but from fear of scandalizing his neighbor, one must know when to use his rights (9) and act with prudence, so that no one fall back into idolatry after having participated at the table of Christ (10, 14–22), as had the Israelites in the desert after they had received the gifts of God (10, 1–13). As for spiritual gifts, they were made for the use of the Church, which is the body of Christ (12). Rather than aspiring to the flashy gifts, like the almost incoherent enthusiasm called "speaking in tongues" (14, 1–25), they must practice that which surpasses them all, charity, which Paul lyrically exalts (13). These casuistic developments were interrupted by a series of rules for liturgical assemblies (11, 2–34). The modest bearing demanded of women clearly contrasts with the customs in vogue among certain religious confraternities in Greece (11, 2–16). As for the

352

eucharistic celebration, Paul's treatment of it shows his attachment to the primitive Christian traditions (11, 17–34).

The same attachment to tradition reappears in the long development devoted to the problem of the resurrection of the dead (15). Greek spirituality holding that the body and the material world were evil repudiated this doctrine (*Acts* 17, 32). But the resurrection of Christ, the point of departure for the Christian faith (15, 3–11), implies the resurrection of all Christians (15, 12–34). It must be understood that our bodies will be transfigured in the image of his (15, 35–53). This apocalyptic evocation of the last day (15, 24–28. 51–53) looses an enthusiasm which the apostle translates in lyric terms (15, 54–57). The end of the letter (16) announces the collection for the Church at Jerusalem and proposes future projects; but these will be contravened by circumstances.

The Second Letter to the Corinthians

The preceding letter did not broach the problems dominating the letters to the Galatians and to the Philippians, so it probably preceded them. But it is difficult to reconstruct the course of events. It is certain that Paul received serious news from Corinth. His authority was vehemently attacked by preachers who probably belonged to the Judeo-Christian party. His rapid visit did not solve the problem. After leaving, he was greatly offended in the person of his envoy (*2 Cor.* 7, 12).

Upon returning to Ephesus Paul wrote a "severe letter." Critics think they see a fragment of that letter in *2 Corinthians* 10–13. In these chapters, to clear himself of a double charge of weakness and ambition, the apostle apologizes for his conduct. After a virulent satire on the "false apostles" who calumniate him (11, 12–15), he draws up a balance-sheet of his apostolate (11, 16—12, 12). The fragment would be fitting in these difficult circumstances, but it is incomplete. Be that as it may, it does not follow either from chapter 7 or from chapter 9.

With chapter 1 a totally different kind of letter begins. Paul

353

left Ephesus after the "great tribulation" which formed the background to the Letter to the Philippians (1, 1–11). He is not in Macedonia, for the preceding difficulties prevented his return to Corinth (1, 12—2, 11). Titus, whom he had sent there, rejoined him with good news (7, 5–16). Receiving this, Paul sent a calm heart-felt letter bearing a message of reconciliation which immediately prepared for his coming. Its core is a long digression where Paul reflects on his apostolic ministry (2, 14—7, 4). Paul's personal attitude in the face of this difficult charge is fully exposed during the course of a meditation lacking logical plan but rich in substance. In contrast with the ministry of the old covenant, which only led to the death of the blind Jews, that of the new covenant brings the Holy Spirit to man (2, 14—4, 6). If he conquered those who inflicted tribulations on him, it is by participation in the death of Jesus, and with the hope of rising with him and being with him for eternity (4, 7—5, 8). Such is the spirit of Paul's ministry (5, 9—6, 10), and thus he demands that they have confidence in him (6, 11–13; 7, 2–4). The conclusion of the letter is dedicated to the organization of the collection for the Church in Jerusalem. There is a delicate sermon on charity, which accompanies a recommendation of the collectors (8). It resembles a similar note destined for all the churches of the province of Achaia (9).

Thus Paul's correspondence with Corinth appears to have been complex. Besides a first letter which has been lost (perhaps 2 Cor. 6, 14—7, 1?), we have a long letter responding to many objections and perhaps composed over a period of time (1 Corinthians); then a "severe letter" to which 2 Corinthians 10–13 is usually linked; finally, a last letter (2 Cor. 1–8) to which is joined an independent note (2 Cor. 9). The present compilation must be due to the recipients, as in the case of the Epistle to the Philippians. Even if 2 Corinthians 10–13 is not linked to the "severe letter," it must nevertheless be considered an independent letter, sent after chapters 2–9, as a result of new circumstances.

354

The Letter to the Romans

Paul spent the winter of 57–58 in Corinth. He hoped to leave for Jerusalem in the spring to bring the fruit of the collection and then set out to the West as far as Spain, passing through Rome (*Rom.* 1, 11–15; 15, 17–32). Preparing for his visit to this important Church, he wrote them a long letter, but we could almost speak of it as a treatise. Having meditated at length on the fundamental themes set out in his Letter to the Galatians, Paul now constructed a broad doctrinal synthesis which sheds light on the whole of Christian life. The Gospel, he says, is the power of God for the salvation of those who believe, Jews or pagans, for in it is revealed the justice of God which justifies men by means of faith in Jesus Christ (*Rom.* 1, 16–17).

The development of this subject follows a definite plan. The first part (1, 18—8, 39) gives an over-all picture of the doctrine. The theme of justification through faith (1, 18–4, 25) is presented in a diptych: without Christ, men are under the wrath of God (1, 18—3, 20), whether Jews or pagans; in Christ is revealed the justice of God, who justifies men by faith in Christ, without the works of the Law, according to the example of Abraham (3, 21—4, 25). The next section (5–8) treats the state of the justified Christian. Snatched by Christ, the new Adam, from the sin and death which weighed upon the race of the first Adam (5, 12–21), dead to sin and risen to a new life since his baptism (6, 1–11), the Christian has passed from slavery to sin to the service of justice, and from death to life (6, 12–23). He has been freed from the Jewish Law, which could not resolve the problem of the conscience and was powerless to do good (7), and he has received the spirit of the children of God, which triumphs over the flesh (8, 1–17). Thus he lives in the hope of the resurrection and the final glorification (8, 18–39).

From this substantial exposition flows an exhortation to the Christian life, parallel to the conclusions of many other epistles (12, 1—15, 13). Paul urges Christians to offer themselves to

355

God in sacrifice (12, 1–2), to serve the body of Christ through the gifts received from the Spirit (12, 3–8), to charity towards all (12, 9–21; 13, 8–10), to submission to the civil powers (13, 1–7), and to a life worthy of a son of the light (13, 11–14). All these themes have a homiletic tone, and echo Paul's preaching at Corinth. The long passage dedicated to dietary observances (14, 1—15, 13) is easily understood if we remember that Judeo-Christians and pagan-Christians were then living together in the communities. After personal news of the apostle (15, 14–33), the letter ends (16, 21–25). In the interval a short note has been inserted, probably addressed to the Church of Ephesus (16, 1–2). It is supposed that Paul sent them a copy of the Letter to the Romans, and in this context the caution against the Judaizers is not surprising (16, 17–20).

Chapters 9–11 still remain to be commented upon. This meditation on the situation of the Jewish people, rebellious against the Gospel except for a remnant, is the fruit of long experience. Paul has meditated in the light of the Scripture, which he cites abundantly. He sees that God, who called Israel to be the missionary of the Gospel to the pagan nations, finally led them into the Church by means of their defection; but Paul hopes for a final conversion of the people "loved because of its fathers" (11, 28). The whole grouping is loosely linked to the context and could have been developed separately. In any case, the letter gives the core of St. Paul's doctrine at the summit of his missionary activity.

3. THE CAPTIVITY LETTERS

The Letter to the Colossians

Paul was still a captive at Caesarea (58–60) or had already come to Rome (61–63) when he wrote this letter. In any case, Epaphras, who had brought the Gospel to Colossae, came to tell Paul of his community and to acquaint him with the difficulties of that community. A city of Asia Minor, Colossae was the resort town for Ephesus, a church which Paul had founded.

356

Its Christians were of pagan origin. They were fervent, but the intellectual ferment of Greek speculation and Jewish practices (2, 16–29) endangered the purity of their faith. That is why Paul's letter was centered on the person of Christ and his role as redeemer (1–2). Two passages stand out: one where light is thrown on the primacy of Christ, head of the body which is the Church (1, 13–20), and another on his superiority over every other power (2, 9–15). The allusions to the Christian experience of baptism (1, 13–14. 21–23; 2, 11–13) introduce the final exhortations, in the form of a baptismal homily (3, 1—4, 6). Life in Jesus Christ (3, 1–4) demands that one put off the "old man" (3, 5–9) and put on the new by doing his works (3, 10–17; 4, 2–6); that implies obligations for every state in life: husbands and wives, parents and child, slaves and masters (3, 18—4, 1). This spirituality develops and completes the instruction in the Letter to the Romans.

The Note to Philemon

By the same courier Paul also sent a personal note to Philemon, a rich Christian of Colossae. Onesimus, a fugitive slave of Philemon, came to believe in the Gospel and was baptized by the apostle. Paul now sent this spiritual son to his master, so that no harm might come to him. But he asks Philemon in delicate terms to welcome him as a brother in Christ—the very diametric opposite of ancient law! Thus the Christian conscience overturned the current concept of the social order, for in Christ there is no more slave, nor free man (*Gal.* 3, 27–28; *Col.* 3, 11). The suppression of slavery would become a legal necessity when the Christian ferment had penetrated into souls and morality. The Letter to Philemon already appeared as the charter for liberation of the slave.

The Letter to the Ephesians

The courier of the two preceding messages, Tychicus (*Col.* 4, 7), also carried a letter addressed to a more general audience. The manuscripts have added "to Ephesus" to its address but

357

the general character of its wording indicates it was destined for an entire group of churches. The essential themes of the Letter to the Colossians reappear in it, but better developed in length and order. It has been suggested that the text was edited by a disciple of St. Paul, imbued with Paul's ideas and style, but other critics think that only the apostle could have imitated himself at this point. In either case, this letter gives us a synthesis of Pauline doctrine parallel to that of the Letter to the Romans, but set in a new perspective.

The "benediction" opening the letter (1, 3–14) introduces an ancient liturgical style. The ensuing exposition sums up the work of God in its broad outlines. By exalting Christ (1, 15–22), God has saved us through him (2, 1–10), reconciling the Jews and pagans in a single people (2, 11–22). Such is the "mystery" revealed at the end of the ages, the Gospel of which Paul had been made minister (3). A series of exhortations are grafted onto this contemplation: calls to unity in the body of Christ (4, 1–16), to the new life which baptism demands (4, 17—5, 20), to the domestic virtues (5, 21—6, 9), to the spiritual combat (6, 10–20). The same baptismal tone which characterized the parallel passages of the letters to the Thessalonians, Colossians, and Romans is affirmed here with such vigor and precision that these chapters become a synthesis of Christian spirituality.

4. THE PASTORAL LETTERS

The group of three pastoral epistles have a totally different character from Paul's other letters. The recipients were not churches, but Paul's disciples whom he often charged with missions in the course of his journeys. This explains the nature of the subjects treated and the much looser composition of these letters, but the differences of style and vocabulary also suggest that an unidentified secretary has played a much greater role here than in the other epistles. The references to Paul's life (*1 Tim.* 1, 12–14; *2 Tim.* 3, 10–12) and his doctrine are evident but these are often presented as a repetition of old texts, which the editor knew by heart (for example, *2 Tim.* 2, 5–13).

The dominant themes correspond to the stage of organization of the churches after the great apostolic missions of Paul. The concern over heretical teachers, who corrupted the faith of Christians, was already noted in the farewell sermon of the apostle to the elders of Ephesus (*Acts* 20, 28–32). But in the pastoral letters the danger has become grave and pressing (*1 Tim.* 1, 3–7; 4, 1–5; 6, 2–10; *Tit.* 1, 10–16: *2 Tim.* 2, 14–18; 3, 1–9; 4, 3–5). Paul here opposes it with the authentic meaning of tradition, concerned with preserving the "deposit of faith" (*1 Tim.* 6, 20; *2 Tim.* 1, 14; 3, 14). Elsewhere, the organization of the Church led to some general recommendations, valuable for all the faithful (*1 Tim.* 2, 1–15; 5, 1–2; 6, 1–2. 17–19; *Tit.* 2, 1—3, 7), and to precise prescriptions for the choice of presbyters and bishops (*1 Tim.* 3, 1–7; 5, 17–25; *Tit.* 1, 5–9), of deacons (*1 Tim.* 3, 8–13) of widows (*1 Tim.* 5, 3–16). Counsels were given to Timothy and Titus tracing a beautiful portrait of the pastor of souls (*1 Tim.* 1, 18–20; 4, 6–16; 6, 11–16; *Tit.* 3, 8–11; *2 Tim.* 1, 6–18; 2, 22–26; 3, 14—4, 5).

Paul's last missionary activities are the background for the first letter to Timothy and the letter to Titus. Titus had been sent to Crete, and Timothy remained in Ephesus. But the second letter to Timothy came from the final captivity of the apostle and constitutes a spiritual testament at the very moment of his preparation for martyrdom. To the memories of the past (1, 5; 3, 10–11) are added new personal notes and a confident tone (1, 15–18; 4, 9–18). In it the apostle, abandoned by all except Luke, envisages the moment of his "departure" and his appearance before the just Judge (4, 6–8). Even the critics who attribute the edition of the prescriptions concerning the organization of the churches to a disciple of Paul, heir to his thought, find Paul's personal tone here, but also full of feeling as in the note to Philemon.

5. THE LETTER TO THE HEBREWS

The Structure of the Work

The Letter to the Hebrews defines itself as a "sermon of exhortation" (13, 22). Its essentially pastoral purpose clearly distinguishes it from theological tracts, which will come in their own good time. But the exhortation appeals throughout to a closely reasoned doctrinal reflection, the theological sections alternating with invitations to Christian perseverance. The author addressed himself to the faithful of Jewish origin, perhaps of the priestly class, who were dreaming nostalgically of the legalistic liturgy of the Old Testament. To strengthen them in the faith, the author showed Christ as the Sovereign Priest of the new liturgy proclaimed by the Scriptures. This subject is developed through variations on the same theme, the author progressively enlarging his perspective.

A solemn introduction (1, 1–4) shows Christ, the Son of God, exalted at the right hand of the Father and established above the very angels (1, 5–14), although his incarnation and his passion had temporarily humbled him to save the human race (2, 5–18). For all the more reason is he superior to Moses, the mediator of the first covenant (3, 1–6). The exhortation is drawn from this first section, woven of scriptural texts interpreted in the light of the cross and the resurrection (2, 1–4), then it flowers into a long homily on Psalm 95 (3, 7—4, 10). At the same time, the theme of Christ the Priest makes its appearance (2, 17; 3, 1; 4, 15). The conclusion strongly asserts the theme, identifying the priestly ministry of Christ with the close of his earthly life: the passion, resurrection, and ascension (5, 1–10).

The following section opens with rhetorical warnings. Beyond the elementary catechesis given to neophytes, the author wished to furnish a more profound teaching, to lead his correspondents to progress in the Christian life (5, 11—6, 19). He wanted to show Christ, "priest according to the order of

360

Melchizedek" (*Ps.* 110, 4), possessing a royal priesthood vastly superior to the Levitical priesthood (7). The comparison of the two priesthoods in their essential activity is the key to his explanation (8, 1—10, 18). While Christ, penetrating into heaven with his blood, accomplished the expiation of all sins and sealed the eternal covenant foretold by the prophets, the priests of old carried out an imperfect worship, the shape and shadow of Christ's sacrifice. This contemplation of Christ the Priest leads to the final exhortation (10, 19—13, 19): they must persevere in the faith, because the day of the Lord draws nigh (10, 19–39); they must imitate the example of faith given by the saints of yesterday (11); they must fear the Judgment which is drawing near (12). Counsels for the Christian life terminate the homily (13, 1–19).

The Origin of the Letter

The doctrine developed in this letter coincides with the teachings of St. Paul, but it is clear that the style, the argumentation, the manner of developing the ideas, the vocabulary, the central themes (like that of the priesthood), bear the stamp of another personality. It is not enough to think of a secretary, acting in place of the apostle. The author is an original theologian, strongly influenced by Alexandrian culture, perhaps a former disciple of Philo. The linking of the work to the letters of St. Paul is, however, an ancient tradition in the East, though it was unknown to the Roman list known as the *Muratorian Canon* (between 160–180), and this situation persisted for a long time in the West. Among the companions of St. Paul, Apollo would best correspond to the data of the text. He was an Alexandrian Jew and versed in the Holy Scriptures, a well-known preacher (*Acts* 18, 24–28; 19, 1; *1 Cor.* 1, 12; 3, 4–6; 16, 12; *Tit.* 3, 13). But we cannot be sure. In any case, the letter was sent from Italy shortly after the captivity of Timothy (13, 23–24). There is no allusion to the destruction of Jerusalem, but the war in Judea had perhaps already begun. The nostalgia for the Jewish liturgy among the addressees is better

361

understood if the temple were still standing, though it could have been written between the years of 67–70. But a possible later date should not be dismissed.

6. THE CATHOLIC LETTERS
(EXCEPT JOHN'S)

The letters called catholic are those outside the Pauline corpus. They have come down to us under the names of James, Peter (2), John (3), and Jude. John's will be examined in the following chapter.

The Letter of James

The Letter of James is undoubtedly the least speculative writing in the New Testament. Rather than a letter, it is a collection of homily outlines, the work of a pastor of souls who was adapting the current moral teaching of Judaism to the use of Christians. As in the book of Ecclesiasticus, two centuries earlier, there is an echo of the voice of the prophets, though most of the fragments reflect the tone of the sapiential literature. In the letters of St. Paul the concluding exhortations were closely connected to the doctrinal expositions preceding them, but here we find such reference points only occasionally in an allusion to the reception of baptism (1, 18; 1, 21), to the coming of the Lord (4, 7–9). The principal themes concern moral life. They must withstand trials (1, 2–18), put the word of God into practice (1, 19–27), do the works of faith to be saved (2:14–26), curb their tongues (3, 1–12), follow true wisdom (3, 13–18), avoid strife (4, 1–12), be patient and loyal (4, 7–12) . . . The author vigorously sides with the poor (2, 1–9; 4, 13—5, 6). Perhaps to correct a false interpretation of the principles of St. Paul, he insists on the observation of all the commandments (2, 10–13) and the necessity of good works (2, 14–26). He knows the rites of the anointing of the sick (6, 13–15; see *Mk.* 6, 13) and the mutual confession of sins (5, 16).

362

Not surprisingly, this writing is linked to the Judeo-Christian milieu of Jerusalem, where James was the head. The date is more difficult to pin down, for the letter does not include historical allusions. James governed the church at Jerusalem from 44 to 61/62. As the text is addressed to the Judeo-Christians of the diaspora (1, 1) and is composed in excellent Greek, an editor must have reshaped it. He probably unified and gave form to fragments echoing James' preaching.

The First Letter of Peter

The first letter of Peter was addressed, from Rome, to a group of churches in Asia Minor (1, 1; 5, 13). It includes a number of parallels with the letters of St. Paul. This is not surprising, for Silas, a companion in Paul's apostolate (*Acts* 15, 40; 18, 5; *1 Thess.* 1, 1; *2 Cor.* 1, 19), edited the letter (5, 12). Besides, a large part of the text appears to be a resumé of current preaching themes connected with the baptismal liturgy. These themes include a thanksgiving addressed to God for the "new birth" (1, 3–8); a call to sanctity and reformation of life (1, 13–21); an exhortation to conduct worthy of the people of God (1, 22—2, 10); the presentation of ideals adapted to different social categories, where the author is concerned with the civil authorities (2, 11–17) or conduct towards masters (2, 18–25), relations between husbands and wives (3, 1–7) or the attitude of the faithful towards one another (5, 5–11). There are analogous passages in the letters to the Romans, to the Colossians, and to the Ephesians. The same is true for the exhortations to the Christians virtues (3, 8–12; 4, 7–11). However, these common themes are not trite but are woven of the strong strands of biblical expression and are rich in Christian spirituality.

The editor has also added original developments alluding to the circumstances around him. The persecution of Nero (64) had begun. For the faithful, this trial was a participation in the sufferings of Christ, which the prophets had foretold (1, 6–12). This is the moment for pondering the mystery of Christ, who

363

passed through suffering to enter into his glory (3, 13—4, 6). The present conflagration is the prelude to divine judgment (4, 12–19). Let the presbyters, the heads of the communities, watch over the flock confided to them by Christ, the chief Pastor (5, 1–4)! This last recommendation is in the style of the pastoral letters. The whole thing shows that the Church reacted in the face of trials not with political machinations against the established authorities, but with a spiritual deepening, a reflection on the mystery of Christ to whom it is united.

The Letter of Jude

The Letter of Jude supposes an historical background similar to that of the pastoral epistles: false teachers were corrupting the authentic faith in Jesus Christ and perverting Christian morals (3–4). The author denounces their blasphemies (8–10) and their perversity (11–16). He foretells their condemnation (5–7) and implores the faithful to resist them and to live in charity (17–23). His references to the apostles (17) suggest a certain distance from their era. He could have written between 80–90, and the term teachers could refer to the current heresy of Gnosticism. Jude, the brother of James, is not the apostle of that name. That he belonged to Judeo-Christianity is confirmed by his use of some of the Old Testament apocrypha: the book of Enoch (6; 14–15) and the *Assumption of Moses* (9).

The Second Letter of Peter

The second letter bearing Peter's name is explicitly given as his message (1, 1) and presents some apparently contradictory peculiarities. On the one hand, it echoes a concrete experience of the head of the apostles: the transfiguration (1, 16–18). And on the other, it clearly uses the letter of Jude, which it must postdate. Besides, the editor looks back to the time of the apostles since he speaks as if he did not belong to their group (3, 2). He knew the first letter of Peter (3, 1) and an established collection of the letters of Paul, which he puts in the ranks of the Scriptures (3, 14–16). All this takes us back to the generation following the death of the two apostles. So the writer has used a pseudonymn. We know that, in the Old Testament, this custom was followed in Ecclesiastes, the book of Daniel, the Wisdom of Solomon, not counting the numerous apocrypha. It belonged to the literary conventions permitted in the biblical milieu. "It may be supposed with likelihood that the author had received a commission, if not from Peter before his death, at least from a religious authority: or that he himself held the authority. Perhaps he had been a disciple of Peter. . . . He transmits an apostolic teaching, and expresses it in the way it would be most effective. There is a pseudonymn here, but a pseudonymn justified by a commission or a situation which allowed, granted the literary conventions of the age, speaking this way" (J. Chaine).

The themes broached amplify those of the letter of Jude. To confirm the faithful in their holy life (1, 3–11) and defend them against false teachers (2, 1–22; 3, 3–7), the author proclaims the Judgment of God in apocalyptic terms (3, 7–13), and recalls the solid doctrinal teaching of the apostles (1, 12–18; 3, 1. 15–16) and the prophets (1, 19–21; 3, 2). The date of its writing is difficult to determine exactly. It is surely located at the outer limits of the apostolic era.

7. FROM THE APOSTOLIC WRITINGS TO APOCRYPHAL LITERATURE

The use of a pseudonymn in the second letter of Peter shows that the apostolic witness could be indirectly transmitted. From the 2nd century on the same process was used in a notable portion of Christian literature. The apocryphal correspondence of St. Paul with the Corinthians is valueless. On the other hand, the letter attributed to Barnabas (between 117 and 130) is a very interesting document. The first part fights against Judaism, by applying to the Scriptures a process of allegorization first used by the Letter to the Hebrews. The second part is a catechetical instruction on the theme of the two Ways: that of light and that of darkness. *The Letter of the Apostles,* or the

Testament of Our Lord in Galilee, is in fact an apocryphal gospel, which dates from around 160. It is an interesting witness of the doctrine and liturgy of this era. The genre inaugurated by St. Luke in the Acts of the Apostles was also repeated in the 2nd century in an entirely fictionalized edifying literature. Thus we have the *Acts* of John, Peter, Paul, Andrew, Thomas. In reaction to the proliferation of this apocryphal literature, the Church, from the 2nd century on, gradually fixed the list of epistles which authentically preserved the apostolic tradition, as well as their exact writers.

However, we again meet the best tradition of the apostolic epistles in the letter of Clement of Rome to the Corinthians, around 95 (Texts 44 and 48), the letters of Ignatius of Antioch, around 110–115 (Texts 44 to 49), and the letter of Polycarp of Smyrna to Philippi a little later (Texts 50 and 52). All these writings include many allusions to the apostolic letters. The account of the martyrdom of Stephen in the Acts (*Acts* 6, 8—7, 60), already influenced by the account of Christ's passion, had itself opened a path, not only for the authors of the apocryphal acts, but also for the editors of the Acts of the martyrs. The most ancient example of this genre recounts the death of St. Polycarp, written the day after the event, around 155–157.

Text 48

FROM THE APOSTLES TO "BISHOPS" OF CHURCHES

In his letter to the Corinthians, which has already been cited (Text 44), Clement of Rome recalls the uninterrupted succession leading from Christ to the heads of the churches founded by the apostles:

The apostles were sent to us by the Lord Jesus Christ as messengers of the Gospel. Christ himself had been sent by God. Christ came from God, then, and the apostles, from Christ. The two things, in good order, proceeded from the will of God. So the apostles, furnished with the teachings of our Lord Jesus Christ, fully strengthened through the resurrection and confident in the word of God, set forth with the assurance of the Holy Spirit, proclaiming this Good News, that the kingdom of God was at hand. They preached in cities and fields and having tested their first converts in the Holy Spirit, they established them as bishops and as deacons with those who believed [42, 1–4].

Our apostles knew from our Lord Jesus Christ that there would be quarrels about the post of bishop. It is for this reason that, foreseeing the future perfectly, they established those we spoke of and then gave this rule, that after their death other men would succeed them in the ministry [44, 1–2].

Thus authority was transmitted in the churches, not through the initiative of the community, but through the apostolic succession. The ecclesiastical organization thus described corresponds to that of the pastoral epistles.

Text 49

THE LETTERS OF IGNATIUS OF ANTIOCH

While on his way to the place of martyrdom (around 110–115), Ignatius of Antioch wrote to Polycarp of Smyrna and various churches. His letters show the cares of a pastor of souls and the great mystical driving force which carried him towards Christ (see Text 44).

On Unity in the Church: Take care to participate in only one Eucharist. For there is only one flesh of our Lord Jesus Christ and only one cup to unite us to his blood. There is only one altar, as there is only one bishop, united to the body of presbyters and deacons, my companions in service.

Letter to the Philadelphians, 4

Compare *1 Corinthians* 10, 16–17. The hierarchy of each church has assumed its classic form in three degrees: the *episcope* has become the bishop; the *presbyters* around him are the priests; the deacons fulfill a subordinate function.

On the Role of the Bishop: All of you follow the bishop as Jesus Christ followed his Father, the body of presbyters as if they were the apostles. As for the deacons, respect them as you respect the Law of God. Let no one do anything which concerns the Church without the bishop. Let only that Eucharist be regarded as legitimate which is presided over by the bishop or his delegate. Where the bishop is, there also is the community, just as where Christ is, there is the universal Church. It is not permitted, without the bishop, to baptize, or celebrate the agape. But what he approves, behold, that is pleasing to God.

Letter to the Smyrnians, 8

On the Desire for Martyrdom: I have written to all the churches, and to all I wrote that I die freely for God, so at least do not prevent me. I beg you, do not have an untimely good will towards me. Let me be the prey of the beasts. It is through them that one can reach God. God's wheat, I am ground by the teeth of the beasts to become the pure bread of Christ. Rather, lead them on so that they become my tomb and that they leave nothing of my body. So I will be a burden to no one by my funeral rites. Then I will be a true disciple of Jesus Christ, since the world will know nothing even of my body. Pray Christ for me, so that by means of the beasts I will become a victim offered to God.

It will serve me nothing to possess the whole world nor the kingdoms of this earth. It is better for me to die for Christ Jesus than to reign over the whole earth. Him I seek who dies for us. Him I desire who rose for us. Behold the time of my birth! Brothers, for

368

heaven's sake, do not prevent me from living, do not desire my death. Myself I wish to belong to God, do not abandon me to the world, do not deliver me to deceptive matter! Let me attain the pure light. It is by attaining it that I will become a man. Permit me to imitate the passion of my God.

My desire has been crucified; there is in me no more fire which clings to matter, but a living water which speaks to me within and says to me, "Come to the Father!" I no longer delight in corruptible nourishment, nor the pleasures of this life. I desire that bread of God which is the flesh of Jesus Christ, the descendant of David, and for drink I desire his blood, which is incorruptible love.

Letter to the Romans, 4, 1–2; 6; 7, 2–3

In this very personal language we hear echoes of St. Paul and St. John. Concerning his attitude in the face of martyrdom, compare *Philippians* 1, 21–24; 2, 17; 3, 8–11; 2 *Timothy* 4, 6–8.

Text 50

THE INFLUENCE OF THE APOSTOLIC LETTERS

The echoes of the apostolic letters are numerous in all the ancient Christian texts. The letter of Polycarp to the Philippians (around 115) is constantly inspired by those of St. Paul and Peter's first letter, and he knew those of John. Paralleling *2 Peter* 3, 15–16, Polycarp speaks of Paul's letters in these terms:

Neither I nor anyone like me can attain the wisdom of glorious Paul. While I was among you, he taught men then by word of mouth the Word of truth, with exactness and sureness. Then after he left, he wrote you letters. But, if you lean on them, you can become strong in the faith that you have received.

Letter to the Philippians, 3, 2

369

Bibliography

F. Amiot, *How to Read St. Paul* (Chicago 1964) and *The Key Concepts of St. Paul* (New York 1962). L. Cerfaux, *Christ in the Theology of St. Paul* (New York 1958) and *The Church in the Theology of St. Paul* (New York 1959). A. George, *The Gospel of Paul* (Notre Dame 1964). W. Groussow, *In Christ* (Westminster n.d.). F. Prat, *The Theology of St. Paul* (London n.d.). G. Ricciotti, *Paul the Apostle* (Milwaukee 1961).

Study Guides

On the spirituality of baptism in the apostolic Church: According to the apostolic letters, various aspects of its spirituality can be listed: the gift of the Holy Spirit (*Acts* 2, 38; *Heb.* 6, 4) and new birth (*1 Pet.* 1, 3; 2, 3; *Tit.* 3, 5–7)—these two aspects are united in St. Paul (*Gal.* 4, 4–7; *Rom.* 8, 14–17); purification (*1 Cor.* 6, 11; *Eph.* 5, 26; *Heb.* 10, 22; *Apoc.* 1, 5; etc.); resurrection in Christ (*Rom.* 6, 1–11; *Col.* 2, 12–13; *Eph.* 2, 1–6; *1 Pet.* 3, 21–22) and illumination (*Heb.* 6, 4; 10, 32; see *1 Thess.* 5, 5–10; *Rom.* 13, 11–14; *Eph.* 5, 8–15)—these two aspects are united in the baptismal hymn cited in *Ephesians* 5, 14. Do not the accounts of the baptism of Jesus (*Mk.* 1, 9–11) show him as the model and source of the baptism of Christians (voice of the Father, divine sonship, fullness of the Holy Spirit)?

The apostolic reflection on the doctrine of the redemption began from the biblical texts: the Christ, Suffering Servant offered in ransom (*Mk.* 11, 45; *Acts* 4, 27. 30; *Phil.* 2, 6–11); the Christ, the new Paschal Lamb whose blood redeemed men (*1 Cor.* 5, 7; 6, 20; 7, 23; *1 Pet.* 1, 18–19; *Apoc.* 5, 6–9; 14, 4). The two aspects are joined in *John* 1, 29. See the bibliography of Chapter XIV.

The eucharistic meal or "Breaking of the Bread" (*Acts* 2, 42. 46; 20, 7–11) ritually reproduced the Last Supper of the

Lord (*1 Cor.* 11, 23–29, and the Synoptic Gospels). It is a meal with the Risen Christ (*Lk.* 24, 28–35; *Jn.* 21, 13; *Apoc.* 3, 20), foretold by the miraculous meal of the multiplication of the loaves (*Mk.* 6, 41–42; *Jn.* 6, 1–14). It furnishes a participation in the body and blood of Jesus (*1 Cor.* 10, 16–17; 11, 27–29; *Jn.* 6, 51–58). It is the prelude to the heavenly banquet (*Mt.* 8, 11; 22, 1–14; *Lk.* 22, 14–18; *Apoc.* 3, 7; 22, 2. 15).

XVIII.

THE JOHANNINE WRITINGS

ONE group of writings is linked to the apostle John. It includes a Gospel, three letters, and an apocalypse. Even though these writings do pose difficult problems for the critics, there is great benefit in not dividing them up. They were known very early in the 2nd century, by Ignatius of Antioch (who knew the fourth Gospel) and Polycarp of Smyrna (who cited the letters). Finally, all the explicit witnesses, whether orthodox writers (Papias, Irenaeus, the Canon of Muratori) or heretics (the Gnostics, Marcion, Tatian), attribute these writings to the apostle John (Texts 45, 51, 52). All the authors are conscious of meeting in them the personal tradition of the apostle John, who died in Asia Minor around the end of the 1st century. Although it is true that legends soon surrounded his death (Text 53) and that those times had different ideas on the notion of a literary author, this does not prevent these writings from authentically transmitting the witness of the apostle John to us.

1. THE APOCALYPSE

The Apocalyptic Genre

Descendant of the ancient prophet's visions which described the heavenly realities and the prophecies which proclaimed the day of Yahweh, the apocalyptic genre, as we have seen, was al-

372

ready used in the Old Testament: the book of Daniel is closely bound up in it. It was popular in Judaism (Texts 31, 33, 39), and the New Testament naturally used this literary style when the subject demanded it—for example, to depict supernatural visions (*Mk.* 1, 10; *Mt.* 4, 8–9; *Lk.* 10, 18; *Acts* 7, 56); to foretell the judgment of the world which is linked to the death of Christ (the synoptic apocalypse: *Mark* 13 and parallels); to speak of the return of Christ, the object of Christian hope (*1 Thess.* 4, 15–17; *2 Thess.* 1, 7–10; 2, 3–10; *1 Cor.* 15, 24–28. 51–55; *2 Pet.* 3, 1–13). The Johannine apocalypse is not, then, an isolated document; but with Christian eschatology as its object, it systematically uses the conventional genre formerly restricted to limited use. This is a difficult book whose doctrine is expressed in myriad grandiose images which, although fascinating in themselves, effectively conceal their secrets. Penetration into these mysteries requires a thorough knowledge of the Old Testament, especially the eschatological oracles of the prophets. By constantly using their texts the author gives them a Christian interpretation. The reader must also have a correct idea of the apocalyptic genre and its laws, otherwise he will drift quickly into arbitrary or absurd interpretations.

The Structure of the Book

In its present state the book is clearly structured. It shows a series of visions one attached to the other with a working-stock of complicated symbols woven throughout. The symbolism of numbers, especially of the number 7, plays a constant role. Despite uncertainties over details we can make out a structured series of septettes.

1. PRELUDE: THE LETTERS TO THE 7 CHURCHES (1–3)

The author, isolated on Patmos during a persecution, fell into an ecstasy on Sunday. He saw Christ in glory, and Christ gave him a mission to write to the 7 churches of Asia (the number 7 is the symbol of totality), grouped around Ephesus (Map 12). The 7 messages keep returning to the same themes: reproaches for lukewarmness, warnings against the heretics, exhortation to fervor, the promise of an eternal reward for those who have persevered. The situation recalls the pastoral letters of Paul, the letter of Jude, the second letter of Peter. This prelude could have existed separately though at present it serves as the preface for the collection of visions.

2. THE PRELIMINARIES OF THE GREAT DAY (4–16)

This section is composed of four self-contained septettes (the third is less distinct than the others).

The Book of the 7 Seals (4–7). In his vision, the author is taken up into heaven. He sees God, who is holding the Book where his decrees are recorded in his hand. No one can break its seven seals, except the slain Lamb (Christ) whom God has made master of history. Gradually the Lamb breaks the seals initiating the signs preceding the divine Judgment, which are the calamities of history. But before the last seal can be opened, the servants of God are set apart, to be saved on the Day of Wrath. Thus the Church is presented as mingled in the history of sinful humanity.

The 7 Angels with the 7 Trumpets (8–11). Judgment does not come yet, but a new septette takes up the signs which will precede it. In the vision they are unleashed upon the world as the trumpets sound. Before the last one had sounded, a vision parallel to that of chapters 4–5 presents the "little book" to the seer, the book which contains the sequel to his prophecy (10) and the "two martyred witnesses" of God (11, 1–13). Perhaps these enigmatic persons, recalling Moses and Elijah, personify the continuity of the evangelistic Gospel witness in history; some see Peter and Paul in them, but they may just be a now decipherable historical witness.

The 7 Signs (12–14). Once more there is a return to the beginning to throw light on the Church grappling with the powers of evil. The new humanity (a Woman about to give birth) is pursued by Satan (the dragon driven from heaven). Unable to reach either her or her first-born son (Christ), Satan decides to carry the war to her children (Christians, members of the Church). This is the deeper reason for the persecu-

374

tions. So he gives his power to two monsters: the beast from the sea, who demands adoration from men (the totalitarian pagan empire), and the beast from the land, his helper (Greco-Roman paganism). But in the face of the followers, behold the Lamb, surrounded by his faithful! They will escape the judgment which will befall the followers of the Beast. This is the judgment the Son of man with helping angels will carry out. The last sign is the seven angels who will act in the following section.

The 7 Angels with the 7 Cups (15–17). Once again the signs preceding the judgment are recapitulated in the 7 cups of the Wrath of God, which parallel the 7 trumpets. So we come to the great day.

3. THE GREAT DAY (17, 1—22, 15)

This second part hinges on three sections each describing a "moment" in the eschatological events. With the four sections of the first part they form a sort of septette which includes the whole book.

The Judgment of Babylon (17, 1—19, 10). Babylon, personified by a woman who rides a monster (the "harlot of the famous name"), symbolically represents Rome, the pagan power persecuting Christians. With the prophecy of her fall, as an effect of the judgment of God, the whole world laments over her, while in heaven a song of joy resounds, for the elect are about to take part in the wedding feast of the Lamb.

The Final Combat (19, 11—20, 15). We are present at the eschatological battle of Christ, the Word of God, against all the hostile powers: the pagan empires which became, following Rome, the vassals of the beast and the dragon. As long as the time of the Church lasts (symbolized by 1000 years), Satan is "bound" and has only a restricted power. As the end approaches his power grows and his struggle against the Church intensifies, but God finally triumphs. When the dead rise for the last judgment, Satan and his allies, and Death itself, are at last hurled down into the "pool of fire and sulphur."

The Heavenly Jerusalem (21, 1—22, 15). After the end of

375

the time during which the two cities confronted one another, we see the heavenly Jerusalem, the spouse of the Lamb, reveal herself. Then the elect, led into the eternal marriage feast, enjoy an Eden-like happiness which will never end. The conclusion of this picture affirms the "approaching" coming of the Lord. The epilogue to the book (22, 16–21) is an ardent appeal to this coming of Christ in glory.

The Purpose and Origin of the Book

The Apocalypse is a skillful composition. However, its strong over-all structure allows for more than one rough spot in detail. In the series of visions (4–22) there are repetitions and parallel passages, as if the final editor had used older sources. This suggests that composition toook place over a period of time. The book is a message of hope and comfort addressed to persecuted Christians. Two eras would explain this context: the end of the reign of Nero (64–68) and that of the reign of Domitian (94–96). Even if the number symbolizing the imperial Beast, 666 (13, 18) is best explained by the name "Nero Caesar," it could allude to Domitian in veiled terms. A series of converging indices point towards the same date, which second century tradition retained. Taking all of this into account, it is likely that a first setting of the texts was edited very early (between 65 and 70) and reworked and completed between 70–95. It would then have received its final form at the same time as the "7 letters" which serve as its preface.

The author calls himself John (1, 1. 4. 9; 22, 9). He classifies himself with the prophets (22, 9), who played an important role in the primitive Church (*1 Cor.* 2, 28–29). If he meant this title in the strict sense, as distinct from the title apostle, the linking of the Apocalypse to the apostle John must be understood in the broad sense. The case would be analogous to that of the Gospel of Mark, which transmits Peter's witness. But then, the tradition of the 2nd century must have soon confused John the apostle and his disciple John (Text 51), attributing to the first the exile at Patmos which would have happened to

376

the second (1, 9–10). There is no certain solution. Even so, the hypothesis of a pseudonym (as in the case of the second letter of Peter), while wholly within the normal conventions of the apocalyptic genre, remains gratuitous here, for in 95 the apostle John had not yet died (Text 45). But it remains probable that one of his disciples did take care of the final edition of the work. Also, it is written in very bad Greek—perhaps a Greek translation which imitates an Aramaic original.

The Meaning of the Apocalypse

In some measure the Apocalypse is a book of symbolized prophetic facts. But it would be wrong to look for precise facts on the successive periods into which the history of the Church would be divided, on the facts of our times, and so on. The book is not a collection of horoscopes! Thus we must beware of *extempore* commentators who discover in it, as in a history book, the exact and precise prediction of present or recently past events, and pretend to deduce the near future by them. In fact, all the "prophetic" passages pertain to the history of the Roman Empire of the 1st century. The author applies to the circumstances of his own time a doctrine which is sketched out in the Old Testament and which the New makes precise (*Mk.* 13 and parallels; *2 Thess.* 2, 1–12) by foretelling the judgment of God on the powers which oppose his plan, and forcibly recalling the promises made to the Church. In symbolic terms, woven of scriptural allusions, he thus expresses a rich doctrine, valuable for all times: the doctrine of the redemption, of the Church, of salvation, of the eternal reward promised to faithful Christians. He sees the Church fighting at close quarters with the persecuting empire as the logical consequences of the passion of Christ, the necessary prelude to his glorious resurrection. It leads certainly to an eschatological triumph, located above and beyond time. These spiritual lessons have lost none of their worth, and they regain their pertinence every time the battle of totalitarian powers against the Church of Christ resumes in history. Thus the Apocalypse above all others appears as the book of Christian hope.

2. THE JOHANNINE LETTERS

The Three Letters

The third letter of John is a short note addressed to an intimate urging him to persevere in fervor. The second, also short, is addressed to a Church (the "Elect Lady") to recommend fraternal charity and to warn against the heretical teachers who refuse to believe in the incarnation of the Son of God. The first letter is the most important. Underlying the written message (see 1, 4; 2, 12–14; 5, 13) is an oral preaching in the Semitic style. The author has collected homiletic fragments revolving around several fundamental themes; the defense of the Church against the heretics (the "anti-Christs") furnished the occasion. Without giving his name, the author presents himself as a *presbyter* ("elder": *2 Jn.* 1, and *3 Jn.* 1), a title of the heads of the community in the pastoral letters of Paul. But he also insists on his character as eyewitness of Christ (*1 Jn.* 1, 1–3), as the author of the fourth Gospel does (*Jn.* 21, 24). Tradition from the 2nd century on has unhesitatingly affirmed this group of writings as the witness of the apostle John (Text 53). It is possible, however, that disciples of the apostle took part in editing the text, as Silas edited the first letter of Peter. The Johannine origin of the preaching reproduced is more important than the personality of its editors.

Johannine Doctrine

In the first letter the themes are intertwined, reappearing in successive waves without definite plan. Together they form a well-structured theology, as personal as St. Paul's or that of the Letter to the Hebrews. The Christ, the Son of God become flesh, is the center of his thought (1, 1–4; 4, 2. 14–16; 5, 1–12.

378

20); he himself receives the title of Word, or Word of God (1, 1). Being himself the Life, he gives us the life of sons of God (3, 1–2; 5, 1. 11–12). Being the Light and the Truth (1, 5–7), to believe in him is to be in the light and truth (1, 7; 5, 9–12). His coming in the flesh was the manifestation of God's love for us (3, 16; 4, 7–16). The sign that we belong to Christ is our practice of love—love of God proven by the fulfillment of his commandments (2, 3–6; 3, 19–24; 4, 17–19); love of our brothers flowing from the love of God (2, 7–11; 3, 10–18; 7, 7–11. 20. 21). Founded on the Gospel data, this spirituality is organized into an original synthesis.

Opposite the divine domain of the life, the light, and the truth, entered by faith and love, rises the domain of the Devil (3, 8–10). This dualist perspective is close to that of the Apocalypse. The Christian must flee this evil world (2, 12–17; 5, 3–5. 19), the domain of darkness and illusion, entered through sin, and lack of belief in Christ or lack of love for his brothers (1, 8—2, 2; 2, 9–11. 16–17; 3, 3–10). It is there that the anti-Christs who deny the coming of the Son of God in the flesh (2, 18–23; 4, 1–6) wish to lead us. So John exhorts all the Christians to fervor in faith and charity, and to flee sin and heresy while awaiting the Coming of the Lord (2, 28). These preoccupations recall the pastoral letters of Paul, the Letter of Jude, the second letter of Peter, and the letters to the seven churches which open the Apocalypse. They show what problems the Church faced towards the end of the first century. And they form the background for the fourth Gospel.

3. THE FOURTH GOSPEL

The Purpose and Character of the Book

The evangelist himself defined the purpose of his book. He wrote so that his readers might "believe that Jesus is the Messiah, the Son of God, and that believing in him they might have life in his name" (20, 31). This key concept recalls the first

379

letter, which could well serve as the preface to the Gospel. He is concerned with a *Gospel,* not a history of Christ as a modern historian would conceive it. Certainly, the historical reality of Jesus is forcefully witnessed here (19, 35; 21, 24; see *1 Jn.* 1, 1–4); a good number of concrete details, confirmed even by modern archaeology, affirm this is a first rank testimony based on a tradition as old as that of the Synoptics. But what the author wants understood above all is the profound meaning of the events recalled, their connection to the mystery of salvation in which we participate through the Church.

This same intention was present in the other three Gospels and ruled especially in the theology of St. Paul. But John, as much as Paul, is a theologian, though his systematic theological exposition takes the form of a Gospel. His choice of episodes is based on the teachings to be drawn from them. When John reports the words of Jesus, it is to make the mystery of his person and his work understood. The actions and sayings of Jesus, contemplated for a long time, have become the substance of his religious thought. This living fidelity gives him a field of play in which to organize the facts in his own way, and to restore Christ's discourse by drawing from it the themes which interest him. The parallel between his book and the Synoptics show that the point of departure for his witness is, indeed, the real life and real words of Jesus. But much time has flowed between the events and the literary crystalization of the witness. Meanwhile, the presentation of the facts has been impregnated with theology, and the presentation of the words has gone on in John's own style.

The Origin and Author of the Book

The book is presented as the witness of "the disciple whom Jesus loved" (21, 24). This disciple (13, 23; 19, 26; 20, 2; 21, 7. 20), is closely associated with Peter, as John was in the Synoptics and the Acts (*Acts* 4; 8, 14). All the clues point to John, who is never named in this Gospel. The tradition he represents has left other traces in the New Testament. For example, the passion and resurrection narrative in Luke depend on him for many characteristics, as does the conclusion of Mark (16, 9–14). But here it takes an organized form. Besides, it was certainly preached long before being recorded in writing. This last step must have taken place between the years 80 to 100, and must not have been accomplished at a single stroke. The conclusion of chapter 21 shows that the final edition of the work was done by John's disciples, and the disciples probably also cooperated in the literary formation and ordering of the fragments which make it up. Some harshness of edition, some poor transitions, some fragments out of context, give the impression of an incomplete composition. These internal indications cross-check the tradition of the 2nd century, which attributed the Gospel to John's extreme old-age, between 95 and 100. In any case, it was known in Egypt twenty years later, since it figures in the most ancient manuscript of the New Testament, the *Rylands Papyrus 457* (around 125).

The Manifestation of the Son of God in the Flesh

The key concepts of the fourth Gospel indirectly parallel those of the Synoptics, but are clothed in a vastly different vocabulary. The theme of the kingdom of God is kept in the background (3, 3. 5), and the theme of life comes to the center of thought. The title of Son of man is found in two places; but that of Son or Son of God (see *Mt.* 11, 27; 17, 5; 21, 37; 24, 36) occurs on the lips of Jesus much more frequently. It is because the whole life of the Master is understood as the manifestation of the Son of God come in the flesh. From this flows the particular attention the evangelist pays to the familiar conversations where Jesus reveals himself (3, 1–11; 4, 5–26; 14–17), to the controversies which interminably face him, to the unbelieving Jews (5, 18–47; 6, 22–71; 7, 14–53; 8, 12–59; 10, 22–42), to the miracles which are revelations in action, veiled but meaningful for hearts docile to grace.

381

This revelation in words and signs is at first given to a restricted number of hearers: some disciples, Nicodemus, the Samaritan woman (1–4). Then it is openly addressed to the crowds of Galilee and Jerusalem and the authorities of Judaism (5–12), but, faced with their refusal to believe, it is finally reserved to the future witnesses of the resurrection (13–21). In this framework, Jesus speaks freely of himself, of his mission, of his work. He defines his role in relation to us: "I am the bread of life [6, 35], . . . the light of the world [8, 12], . . . the Good Shepherd [10, 11], . . . the resurrection and the life [11, 25], . . . the true vine" [15, 1]. He reveals the nature of his relation to the Father (5, 19–30; 6, 44–46; 8, 28–29. 54–58; 10, 25–38; 14–16). Paradoxically, this revelation culminates on the cross, which is both the victory and the glorification of Jesus (12, 13–36; 17, 1–2). That is why the glorified Christ can now give life to the world. Christians experience this when they participate in the sacraments of the Church. Scrutinizing the facts of the earthly life of Jesus in the light of this Christian experience, John sees the sacraments engraved in detail: the baptism of water, which gives the Holy Spirit (1, 33; 3, 5; 4, 13–14; 7, 39; 9, 7–37; 11, 25–43; 14, 16–17) and remits sins (20, 23); the Eucharist which gives participation in the body and blood of Jesus Christ (2, 6–11; 6, 41–58). Not only are the miracles seen as sacramental symbols, but also the water and blood which flowed from the side of Jesus on the cross (19, 34). In brief, the Gospel appears as a rich catechesis, more profound than that of the Synoptics and also more precise in its doctrinal vocabulary. It is John the theologian who defines Jesus as the personal Utterance of God, the Word (*1 Jn.* 1, 1–14; *Jn.* 1, 1–14).

The Drama of Light and Darkness

Nevertheless, the manifestation of Jesus effects a judgment among men. On the one hand, John shows the faith awake to the vision of signs: that of the disciples (2, 11), of the crowds

(2, 23), of Nicodemus (3, 2), of the Samaritan woman and her compatriots (4, 39), of the royal official (4, 48–53). But the same miracles are an occasion of opposition for the souls in darkness who do not see the witness of the Father there (5, 16–18; 36–47). After the miracle of the multiplication of loaves, the concrete revelation of Jesus as the Bread of Life, a crisis is precipitated and many leave him (6, 60–66) while the faith of the disciples is purified (6, 67–69). From this moment, the opposition of the unbelievers grew, until the resurrection of Lazarus clinched the decision among the authorities to put Jesus to death (11, 45–53).

This progression of the drama throughout the whole Gospel rouses John's reflection. He sees realized in the earthly life of Jesus a fact that his letters found in the present life of the Church and which the Apocalypse shows throughout history: the duel between light and darkness, life and death, Christ and Satan. When Christ, the life and light, appeared in the world, men were summoned to take up a position in his regard. He then causes a division between those who believe and are illumined by him and go to life, and the others who plunge themselves into darkness and death. This forms the judgment of God (3, 16–21; 9, 39). Throughout the Gospel the unbelieving Jews appear as the incarnation of the evil world which, driven on by Satan (13, 2), wants to dispose of him who is the light and the life (compare *Apoc.* 12, 4–6. 13–16). But at the very moment of this plot's success, the world is being judged, and Satan dethroned (12, 31). For by the cross Jesus "passes from this world to the Father" (13, 1), and once for all risen he will strengthen the faith of his witnesses and send them to bring the message of salvation to the world (20, 19–29). We can sense the theological atmosphere in which the account flowers. The least phrases, the least gestures of Jesus, are laden with meaning. At each moment unlimited spiritual perspectives are being opened because the very mystery of Jesus which has already unfolded in history remains for Christians a present reality, in which they participate.

4. APOCRYPHAL APOCALYPSES

If the tradition of John has been authentically transmitted by certain channels (like that which, through Polycarp, reached to Irenaeus; see Text 45), his legend developed early during the 2nd century, as the *Muratorian Canon* shows (Text 53), between 160 and 180, and the apocryphal Acts of John in the second half of the century. On the other hand, from the years 130–150, heretical Gnosticism claimed the fourth Gospel for itself (notably its prologue on the theology of the Word), just as the illuminists have repeatedly abused the book of the Apocalypse. These attempts at perversion have not troubled the Church's confidence in the witness of "the disciple whom Jesus loved." But just as apocryphal literature produced gospels and epistles and acts of apostles imitating the genres of the New Testament, it also produced apocalypses describing the end of time or the mysteries of heaven and hell, by putting them under the patronage of the apostles. That of Peter would date from around 150; that of Paul from the 3rd century. They do possess literary merit and have had a considerable influence on Christian art.

Text 51

ANCIENT WITNESSES ON
THE APOSTLE JOHN

St. Justin, who was converted in the East around 135, refers to the Johannine Apocalypse (20; 5) in his *Dialogue with Trypho* (around 155):

384

Among us also, a man by the name of John, one of the apostles of Christ, thanks to a revelation (= apocalypse) which came to him, prophesied that those who believed in our Christ would dwell a thousand years in Jerusalem, after which there would be a general resurrection and, in a word, eternal, for all without exception, then a judgment.

Dialogue with Trypho, 81, 4

For Justin, the seer of the Apocalypse was John. The same goes for Clement of Alexandria and St. Irenaeus at the end of the century. But this letter was directly linked to John by his master Polycarp (Text 45). He also affirms the Johannine origin of the fourth Gospel (Text 46) and John's stay at Ephesus:

The Church at Ephesus, which Paul had founded and where John dwelt until the era of Trajan [98–117] is also a truthful witness to the tradition of the apostles.

Text 52

THE LETTERS OF JOHN IN CHRISTIAN LITERATURE

The letters of Ignatius of Antioch (around 110–115) include echoes of the letters of St. Paul and the fourth Gospel. The letter of Polycarp to the Philippians (around 115) uses entire phrases from the apostolic writings; for example, in this warning against heretics:

Be zealous for good; avoid the snares, the false brethren, and those who hypocritically conceal themselves under the name of the Lord: they mislead frivolous souls. For "whoever does not confess that Jesus has come in the flesh, that one is an anti-Christ" (*1 Jn.* 4, 3; *2 Jn.* 7); and whoever does not confess the testimony of the

385

cross, that one "is of the devil" (*1 Jn.* 3, 8); and whoever bends
the words of the Lord to his own desires and says there will be
neither a resurrection, nor a judgment, that one is the first-born of
Satan. Thus, leaving aside the nonsense of the crowd and false
doctrines, let us return to the Word which has been transmitted to
us from the beginning.

St. Polycarp, *Letter to the Philippians,* 6, 3–7, 2

Text 53

THE LEGEND OF JOHN
IN THE 2ND CENTURY

The memory of John at Ephesus was transmitted by oral tradition. So it was soon loaded down with legendary elements
which, in the second half of the 2nd century, furnished the
material for the Acts of John. The *Muratorian Canon* (between
160 and 180), while insisting upon the unity of the Gospel
tradition, already spoke of the origin of the fourth Gospel in
these terms:

The fourth Gospel: of John, one of the disciples. Since those
who had been disciples with him and his colleagues in the episco-
pate entreated him [to write], he said: "Fast with me for three days,
and that which will have been revealed to anyone among us, we
will recount." That very same night, it was revealed to Andrew, one
of the apostles, that, by means of a revision made by all, John
would put all in writing in his own name. This is why, even though
the beginnings are presented differently in each of the Gospels,
there is no point of difference as regards belief, since in each
everything is set forth under the influence of the one Spirit: the
nativity, passion, resurrection, the conversations of Jesus with his
disciples, and his twofold coming—the first, which has already
taken place, in humility and contempt; the second, which will take
place, in royal power and glory.

Why is it surprising if John affirms so strongly each of these

386

things, even in his epistles, who says: "That which we have seen with our eyes, heard with our ears and touched with our hands, it is that which we have written to you" (*1 Jn.* 1, 1–2)? Thus he not only attests that he saw and heard the Lord, but that he set down in writing all his wonders in a certain order (lines 9–34).

This long development is perhaps a defense of the fourth Gospel against certain adversaries of the writings of John. A little later, the document also mentions the Apocalypse of John. It adds to it the Apocalypse of Peter which, it says, "some of us have forbidden to be read in Church."

Bibliography

L. Bouyer, *The Fourth Gospel* (Westminster 1964). A. Feuillet, *Johannine Studies* (Staten Is. n.d.). A. George, *Jesus Our Life* (Notre Dame 1965), a reading guide with a bibliography. W. Groussouw, *Revelation and Redemption* (Westminster n.d.).

Study Guides

Taking the revelation of Jesus as the Son of God in the Synoptics as a starting point (see Chapter XVI), reread the fourth Gospel to see how John gives it a central place (1, 49; 5, 19–47; 6, 24–47; 7–11).

On the royalty of Jesus in Johannine thought. Jesus refuses messianic royalty in a temporal perspective (6, 15), even though he is the Messiah-King (12, 12–17), because his royalty is not of "this world" (18, 33–37). But his resurrection makes him, on another level, "the King of kings and Lord of lords" (*Apoc.* 19, 11–16) and the kings of the earth will be destroyed if they are opposed to this spiritual kingship, as pagan totalitarianism is (*Apoc.* 19, 17–21; 20, 7–10).

On the symbolic meaning of Christ's miracles according to the fourth Gospel. Eucharistic signs: the wedding feast of Cana (2, 1–11) and the multiplication of loaves (6). Baptismal signs: the healing of the paralytic (5), in connection with the remission of sins (5, 14) and giving of life (5, 21); the healing of the man born blind (9), in connection with baptismal illumination; the resurrection of Lazarus (11), in connection with the resurrection of men in Christ (see 5, 25). Do not these themes match those of the apostolic preaching (see above, Chapter XVII)?

In comparison with the parables of the Synoptic Gospels, study the allegories of John's Gospel (*Jn.* 10; 15, 1–8).

XIX.

THE BIBLE, WORD OF LIFE

WE have followed the history of the biblical revelation step by step, taking note of its broad stages. The themes of revelation, drawn out and developed throughout the Old Testament, have come together in the person of Jesus Christ and have thus acquired their full and final meaning—the meaning which the Church has proclaimed since apostolic times (Text 42). Gradually, as revelation has progressed, we have seen the collection of sacred books take shape. Now that we have made this concrete contact with the Scriptures, we will try to survey them in a single glance, in order to ask some more general questions and to come to the answers our preceding study permits. What is the word of God, and how can the sacred books be called the word of God? What is the role of the Church with regard to this word of God and these books? How can their authentic meaning be determined, so that they can nourish the faith and the Christian life?

1. THE MYSTERY OF THE WORD OF GOD

The Two Languages of God

Language is the essential medium of communication between human persons—and also, making the due allowances, between men and God. God can only be known to men if, in the

389

first place, he speaks to them in some way. His word is the necessary point of departure for every religious relationship between himself and men. But God has two closely linked yet distinct languages: a natural language, bound up in creation, and a supernatural language, which belongs to the order of redemption and grace.

The Creator, in fact, speaks to every man, in whatever time or place. This first language is accessible to whoever "seeks the Truth with his whole soul," according to Plato's expression. Creation is not merely an area for man's exploration. It is also a sacred sign through which the Creator allows himself to be glimpsed, and in which he renders witness to himself (*Acts* 14, 15–17; 17, 24–29; *Rom.* 1, 19–20). In the same way, the conscience is not only the "voice of reason" as a sense of the moral law, it also makes man conscious of his dependence upon his Creator and as a drive towards an Absolute, it concretely orients man towards him who is his last end. Alas! In the present state of sinful mankind this twofold natural language of God runs the great risk of going unheard. At the least, the bare glimpse of the living God runs the risk of being distorted into a caricature, as happened in the ancient paganisms (*Rom.* 1, 21–23). God alone could remedy this peril through grace. This is one of the reasons for revelation. For God wanted to establish a much more intimate relation between men and himself than the spectacle of his works or the intuitions of men's consciences would ever allow. He wanted men to participate in his own life. Men could not know that; God alone could reveal it.

There exists, then, a second language of God, tied to the realization of his plan of salvation. It was not addressed to all men in an immediate and uniform way. God confided it to messengers, whom he charged with passing it on to other men. Through them the word of God has been inscribed in history. To accredit them, God worked signs which accompanied their mission: miracles, promises fulfilled, events filled with meaning. These were historical signs, setting forth divine revelation in a given time and place as an event in human history. Or rather, revelation was a series of events, which began with the call of

Abraham, and culminated in the life of Jesus Christ, the Word of God made flesh, as St. John says (*Jn.* 1, 14). By means of this second language, God revealed our redemption as he was realizing it here on earth. He revealed our call to the supernatural life, while establishing the means for attaining it. With the same stroke, he clarified the meaning of his creation and the message of human conscience, restoring to its full order a nature which sin had corrupted.

The People of God

In the Bible the word of God refers to the supernatural message of revelation. But this message had to be received and preserved from age to age. It had to mature in a suitable climate, before finally being brought to the whole world. That is why God chose a human community, which he made his people. Through them, he showed that the purpose of his revelation was to unite men among themselves by linking them to him. We saw this happening in the Old Testament (*133, 221, 225, 325–327*), and the New Testament finally manifested it in its fulness (*Rom.* 3, 21—4, 12).

For two thousand years the people of God was visibly supported by a temporal collectivity. The Israelite nation, born at Sinai (*188*), organized into a kingdom in the time of David (*71*), and finally became Judaism (*290–299*). But this disposition was only temporary and was to disappear when the time of preparation was completed (*Gal.* 3, 23—4, 7). Thus when Christ inaugurated the reign of God in person and offered himself as redeemer in sacrifice (*Heb.* 8, 1–13; 10, 1–18), the people of God was opened to all the nations, uniting them to Israel within a new humanity (*Eph.* 2, 11–22: *Apoc.* 7, 1–12). This people, the Church today, is a reality of a different order than that of human civilizations. Through it, the word of God and the grace of Christ are brought to all men and by receiving its witness and participating in its life, all can enter into communion with God, here on earth and for eternity (*Apoc.* 21, 1–6. 22–29).

Believing in the Word of God

We must place ourselves in this perspective to understand the nature of the Christian faith. It is neither the blind acceptance of a certain number of unverifiable ideas, nor an emotional drive in which the reason plays little part. These ideas, common to a good number of unbelievers, are mere caricatures. In reality, the faith is a man's adherence to the Word of God coming to him in Jesus Christ. Or better, faith is a personal encounter with Jesus Christ, the Word of God made flesh (*Jn.* 1, 14), and through that, communion of life with God himself. Such an encounter is not purely an intellectual affair. The whole man is involved in his reason, will, his very emotions—what Pascal called "the heart." In the living relationship thus established between himself and God, man's intellect is illumined by grace, and receives new understanding. The word of God is not simply a word, evoking abstract ideas. It calls up in him profound resonances, for the spiritual realities of which it speaks to him are the very things in which he is interiorly participating. The truth which Christ, the Word of God, reveals to him is the light of his life.

Nevertheless, access to the certitude of faith clearly requires certain conditions, for he alone can believe who is disposed to believe. Every obstacle opposing the establishment of a personal relationship between a man and Christ is an obstacle to faith. This is true not only for the passage from unbelief to faith, but for its preservation. When the faith no longer flowers in life, when the theoretical acceptance of the word of Christ is no longer rooted in an effective love of him, faith is threatened with a progressive withering up, and perhaps death. He alone "comes to the light who does the truth," as St. John says (*Jn.* 3, 21).

The personal relationship of a man with Christ must not be conceived as a private conversation between the two. Christ is still present on earth in his Church, which is his body. There is no adherence to Christ except by participation in the faith of the Church, the depository and guardian of the Word of God.

392

She distributes this Word to us because it is the substance of her life.

2. THE WORD OF GOD AND SACRED SCRIPTURE

Scripture in Living Tradition

In studying the history of revelation, we have seen time and again that the word's first vehicle was not the Scriptures, but living tradition. The Scriptures came in second place, charged with a precious role within the tradition which bore them. We have to return to this idea of tradition to wipe out any false idea of it. In whatever age we consider, the religion of the people of God was founded on the very word of God, known through the witness of inspired men. That goes for the religion of the patriarchs, of Moses, of the prophets and the Sages, as well as for the New Testament. But before taking written form, this divine word was transmitted from one generation to another in a thousand different ways. Oral teaching, the common performance of ritual worship, the repetition of prayers inherited from their ancestors—all play a key role, as modern exegesis has strongly emphasized. In a word, the common life of the people of God is the primary channel through which his word reached men.

Scripture clearly has its place in this framework. Yet it did not, at a certain stage of development, collect all the contents of tradition and then substitute itself for every other means at the disposal of tradition. Rather, without interrupting tradition's living continuity, Scripture crystallized certain elements of it in an authentic and lasting manner—a partial and occasional crystallization, without doubt. Thus Deuteronomy is not the *whole* Law of Moses, nor is the Gospel according to St. Mark the *whole* of the Gospel of Jesus Christ. Yet this fixing of the word of God plays an irreplaceable role in tradition itself.

In fact, Scripture lets living tradition return to a contact with

393

its sources. This is true of the Old Testament. If post-exilic Judaism already seems to be a religion of the Book, it is because the word of God by which it lived was no longer delivered to it by oral tradition alone. It had assumed a written form, in the Torah of Moses and in the prophetic collections. There, the Jewish community founded itself once more upon its early beginning. Not that the books alone were enough to nourish its life. The community had to interpret them, to sound out their message in relation to life's practical problems. But in so doing the community looked for the rule of its own fidelity to the word of God, just as in the early Church, after the fixation of the apostle's tradition in some written form, the resulting book became a rule of faith and life. Not that the whole content of tradition was enclosed in it; rather, nothing of apostolic authenticity could contradict what the writings attested. For this reason, the Church in the 2nd century, once the age of the apostles had ended, when the teaching of the apostles could still be gathered up by those who had known them, set out to collect all the writings representing the apostolic tradition, as incomplete and occasional as they were. Under its living form, tradition has continued. The Church has always benefited from the assistance of the Holy Spirit in preserving the word of God and understanding it with exactness (*Jn.* 14, 26). But to aid his Church in keeping the entrusted deposit intact, God had fittingly willed that this word would exist fixed in writing, not under a simple human guarantee, but under his own guarantee. The holy books would in themselves be the word of God, because they came from inspired authors.

Prophetic Inspiration and Scriptural Inspiration

The word *inspiration* is often used to designate purely human realities such as poetic or artistic inspiration. The artist, by his creative activity, lets us participate in his contemplation of beauty. This is a gift of God, but a natural gift, an aspect of human genius. Besides artistic genius, there also exists a moral or religious genius. Privileged individuals forcibly perceive what we called the natural language of God, which resounds in creation and in the human conscience. In this broad sense, one can then speak of inspiration, if he so desires, so long as he clearly defines its object and limits.

But God wanted to give men a message of another order, his personal revelation. He acted through the intermediary of inspired men. Now natural religious genius would no longer suffice to explain either the intuitions or the power of expression of these men. A particular grace would be at the base of all their prophetic activity. Whatever the means of manifesting this activity, the men would only be *instruments* in the hands of God. Whatever they say, or write, or symbolically perform, it is God who addresses men through their intermediary. To clarify this mysterious reality, one can think of the role played by the humanity of Jesus Christ, the Word of God made Flesh (*Jn.* 1, 14) in our salvation. It was only a pure instrument, totally taken over by the person of the Son of God to speak to men and effect their redemption. There is something analogous, but to a lesser degree, in the case of the inspired men of whom we are speaking, the "prophets" in the broad sense of the term. God used them as instruments to work on earth. In the measure that they carried out this work of God, their acts, like their writings, are divine as well as human, for their whole activity had its source in God.

The term *instrument* must not make the inspired person appear to be passive under the impulse of the Holy Spirit. On the contrary, inspiration made him supremely active, for God used him while respecting his nature as an intelligent and free man, with his own temperament, mentality, language, and all the peculiarities characterizing him as an individual. At the hour of his calling, Jeremiah did not react like Isaiah (*114, 155*), and the conduct of Elijah before Ahab (*89–92*) was not the same as the prophetic mimes of Ezekiel (*195–197*). At this point in our analysis we can pass from prophetic inspiration, in the wide sense, to scriptural inspiration, which is applied

395

only to the sacred books. God used certain men as instruments *in their very literary activity,* so that his word took written form. That does not mean that the content of their books was always revealed to them, or that every sentence was dictated to them by a heavenly voice. This materialistic representation of inspiration does not take account of psychological truth. Nor were inspired men necessarily important personages; they were not even necessarily conscious of the extraordinary grace given them. Though there were some who were great *prophets,* in the strict sense of the term (like Moses or Isaiah), there were also humble, anonymous scribes, collectors of traditions or obscure lawyers, editors of proverbs or composers of psalm. Who would St. Mark be to us, if we were not in his debt for having collected the evangelistic testimony of Peter, and who would Silas be, if he had not edited the first letter of Peter?

It does not matter. God has willed that these men put in writing, under his own guarantee, certain testimony relating to his revelation and his work of salvation. From the Old Testament on, "the Spirit of Christ was in them, attesting in advance the sufferings of Christ and the glories which would follow them" (*1 Pet.* 1, 11). This is why, whether it is the Old or the New Testament, "all Scripture is inspired by God (*2 Tim.* 3, 16). So we speak with reason of *sacred books,* since every literary activity of these men was enveloped in divine inspiration. One can say that in these books everything is from man and everything is from God.

The Profound Unity of the Bible

The modern reader who begins to read biblical literature is always tempted to evaluate it in accord with his own mental categories. Instinctively, he harmonizes it with the accustomed literary forms of his own times. This poor methodology forgets the purpose that all the sacred books have in common! Whatever be their variety, which is great, they all relate to religious literature. Or rather, they all have a place and a determined function in the life of the people of God, as it unfolds in both Testaments. From this point of view, they form what may be called a *functional* literature, whose forms are governed above all by the diverse aspects of community life. Clearly, the forms used in the Old Testament are related to the community life of Israel in the different stages of its development. In the New, they are related to the life of the early Church: evangelization, liturgy, moral instruction of the faithful, apologetics, theological reflection, and so forth. If one remembers this background, he discovers intimate connections among all the sacred books, connections more profound than the differences due to the personality of the different authors.

This explains why the centers of interest in these books are, with only slight variations, the same throughout. From one end to the other, the Bible is the witness of *the acts of God in human history,* that is, revelation, with its century by century progress; the preparation of Israel for the Gospel, throughout the vagaries of its destiny; the coming to earth of the Son of God, who completed revelation and saved men by his redemptive sacrifice; the foundation of the Church, the body of Christ, the definitive regime under which will be ranged the people of God as long as the present world lasts. Whoever begins the sacred books with this key will have no trouble in unlocking their profound unity. If the Old Testament pedagogy is seen leading men towards Christ; if the progress of religious doctrine is patiently followed from century to century, up through the complications of the New Testament; if the lessons of the ancient texts are correctly understood by placing them in the light of Jesus Christ, then the Bible can become unequaled nourishment for the reader's faith. Just as all the events of sacred history, from the call of Abraham to the foundation of the apostolic Church, took place in the same divine plan which assures them unity, so all the sacred books form a single Book, *the Bible,* patiently composed under the unique direction of its divine author.

The Human Variety of the Bible

The Bible, the functional literature of the People of God, nevertheless presents a more varied picture than any other human book. It is the word of God expressed in human language. We must expect to find the trace of diverse human mentalities there, corrected perhaps, but assumed by the revelation which they serve to transmit. From this point of view, the evolution of civilization in Palestine between the beginning of the second millennium and our era has experienced profound modifications in modes of feeling, reasoning, speaking. The mentality of the patriarchs differs from that of the Fathers of the Church. Nevertheless, the poet of Job wrote before Judaism had made deep contact with Greek civilization.

To read the Bible without taking into account this cultural evolution, which at every instant conditions its language, would be to risk constant misunderstandings. Each page takes meaning from the mentality of the age in which it was composed and from the cultural situation in which the divine revelation presented itself. The anthropomorphic representation of God, current in the ancient traditions of the Pentateuch, is at the service of a real theology, but the souls whose needs it satisfied were not those of the Alexandrian mentality, for whom the Wisdom of Solomon was written. Here we see how the historical knowledge of the ancient Near East comes to the aid of biblical exegesis. It throws light, at different levels, upon the milieus to which the sacred books were originally adapted.

This adaptation is translated into highly varied language and modes of expression. Not only the types of style (which already have their importance) varied, but also the *literary forms* themselves. God did not restrict his inspiration to some well-defined genres, chosen especially so as not to confuse modern readers. No literary genre was, in itself, unworthy of inspiration, provided that it met the demands of the functional literature of the people of God, the vehicle of the divine revelation (Text 5).

At this point there is a frequent and tenacious error which must be dispelled. Since the Bible is the Word of God, it says,

398

one should find only true histories in it. A strange idea! For purely fictional accounts or ones freely developing the facts of history can just as well, through a convention of language permitted by every literature, teach lessons beyond the boundaries of history: philosophical reflection, religious doctrine, moral teachings—see the *Prometheus Bound* of Aeschylus, La Fontaine's *Fables, Candide,* or *The Brothers Karamazov* . . . Why should this be forbidden to the biblical authors? Did not Christ compose parables? What is shocking about the book of Job unrolling in the framework of a popular story or that of Jonah using a folklore theme (that of a man saved by a fish), since the lessons taught are not related to history?

These are two clear-cut cases. Some are more complex. In fact, if a number of the biblical books have to furnish a *religious interpretation* of history as their primary object, they nonetheless intend to give the key of *real* history: of the people of God, of revelation, of the plan of salvation. But to present this history they use very diverse materials, which were not submitted in advance to the laws formulated by modern critics. There are many ways of representing the past without betraying it. From this point of view, it must be clearly understood that the biblical narratives, even if they have an historical purpose, do not all fit into the same category. The history of the reign of David, recounted by a witness to the events, during the reign of Solomon, is not identical to that of Abraham which is based on popular traditions transmitted orally for centuries. Even in the New Testament, we do not treat the *Log of the Journey* of Paul to Rome the same as the traditions of the early community preserved in the first chapters of Acts, the accounts relating to the public life of Jesus, crystallized very quickly in the apostolic catechesis, while the accounts of the infancy according to St. Matthew were gathered much later from tradition and were clearly used for didactic purposes.

The accurate appreciation of such varied texts calls for great care and is a matter of delicate shadings. To treat all the accounts identically under the pretext that they form sacred his-

399

tory, would be to ignore one of the fundamental laws of human language. One does not treat the *Chronicles* of de Joinville and the *Little Flowers of St. Francis of Assisi* in the same way. This did not prevent the *Little Flowers* from occupying an important place in the literature of edification in the 13th century. And their legendary developments did not deny the historical existence of St. Francis. In this connection, the Bible contains many particular cases causing as many different problems. We may leave it to the specialists to resolve them, but it is good to be warned of their presence, if one wishes to read the sacred books intelligently. The fact that the Bible belongs to a cultural milieu very far removed from our own makes access to it difficult for modern minds. We must strip off some of our habitual modes of thought in order to follow the nuances of the ancient Semitic mentality. A rough task from some points of view! At least we must understand that the encounter with God does not belong to the order of human science. These men of other times did what they did, not on their own initiative to be sure, but because God first spoke to them.

The Divine Truth of the Sacred Books

Our approach to the sacred books, not only in their divine reality, but in their human peculiarities, will give us a correct understanding of the *truth* of the Bible. Inspiring the sacred authors, God assumed the primary responsibility and the guarantee for their writings. He would not teach error. And since his teaching passes through the channel of an inspired man, we must accept in faith all that *the man affirms as true*. But what does he intend to affirm as true? To put it another way, what is *taught* in the Bible? The problem is not simple, since the Bible is not a question and answer catechism. To resolve it, many elements must be considered.

In the first place, we must see revelation's *point of view*. Its only object is the mystery of God and the mystery of our salvation. The Bible cannot, then, teach anything which does

400

not treat of them. This means for example, that it would be foolish to question the first chapters of Genesis on the geological periods or on the way the body of man came into existence. In properly scientific material, the Bible speaks the language of its times, using representations then current. The problems which interest the Bible are of another order. They are metaphysical, moral, religious. Yet it is possible for its teachings to have relevance even on the scientific level. For example, Scripture clearly teaches the unity of human kind, fallen in its head and restored in Jesus Christ. Even so, it does not precisely clarify the biological basis for this unity. Here the researchers are left to their inquiries and the theologians to their reflections.

In what concerns history, the question is not the same as that of the natural sciences. In fact, the history of the plan of salvation is the very object of the Bible. In recounting God's interventions on earth, it intends to record a *real* history. But all the facts of human history obviously do not have an equal connection to the plan of God. Even when there is a question of the people of God, the Bible makes them the object of a direct teaching only when this link exists, and views them exclusively from this point of view. This is why the conduct of events by divine providence interests it much more than the chain of cause and effect on the plane of human politics. Biblical authors saw events from a very different angle than that of modern historians. We must assume this perspective to understand the Bible.

In the second place, the Bible is a book of *pedagogy*. Therefore, revelation presents itself progressively. So it would be misleading to search all the documents, and especially the most ancient, for a perfect and complete formulation of Christian doctrines. The points revealed in the Old Testament took on their definitive outlines only in the light of Christ. Before Christ, the texts gave only an approximate definition, one open to future clarifications. They retain their value for us, certainly; but they need to be completed, and sometimes corrected. For example, take the concepts of individual retribution and life beyond the grave, which were clarified so late in the Old Testament (*383, 400, 401*), or again the promise of salvation and the Messiah, expressed in figurative language until Christ defined their real meaning. This realization helps us understand the difference between those Old Testament texts containing a certain measure of positive affirmation, confirmed and completed by the Gospel, and those with provisory presentation, sometimes defective, which the New Testament replaced by a better presentation. Thus it is accurate to say that God rewards each according to his actions. Affirmed from the beginning, this principle did not vary. But for long centuries it was believed that this took place here on earth: an imperfect representation later to be corrected. The psalms which sing of the justice of God (*313*) thus retain their value; but supplementary precisions, corrections, and transpositions must be introduced into them.

Finally, we must take into account the *literary genres* used by the sacred authors to express their thought. All these genres are somehow related to the life of the people of God whose faith they nourish. But they do so by very diverse means. In our modern literatures, one does not read with the same key the *Song of Roland*, the *Chronicles* of de Joinville, the *Fables* of La Fontaine, the *Philosophical Tales* of Voltaire, and the novels of Conrad. We know better than to look for the same thing in each. We know that their *truth* lies on different planes.

Making the proper allowances, we must likewise use different approaches to the traditions of Exodus, the books of Kings, Jonah, Job, and Esther (to take only Old Testament examples). Even there, where real history is in question, we must remember that different means are used for depicting that history, that the representation of the past is infinitely varied. Certain forms of narratives permit, or even require, the use of imaginative material. This does not necessarily reduce the extraordinary to the realm of fiction, but we must recognize where fiction is used. It would be absurd to consider the Gospel miracles legendary because the fish in Jonah comes from folk-lore, just as it would be equally absurd to hold the account of Jonah to be a page from a chronicle because there are real miracles in the Gospel. It would also be just as dangerous for the faith to regard the hyperboles of poetry as miraculous happenings as it would be to deny the existence of miraculous events without any investigation. Such conclusions manifest a regrettable confusion between the various literary forms used by the biblical authors from time to time. It is not enough to approach the holy books with the spirit of faith and good will. We must also have a spirit of discrimination.

The recognition of literary forms opens up the exact shade of meaning of the biblical affirmations. An author does not equally commit himself in every sentence. Most often, the essentials of his writing stand out only after a general view permits a judgment of the whole work. In the case of the historical works, the problem is even more complicated since the authors, in depicting the past, are indebted to their sources. In using documentation to present sacred history, they do not in any way change its nature. Thus the witness of the apostles concerning Jesus, as it was gathered in the Gospels, is much more direct and stronger than the witness of the author of the book of Kings concerning the prophet Elijah. In the first case, it is the eyewitnesses who are speaking (in their own way, which is not that of scientific history!); in the second, the later chronicler reproduces the source he is indebted to, and this source is a conserver of a popular tradition. Thus the *degree of affirmation* is not equal throughout. This must be applied separately for each book, for each episode, for each fact of the sacred accounts. The literary critic and the historical critic working this way are not showing lack of respect for the word of God. On the contrary, they attempt better to understand the word of God, in all its human overtones.

We can see why exegetes must know Israelite civilization, the Semitic mentality, the ancient Oriental literatures, since they try to clarify what the Bible teaches on every page. Such a knowledge is not required by every reader, though it is never useless. But he must at least be open to it, and should approach the Bible in a spirit of faith, to be admitted by it and correctly to grasp the heart of Scripture.

3. THE BIBLE IN THE CHURCH

The Church, the Interpreter of Sacred Scripture

The sacred texts, then, raise difficult problems. Those who hope to find an answer to everything in the Bible, to clarify the enigmas of existence and to encounter God in a face-to-face conversation, fool themselves and are open to failure. God did not leave sacred Scripture to be interpreted according to the individual conscience. He has placed it into the hands of his Church, whose understanding is guided by the Holy Spirit.

The Church, in fact, preserves the same word of God which is found crystallized in Scripture in its living tradition. Called to proclaim the Gospel, she also has the task of bringing to light its riches and guaranteeing its correct comprehension. Thus every reading or individual study has to be carried out and guided under her protection, lest it risk falling into impasse or error. To be sure, the New Testament already furnishes the key to the Old, since the apostolic teaching is found condensed in it. But it must itself be understood in accord with a sure and authentic rule of interpretation. This rule is found in the living tradition of the Church, which, without a break, prolongs the apostolic tradition under the authority of a magisterium assisted by the Holy Spirit. She herself continually returns to Scripture for enlightenment. In return she clarifies its obscurities. To read the Bible in and with the Church is the only sure method (Text 54).

Even the point of departure for this reading is furnished by the Church. In her liturgy and preaching, she places the whole substance of the sacred texts at the disposal of her faithful.

404

This does not make personal reading unprofitable when undertaken not to satisfy curiosity but to nourish the faith. If recourse to the Church is indispensable, this does not dispense us from personal reflection. Rather, such recourse permits an exact understanding of the texts, whether they are read for edification, without examining the literary or historical problems raised, or whether the problems are directly examined for solutions. But it must be noted that the Church does not with its supreme teaching authority intervene on every proposal, thereby solving the problems in question. It does this only in grave cases where the fundamentals of doctrine are at stake. For the rest, it is sufficient for exegetes and theologians to carry on within the true faith, and for pastors accurately to preach the whole message included in the word of God. As for the details of technical questions, no one is infallible. To prevent possible deviations, the Church holds also that the faithful use, in ordinary cases, an edition of the Bible approved by it. This edition must contain some explanatory notes to guide the readers. When we are aware of the difficulties facing the reader, who is surprised by such precautions?

The Canon of the Sacred Books

The first intervention of the Church with regard to Scripture was the determination of the list of sacred books. A preoccupation of this kind had already arisen in Judaism. When it fixed the definitive edition of the five books of the Law, probably in the time of Ezra, Judaism set out to give an invariable form to the writings which enclosed the authentic Mosaic tradition. Later, the collections of the prophets were in their turn fixed. Around 132 A.D., the Greek translator of Ecclesiasticus knew three categories of sacred books: the Law, the prophets, and the other writings. This last category, the only one which could still grow, had indefinite outlines. The authorities of Palestinian Judaism, in determining the official list of the sacred books around the end of the first century A.D., excluded a certain

405

number of works which Alexandrian Judaism held on the same level of veneration as the others. Since the Church of apostolic times, which developed in a Greek milieu, received her Bible from Alexandrian Judaism, she was open to these works, which are sometimes designated by the name *Deuterocanonical*. Certain milieus gave credit to many apocryphal works, too.

But while using the inspired books of the Old Testament, the primitive Church was simultaneously shaping her own literature. The writings coming from the apostles or containing the authentic apostolic tradition were carefully preserved. The author of the second letter of Peter already knew a collection of the letters of St. Paul, which he put on a par with "the other Scriptures" (*2 Pet.* 3, 15–16), doubtlessly referring to the Old Testament (*2 Pet.* 1, 20–21) and perhaps to the Gospel collections. From the 2nd century on, the concern was to fix a *canon* (meaning a rule) of the New Testament, and to remove unauthorized books from the use of the Churches. These books were beginning to multiply, and sometimes served as vehicles for suspect or frankly heretical doctrines. Thus the *Muratorian Canon,* which we have cited several times (Texts 46 and 53), is a Roman list dating from 160–180. For some time, the official list had indefinite boundaries. But by the third century, it had been accepted in the majority of the local churches, both for the Old and New Testaments. Nevertheless, it was not until the Council of Trent, in the 16th century, that a final decision was prompted by the Protestant attitude which rejected the authority of the Deuterocanonical books. Here is the Canon of the Scriptures:

OLD TESTAMENT

I. THE LAW, divided into five books (whence the name Pentateuch): Genesis, Exodus, Leviticus, Numbers, Deuteronomy.

II. THE PROPHETS (Comprising two distinct sections):
1. History of the prophetic era: Joshua, Judges, Samuel (2), Kings (2).

406

2. Prophetic collections: Isaiah, Jeremiah, Ezekiel, the "twelve prophets" (Hosea, Joel, Amos, Obadiah, Jonah, Micah, Nahum, Habakkuk, Zephaniah, Haggai, Zechariah, Malachi).

III. THE OTHER WRITINGS (of various kinds):
1. Those admitted by Palestinian Judaism (the Hebrew Bible): Psalms, Job, Proverbs, "the five rolls" (Ruth, Song of Solomon, Ecclesiastes, Lamentations, Esther), Daniel, Ezra, Nehemiah, Chronicles (2).
2. Others admitted by Alexandrian Judaism (the Greek Bible): Tobit, Judith, Wisdom, Sirach, Baruch, and the Letter of Jeremiah, Maccabees (2), the supplements to Daniel and Esther.

NEW TESTAMENT

I. GOSPELS: According to Matthew, Mark, Luke, and John

II. THE ACTS OF THE APOSTLES

III. APOSTOLIC LETTERS
1. The letters of St. Paul (named for those to whom they are addressed): Romans, Corinthians (2), Galatians, Ephesians, Philippians, Colossians, Thessalonians (2), Timothy (2), Titus, Philemon. The Letter to the Hebrews is also attached to this group.
2. "Catholic" letters: (designated by the names of those they are attributed to): James, Peter (2), John (3), Jude.

IV. THE APOCALYPSE OF JOHN

This list does not pretend to resolve the problems of literary origin raised concerning some of the books mentioned. It only affirms that the books in question, in all their parts, whoever their authors might be, are inspired and for this reason enjoy a peculiar authority as the word of God. Once this is admitted,

407

it is always possible to inquire into their exact origin and their composition, even if this inquiry must show that such a book was not written by the person under whose name it has come to us. The traditional attributions do not, in themselves, pertain to the faith.

Biblical Exegesis

Once the canon of the Scriptures was fixed, the Church has been preoccupied with putting the Bible at the disposal of the faithful. That presupposes two things: that it be translated into the different languages of the evangelized people, and that it be explained through preaching and works of all kinds. Versions have multiplied down through the ages. At the Council of Trent, the version called the *Vulgate* (due to St. Jerome) was declared the *authentic* version for the Latin Church. What is in question here is a *juridical* authenticity, which means that, on the testimony of the Church, this version does not contain any doctrinal error. This clearly does not mean that it is a perfect translation. In this regard, the progress of biblical studies has gradually shown the need for improvement, or even replacement. This is why the psalter of the Vulgate was replaced in 1945 by a new official version, made from the original texts.

The explanation of the sacred books in the Church has been left to the initiative of the various pastors and Christian scholars. The innumerable commentaries from patristic antiquity and the Middle Ages are especially concerned with the theological exploration of the texts or the simple edification of the faithful. Nevertheless, on occasion, the authors also tried to resolve the historical or literary problems posed by the holy books. Since the 16th century the perfected critical methods applied to secular documents have also been applied to the Bible. A better interpretation of Semitic languages, the growth of the historical sciences and literary analysis, the discovery of ancient civilizations thanks to the excavations of archeology,

408

have entirely renewed the knowledge of the milieu of the Bible's birth. Many texts have thus been clarified. But it has also posed a myriad of questions in matters of history which Christian antiquity did not suspect and did not have the means of resolving. These questions are still being studied. Whatever solutions will be found, we can be sure that the doctrinal value of the holy books will remain unmodified. Revelation is independent of such research. But the history of the tradition which produced the Bible can only make it better understood in detail, and this will be beneficial to the faith.

A century's progress of biblical exegesis has, however, made mistakes and caused injuries. A rationalistic concept of the religious fact led certain interpreters, detached from all belief or belonging to Liberal Protestantism, to propose theories ruinous to Christian faith. At the beginning of the century, a certain number of Catholics were carried away by this spirit. The Church reacted against them with its condemnation of Modernism. So it happened that, without going beyond the limits of the faith, some became too exclusively attached to the historical and literary questions posed by the holy books, while overlooking their doctrine. Work carried on under these conditions, valuable as it was, could seem more damaging than profitable. On the other hand, certain spirits, frightened by the Modernist danger or disturbed in their intellectual ruts, confused the dogmatic tradition of the Church with the conservative positions of yesteryear's exegetes and clung without profit or serious argument to their obsolete and scientifically valueless solutions.

True work was accomplished nonetheless. Besides important, private undertakings (like the creation of the Ecole Biblique of Jerusalem, in 1892), the papacy intervened time and time again, either to block the path of dangerous theories by inviting exegetes to give up the work they were doing or by promoting a scientific and religious study of the sacred books. To promote this work the Pontifical Commission for Biblical Studies (1902) and the Pontifical Biblical Institute (1909) were created at Rome, and the popes published the encyclicals

Providentissimus (1893), *Spiritus Paraclitus* (1920), and *Divino Afflante Spiritu* (1943).

Today the work of Christian exegesis is in full swing. Many detailed questions raised by critical study of the Bible have not yet received definitive solution. Exegesis must be content with approximate solutions harboring an element of hypothesis. In the course of this book, we have come across a certain number of them, and we have seen that *they never throw the doctrinal value of the sacred books into question*. In fact, this scientific study of the Bible, pursued rigorously and methodically, without prejudice but prudently, can only illuminate the religious message they contain, as the word of the living God. The excess of a venturesome critic working on careless foundations must not mask this fundamental fact. Most often such a critic is forced to abandon his positions in the face of new discoveries, which though they do not directly prove the reality of the divine revelation, at least force the unbelieving historians themselves to face the problem posed by the religion of Israel. Here they face an unparalleled phenomenon in the immense ancient civilization, especially so when it is linked with Christianity, its final flowering. The enigma dissolves when the phenomenon is studied under the light of faith. For in the history of this religion, justified and fulfilled in Jesus Christ, we discover the traces of God in human history.

4. THE CHRISTIAN READING
OF THE BIBLE

The Literal Sense of Scripture

The preceding ideas show how the Bible must be read, not by forcing the texts to say something, but by paying attention to its literal sense, listened to in its fulness. The *literal* sense is the meaning which flows from the texts as their inspired author left them to us, the meaning he himself intended to give his work, while using a given, definite literary technique to express

410

his thought. This literal sense, then, embraces all the nuances of human language, all the contours of the various literary genres. It can never be reduced to the historical content which the critics are able to disengage from the sacred books. For the lessons, enclosed in the text through the sacred authors by God himself, contain a doctrinal importance. The Christian reader must constantly seek to uncover this doctrinal content for it constitutes the true worth of the Bible.

Let us add only that the literal sense must be listened to *in all its fullness,* which implies the profound richness discovered when the Scriptures are linked to Jesus Christ and the mystery of salvation. For the texts of the New Testament, this manner of listening to the texts poses no problem. But for those of the Old, we must bear in mind the ever limited horizon of the biblical authors. Their work takes on its full meaning only if given its proper place in the history of the plan of God, culminating in Jesus Christ.

To be sure, we must see the exact boundaries of the limited horizon of such a book or author. This is the job of biblical criticism. But the critic also must have the good sense to go beyond this first objective, to understand what the text in question says *to us,* what its permanent value-giving message is. Here the light of faith completes the insufficiencies of criticism. In the literal sense itself, faith discovers, written between the lines, the mystery of Jesus Christ. From the Old Testament, the eschatological promises of the prophets proclaimed him in a veiled way; the People of God themselves lived his life in a hidden way. It is this presence of Christ that the Christian reader must seek everywhere in the Scripture.

Scripture and Christian Life

Discovering Christ in Scripture throws light on all Christian life for the texts often directly apply to practical life. The precepts of the Decalogue, like the sayings of the Gospel or the counsels of St. Paul to Christians, directly concern our lives today. But often, in the Old Testament, the imperfect data of the texts must be corrected, to put them on a level with the Gospel revelation. We must see the analogies between our lives and those of the people of God, their attitudes, and the destiny to which God was leading them. When we see Israel rebel in the desert, we uncover the history of all sinners of all times, *our* history. So the texts which speak of the tragedy in the desert assume a constant relevance. Israel was chastized by different calamities: punishment will befall us too if we act the same way, and the calamities which befell the guilty people are the image of those which threaten us.

We must go further. The analogy of the two Testaments is such that the great experiences of the people of Israel, the fundamental institutions with which God endowed them, have a *figurative* value in relation to the mystery of Jesus Christ, as realized in his life and as given to us through his Church. The exodus of the people of God, took place on the temporal plane, but they recognized a divine grace in it, and their faith was directed towards another future deliverance. We ourselves experienced that deliverance in our baptism: that of the redemption of Jesus Christ. This is why St. Paul says that the events of the exodus constitute *figures* for us (*1 Cor.* 10, 1–11). So too, the Letter to the Hebrews sees how the rites of Sinaitic worship are foreshadowings and figures of the sacrifice of Christ (*Heb.* 8–10).

We must not see figures everywhere in the Bible, as if all the details of the history, institutions, and texts were allegories. But where they do exist, they permit us to discover a new depth under the literal sense. In fact, under the veil of figures, our fathers in the faith believed in the mystery of Christ. All the texts expressing this faith point to the mystery of Christ under the veil of figures. It is for this reason that, during the paschal vigil, the Church can celebrate the spiritual liberation of Christians by chanting the canticle of the exodus (*31*). It is for this reason that she takes up again the old royal psalms and applies them to the mystery of Christ the King. Such applications are not left to the whims of readers any more than the investigation of the literal sense. In this area too, the Church is our guide. In her school we can patiently learn to discover Christ in the sacred Scriptures.

Text 54

SCRIPTURE AND TRADITION

To understand the role of Scripture in the Church, its exact relation to Tradition must be presented:

Tradition and Scripture are not two independent sources which complete one another as two separable parts of a whole. If we are tempted to think so, it is because we have not escaped from the unfortunate cleavage made by Protestantism. To the Christians of antiquity, the Bible is so inseparable from Tradition as to be, in fact, a part of it: it is its essential element, its nucleus, so to say, But, on the other hand, if it were to be torn from the living whole which is constituted by the many factors of tradition, guarded and transmitted by the conscience of the Church, always watchful, always active—then the Bible would indeed become incomprehensible. It would be, in fact, separated from the life of the very realities of which it speaks. For the Catholic, then, the Bible and Tradition does not mean the Bible plus a foreign element without which it would remain incomplete. It means the Bible replaced, or rather remaining, in its proper atmosphere, its living environment, its native light. It is the Bible and nothing but the Bible; but it is the whole Bible, not in its letter only, but with the Spirit which dictated it and which does not cease to inspire the reading of it. Where, in fact, asks St. Augustine, will one find the Spirit of Christ if not in the body of Christ? It is, then, in the Church, the body of the living Word of God made flesh, that the Word, once given by inspiration to men of flesh, dwells on as Spirit and life.

Louis Bouyer, *The Meaning of Sacred Scripture*

Text 55

THE TWO FOODS OF THE SOUL

In this passage, *The Imitation of Christ* is interested in the religious value of the Scriptures. It shows it as a spiritual food comparable to the Eucharist:

I feel that two things are especially necessary for me here below and that without them I could not bear the weight of this miserable life.

Shut up in the prison of the body, I need food and light. This is why you have given this poor weak thing your sacred Flesh to nourish soul and body, and your Word to shine like a lamp for my feet.

I could not live without these two things, for the Word of God is the light of the soul, and your sacrament the Bread of Life.

They may be regarded as two tables set in the treasure house of the Church. The one is the table of the sacred altar on which a holy bread rests, that is the precious body of Jesus Christ. The other is the table of the divine Law, which contains the holy doctrine, which teaches the true faith, which lifts the veil of the sanctuary, and leads us surely to the Holy of Holies.

I thank you, Lord Jesus, Light of eternal light, for having given us through the ministry of the prophets, the apostles, and other teachers, this table of the holy doctrine.

The Imitation of Christ, **IV,** 11, 4

Bibliography

On the problems treated in this chapter, *The Word of God* by G. Auzou (St. Louis 1963). More succinct treatments may be found in H. Daniel-Rops, *What is the Bible?* (New York 1958) and J. Steinmann, *Biblical Criticism* (New York 1959). On the biblical question in the Church in modern times, see J. Levie, *The Bible, Word of God and Word of Man* (New York 1966). See also the general works cited in the bibliography of Chapter I.

TABLE OF BIBLICAL
REFERENCES

37. Ex. 20, 1–17
38. Ex. 21, 23–25; 22, 20–26; 23, 6–9; Deut. 24, 10–22
39. Ex. 21, 15–17; Deut. 21, 18–21; 22, 22–29; 24, 1–4; 25, 5–6
40. Ex. 13, 11–16; 22, 28–29; 34, 19–25
41. Ex. 12, 1–20; 24–27; 43–49
42. Lev. 4, 2–12
43. Ex. 23, 20–33
44. Ex. 32
45. Num. 11
46. Num. 13–14; 20–25
47. Num. 23, 7–10; 24, 3–9. 15–19
48. Deut. 34
49. Jdg. 1
50. Jos. 1, 1–5
51. Jos. 3–4
52. Jos. 5, 13—6, 27
53. Jos. 10
54. Jos. 8, 30–35; 24, 19–31
55. Jdg. 2, 6–23
56. Jdg. 5
57. Jdg. 6, 25–32
58. Jdg. 7–9
59. Jdg. 13
60. 1 Sam. 1–3
61. Jdg. 9, 7–15
62. 1 Sam. 8; 10, 17–25
63. 1 Sam. 9, 1—10, 16; 11, 1–15
64. 1 Sam. 13–27
65. 1 Sam. 28, 4—29, 1; 31
66. 2 Sam. 1
67. 2 Sam. 2–5; 8
68. 2 Sam. 5, 6–9; 6
69. Ps. 24, 7–10
70. Ps. 110
71. 2 Sam. 7, 1–17
72. 2 Sam. 11–12
73. 2 Sam. 18–19
74. 1 Kgs. 1
75. Ps. 132
76. 1 Kgs. 3, 4–15
77. 1 Kgs. 5, 15–26; 6–7
78. 1 Kgs. 8, 1–20; 54–66
79. 1 Kgs. 9, 1—11, 13
80. 1 Kgs. 11, 26–40
81. Ps. 18
82. Ps. 20
83. Ps. 21
84. Ps. 61
85. Ps. 63
86. 1 Kgs. 12
87. 1 Kgs. 14, 1–18
88. 1 Kgs. 16, 29–33
89. 1 Kgs. 17, 1—18, 19
90. 1 Kgs. 18, 20–46
91. 1 Kgs. 19, 1–18
92. 1 Kgs. 21
93. 1 Kgs. 22
94. 1 Kgs. 19, 19–21
95. 2 Kgs. 2, 1–18
96. 2 Kgs. 4–5
97. 2 Kgs. 9–10
98. Amos 6, 1–7
99. Amos 5, 4–7. 10–15
100. Amos 8, 4–12
101. Amos 5, 18–20
102. Amos 2, 9–12; 3, 2
103. Amos 4, 6–12
104. Amos 9, 8–10
105. Amos 4, 4–5; 5, 21–25
106. Amos 3, 3–8; 7, 10–15
107. Hos. 4, 1–4
108. Hos. 8, 4–7. 11–13

419

184. Gen. 1, 1—2; 3
185. Gen. 6–8 (Priestly); 9, 1–17
186. Gen. 17
187. Ex. 12–14 (Priestly)
188. Ex. 19, 3–8
189. Ezek. 2, 3—3, 9
190. Ezek. 3, 16–21
191. Ezek. 22, 23–31
192. Ezek. 16
193. Ezek. 8–11
194. Ezek. 18
195. Ezek. 21, 13–22
196. Ezek. 3, 22—5, 4
197. Ezek. 12, 1–20
198. Ezek. 27
199. Ezek. 28
200. Ezek. 1, 1—2, 2; 3, 10–15
201. Ezek. 37, 1–14
202. Ezek. 34
203. Ezek. 36, 16–36
204. Ezek. 37, 20–28
205. Ezek. 40, 1–4; 43, 1–9; 47, 1–12; 48, 35
206. Ezek. 38–39
207. Lam. 4
208. Lam. 1
209. Ps. 137
210. Ps. 44
211. Ps. 80, 2–8. 15. 18–20
212. Ps. 80, 9–14. 16–17
213. Ps. 89
214. Is. 14, 3–21
215. Is. 40, 1–11
216. Is. 41, 1–5. 25–29
217. Is. 41, 8–20
218. Is. 43, 1–7. 16–21
219. Is. 48, 20–22; 49, 9–13
220. Is. 44, 6–8. 21–23; 45, 7–8

221. Is. 51, 1–8
222. Is. 49, 14–26
223. Is. 51, 17—52, 10
224. Is. 54
225. Is. 42, 1–7
226. Is. 49, 1–6
227. Is. 50, 4–9
228. Is. 52, 13—53, 12
229. Ezra 1; 6, 3–5
230. Is. 35
231. Ezra 4, 4—5, 24
232. Zech. 1, 7–17
233. Ezra 3
234. Hag. 1, 1–11
235. Hag. 2, 1–9
236. Zech. 6, 9–14
237. Ezra 4, 1–3; 5, 3–17
238. Ps. 85
239. Ezra 6
240. Is. 61, 1–3
241. Is. 60; 62, 2–5
242. Is. 56, 1–8
243. Is. 66, 18–21
244. Ruth 1, 15–18
245. Jon. 1; 3–4
246. Prv. 11, 24; 13, 7; 14, 20. 28; 16, 13–15; 18, 11. 16–17. 23; 19, 12; 20, 14
247. Prv. 10, 2. 4. 9. 26; 11, 13. 17; 12, 9. 18. 24; 13, 3. 11. 20; 14, 21. 30; 15, 14. 17; 16, 23; 17, 1. 4. 28; 18, 12; 19, 24; 20, 4. 17; 21, 13. 17; 22, 8; 25, 6–7. 14–15. 23. 27–28; 26, 14. 17–19. 27; 27, 2; 29, 13
248. Prv. 12, 25; 13, 12; 14, 10–13; 15, 15. 30; 17, 22; 18, 19. 24; 27, 5–7. 9. 17

420

316. Ps. 16
317. Ps. 42–43
318. Ps. 122
319. Ps. 84
320. Ps. 50
321. Ps. 40
322. Ps. 147, 1–6
323. Ps. 147, 12–20
324. Ps. 130
325. Zech. 14, 6–21
326. Ps. 93
327. Ps. 97
328. Zech. 9, 9–10
329. Ps. 72
330. Ps. 2
331. Bar. 4, 5—5, 9
332. Tob. 13, 9–17
333. Song 1, 5–11
334. Song 1, 12—2, 6
335. Song 2, 8–17
336. Song 5, 2–8
337. Song 7, 11—8, 7
338. Eccl. 1–2
339. Eccl. 4, 1–4; 9, 11–16; 10, 5–7
340. Eccl. 5, 9–16
341. Eccl. 7, 15; 8, 10–14
342. Eccl. 9, 1–10; 11, 7—12, 8
343. Tob. 2
344. Tob. 3
345. Tob. 4
346. Tob. 5–6
347. Tob. 7–8
348. Tob. 11–12
349. Sir. 39, 1–10
350. Sir. 1, 11–20. 26–28
351. Sir. 14, 20—15, 10
352. Sir. 24
353. Sir. 40, 1–11

354. Sir. 41, 1–4
355. Sir. 15, 11–20
356. Sir. 16, 17–21
357. Sir. 5, 4–7
358. Sir. 17, 25—18, 14
359. Sir. 34, 13–17
360. Sir. 13; 27, 1–2; 31, 8–11
361. Sir. 6, 5–17; 9, 10
362. Sir. 7, 19; 9, 1–9; 25, 13 —26, 18
363. Sir. 30, 1–13
364. Sir. 3, 1–16
365. Sir. 21, 11–28; 22, 9–18
366. Sir. 20, 1–18. 18–26; 23, 7–11
367. Sir. 3, 30—4, 10; 4, 31; 7, 32–36
368. Sir. 28, 1–7
369. Sir. 3, 28; 10, 6–18; 11, 1–6
370. Sir. 2, 1–6; 4, 28
371. Sir. 34, 18–26; 35, 1–10
372. 2 Mac. 4
373. 1 Mac. 1
374. 1 Mac. 2, 29–38
375. 2 Mac. 6, 18–31
376. 2 Mac. 7
377. Dan. 2
378. Dan. 4
379. Dan. 5
380. Dan. 3; 6
381. Dan. 7
382. Dan. 9
383. Dan. 12, 1–3
384. 1 Mac. 2, 25–28. 42–44
385. 1 Mac. 4, 28–35
386. 2 Mac. 11, 5–12
387. 1 Mac. 4, 36–61
388. 1 Mac. 6, 6–16
389. 2 Mac. 9

422

LIST OF TEXTS

425

426

CHRONOLOGICAL TABLES

429

INDEX OF BOOKS
OF THE BIBLE

The books of the Bible have been treated in chronological order in the text, and so were mentioned in many places. They are listed below in their order in the canon of Scripture.

New Testament

ANALYTICAL INDEX

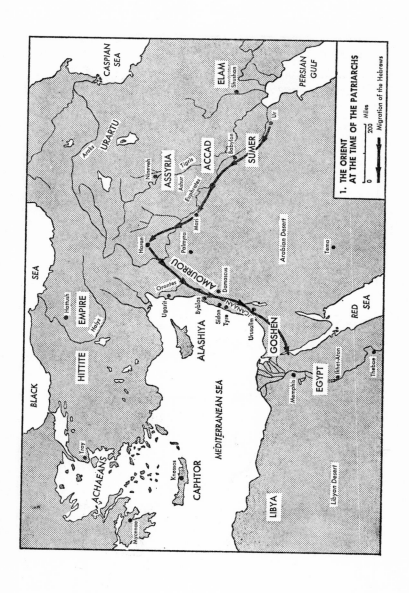

1. THE ORIENT
AT THE TIME OF THE PATRIARCHS

0   200
    Miles

Migration of the Hebrews

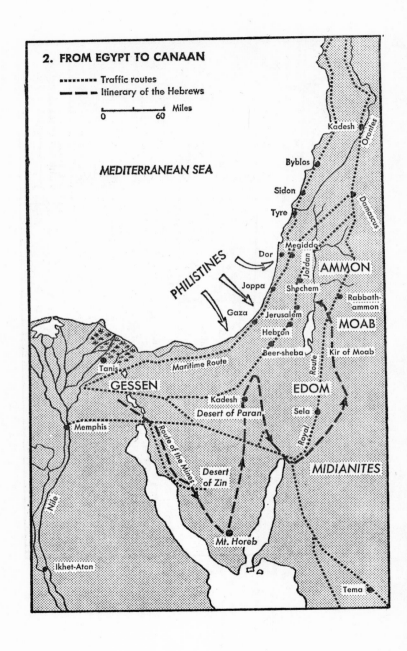

2. FROM EGYPT TO CANAAN

▪▪▪▪▪▪▪▪ Traffic routes
▬ ▬ ▬ Itinerary of the Hebrews

0   60   Miles

MEDITERRANEAN SEA

Kadesh

Byblos

Sidon

Tyre

Orontes

Damascus

Megiddo

Dor

PHILISTINES

AMMON

Jordan

Joppa

Shechem

Rabbath-
ammon

Gaza

Jerusalem

MOAB

Hebron

Beer-sheba

Kir of Moab

Maritime Route

Tanis

GESSEN

EDOM

Kadesh

Desert of Paran

Sela

Route

Route of the Mines

Memphis

Desert
of Zin

MIDIANITES

Royal

Nile

Mt. Horeb

Ikhet-Aton

Tema

CILICIA

Tarsus

Karkemish

Euphrates

Haran

Alep

Ugarit

Orontes

Karkor

CYPRUS

Hama

ARAMAEANS

Arpad

PHOENICIA

Kadesh

Palmyra

MEDITERRANEAN SEA

Byblos

Damascus

Sidon

ARAM-ZOBAH

Tyre

Dan

Bosra

Dor

ISRAEL

Shechem

Jordan

Jabbok

PHILISTINES

Rabbath-ammon

Gaza

Hebron

AMMONITES

Torrent of Egypt

JUDAH

Kir of Moab

Beer-sheba

MOAB

Kadesh

EDOM

Sela

3. THE EMPIRE
OF DAVID
AND SOLOMON

 Eziongeber

━ ━ Boundaries of the empire
▪▪▪▪▪ Boundaries of annexed
or vassal states

0   60   Miles

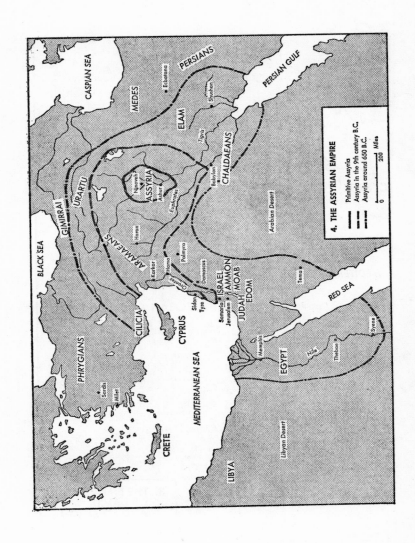

4. THE ASSYRIAN EMPIRE

Primitive Assyria
Assyria in the 9th century B.C.
Assyria around 650 B.C.

0   200
Miles

CASPIAN SEA

PERSIANS

MEDES

PERSIAN GULF

Ecbatana

ELAM

Shushan

Tigris

CHALDAEANS

URARTU

Nineveh
ASSYRIA
Ashur

Babylon

Euphrates

GIMIRRAI

ARAMAEANS

Haran

Arabian Desert

BLACK SEA

Karkar

Hamat

Palmyra

Orontes

Damascus

CILICIA

Samaria
ISRAEL
AMMON

Tyre
Sidon

Jerusalem
JUDAH
MOAB

EDOM

Tema

RED SEA

PHRYGIANS

CYPRUS

Memphis

Sardis

Miletus

EGYPT

Nile

Thebes

Syene

MEDITERRANEAN SEA

CRETE

LIBYA

Libyan Desert

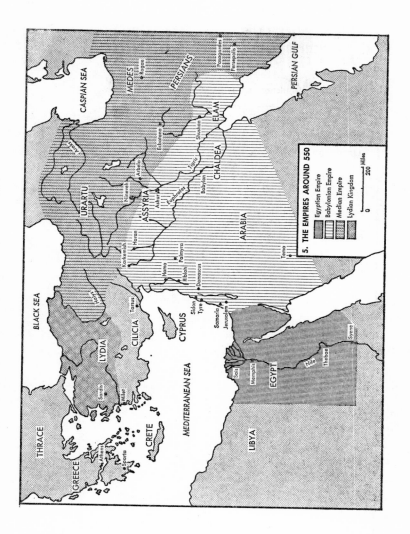

5. THE EMPIRES AROUND 550

Egyptian Empire
Babylonian Empire
Median Empire
Lydian Kingdom

Miles
0   200

THRACE

GREECE
Athens
Sparta

CRETE

BLACK SEA

LYDIA
Sardis
Miletus

CILICIA
Tarsus

Halys

URARTU

CASPIAN SEA

MEDES
Ragae
Ecbatana

PERSIANS

Pasargadae
Persepolis

PERSIAN GULF

ELAM
Shushan

ASSYLIA
Nineveh
Arbela
Ashur

CHALDEA
Babylon

Tigris
Euphrates

MEDITERRANEAN SEA

CYPRUS

Sidon
Tyre
Samaria
Jerusalem

Hama
Riblah
Damascus
Palmyra
Karkemish
Haran

ARABIA

Tema

EGYPT
Sais
Memphis
Thebes
Syene

Nile

LIBYA

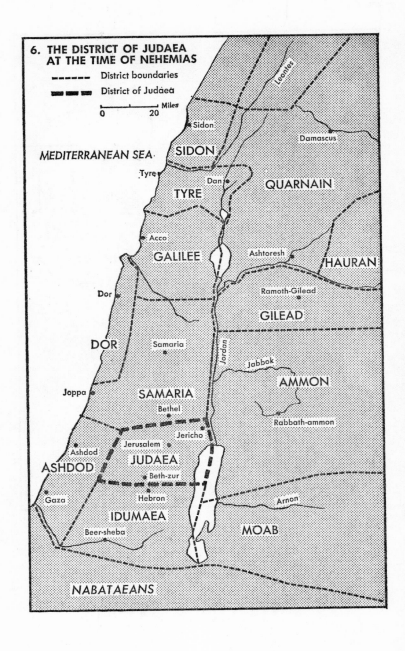

6. THE DISTRICT OF JUDAEA AT THE TIME OF NEHEMIAS

- – – – – – District boundaries
- ▬ ▬ ▬ District of Judaea

0   20 Miles

MEDITERRANEAN SEA

Leontes

Sidon

SIDON

Damascus

Tyre

Dan

TYRE

QUARNAIN

Acco

GALILEE

Ashtoresh

HAURAN

Dor

Ramoth-Gilead

GILEAD

DOR

Samaria

Jordan

Jabbok

AMMON

Joppa

SAMARIA

Bethel

Rabbath-ammon

Jericho

Ashdod

Jerusalem

JUDAEA

ASHDOD

Beth-zur

Gaza

Hebron

Arnon

IDUMAEA

MOAB

Beer-sheba

NABATAEANS

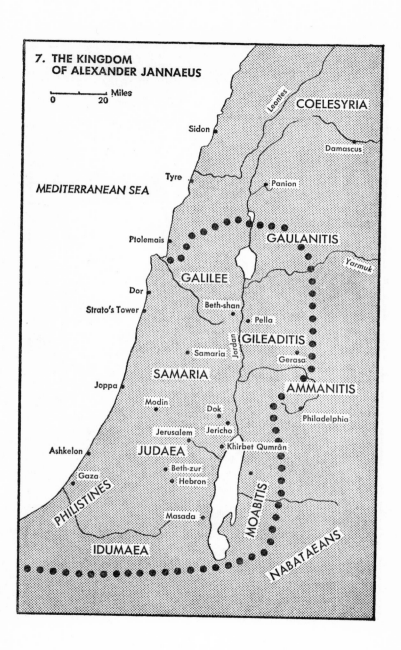

7. THE KINGDOM OF ALEXANDER JANNAEUS

0 — 20 Miles

COELESYRIA

Leontes

Sidon

Damascus

Tyre

MEDITERRANEAN SEA

Panion

Ptolemais

GAULANITIS

Yarmuk

GALILEE

Dor

Strato's Tower

Beth-shan

Pella

Jordan

GILEADITIS

Samaria

Gerasa

SAMARIA

AMMANITIS

Joppa

Modin

Dok

Philadelphia

Jerusalem

Jericho

Ashkelon

Khirbet Qumrân

JUDAEA

Beth-zur

Gaza

Hebron

MOABITIS

PHILISTINES

Masada

IDUMAEA

NABATAEANS

8. PALESTINE AT THE TIME OF JESUS

— — Boundaries of Provinces
••••••• Roads

Miles
0   25

MEDITERRANEAN SEA

Beirut

ITURAEA

ABILENE

Sidon

PHOENICIA

Leontes

Damascus

Tyre

Caesarea Philippi

TRACHONITIS

Ptolemais

GAULANITIS
Bethsaida

BATANAEA

Capharnaum

Tiberias

AURANITIS

GALILEE

Nazareth

Gadara

Beth-shan

DECAPOLIS

Caesarea

Pella

SAMARIA

Jordan

Gerar

Joppa

Lydda

PERAEA

Jabneel

Jericho

Philadelphia

Emmaus

Bethany

Ashkelon

Jerusalem
Bethlehem

Khirbet Qumran

JUDAEA

Hebron

DEAD SEA

Machaerus

Gaza

Engedi

Masada

Beer-sheba

NABATAEANS

IDUMAEA

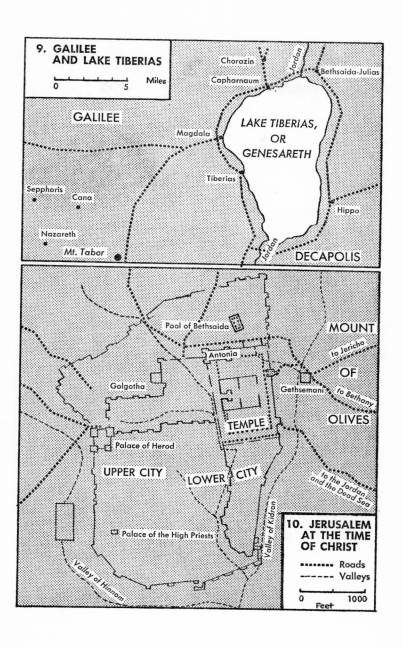

9. GALILEE AND LAKE TIBERIAS

0 — 5 Miles

GALILEE

Chorazin
Capharnaum
Jordan
Bethsaida-Julias

LAKE TIBERIAS, OR GENESARETH

Magdala

Tiberias

Sepphoris
Cana

Nazareth
Mt. Tabor

Hippo

Jordan

DECAPOLIS

Pool of Bethsaida

Antonia

MOUNT

to Jericho

OF

Golgotha

Gethsemani

to Bethany

TEMPLE

OLIVES

Palace of Herod

UPPER CITY

LOWER CITY

to the Jordan
and the Dead Sea

Valley of Kidron

Palace of the High Priests

10. JERUSALEM AT THE TIME OF CHRIST

••••••• Roads
------- Valleys

0 — 1000
Feet

Valley of Hinnom

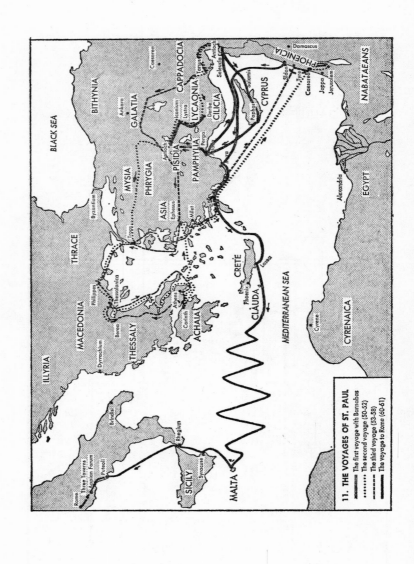

11. **THE VOYAGES OF ST. PAUL.**

━━━━ The first voyage with Barnabas

·········· The second voyage (50-52)

- - - - - The third voyage (53-58)

━━━━ The voyage to Rome (60-61)

12. **GREECE AND ASIA MINOR AT THE TIME OF THE APOSTLES**

✝ Ephesus: The seven churches of the Apocalypse